Careers Overseas

Careers Overseas

SALEM PRESS

A Division of EBSCO Information Services, Inc.

Ipswich, Massachusetts

GREY HOUSE PUBLISHING

Publisher's Cataloging-In-Publication Data
(Prepared by The Donohue Group, Inc.)

Title: Careers overseas.
Description: [First edition]. | Ipswich, Massachusetts : Salem Press, a division of EBSCO Information Services, Inc. ; [Amenia, New York] : Grey House Publishing, [2017] | Includes bibliographical references and index.
Identifiers: ISBN 9781682175972 (hardcover)
Subjects: LCSH: Employment in foreign countries. | Americans--Employment--Foreign countries.
Classification: LCC HF5382.55 .C37 2017 | DDC 331.702--dc23

First Printing

PRINTED IN THE UNITED STATES OF AMERICA

CONTENTS

PUBLISHER'S NOTE

Careers Overseas is organized into ten chapters that contain thirty-four profiles describing specific fields of interest available to those who wish to work overseas. Merging scholarship with occupational development, this single comprehensive guidebook provides students planning to pursue one of many potential careers overseas with the necessary insight into opportunities, and provides instruction on what job seekers can expect in terms of training, advancement, earnings, job prospects, working conditions, relevant associations, and more. In addition, it offers guidance regarding requirements concerning where to find information about establishing an overseas career, from visas and vaccinations to work permits and residency requirements. *Careers Overseas* is specifically designed for a high school and undergraduate audience and is edited to align with secondary or high school curriculum standards.

Scope of Coverage

Understanding the wide array of jobs available to those interested in working overseas is important for anyone preparing to launch an international career. *Careers Overseas* comprises ten lengthy chapters on a broad range of occupations including traditional and long-established jobs such as flight attendant, pilot, and tour guide, as well as in-demand jobs: registered nurse, cartographer, and surgeon. This excellent reference also presents possible career paths and occupations within high-growth and emerging fields in the overseas job market.

Careers Overseas is organized to bring together information about working and living overseas. The first chapter offers general information about working overseas, and the second chapter takes a closer look at studying and volunteering overseas. The remaining chapters consider wider categories, including business and finance; government and security; arts and entertainment, healthcare; resource management and exploration; science and research; travel and tourism. Each chapter includes a number of occupational profiles that offer an overview of the occupation as well as details about duties and responsibilities, occupation specialties, human and technological working environments, and transferrable skills and abilities. Interesting enhancements, like **Fun Facts**, **Famous Firsts**, and dozens of photos, add depth to the discussion. A highlight of each chapter is **Conversation With**—a two-page interview with a professional working in a related job. The respondents share their personal career paths, detail potential for career advancement, offer advice for students, and include a "try this" for those interested in embarking on a career in their profession.

Essay Length and Format

Each chapter ranges in length from 3,500 to 4,500 words and begins with a Snapshot of the occupation that includes career clusters, interests, earnings and employment outlook. This is followed by these major categories:

- **Overview** includes detailed discussions on: Sphere of Work; Work Environment; Occupation Interest; A Day in the Life. Also included here is a Profile that outlines working conditions, educational needs, and physical abilities. You will also find the occupation's Holland Interest Score, which matches up character and personality traits with specific jobs.
- **Occupational Specialties** lists specific jobs that are related in some way, like Set Designer, Animators, and Photographer. Duties and Responsibilities are also included.
- **Work Environment** details the physical, human, and technological environment of the occupation profiled.
- **Education, Training, and Advancement** outlines how to prepare for this field while in high school, and what college courses to take, including licenses and certifications needed. A section is devoted to the Adult Job Seeker, and there is a list of skills and abilities needed to succeed in the job profiled.
- **Earnings and Advancements** offers baseline information about earnings potential so readers can gauge the difference between earnings in the U.S. and overseas.
- **Employment and Outlook** discusses employment trends, and projects growth to 2020. This section also lists related occupations.
- **More Information** includes associations that the reader can contact for more information.

Special Features

Several features continue to distinguish this reference series from other career-oriented reference works. The back matter includes:

- Appendix A: Guide to Holland Code. This discusses John Holland's theory that people and work environments can be classified into six different groups: Realistic; Investigative; Artistic; Social; Enterprising; and Conventional. See if the job you want is right for you!
- Appendix B: General Bibliography. This is a collection of suggested readings, organized into major categories.
- Subject Index: Includes people, concepts, technologies, terms, principles, and all specific occupations discussed in the occupational profile chapters.

Acknowledgments

Thanks are due to Allison Blake and Vanessa Parks, who developed the "Conversations With," as well as to the professionals who communicated their work experience through interview questionnaires. Their frank and honest responses provide immeasurable value to *Careers Overseas*. The contributions of all are gratefully acknowledged.

WORKING OVERSEAS: CHALLENGES AND OPPORTUNITIES

Working overseas, or abroad, means living and working in a country other than one's native country or the country in which one has national citizenship. There are many different approaches to working overseas, from short-term volunteer or internship programs that may last only a few months to a year to full time jobs for which a person might relocate for long periods, or permanently, becoming an "expat" or "expatriate" from his or her native nation.

Working overseas is fundamentally different than traveling internationally for recreation or participating in study abroad programs. To succeed at working overseas, a person needs not only to have an interest in exploring a new culture, but must also be prepared to work while doing so. Deciding whether or not to pursue overseas work therefore involves two related, but different decisions. First, an individual must decide if he or she is interested in exploring a new culture and environment and is comfortable with the idea of adjusting to new customs and lifestyles. Second, the prospective overseas worker must be interested in the job that is being offered as the experience of living and socializing abroad will not be nearly as enjoyable or fulfilling if the person has little or no interest in their work. Therefore, overseas workers must balance interest in a career or job with interest in travel, exploration, and foreign cultures. For those interested in both, working overseas can be an adventurous, pleasurable, and highly enriching experience.

Finding Work in an Increasingly Interconnected World

The era in human history now called the "Digital" or "Information Age," is partially defined by the advent and spread of digital tools and computing. The Internet, and other digital technology, has accelerated the process of globalization, which can be viewed as the breakdown of traditional national and international isolationism and the formation of a global culture and economy. Digital tools have allowed even independent, small companies to conduct some business overseas and this process has therefore greatly expanded opportunities for overseas work. This is especially true in the financial and business fields, as companies more regularly open international branches and management offices, but also applies to a variety of other fields. For instance, consider a technology company expanding from the United States to Europe. Such a project may create overseas employment opportunities for construction and architectural specialists, retail and consumer professionals, linguistic experts, engineers, scientists, and a variety of other professionals.

In 2015, the U.S. Government's National Travel and Tourism Office (NTTO) reported that more U.S. citizens traveled abroad in 2015 than in any other year for which data was recorded, with a record 73.4 million Americans traveling abroad during the year. Increasing interest in foreign travel and work has fueled the growth of the multi-billion-dollar travel and tourism industry, which helps to facilitate the travel and/or relocation process for tourists and business travelers moving overseas for recreation or work. According to the Association of American Residents Overseas reported that, in March of 2016, there were more than 8.7 million Americans living or working overseas, not including the thousands of military and State Department personnel stationed overseas in government installations.

Preparing for International Employment

Though a professional may be qualified for domestic jobs in his or her field, companies and organizations hiring individuals for international work may have a different set of needs and/or requirements.

Preparing for international work begins with education. No matter what the field, individuals with higher level degrees are more likely to be hired for desirable positions, and this may include many overseas positions offered by companies and other organizations. In addition, while studying towards a degree, individuals with an interest in working abroad should aim for classes, even outside of their chosen field, that demonstrate their familiarity and interest with current events, international politics, or foreign history/culture. Individuals studying business might therefore take classes in international finance, foreign languages, or in the history of a specific area/region to increase their chances of working overseas.

Individuals who might want to work abroad in the future can also prepare as early as early as secondary school/high school by taking language and world history courses. Prospective employees with training in Mandarin or Cantonese, for instance, are likely to appear far more attractive to employers hiring overseas workers in Mainland China or Hong Kong. While experience with the native language is not always necessary, such experience is a benefit for all foreign travelers and/or workers when it comes to adjusting to life in a foreign nation.

Students can also increase their chances of future employment overseas by taking part in other activities that demonstrate their interest or familiarity with foreign cultures to future employers. For instance, students can befriend or take part in organizations for foreign students. Spending time with individuals from a foreign nation helps to build familiarity with cultural customs and language and provides a resource for information for a student interested in traveling or working overseas after completing their education. Many universities, colleges, and some secondary schools, also have programs that enable students to travel abroad for brief periods, either for internships, as volunteers, or simply as students traveling to learn about foreign cultures, languages, and/or history through the many "study abroad" programs offered at colleges and universities. Students who have participated in foreign internships or study abroad programs will likely have a distinct advantage when applying for professional positions overseas as familiarity and experience help ensure employers that the prospective employee understands and will be able to adjust to life in a foreign culture. For those who find no official or educational opportunities to work or study abroad, traveling abroad for leisure is a good way to get a feel for a foreign culture and will also demonstrate experience to potential employers. When preparing a resume for international positions, applicants should list all experience with foreign travel, whether for education, work, or leisure.

The Logistics of Working Overseas

The legal and governmental requirements needed to work overseas vary from nation to nation. Traveling into some regions or nations requires medical clearance and/or inoculation against certain kinds of illnesses, while other nations may have no such requirements. In addition, different countries require different types of documentation demonstrating a person's identity and reason for traveling to the country. Proper documentation might include a valid passport and visa, which is an endorsement stamped on a passport indicating that the individual is allowed to enter, leave, or stay in a country. When working in a foreign nation, it is also necessary to obtain a work permit that shows that an individual has a legal right to work in the nation. Some nations may also require an individual submit to a police or security background check or may require proof of employment and/or professional licenses before granting a work permit. To discover specific requirements, an individual can contact travel industry professionals or seek out organizations for expatriates living overseas. These organizations can help connect a prospective overseas worker with others who might have lived and/or worked in the same area. It is also possible to obtain information about travel/work requirements from foreign government websites or through the U.S. Department of State website, which has numerous articles providing data on overseas travel and work.

In most cases, when hired to work overseas a person's employer will provide guidance to help the individual manage the logistics of travel and relocation. However, in some cases, the prospective employee may be responsible for handling some or all of this process independently.

Information and documentation that may be required may include the following:

- Passport
- Visa or Work Permit documentation
- Educational records
- Birth Certificate
- Proof of professional licensing
- Marriage contract or documentation
- Police or other security clearance documentation
- Contract for employment
- Certificate of immunization or medical clearance

Finance and Benefits

Another essential consideration when preparing for overseas work involves making arrangements to handle taxes, finance, and banking. Depending on how long a person is planning on living/working overseas, it may be necessary to organize a bank account overseas. Speaking to professionals at an individual's domestic bank can be helpful in locating and preparing the proper documentation. Foreign banks may need proof of an individual's accounts in his or her native country and information about the individual's credit status when considering an application for a new account.

In some cases and in some countries, an individual may be able to continue using his or her existing credit or bank accounts, but some nations have specific laws regarding using overseas accounts. Before accepting an overseas position, prospective workers need to determine how they will handle their finances while working overseas and how to manage any accounts or assets remaining in their native nation. For instance, before leaving to work abroad, an individual may need to inform his or her banking institution so as to protect their existing accounts/assets. For those working or living overseas permanently, it may be necessary to close out any existing accounts before or after relocation. When possible, an overseas worker may want to maintain a bank account in his or her native nation, at least temporarily, while adjusting to life in their new country.

Depending on the length of time that a person intends to live/work abroad, it may be necessary to pay taxes in both the native and adopted nation, which can potentially lead to an individual paying double the taxes on their income. To avoid this and other legal/financial complications, an individual planning to work overseas should consult with a tax attorney or accountant to determine how best to manage their tax obligations. Many nations have special tax laws or programs offered to individuals working or living abroad and overseas workers may be able to save on their tax obligation by taking advantage of specific incentive programs.

Depending on the location and the length of an individual's contract, it may also be necessary for an individual to make arrangements regarding his or her social security and other governmental benefits. Some nations have "social security reciprocity" agreements with the U.S. government and travelers/workers in that nation may therefore be required to keep paying U.S. social security and Medicare for up to five years after relocation. Those working abroad may also need to pay into foreign social security or social welfare taxes unless the nature of a person's contract or employment includes an exemption from some taxes in their adopted nation. The United States Social Security Administration can provide information for travelers and overseas workers about complying with domestic and foreign social security laws.

Individuals who live and work abroad must also consider medical insurance and benefits. Some insurance companies based in the United States, like Blue Cross Blue Shield, offer special insurance plans for individuals working in foreign nations. For those considering a longer, or indefinite relocation, it might be necessary to purchase local medical insurance. In some cases, an overseas worker's employer might provide benefits through a corporate program or might be able to provide useful information on how to manage medical care and medical insurance while working abroad. Individuals who have been paying into other types of insurance plans, such as medical, dental, or life insurance, may also need to update their policies or even cancel their policies to prepare for an overseas relocation.

Homeowners considering working overseas must either divest themselves of their property or ensure that their property will be managed in their absence. Owning property and assets in one nation might also affect an individual's tax obligations while living abroad. When considering living abroad, an individual should consider how he or she will handle shipping, storing, selling, donating, or otherwise managing any property that the individual does not want to bring with them overseas. In many cases, it is not possible to bring pets, plants, furniture, vehicles, and other bulk or sensitive goods that cannot be easily or legally transported. How one handles his or her property and possessions when moving abroad for work may differ depending on the length of a person's contract, whether the individual plans to return to their native nation in the future, and what resources are available to help manage one's assets while living overseas.

Individuals living abroad temporarily may want to remain involved in the politics of their native nation. The United States allows citizens living abroad to post absentee ballots in political elections and this allows U.S. citizens living and/or working abroad to remain involved in the political process. For those who plan to remain in their adopted nation permanently, it will most likely be necessary for an individual to obtain citizenship in their adopted nation. Obtaining citizenship can be a lengthy and difficult process that may require the individual to find legal representation and to pass tests to demonstrate knowledge of laws and local government/culture. Overseas workers who plan to obtain citizenship should consult with an immigration lawyer or specialist, or seek out resources from governmental agencies responsible for immigration and naturalization.

Succeeding at Overseas Work

Many nations around the world have expatriate groups and communities that provide a useful resource to individuals who are new to living and/or working abroad. Expatriates sometimes have their own bars, Internet cafes, and other social venues where expats living in the same communities can socialize and stay in touch with news and culture from their native nations. Individuals in these communities can provide overseas workers and residents with practical advice and guidance on things like leasing or purchasing property or vehicles and can also provide helpful information on how to access local resources.

While there is an adventurous aspect to living and working abroad, individuals who travel for education or work often experience "culture shock," which refers to the emotional and cultural difficulties involved in adjusting to a new culture. Faced with new languages, new customs, and new environments fraught with both opportunities and potential hazards, adjusting to life abroad can be a difficult challenge and many who begin overseas educational or employment programs may find they want to return home before their contract is complete. To succeed in living, working, or studying abroad, travelers should be prepared for this process and should use resources, such as expat communities and publications, to help orient them to life in their new home.

Before applying for overseas positions, it is helpful to gain a basic understanding of the culture one will encounter overseas. Some expressions and behaviors that are considered insignificant in the United States may appear rude or inappropriate in other nations. It is therefore useful to study things like eating habits, appropriate and inappropriate conversational topics, and gift giving protocols. Those who take the time to learn about ethics, customs, and popular culture in their adopted nation will be better prepared for day to day life and interacting with native residents. It is also important for prospective overseas workers to gain a basic familiarity with the laws of their new country. Traffic laws as well as laws regarding public behavior are important to know for those considering an extended stay and it is also important for overseas workers to learn about and familiarize themselves with the legal services and rights of their adopted country.

Living overseas is more enjoyable and less problematic for those who also learn about public services and facilities before relocation. For instance, knowing about public transportation, the cost of food and other living expenses, and about the type of medical care and other social services available to foreign workers will help new arrivals to feel more prepared and comfortable in their new environment.

Finally, recreating in expatriate communities or venues may provide a comfort for those feeling culturally isolated, but is not a solution for cultural isolation itself. Though some expatriates living abroad may try to maintain the same type of lifestyle they had in their native country, such an approach may deepen, rather than relieve, the sense of isolation, especially when newly relocated to a foreign country. Experienced expatriates recommend involving oneself in local, native culture, as much as possible, and forming friendships and social relationships with native residents, rather than isolating oneself within expatriate communities. Over the long term, integrating with local residents and participating in native culture lessens feelings of isolation and helps those living abroad to feel connected and involved in their new home. Such interactions also deepen linguistic familiarity and knowledge of customs and popular culture.

There are a variety of resources available for expatriates living in foreign nations. For instance, *Escape Artist*, a magazine and website (www.escapeartist.com), provides articles and other resources aimed specifically at helping expats with various activities, such as managing international taxes, accessing international news, and investing overseas. Similarly, the non-profit organization American Citizens Abroad (ACA, www.americansabroad.com), provides information on issues affecting expatriates, such as voting rights and procedures, tax liability and benefits, and social security. The organization also provides advocacy services for those experiencing legal issues while living overseas.

For many, the idea of working or living abroad may hold an adventurous or romantic allure, but the process of adjusting to life in a new country can be difficult and challenging. The degree to which a person succeeds as a foreign worker or student depends largely on a person's approach and willingness to change and adjust to new situations. For those interested in foreign cultures and who long for unique experiences, working abroad may be an excellent option, providing unique and lasting experiences that can enrich one's life and fundamentally alter one's view of the world.

For more information on living, working, or studying abroad, there are organizations and websites that provide useful information about the logistics of relocation and on how to find work, volunteer, internship, and student opportunities in other countries.

The following websites are a good place to start for those interested in overseas employment:

- Working Abroad (www.workingabroad.com)
  - Provides information on teaching, environmental, and humanitarian positions overseas, aimed at U.S. residents.

- Transitions Abroad (www.transitionsabroad.com)
  - Teaching website that provides articles and information on working, studying, and traveling internationally.

- Go Abroad (www.goabroad.com)
  - Provides information and links students and professionals to international education, volunteer, internship, and job opportunities.

- BUNAC (www.bunac.org)
  - The British Universities North America Club operates as a support service for those living and working abroad and provides information about visas, taxes, job applications, travel and lodging, and helps to connect potential employees with opportunities for work and study overseas.

- Easy Expat (www.easyexpat.com)
  - Provides a variety of guides on issues like visas, jobs, accommodation, and schooling, as well as classified ads for jobs open to international applicants.

Works Used

"8.7 Million Americans (excluding military) Live in 160-plus Countries." *AARO.org*. The Association of Americans Resident Overseas. 2016. Web. 1 Aug 2017.

"Five First Steps to Finding a Job Abroad." Forbes. *Forbes*, Inc. Sep 25, 2009. Web. 1 Aug 2017.

"International Jobs – Working Overseas." *State.gov*. U.S. Department of State. 2017. Web. 1 Aug 2017.

LaGrave, Katherine. "More Americans Traveled Abroad in 2015 Than Ever Before." *CNTraveler*. Conde Nast. Mar 28 2016. Web. 21 Jul 2017.

Peolzl, Volker. "How to Get Work Permits Abroad." *Transitionsabroad.com*. Transitions Abroad. 2017. Web. 1 Aug 2017.

Escape Artist.com. Escape Artist, Inc. 2017. Web. 1 Aug 2017.

Americansabroad.org. American Citizens Abroad. 2017. Web. 1 Aug 2017.

STUDYING AND VOLUNTEERING OVERSEAS

Overseas volunteering, internship, and study programs give participants a chance to live and work in a foreign nation for a limited time while gaining experience that may help them meet later personal or career goals. For those interested in working overseas on a permanent basis, participating in internships and/or study/volunteer programs is an excellent way to experience the process before making permanent or long-term commitments. In most cases, companies and organizations offering overseas volunteer, internship, and educational opportunities help participants with logistics and relocation, guiding applicants through the process of obtaining paperwork, licenses, permits, and immunizations. While many see volunteer and internship positions overseas as an opportunity for recreation in a foreign nation, most internships, volunteer positions, and study abroad programs are also challenging and potential applicants should be prepared to work hard while they explore and enjoy living in a new culture.

Volunteering Abroad

The earliest known international volunteering organization was formed by the British Red Cross in 1909, and known as the Voluntary Aid Detachment (VAD). Those who joined the VAD, primarily British women, were trained in first aid and nursing and served the British military in the first two world wars. Since the first international volunteer organizations began operation, many volunteer activities have been based on social service and outreach to needy populations. The first overseas volunteer organization in the United States was International Voluntary Services (IVS), a Mennonite organization based on similar British organizations that began operation in 1953 and lasted until 2002 placing thousands of volunteers in 16 nations around the world to work on construction and educational programs.

One of the most familiar volunteer organizations in the United States is the Peace Corps Volunteers, established in 1961 by an executive order from President John F. Kennedy as a way to facilitate sending American volunteers to foreign nations to help needy populations. The Peace Corps have programs in 140 nations around the world, and more than 220,000 volunteers have participated in the program between 1953 and 2015. The Peace Corps asks participants to commit to two years of service, with the opportunity to extend their contracts, and typically only accepts applicants who have earned a college degree. Participants typically work in underserved communities, assisting with economic programs, such as building or repairing infrastructure, helping to ensure that communities have adequate food and sanitation, and performing outreach medical and educational work. The stated goals of Peace Corps service is both to help those less fortunate, while also developing and fostering greater international understanding, acceptance, and familiarity.

There are many different types of volunteer opportunities, requiring different types of service and work. Some programs ask volunteers to participate in manual labor, such as in constructing houses or other facilities, while other programs concentrate less on physical activities and more on intellectual work, such as working with computer systems or participating in educational programs. Other volunteer opportunities, typically aimed only at experienced participants, send volunteers to areas affected by warfare or other types of disasters. The range of opportunities means that there are volunteer programs that may appeal to volunteers with different skills and personalities. Volunteering abroad can be a helpful step towards working overseas and some organizations may offer paid positions to volunteers after their volunteer service. Alternately, a person who has participated in a volunteer program can use that experience as a qualification when applying for overseas work with a company or organization.

While most volunteer programs are focus on helping people and underserved communities, there are also volunteer programs that focus on conservation, environmental reclamation, or animal welfare. Often offered through educational or scientific institutions, the increasing popularity of such programs reflects deepening global concern over the depletion of natural resources and the continuing pattern of environmental degradation. Environmental or conservation-based volunteer programs can also benefit those exploring potential careers in conservation, ecology, biology, or wildlife management.

Writing in the journal *Tourism Recreation Research* in 2010, researchers Jim Butcher and Peter Smith found that there has been an increase in interest in international volunteering as an alternative to traditional tourism, with companies offering short or long term tourist programs in which the income from tourism funds development programs for native communities or contributes to conservation programs. Whereas many volunteer programs ask volunteers to commit to 6 months to two years in their program, the popularity of volunteer tourism has resulted in a proliferation of shorter programs that offer leisure activities blended with volunteer work.

While there is a tendency for inexperienced individuals to view volunteering abroad as an extended vacation, not all participants find volunteer programs as rewarding or enjoyable as they hoped and some applicants are underprepared for the level of work involved. For instance, of 10,120 volunteers accepted by the Peace Corps in 2015, 10 percent (1008) left the program early due to personal, professional, or medical conflicts. Volunteer work is also work and those interested in volunteering must carefully consider whether they will be comfortable performing the job required and for the length of time necessary to fulfill a contract. For those uncertain whether they will enjoy the experience, many organizations offer trial programs that introduce potential volunteers to the type of work and the types of experiences they might expect when participating in a volunteer abroad program.

Fun Fact

In 2017, the University of Wisconsin-Madison produced more Peace Corps volunteers than any other large university in the U.S. Among medium-size schools, American University in D.C. topped the list, while Denison University in Ohio was first among small schools.
Source: Peace Corps

Overseas Internships: Sampling the Experience of Working Abroad

An internship is a position within a company, organization, or project in which a student or trainee can gain experience and learn about the company or organization's activities and environment. Internships may be either paid or unpaid and may be aimed at students or professional of various ages and with varying levels of experience. For instance, some internships are designed specifically to provide secondary/high school students with direct experience of a career path as the student makes decisions about higher education. Other internships are aimed at postsecondary/college students or at recent graduates preparing to enter the workforce.

Participating in an international internship is one of the best ways to experiment with working abroad without committing to a long term contract or job. Most internships involve limited contracts of between one or two months to as long as two years, and organizations offering internship opportunities typically assist new interns with the logistics and planning involved in moving abroad. Many companies offering overseas positions recommend that interested applicants begin the process by completing an internship in the field, thus testing out the process of living and working abroad before applying for full positions.

Many internship programs take place during breaks in the typical college year, thus allowing students to participate before returning to their education. Financial company Goldman Sachs, for instance, has a summer intern abroad program where students spend two months working as financial analysts in places such as India, Japan, Australia, New Zealand, Europe, the Middle East, and Africa. For Business students, the Deloitte company offers paid-internship programs in Brazil, China, Italy, South Africa, Spain, Sweden, and Turkey where interns spend a month working in professional services.

There are also a variety of internship programs offered through U.S. government agencies. The U.S. Department of State offers internship positions for students interested in foreign relations through the Pamela Harriman Foreign Service Fellowship, which provides a $5,000 stipend for an intern to work in a foreign embassy in either Paris or London. In many cases, the best way to find internship opportunities is through a college or university. For instance, the University of

Pennsylvania offers an International Internship Program (IIP) that pairs students with non-profit or non-governmental organizations in a variety of locations in Europe, the Middle East, Africa and many other locations around the world. IIP internships are typically unpaid, but the university supplements and supports their interns with funding to offset the cost of travel, housing, and food.

Though internships can be challenging and many involve difficult work, most companies offering internship programs also make an effort to allow interns to explore their new environment and provide time for leisure, helping them to get a feel not only for a specific job or field, but also for traveling and exploring new cultures.

Conversation With . . .
ANDY RADELET

Former Marketing & Business Development Intern
Fun Guide Co., Beijing City, China
Intern, 2 months

1. What was your path in terms of education/training, entry-level job, or other significant opportunity?

During the summer of 2016, I participated in CRCC Asia's China Internship Program in Beijing. As an Economics and Mandarin Chinese student going into my senior year at Michigan State University, I wanted a marketing internship that would give me real-world working experience in the increasingly important Chinese business environment. My placement was with a mobile software company that creates and manages apps for various firms, including many major banks within the country. In early 2016, the company initiated plans for a start-up venture in which they would create their own app—the first they created for their own company. It would fill a need in the marketplace for English-speaking foreigners seeking daily news updates, vouchers, and reviews of different restaurants and activities that might appeal to them while visiting Beijing. It made my life great, to say the least. Being able to research up-and-coming hot spots in the city and visit them with my friends after work was something I could get used to!

What impressed me the most about CRCC Asia was the perfect blend of professionalism and friendliness. Each team member I spoke to from the pre-departure stage until the day I left Beijing could not have been more knowledgeable and helpful. Post-graduation, I knew I wanted to work in an environment like that and CRCC Asia's mission is something I believe in: bringing the world closer together by creating global citizens. I ended up landing a job as CRCC's USA Admissions Advisor in Philadelphia.

2. What are the most important skills and/or qualities for someone doing an internship overseas in your field?

It may be cliché, but the most important skill an international intern should have is quite simply cultural awareness. Cultural agility is becoming a crucial skill. Many highly regarded companies are hunting for employees with professional experience abroad and the ability to connect with people from distinct cultures.

3. What do you wish you had known going into the internship?

When I boarded the plane to Beijing, I didn't know what was going to be waiting for me 13 hours later, or even what my expectations should be. It would have eased my nerves to know that no matter where you are working, a good work ethic, a positive attitude, and friendliness go a long way. Companies know that interns have rather limited skills, mainly due to lack of experience. But the company I was placed with was very welcoming and let me know they were interested in hearing my thoughts and suggestions on business ideas, knowing that I brought a foreign perspective that they could potentially use as an asset.

4. Are there many opportunities for international internships? In what specific areas?

Many large global companies have attempted to enter the Chinese market but have failed. Marketing tactics that work in the U.S. rarely have the same success in the Chinese market. One of the most important components of marketing is knowing the culture of the market you are trying to sell to. Having on-the-ground experience, no matter how long or brief, is imperative. China has opened a gateway to a whole new world of revolutionized products and services, making it one of the most frequently visited countries for student and graduate internships. The job market in China has skyrocketed due to the expansion of various industries.

5. How do you see the importance of international experience changing in the next five years? What role will technology play in those changes, and what skills will be required?

As the world becomes more and more globalized, international internship experience is becoming crucially important, no matter what your career. Technology has been the largest reason for the increasing globalization and while it may make communication easier, cultural awareness and market knowledge still will be of utmost importance.

6. What did you enjoy most about the internship? What did you enjoy least?

I most enjoyed the relationships I formed not only with my Chinese coworkers, but also with other CRCC Asia interns in my program, who came from all over the world, including the United Kingdom, Italy, France, and Australia, among others. We all became united in the fact that no matter where we were from, together we were the minority in China.

While I very much enjoyed my internship, I would have liked to be more exposed to the future growth strategies of the company and ideas on how to combat the prevalence of plagiarism in the marketplace and protect intellectual property.

7. **Do you have any other advice for students considering an internship abroad?**

My internship in China left me with a wealth of skills and knowledge, and proved I had the courage and ability to immerse myself in a very different culture for an extended amount of time. It enriched my resume and gave me an edge that is sure to benefit me in my future career. It was far from an easy ride, but the challenges I met and sense of accomplishment will stay with me for the rest of my life. I decided to pursue a career in international education in hopes that I can assist students in having the same life-changing experience that I had.

Studying Abroad

In 1923, Raymond W. Kirkbride, a World War I veteran who had spent years overseas, and professor of modern languages at the University of Delaware, proposed a unique new academic program to the school's then president, Walter S. Hullihen, in which junior year students would spend the year studying in France. Hullihen embraced the idea, thus creating the Delaware Foreign Study Plan, better known as "Junior Year Abroad." Using funding from private donors (as the University board refused to fund the program), Kirkbride and Hullihen sent their first group of eight junior year students to France in 1923, starting a tradition that captured national attention. Between 1923 and 1948, the University of Delaware sent 900 students abroad, many participating in the program from other universities, and soon other universities started similar study abroad programs for their students.

Kirkbride, believed that spending time in a foreign nation could broaden a person's horizons, presenting unique experiences and challenges. While the initial study abroad programs were aimed only at language and foreign culture students (as many still are) study abroad programs have since expanded and diversified, offering opportunities for students in a variety of academic fields. Students participating in study abroad programs receive financial support and assistance with the travel and relocation process, and typically receive university or college credit if they complete the educational requirements of their program. For students interested in languages, foreign relations, international history, or in potentially working and living abroad as professionals, study abroad programs provide a safe, supported, introduction to the process and can be helpful for those hoping to work overseas as professionals later in life.

The Institute for the International Education of Students (IES), conducted a survey in 2004 asking individuals who participated in study abroad programs between 1950 and 1999 to describe their perception of their experience. In total, 96 percent believed the experience helped them gain self-confidence and 95 percent believed that their time studying abroad had a lasting impact on their worldview. Another similar study by the IES in 2012 found similar results with 84 percent stating that their study abroad experience helped them build job skills that they used later in their careers.

College tuition is soaring in the U.S., but American students can get a free education at universities in eight other countries: Germany, Iceland, France, Norway, Finland, Sweden, Slovenia and the Czech Republic. (Source: student.com)

Conversation With . . .
PATRICE BURNS

Career Services Coordinator
Saint Louis University, Madrid, Spain
Career counselor in international higher education
10 years

1. **What was your individual career path in terms of education/training, entry-level job, or other significant opportunity?**

As an undergrad Spanish major at the University of Wisconsin, I studied abroad for a year at the Complutense of Madrid (Reunidas) and decided I'd return to Madrid upon graduation. I stayed in Madrid for several years and finally landed a job at an investment bank, but knew I'd have more opportunity in the U.S. I returned to Wisconsin, got a master's degree in Spanish from Marquette University, and found my passion: working and teaching at universities. As Director of Foreign Languages at UW Milwaukee School of Education, I was able to share my love for language, culture and travel with like-minded adults, which re-ignited my interest in living abroad. When I returned to Spain, I knew my future would be in higher education. Saint Louis University-Madrid, the only American university offering full degree programs in Europe, was the perfect fit.

We are a small campus of 750 students with students from over 65 different countries, including the U.S., Spain, Egypt, Morocco, Saudi Arabia, Philippines, Germany, United Arab Emirates, France, and Austria. My aim is to get students thinking about life after college from the day they start. This means considering and deciding on a major, obtaining good grades, and building resumes by working or volunteering. I also work with them on crafting resumes, creating LinkedIn profiles, networking online and in person, practicing interviews, and even how to look for work. I also help them research and apply to grad schools.

We pride ourselves on providing the U.S. college experience—clubs, student government, service learning, campus ministry—which are not part of a Spanish college campus. Students earn a U.S. degree outside of the U.S. Regardless of where a student is from, he or she interacts with a much more diverse group of people than at any other typical college, be it in the U.S., Spain, Egypt, or Great Britain.

2. **What are the most important skills and/or qualities for someone in your profession, particularly someone who decides to work overseas?**

An eagerness to learn what the "real world" is looking for both in new employees and in the hiring process. It's important to connect with each student as an individual and understand both what he/she wants and what obstacles they face, whether that is gaining employment, dealing with family pressure to move home, or paying off college loans.

3. What do you wish you had known before deciding to work abroad?

The salaries are much, much lower in Spain than they are in the U.S. (and I'm sure the UK), and there is much less opportunity for growth. Every Spaniard I know who has worked in the U.S. is amazed at what they call the meritocracy. This does not exist in Spain.

4. Are there many job opportunities overseas in your profession? In what specific geographic areas?

Yes. More and more universities are opening programs in countries abroad. Provided a young graduate has the language skills and cultural knowledge—or even openness—required to work in that country, it's mainly a matter of choosing one's area of focus and applying. Universities require postgrad degrees for administrative and teaching positions.

5. Will the willingness of professionals in your career to travel and live overseas change in the next five years? What role will technology play in those changes, and what skills will be required?

The main innovation I am seeing is great flexibility in study abroad options. Undergrads can now choose exactly what they want to study and where, say economics in Japan or biology in Ecuador.

In the past, a college professor—often a specialist in the country's language— was sent from the home campus to run a study-abroad center, but that's no longer viable because we need to offer our students a wide range of programs and classes. So, a more generalist staff is needed, with knowledge of U.S. degree requirements as well as local academic options and local resources, such as doctors and student sports leagues.

We all use technological tools on a daily basis to communicate with our colleagues and effectively manage delivery of our academic programs. Given this, excellent communication skills, both spoken and written, are more highly valued than they were 10 years ago.

6. What do you enjoy most about your job? What do you enjoy least about your job?

I love that I am surrounded by people from all over the world every day. I hear new languages and learn new ways of viewing the world and understanding things.

I least enjoy least dealing with the awful market situation for young, talented graduates in Spain. I deal with many grads who are at least trilingual and incredibly bright and eager to learn. The positions and salaries available to these young men and women are not at all commensurate with their ability. Spain's current unemployment rate is over 40 percent for those under 25, so it's nearly impossible for non-Europeans to get work permits, and many Spaniards move to other countries—wherever they have connections.

7. Can you suggest a valuable "try this" for students considering a career overseas in your profession?

Spend a day in the international office of your local university or community college, even as a fly on the wall. In a matter of hours, you will see the various nationalities of students attending the university and the issues they must navigate to live and study in another country. I'd also suggest seeing what study abroad opportunities the universities in your area offer. Go to their abroad websites and see what types of staff and faculty work there.

International Childcare: The Au Pair Industry

For centuries, some upper and middle class families in the United States and Western Europe have hired domestic servants to care for their children. In general, the term "nanny" is used for any domestic servant hired to supplement childcare. Nannies may live in a family's home, but more often live independently, visiting the family daily or a certain number of times per week. Au pairs are similar to nannies in that they help with childcare and other domestic activities, but, unlike nannies, au pairs typically come from overseas and usually live with the host family for the duration of their contract.

The au pair industry blurs the lines between professional domestic servants and international students. The industry originated in post-World War II Europe where the impoverishment left behind by the war led more and more women from Eastern Europe to search for employment opportunities overseas. The term originates from the French language, meaning "on par with," and refers to the idea that an au pair becomes part of his or her host family for the length of their stay. There are many private organizations that help connect interested families with overseas au pairs and some nations have government agencies that help support the industry. For instance, the U.S. Au Pair Program, managed by the U.S. Department of State, helps families locate and hire au pairs and vice versa and can help facilitate the process of relocation and obtaining the proper permits.

One of the central ideas behind the au pairs industry is that such an arrangement not only provides a way for students and childcare professionals to live and work abroad, but also fosters meaningful cultural exchange. Foreign au pairs living abroad may deepen their knowledge of the language and culture in their host nation, while helping children in their host families to learn the language and culture of their native nation. When conducted ethically, international childcare positions can therefore help to deepen cross cultural sensitivity, understanding, and experience for all who take part in au pair programs.

Despite remaining common, the au pair industry has also had significant problems in that limited regulation sometimes leaves au pairs, who are often young, student-age women from developing nations, vulnerable to exploitation by host families. In the United States, for instance, a 2013 study by Harvard University law professor Janie Chuang found that au pairs working in the United States are often paid less than minimum wage and may be required to work excessive hours with little freedom. Such a pattern has been allowed to continue because au pairs are classified as foreign "students" of the U.S. Department of State cultural exchange program, rather than as migrant workers, who are protected by laws established by the Department of Labor. A lobby for stronger regulation is underway, but those interested in au pair positions should be careful in researching available opportunities or when selecting a company to work with in finding potential positions.

The Importance of International Experience

Testimonies of people who have participated in study abroad, internships, or volunteer programs overseas overlap in significant ways. In all, individuals who travel internationally to participate in work or educational programs tend to feel they gained more from the experience than those who travel for leisure alone. Participating in a structured program, whether an internship, study, or volunteer program, may be more valuable in terms of career and personal growth than vacationing overseas. Further, the increasing overlap between leisure and purpose-based international travel means that people from different backgrounds and fields can potentially have the opportunity to experience overseas life and work. As global cultures come closer together, due to shared environmental, economic, and military goals, it will be increasingly important for professionals in a variety of fields to have international experience. If this trend continues, international internships, study programs, and volunteering may come to have increased value for young professionals, demonstrating the individual's willingness and preparedness to participate in the global economy and environment of the future.

Works Used

Butcher, Jim and Peter Smith. "'Making a Difference': Volunteer Tourism and Development." *Tourism Recreation Research*. Vol 35, No. 1 (2010). Pp: 27-36.

Dwyer, Mary M. and Courtney K. Peters. "The Benefits of Study Abroad." *Transitions Magazine*. 2004. Web. 20 Jul 2017.

"FY 2015 Peace Corps Early Termination Report GLOBAL." *Peacecorps*. 2016. Pdf. 20 Jul 2017.

"History." *Peacecorps.gov*. Peace Corps. 2016. Web. 20 Jul 2017.

Light, Sue. "The Fairest Force: Great War Nurses in France and Flanders." *Fairestforce.co.uk*. 2015. Web. 20 Jul 2017.

"Our History." *Udel*. University of Delaware Institute for Global Studies. 2016. Web. 20 Jul 2017.

Taft, Rachel. "10 Paid Internships Abroad in Summer 2017." *Gooverseas.com*. Go Overseas. Feb 20 2017. Web. 20 Jul 2017.

Chuang, Janie A. "The U.S. Au Pair Program: Labor Exploitation and the Myth of Cultural Exchange." *Harvard Journal of Law and Gender*. Vol 36, 2013. Pdf. 21 Jul 2017.

DePillis, Lydia. "Au pairs provide cheap childcare. Maybe illegally cheap." *The Washington Post*. Nash Holdings. Mar 20 2015. Web. 21 Jul 2017.

"What's the Difference Between Au Pairs and Nannies?" *New Parent*. New Parent Media, Inc. 2017. Web. 21 Jul 2017.

BUSINESS AND FINANCE IN A GLOBAL ECONOMY

In the twenty-first century, business and finance are increasingly international in scope. According to a study by Wells Fargo in 2016, in that year, 47 percent of U.S. companies were utilizing international business opportunities, an increase from 39 percent in 2015. In addition, 87 percent of business owners and managers surveyed stated that emerging international markets were necessary and beneficial for long term corporate growth. For the nation's largest corporations and financial giants, overseas markets can provide as much as 40-50 percent of annual profit, enabling the U.S. economy to thrive despite limited domestic growth. In 2011, for instance, Bank of America obtained 20 percent of its annual $134 billion from overseas business, while the Ford Motor company derived 51 percent of the company's annual $129 billion from international sales.

Despite the common perception that globalization necessarily means outsourcing American labor, thus diminishing jobs for U.S. citizens, international business is no longer a rarity, but has rapidly become the norm for corporations in a variety of fields. For those interested in working overseas, the globalization of commerce is a boon, creating thousands of opportunities for U.S. workers who are willing to relocate to foreign branches or offices. Further, globalization has vastly increased the need for economic analysts with international expertise who can help guide companies hoping to take part in emerging opportunities.

Understanding International Markets

Economists and financial analysts are responsible for gathering data on financial trends and the increasing tendency for corporations to do business overseas has created growing demand for economic experts with experience or knowledge of foreign business and finance. Colleges and universities across the United States offer programs in international business, economics, and finance, and financial corporations interested in international markets regularly post professionals overseas where they can track day to day economic development, providing immediate data to U.S. investors and companies. Investment firms also station personnel overseas to serve U.S. customers who wish to invest in foreign companies or markets and many high profile investment firms increasingly prefer to hire investors, analysts, and portfolio managers with international experience.

Another avenue for those interested in overseas finance and business is through the fields of international business law and regulation. For companies operating overseas, coping with local laws and business rules can be difficult, and this has created a niche for legal professionals who specialize in financial/business law and have knowledge of relevant foreign laws and regulations. Persons who already have law degrees, especially with a focus on business or finance, can pursue overseas employment by adopting a secondary focus in international studies. Similarly, officials working in regulation and compliance are needed to help companies operating overseas ensure that they adhere to local regulations, which may or may not be specific to certain types of businesses. U.S. natives working as regulatory and/or compliance officers may therefore be eligible for overseas positions, especially those candidates who have travel, linguistic, or other experience living, working, or coping with international regulatory systems.

In some cases, U.S. companies setting up businesses overseas may employ consultants with entrepreneurial experience. Business and financial consultants are a familiar feature of the domestic professional environment and there is an increasing demand for business and financial consultants who are willing to travel abroad to help establish native businesses. Similarly, U.S. businesses opening overseas offices might hire consultants from their native nation to assist in the process or help train staff. Applicants with linguistic expertise, or knowledge of foreign business practices and customs, may therefore have an advantage when applying for overseas positions and students can prepare for international consultation or management by taking relevant classes and/or by participating in study abroad, internship, or other overseas learning opportunities.

Trade and Consultation

The most ancient form of international business involves the buying and selling of goods across international lines. In prehistory, tribal and nomadic societies in Eurasia established trade routes where merchants and traders could exchange livestock, precious metals and stones, and a variety of other goods. These trade routes endured for millennia, gradually growing into the familiar Silk Roads leading from Asia through Africa and named for the centuries-long market for Asian silk that began in the third century BCE. In the modern world, procurement and purchasing specialists continue to travel abroad, sourcing and purchasing goods and materials for sale in their native nations. Similarly, corporations and manufacturers hire sales professionals to travel abroad marketing and selling their products, services, or materials to interested foreign companies.

For business students and professionals interested in frequent or extended international travel, a career in international trade may provide an excellent opportunity. There are many different career opportunities in trade, both in buying and selling and in the many other careers surrounding the industry, such as shipping and receiving specialists, regulatory and compliance professionals, and the financial experts that monitor trade contracts and payment between international companies. Opportunities in international trade are also not restricted to the private sector, as there are many government agencies that hire trade professionals to help manage contracts, finances, and other aspects of trade agreements. Professionals with training in business and trade may therefore have a multitude of opportunities, from working with private companies to assisting with the diplomatic process of organizing government trade agreements.

International Independence

In some cases, entrepreneurs from the United States or other economically dominant nations have found that, by moving to nations with developing economies, where the U.S. dollar has more purchasing power, they can establish their own companies or businesses for a fraction of the cost of doing business domestically. For instance, in a 2013 article in *International Living* former U.S. resident Kevin Sheehy described how he was able to open a Vietnamese restaurant in Quito, Ecuador with an investment of only $14,000, which is far less than one might spend to open a similar business in the United States.

Independent entrepreneurs can also invest in franchise opportunities with established companies. Dozens of U.S.-based franchises, like Crunch Fitness, McDonalds, or Jimmy Johns Sandwiches actively advertise for entrepreneurs looking to open or manage franchise locations overseas. Operating a franchise has benefits, in that the parent company typically provides support and assistance and can help with the logistics of staffing, sourcing, and set-up costs.

Whether working for a massive multinational company, or going into business for oneself, there are many opportunities for professionals with business and financial experience to find fulfilling and profitable job opportunities overseas. The first step on this path is education. Companies hiring overseas business and finance specialists typically look for candidates with more diverse experience and, specifically, previous experience with foreign languages, and/or with living or working overseas. Students and professionals should therefore seek out opportunities to travel or study abroad and, when possible, should apply for internships with companies operating overseas. In addition, while a general education in business and/or finance might be sufficient, training specifically in international business, economics, and/or law will provide an advantage to applicants interested in the international side of the field.

Works Used

"Despite Weak Global Economy, U.S. Companies Still Turning to International Markets for Growth." *NewsroomWF*. Wells Fargo. Apr 25, 2016. Web. 21 Jul 2017.

Newman, Rick. "Why U.S. Companies Aren't So American Anymore." *U.S. News*. U.S. News and World Report. Jun 30 2011.

Presher, Dan. "Expats Find Business Opportunities Overseas." *Internationalliving*. IL Magazine. Mar 13 2013. Web. 21 Jul 2017.

General Manager and Top Executive

Snapshot

Career Cluster(s): Business, Management & Administration, Government & Public Administration

Interests: Having a lot of responsibility, working long hours, running an organization, communicating with others

Earnings (Yearly Average): $137,525

Employment & Outlook: Slower Than Average Growth Expected

OVERVIEW

Sphere of Work

General managers and top executives are responsible for making strategic business decisions to ensure that their organizations run smoothly and profitably. They occupy the very top tier of management and, as such, bear the ultimate responsibility to the owners and stakeholders for the organization's performance. Highly compensated, they are expected to provide a corresponding level of leadership and direction to

other senior executives and managers, as well as to formulate and communicate high-level policy. General managers and top executives in private enterprises may be known by more specific job titles, such as president, chief executive officer, or director. In the non-profit and government sectors, they may have job titles such as agency director, chief, or superintendent.

Work Environment

General managers and top executives usually spend most of their work day in office environments. Typically, they have their own office or suite of offices close to other members of the organization's executive management team. General managers and top executives can expect to spend a considerable amount of time traveling away from home, especially if their organization is national or multinational. They are frequently expected to put in as many hours as required to fulfill their duties. As a result, many top executives work sixty or more hours a week, including evenings, weekends, and holidays.

Profile

Interests: Data, People
Working Conditions: Work Inside
Physical Strength: Light work
Education Needs: Bachelor's Degree, Master's Degree, Doctoral Degree
Licensure/Certification: Usually Not Required
Physical Abilities Not Required: Not Climb, Not Kneel
Opportunities For Experience: Internship, Military Service, Part Time Work
Holland Interest Score*: ESR

* See Appendix A

Occupation Interest

This occupation suits people who combine technical knowledge and abilities relevant to the industry they work in with sophisticated business and leadership skills and the desire and commitment needed to effectively run an organization. They must have the experience, foresight, and ability to develop an organization's strategic direction by taking into account the competitive environment, market opportunities and challenges, micro- and macroeconomics, sociopolitical factors, resource requirements, and operations. Strong analytical abilities and the capacity to set goals for short- and long-term planning are a must in this profession. This job usually requires long hours and a level of responsibility that may cause stress.

A Day in the Life—Duties and Responsibilities

A top executive's day may be dedicated to dealing with one issue or a wide variety of issues. It is likely, however, that a significant proportion of the day will be spent communicating with others, either one-on-one or in group meetings. The general manager is likely to schedule regular meetings with key staff and committees about issues such as budgets, financial results, sales forecasts, and special projects. He or she will meet regularly with the key staff who report to them. This may include, for example, the chief financial officer, human resources director, operations director, sales and marketing directors, and any other key staff. The general manager is likely to delegate duties as needed to his or her support staff, as well as task them with special projects, research, and analysis. Individuals in this position are additionally responsible for developing lower-level employees into future managers.

The organization's top executives may also be involved at a strategic level in special projects and initiatives. Depending on the type of organization, this may include, for example, crisis and reputation management, new product development and launches, mergers and acquisitions, site openings and closures, strategic operational and logistic changes, and policy development.

The general manager is responsible for reporting to the company's board of directors, owners, and investors. In the case of publicly listed companies, this includes shareholders. The general manager is responsible for ensuring that the company fulfills its legal and fiduciary responsibilities. In doing so, the general manager makes a personal guarantee to the company's board and shareholders that the information provided in official legal and financial reports is accurate and reliable.

Duties and Responsibilities

- Setting general goals and policies in collaboration with other top executives and the board of directors
- Meeting with business and government leaders to discuss policy-related matters
- Directing the operations of firms and agencies
- Overseeing department executives
- Achieving organizational goals quickly and economically

OCCUPATION SPECIALTIES

Chief Executive Officers/Presidents (189.117-026)

Chief Executive Officers/Presidents decide policies and direct operations of organizations.

Department Store Managers (185.117-010)

Department Store Managers direct activities, formulate and implement policies for sales and other departments.

Bank Presidents (186.117-054)

Bank Presidents plan and direct policies and practices of banks or other financial institutions.

Special Agents (166.167-046)

Special Agents recruit sales agents and coordinate agencies and home offices of insurance companies.

College Presidents (090.117-034)

College Presidents plan and direct the administration of a school, college or university.

School Superintendents (099.117-022)

School Superintendents direct and coordinate the administration of school systems.

Police Chiefs (375.117-010)

Police Chiefs direct and coordinate the activities of a municipal police department.

Harbor Masters (375.167-026)

Harbor Masters direct and coordinate the activities of a harbor police force.

Library Directors (100.117-010)

Library Directors plan and administer library services with the approval of a board of directors.

WORK ENVIRONMENT

Immediate Physical Environment

General managers and top executives usually work from their own office, which tends to be pleasant and well-appointed. The general manager's physical environment will be influenced by the size and type of employer and the industry in which they operate.

Transferable Skills and Abilities

Communication Skills
- Speaking effectively (SCANS Basic Skill)
- Writing concisely (SCANS Basic Skill)

Interpersonal/Social Skills
- Asserting oneself
- Cooperating with others
- Motivating others

Organization & Management Skills
- Making decisions (SCANS Thinking Skills)

Research & Planning Skills
- Developing evaluation strategies
- Solving problems (SCANS Thinking Skills)

Work Environment Skills
- Traveling

Human Environment

This role involves a great amount of interaction with others. General managers and top executives must possess advanced oral and written communication skills, including the ability to collaborate, negotiate, and resolve conflict. They must be able to conduct themselves with diplomacy and tact and interact confidently with powerful people.

Technological Environment

Daily operations may demand the use of standard office technologies, including computers, telephones, e-mail, photocopiers, and the Internet. General managers and top executives are supported by an executive secretary or administrative team who completes much of the more routine paperwork and requests. The technology used by someone in this position can vary depending on the industry the organization occupies.

EDUCATION, TRAINING, AND ADVANCEMENT

High School/Secondary

High school students can best prepare for a career as a general manager and top executive by taking courses in applied communication subjects such as business writing as well as computer science. Foreign languages may also be beneficial. Courses that develop general business skills may include accounting, entrepreneurship, bookkeeping, business management, and applied mathematics. Administrative skills may be developed by taking subjects such as business computing and typing. Becoming involved in part-time administrative or clerical work after school or during the weekends builds people skills and is a helpful way to begin learning about business operations and management. Leadership experience can be developed through taking part in extracurricular activities.

Suggested High School Subjects
- Applied Communication
- College Preparatory
- Composition
- Computer Science
- English
- Entrepreneurship

Related Career Pathways/Majors
Business, Management & Administration Cluster
- Business Analysis Pathway
- Management Pathway
- Marketing Pathway
Government & Public Administration Cluster
- Foreign Service Pathway
- Governance Pathway
- Planning Pathway

- Public Management & Administration Pathway
- Regulation Pathway
- Revenue & Taxation Pathway

Postsecondary

In keeping with the level of responsibility of the position, most employers expect their general managers and top executives to possess postsecondary qualifications. The minimum requirement is considered to be a bachelor's degree in business or another relevant field. A master's degree in business administration is sometimes, but not always, considered to be a requirement. Because this position is extremely results-oriented, some individuals earn more advanced degrees, while others advance as a result of proving their abilities through on-the-job experience.

Related College Majors
- Aviation Management
- Business
- Business Administration & Management, General
- Education Administration & Supervision, General
- Enterprise Management & Operation
- Entrepreneurship
- Finance, General
- General Retailing & Wholesaling Operations & Skills
- Sport & Fitness Administration/Management
- Travel-Tourism Management

Adult Job Seekers

Adults seeking a career as a general manager and top executive should emphasize any prior management experience or advanced knowledge of the core competencies of business management, such as financial management, human resource management, operations, and sales and marketing. Adult job seekers may need to supplement their current skill set by taking classes in relevant areas. Candidates should keep in mind that many companies promote their existing managers into top executive positions. Networking, job searching, and interviewing are, therefore, critical, and this should include registering with executive recruitment agencies.

Professional Certification and Licensure

There are no formal professional certifications or licensing requirements for general managers and top executives. Professional associations offer general manager certifications and some industry authorities require staff to hold special licenses. The American Management Association (AMA) and National Management Association (NMA) provide certificate programs in a range of specialty areas, as well as general management.

Additional Requirements

The workload and pressures placed on general managers and top executives are often relentless or intense, so these individuals should be highly motivated, confident, and able to thrive under pressure. Work/life balance may be difficult to achieve or maintain in such a demanding and responsible role, which often requires a great commitment of time and energy.

EARNINGS AND ADVANCEMENT

General managers and top executives are among the highest paid workers in the nation. Earnings depend on the level of managerial responsibility, length of service, and type, size and geographic location of the firm. Salaries in manufacturing and finance are generally higher than in state and local government.

Median annual earnings of general managers were $100,064 in 2012. The lowest ten percent earned less than $50,117, and the highest ten percent earned more than $176,384. Median annual earnings of top executives were $174,985 in 2012; although top executives in some industries earned considerably more.

General managers and top executives receive paid vacations, holidays, and sick days; life and health insurance; and retirement benefits.

These are paid by the employer. They may also receive the use of company aircraft and cars, expense allowances and stock options.

EMPLOYMENT AND OUTLOOK

General managers and top executives held about 2.1 million jobs nationally in 2010. Employment is most concentrated in restaurants, groceries, business services, retail stores, financial institutions, educational institutions, hospitals and the government. Employment is expected to grow slower than the average for all occupations through the year 2020, which means employment is projected to increase 3 percent to 9 percent. Demand for jobs is expected to increase in the health services industry but expected to decline in many manufacturing industries.

Related Occupations
- City Manager
- Computer & Information Systems Manager
- Education Administrator
- Financial Manager
- Human Resources Specialist/ Manager
- Information Technology Project Manager
- Management Analyst & Consultant
- Medical & Health Services Manager
- Online Merchant
- Postmaster & Mail Superintendent
- Public Administrator
- Public Relations Specialist
- Retail Store Sales Manager

Related Occupations
- Law Enforcement & Security Officer
- Law Enforcement & Security Specialist
- Military Police

Conversation With . . .
VJ MAURY

Former CEO, Palace Cinemas
Budapest, Hungary (2001-2011)
Entrepreneur internationally, 10 years

1. What was your individual career path in terms of education/training, entry-level job, or other significant opportunity?

After graduating from Clemson University, I served as a Foreign Service Officer for seven years in U.S. embassies in Turkey and Malta, supporting the diplomatic mission. In Malta, because it was such a small embassy, I was also defense attaché. Later, I went to the Stern School of Business at New York University and earned an MBA. When I graduated, there were a lot of media investments in Central Europe because the region had just opened up after the fall of the USSR. Since I had foreign experience already, I was a good fit for a multinational media company. Business school in New York was a great place to meet both media and international companies and to hear about opportunities.

I took a position with Central European Media Enterprises, a media and investment company that invested in private TV in Central Europe. I oversaw the building and operation of a TV station in Ljubljana, Slovenia, from 1995 to 1999. In the course of that job—looking at other regional investment opportunities—the idea of a cinema chain presented itself. Another CME employee and I raised money to pursue that.

2. What are the most important skills and/or qualities for someone in your profession?

Collaboration and communication. Getting people into workable teams takes good communication, and sometimes you are communicating in a low level of English. When working with native English speakers, you don't realize how much you fill in the blanks of what others are saying or quickly understand the nuances in your own language. When you are dealing with teams of people who are communicating in a second or third language—sometimes awkwardly—the communication is more basic and things have to be really spelled out. It helps if you have a second language to work with or learn the local language a little bit. But it takes coaxing and a collaborative attitude to get people to work together. You also have to be able to stay focused on the big picture of your mission since much of the time, you don't really grasp what people are saying in the local language. I would say I understood about 10 percent of what people were saying when they were not speaking English or German.

3. What do you wish you had known going into this profession?

There isn't really anything I wish I'd known; it was all a surprise because I worked for a start-up company in a newly created role, so I had to design it as I went. A lot of surprises arise, so you have to stay flexible. To work in a foreign country and also work for a start-up, you need to be comfortable with risk and adventure.

4. Are there many job opportunities in your profession? In what specific areas?

There are opportunities for well-trained CEOs and managers in foreign countries but, increasingly, even remote countries have access to decent management training (via online business programs), so native-born managers are becoming more the norm. If the business is international, companies usually want a mix of international talent. Solid management experience with increasing levels of responsibility is transferrable.

5. How do you see your profession changing in the next five years, what role will technology play in those changes, and what skills will be required?

Technology helps decentralized corporations function more seamlessly. Our company had the CEO (me) in Budapest and the CFO in Prague, and country managers all over the region. We did need to get together to team-build from time to time, but technology and collaborative software helped us stay connected and focused. In Europe, there has been a lot more labor mobility so this means it's more competitive. Just because you have the language skills for say, Spain, candidates also need to add value in other ways because they'll be competing with well-trained Europeans from all over the continent. Also, many companies that are trans-regional use English as the *lingua franca*, making it even more competitive.

6. What do you like most about your job? What do you like least about your job?

I liked interfacing with many different nationalities and traveling to see how our business was different in each local area. I disliked reporting to a remote board of directors (based in London), who, although they had deep experience in media leadership, did not always understand the challenges and opportunities on the ground, like why the Czechs like bacon-flavored popcorn at the movies.

7. Can you suggest a valuable "try this" for students considering a career in your profession?

I think internships in multinational corporations are a great thing to try. If you can combine this with a year of study and/or living with a family, you really get a sense of both the work culture and living culture of a place. You need to like living in a foreign country in order to thrive professionally in a foreign country, so you can't be too fussy about which laundry detergent you like or what kind of coffee you drink; you have to kind of go with it.

MORE INFORMATION

Business and Professional Women's Foundation
1718 M Street NW, #148
Washington, DC 20036
202.293.1100
foundation@bpwfoundation.org
www.bpwfoundation.org

Career Advancement Scholarship
Program
www.free-4u.com/bpw-career_
advancement_scholarship_program.htm

National Management Association
2210 Arbor Boulevard
Dayton, OH 45439
937.294.0421
nma@nma1.org
www.nma1.org

Various national awards; eligibility is
contingent on membership
www.nma1.org/Awards/NMA_Awards.
html#National_Awards

Kylie Hughes/Editor

Economist

Snapshot

Career Cluster(s): Agriculture, Food & Natural Resources, Finance, Government & Public Administration, Science, Engineering, Technology & Mathematics

Interests: Mathematics, banking, finance, research, analyzing data

Earnings (Yearly Average): $94,817

Employment & Outlook: Slower Than Average Growth Expected

OVERVIEW

Sphere of Work

Economists are social scientists who study how society produces, distributes, and uses its resources. They research and analyze a wide range of economic areas, such as trade, taxation, industrial productivity, business, and employment trends. Economists study these and other areas using statistical analyses, models, and sampling techniques. Each economist tends to focus on one specific area, or sub-field, of economics.

Economists work in a number of professional capacities. Some work as advisors to government leaders, providing insight into the effects of legislation on the economy. Others are academics, teaching economic theories and concepts to postsecondary students. Major corporations and private research firms hire other economists to assess such areas as client demand, productivity, and market conditions.

Work Environment

Economists generally work in office settings in government buildings and state capitals, in colleges and universities, and at businesses and private "think tanks." In each setting, economists must use their analytical, communication, and critical thinking skills as they conduct studies of current conditions and present their findings and opinions to their superiors and other audiences.

Economists often work alone in their research, although they may work in teams in collaborative efforts to study comprehensive and complex issues. They generally work forty-hour workweeks, although they may be called upon to work extra hours when faced with project deadlines or asked to present their ideas at conferences or meetings.

Profile

Interests: Data
Working Conditions: Work Inside
Physical Strength: Light work
Education Needs: Bachelor's Degree, Master's Degree
Licensure/Certification: Usually Not Required
Physical Abilities Not Required: Not Climb, Not Kneel
Opportunities For Experience: Part Time Work
Holland Interest Score*: IAS

* See Appendix A

Occupation Interest

Economists have the professional ability to understand extremely complex systems that are often of great importance to world leaders, high-level business executives, and the intellectual community. Those economists who focus on microeconomics help major corporations maximize their profits while forecasting consumer demand and prices. Economists who focus on macroeconomics are invaluable to organizations and agencies that seek to understand economic growth, inflation, banking and finance, unemployment, and productivity. Because of their expertise in the many fields and subfields of economics, these individuals are often in high demand.

A Day in the Life—Duties and Responsibilities

An economist's most important duties are research and analysis. An economist must study the many elements that contribute to company or political system's operational strengths and weaknesses. The economist uses computer software to compile and organize data from consumer surveys, the media, and internal documents, such as production reports and profit and loss statements. This information helps the economist to create a comprehensive model of the subject. The data and models that an economist generates help all parties involved to understand the relationships between certain concepts and the root causes of many issues.

After the economist creates workable models and frameworks, he or she uses them to forecast conditions for the short- and long-term future. The economist may report his or her findings to help government officials draft and implement effective policy. A corporate economist can use findings to help executives determine the areas in which investments may yield the best returns. Such models enable an economics-oriented "think tank" to compile reports for the government and its corporate clients. Meanwhile, an academic economist uses such information to write scholarly articles and books while he or she conducts the typical duties of a college professor. In each situation (faculty, corporate, or government), an economist may be called upon to present his or her findings, theories, and opinions at conferences, board meetings, and hearings.

Duties and Responsibilities

- Developing methods for collecting and processing economic and statistical data
- Interpreting economic and statistical data
- Analyzing the relationships between the supply and demand for goods and services
- Developing ways to control inflation, unemployment and business cycles
- Planning and conducting studies to determine the need for change in business or government policy

OCCUPATION SPECIALTIES

Agricultural Economists

Agricultural Economists study agricultural problems to determine better uses of farm resources.

Tax Economists

Tax Economists collect and study data and the effects of taxes and policies on national income and overall business activities.

Labor Economists

Labor Economists collect and interpret labor data to forecast labor trends and suggest changes in labor policies.

Industrial Economists

Industrial Economists study the organizational structure, methods of financing, production costs and techniques, and marketing policies of various types of businesses to develop improvements.

Environmental Economists

Environmental Economists assess and quantify the economic benefits of using more environmental alternatives, such as the use of renewable energy resources.

WORK ENVIRONMENT

Immediate Physical Environment

Economists spend the majority of their time in government or private offices, classrooms (in the case of university economists), and other locations where social science research can be conducted. Additionally, they may be asked to present information to government agencies, conferences, and other venues.

Transferable Skills and Abilities

Communication Skills
- Speaking effectively
- Writing con

Organization & Management Skills
- Coordinating tasks
- Making decisions
- Managing people/groups
- Paying attention to and handling details

Research & Planning Skills
- Analyzing information
- Developing evaluation strategies
- Using logical reasoning

Technical Skills
- Performing scientific, mathematical and technical work
- Working with data or numbers

Human Environment

Economists may conduct their research alone or with collaborators. In either case, economists come into contact with many different types of professionals, including corporate leaders, elected and appointed government officials, students, academic peers, and the media.

Technological Environment

Economists should be familiar with computers, including many different types of office, research, and modeling software. Such programs include basic word processing and spreadsheet systems, chart and graph generators, and specialized databases. Additionally, economists need to use other forms of basic office technology, such as cellular and smart phones, presentation technologies, personal organizers, and scanners.

EDUCATION, TRAINING, AND ADVANCEMENT

High School/Secondary

High school students who are interested in economics should take courses in economics, accounting, business, statistics, math, computer science, and data processing. As half of all professional economists work for federal, state, or local government organizations, high school students may also benefit from studying political science, social studies, government, and history. High school students interested in becoming economists may also find English and communications courses helpful preparation for report writing and public speaking responsibilities they will have as economists.

Suggested High School Subjects
- Accounting
- Algebra
- Applied Math
- Business Data Processing
- Calculus
- College Preparatory
- Composition
- Computer Science
- Economics
- English
- Geometry
- Government
- History
- Mathematics
- Political Science
- Social Studies
- Sociology
- Statistics
- Trigonometry

Related Career Pathways/Majors

Agriculture, Food & Natural Resources Cluster
- Agribusiness Systems Pathway

Finance Cluster
- Business Financial Management Pathway

Government & Public Administration Cluster
- Planning Pathway
- Revenue & Taxation Pathway

Science, Technology, Engineering & Mathematics Cluster
- Science & Mathematics Pathway

Postsecondary

In the field of economics, advanced degrees make an individual more attractive to potential employers. Undergraduates should take courses of relevance to the field, including statistics, accounting, calculus and econometrics (the application of math and statistics to the study of finance and economics). They should also take courses in specific areas such as monetary policy, microeconomics, industrial/organizational economics, and macroeconomics. Graduate students in pursuit of their master's or doctoral degree should take more specialized courses that help hone their expertise on a particular field of economics, such as international economics, economic history, or public finance.

Related College Majors
- Agricultural Business & Management, General
- Agricultural Economics
- Applied & Resource Economics
- Business/Managerial Economics
- Consumer Economics & Science
- Econometrics & Quantitative Economics
- Economics, General
- International Economics

Adult Job Seekers

Many economists obtain positions after college by working as interns or research assistants while they pursue a postgraduate degree. They may also gain access to job openings through professional economics associations, such as the American Economic Association, the National Association for Business Economics, or the Society of Government Economists. Professional placement services may assist candidates in pursuing available jobs.

Professional Certification and Licensure

There are no professional licensure or certification requirements for most economist positions. However, economists are encouraged to become members of a relevant professional association.

Additional Requirements

Economists must be detail-oriented, which help them compile high volumes of data. Additionally, economists' research skills should be finely tuned – they should be able to conduct interviews, develop and administer surveys, and use a wide range of media to study trends and conditions in the field of focus. An economist should also have strong written and spoken communications skills, which enable them to create coherent reports and present findings to many different types of audiences.

EARNINGS AND ADVANCEMENT

Earnings depend on the geographic location of the employer, the type of work performed and the education and experience of the employee. The highest paid business economists were in securities and investment and nondurable manufacturing industries; the lowest paid were in education, wholesale and retail trade and publishing.

Median annual earnings of economists were $94,817 in 2016. The lowest ten percent earned less than $51,145, and the highest ten percent earned more than $164,819. The average annual salary for economists employed by the federal government was $113,250 in 2016.

Economists may receive paid vacations, holidays, and sick days; life and health insurance; and retirement benefits. These are usually paid by the employer.

EMPLOYMENT AND OUTLOOK

There were approximately 15,000 economists employed nationally in 2010. The U.S. Departments of Labor, Agriculture, and State are the largest federal employers of economists. The remaining jobs were spread throughout private industry, particularly in scientific research and development services and management, scientific, and technical consulting services.

Employment of economists is concentrated in large cities. Some work abroad for companies with major international operations, for U.S. government agencies and for international organizations, such as the World Bank, International Monetary Fund and United Nations.

Employment is expected to grow slower than the average for all occupations through the year 2024, which means employment is projected to increase 3 percent to 9 percent. Opportunities for economists should be best in private industry, especially in scientific research and development, and consulting firms, as more companies contract out for economic research services.

Related Occupations
- Actuary
- Financial Analyst
- Management Analyst & Consultant
- Market Research Analyst
- Mathematician
- Operations Research Analyst
- Securities Sales Agent
- Sociologist
- Statistician
- Urban & Regional Planner

MORE INFORMATION

American Economic Association
2014 Broadway, Suite 305
Nashville, TN 37203
615.322.2595
aeainfo@vanderbilt.edu
www.vanderbilt.edu/AEA

National Association for Business Economics
1233 20th Street NW, Suite 505
Washington, DC 20036
202.463.6223
www.nabe.com

NABE Foundation Americans for the Arts
Scholarships:
www.nabefoundation.com/ourPrograms.
html

Society of Government Economists
P.O. Box 77802
Washington, DC 20013
202.643.1743
www.sge-econ.org

Michael Auerbach/Editor

Lawyer

Snapshot

Career Cluster(s): Government & Public Administration, Law, Public Safety & Security

Interests: Law, business, writing, research, resolving conflict, communicating with others, helping others

Earnings (Yearly Average): $119,526

Employment & Outlook: Average Growth Expected

OVERVIEW

Sphere of Work

Lawyers (also called attorneys) work within the legal system. They represent the rights and interests of individuals, corporations, and other entities under federal, state, and even international law. Lawyers work in a wide array of areas, such as regulatory compliance, criminal law, lobbying, business and industries, probate, and human rights. Attorneys work in law offices, business offices, government agencies, and courtrooms. Over one-quarter of attorneys are

self-employed, either working in their own practices or as partners in a law firm. To some, attorneys act as counsels, providing advice on everyday business and personal activities. For others, lawyers act as an advocate, speaking on their behalf in court during criminal or civil proceedings.

Work Environment

Lawyers typically work in office environments. Large law firms are often fast-paced, with lawyers meeting with clients, preparing and filing paperwork, conducting research, and performing other legal tasks. Attorneys at smaller firms or practices must often perform more tasks than their counterparts at larger firms or practices. Government agencies and major business corporations typically retain or employ attorneys who perform research, write position papers, and issue recommendations for changes in action based on new law and regulations.

Lawyers usually work long and sometimes erratic hours, including late nights and weekends. They should expect to work within a highly competitive environment, both during and after their job search. Private law firms and government law offices may be strikingly different in terms of financial resources, and tend to offer different rates of compensation. Different lawyers may also specialize in different areas of the law, such as corporate law, environmental law, or malpractice cases.

Profile

Interests: Data, People
Working Conditions: Work Inside
Physical Strength: Light work
Education Needs: Doctoral Degree
Licensure/Certification: Required
Physical Abilities Not Required: Not Climb, Not Kneel
Opportunities For Experience: Military Service, Part Time Work
Holland Interest Score*: ESA

* See Appendix A

Occupation Interest

Although the work of an attorney is often very challenging, it can also be exciting and rewarding. Lawyers are considered experts in the field of law, and use this expertise to help others conduct business, deal with legal troubles, protect the environment, and write legislation. Many attorneys become judges or politicians, while others use their knowledge to help a business grow and profit in the marketplace.

A Day in the Life—Duties and Responsibilities

An attorney's daily responsibilities vary based on the type of law in which the individual works or specializes in. A staff attorney or legal counsel for a major business corporation spends much of his or her day analyzing regulations and legislation, researching legal precedents, studying tax codes, meeting with government officials, writing legal correspondence, attending negotiations, and drafting contracts and other legal documents. Private lawyers may perform these activities as well, although in the absence of large numbers of co-workers, they may also perform administrative tasks, including billing and office management.

Lawyers who work as advocates in the court system perform many of the tasks as other attorneys, but also focus on proceedings in the courts. They research previous judicial decisions, interview witnesses and litigants, meet with judges and opposing attorneys, prepare courtroom questions and comments, review testimony, file motions, select juries and, during hearings and trials, present evidence on their clients' behalf.

In addition to their work on behalf of clients, many attorneys perform a number of other activities. For example, they often perform academic work, teaching at law schools and other universities, and write scholarly papers for law journals and similar periodicals. Many attorneys work with the poor or impoverished, assist in disputes between clients and landlords, and provide advice on personal financial decisions.

Duties and Responsibilities

- Interviewing clients and witnesses
- Advising clients as to legal rights and responsibilities
- Gathering evidence to commence legal action or form a defense
- Examining and cross-examining witnesses
- Summarizing cases to juries
- Writing reports and legal briefs
- Representing clients in court and before other agencies of government
- Preparing various documents such as wills, property titles and mortgages
- Acting as trustee, guardian or executor

OCCUPATION SPECIALTIES

Criminal Lawyers

Criminal Lawyers specialize in legal cases dealing with offenses against society or the state, such as theft, murder and arson. They are responsible for preparing the case for trial, examining and cross-examining witnesses and summarizing the case to the jury.

District Attorneys

District Attorneys, also known as prosecuting attorneys, city attorneys or solicitors, conduct prosecution in court proceedings for a city, county, state or the federal government.

Corporation Lawyers

Corporation Lawyers advise corporations on legal rights, obligations and privileges in accordance with the constitution, statutes, decisions and ordinances.

Patent Lawyers

Patent Lawyers specialize in patent law and advise clients such as inventors, investors and manufacturers whether an invention can be patented, and on other issues such as infringement on patents, validity of patents and similar items.

Environmental Lawyers

Environmental Lawyers specialize in the policies of environmental law and help their clients to follow those statutes. They may help clients to properly prepare and file for licenses and applications and represent parties such as interest groups and construction firms in their dealings with the U.S. Environmental Protection Agency.

WORK ENVIRONMENT

Immediate Physical Environment

Lawyers work primarily in office settings, such as law firms, government agencies, corporate headquarters, and similar business environments and home offices. They also attend hearings and trials in courtrooms, conduct research in law libraries, and meet with clients and other individuals at their homes or at other locations, including prisons.

Transferable Skills and Abilities

Communication Skills
- Persuading others
- Speaking effectively
- Writing concisely

Interpersonal/Social Skills
- Being honest
- Cooperating with others
- Providing support to others
- Working as a member of a team

Organization & Management Skills
- Organizing information or materials
- Paying attention to and handling details
- Performing duties which change frequently

Research & Planning Skills
- Analyzing information
- Developing evaluation strategies
- Gathering information
- Using logical reasoning

Human Environment

Lawyers work with a wide variety of other people. During legal and civil cases, these individuals interact with clients and opposing litigants, judges, witnesses, law enforcement officials, and courtroom professionals. Outside the courtroom, lawyers interact with business executives, elected and government officials, paralegals, labor representatives, and administrative personnel.

Technological Environment

Lawyers will rely on office computer systems and related software to prepare cases, draft motions, and write correspondence. They may use presentation equipment, such as laptop projectors, video units, and similar equipment, for presenting courtroom evidence and for offsite presentations.

EDUCATION, TRAINING, AND ADVANCEMENT

High School/Secondary

High school students who plan to become lawyers are encouraged to take courses that help build their understanding of the law, such as history, political science, social studies, business, and economics. They would also benefit from taking courses that build communication and writing skills, such as composition and public speaking classes.

Suggested High School Subjects
- Algebra
- Business Law
- College Preparatory
- Composition
- Economics
- English
- Foreign Languages
- Government
- History
- Literature
- Political Science
- Psychology
- Social Studies
- Sociology
- Speech

Related Career Pathways/Majors
Government & Public Administration Cluster
- Revenue & Taxation Pathway

Law, Public Safety & Security Cluster
- Legal Services Pathway

Postsecondary

Aspiring attorneys need a bachelor's degree in a related field, such as history, political science, government, or public safety, with a focus on pre-law studies. After they receive their undergraduate degree, they must enter an accredited law school, where they will pursue their juris doctorate degree.

Related College Majors
- Law (L.L.B., J.D.)
- Pre-Law Studies

Adult Job Seekers

Many adults find employment as a lawyer through their law school's placement office. Attorneys who seek employment positions with the government may apply through government websites. Professional associations such as the American Bar Association (ABA) also offer resources on how to pursue a job in the legal field.

Professional Certification and Licensure

In addition to their law degrees, lawyers must pass the bar examination of the state or states in which they work. They may also join a professional legal association such as the ABA or similar state organizations.

Additional Requirements

Lawyers must have excellent analytical, research, and communications skills. They must have strong understanding of the law (particularly in the areas in which they work) and the US Constitution, and tend to be both driven and highly organized. Lawyers often work long hours, and should be comfortable dealing with conflict. Furthermore, lawyers must often work with accused criminals, which can lead to tension and confrontations with such people if the case is not proceeding as desired. Because they are legally bound to protect clients' privacy regardless of guilt or innocence, lawyers must sometimes be willing to subordinate personal ethical feelings to the demands of their job.

EARNINGS AND ADVANCEMENT

Earnings depend on lawyers' area of expertise and whether they are in private practice or employed by law firms or governmental agencies. Lawyers who practice alone usually earn less than those who are partners in law firms.

Median annual earnings of lawyers were $119,526 in 2016. The lowest ten percent earned less than $57,378, and the highest ten percent earned more than $176,384.

Lawyers may receive paid vacations, holidays, and sick days; life and health insurance; and retirement benefits. These are usually paid by the employer.

EMPLOYMENT AND OUTLOOK

There were approximately 728,000 lawyers employed nationally in 2010. About one-fourth of lawyers practiced privately, either in law firms or in solo practices. Most of the remaining lawyers held positions in government, the greatest number at the local level. Employment of lawyers is expected to grow about as fast as the average for all occupations through the year 2024, which means employment is projected to increase 10 percent to 19 percent. This is due to an ever increasing population and growing business activity that will result in more legal transactions, and civil and criminal cases. Demand will also be strong because of the growth of legal action in areas such as healthcare, intellectual property, environmental law and bankruptcy. Due to intense competition for jobs, willingness to relocate may be an advantage in securing a job. In addition, employers increasingly seek graduates who have advanced law degrees and experience in a particular field such as tax, patent or other types of law.

Related Occupations
- Human Resources Specialist/ Manager
- Judge
- Paralegal

Related Occupations
- Lawyer

MORE INFORMATION

American Bar Association
740 15th Street, NW
Washington, DC 20005-1019
202.662.1000
service@americanbar.org
www.americanbar.org

Association of American Law Schools
1201 Connecticut Avenue, NW
Suite 800
Washington, DC 20036-2717
202.296.8851
aals@aals.org
www.aals.org

Association of Corporate Counsel
1025 Connecticut Avenue NW
Suite 200
Washington, DC 20036
202.293.4103
www.acc.com

Commercial Law League of America
205 N. Michigan Avenue, Suite 2212
Chicago, IL 60601
312.240.1400
info@clla.org
www.clla.org

Federal Bar Association
1220 N. Fillmore Street, Suite 444
Arlington, VA 22201
571.481.9100
fba@fedbar.org
www.fedbar.org

Law School Admission Council
662 Penn Street
Newtown, PA 18940
215.968.1101
lsacinfo@lsac.org
www.lsac.org

National District Attorneys Association
44 Canal Center Plaza, Suite 110
Alexandria, VA 22314
703.549.9222
www.ndaa.org

Michael Auerbach/Editor

Purchasing Agent

Snapshot

Career Cluster(s): Agriculture, Food & Natural Resources, Architecture & Construction, Business, Management & Administration, Manufacturing, Marketing, Sales & Service

Interests: Sales, supply chain management, business management, negotiations, economics

Earnings (Yearly Average): $61,862

Employment & Outlook: Slower Than Average Growth Expected

OVERVIEW

Sphere of Work

Purchasing agents evaluate raw materials and other supplies for companies to use as an ingredient or component of their products. They assess the materials for quality, durability, and market value.

The main responsibility of purchasing agents is to find the highest-quality supplies and equipment at the lowest cost while adhering to the desires of current customers and target markets. Purchasing agents work in nearly all realms of manufacturing.

Work Environment

Purchasing agents split their time between administrative and office settings and warehouse and manufacturing facilities. Agents employed in food production or medical manufacturing may spend time on farms and in other environments where products are grown and harvested. Purchasing agents also spend a lot of time at trade shows, product-demonstration seminars, and other industry meetings in order to evaluate new products and foster professional contacts with potential suppliers.

Profile

Interests: Data, People
Working Conditions: Work Inside, Work Both Inside and Outside
Physical Strength: Light work, Education Needs:Junior/Technical/Community College, Bachelor's Degree
Licensure/Certification: Recommended
Physical Abilities Not Required: Not Climb, Not Kneel
Opportunities For Experience: Military Service, Part Time Work
Holland Interest Score*: ESR

* See Appendix A

Occupation Interest

A job in purchasing attracts candidates who enjoy and are skilled at mathematics, economics, and sales. It is not uncommon for purchasing agents to be fluent in more than one language. The field also attracts professionals who enjoy the process of negotiation and maximizing profits. Purchasing agents are typically outgoing and confident individuals with deft interpersonal communication skills who are comfortable interacting with new people regularly.

A Day in the Life—Duties and Responsibilities

Purchasing agents fill their days with numerous duties and responsibilities, many of which need to be tended to simultaneously. Purchasing agents are in constant communication with people inside their own companies to understand and anticipate the company's needs from a purchasing standpoint. If current suppliers are not meeting quality standards, purchasing agents are responsible for recruiting their replacements.

One of the major tasks assumed by purchasing agents is the evaluation of potential suppliers and their products. Such evaluations can entail extensive travel and an in-depth familiarity with the manufacturing processes and quality standards of their employing organization.

Once suppliers are vetted and narrowed down to a small group of potential candidates, purchasing agents are responsible for negotiating bid proposals and contracts. Contract negotiations can involve large sums of money, depending on a purchasing agent's particular realm of industry. Agents must ensure that potential suppliers can meet requirements surrounding delivery dates and potential demand.

Purchasing agents should pay attention to markets and financial trends relevant to their particular industry in order to stay knowledgeable about potential cost-cutting avenues and to anticipate fluctuations in consumer demand. They are also responsible for the ongoing evaluation of vendors, and they maintain records of various vendors' track records in pricing and overall quality

Duties and Responsibilities

- Developing standards for selecting specific material or services
- Reviewing written requests for products and services
- Obtaining information about products and prices
- Determining seller's ability to produce products and services
- Maintaining records on items purchased
- Discussing and taking corrective action on defective purchases

OCCUPATION SPECIALTIES

Contract Specialists

Contract Specialists negotiate with suppliers to draw up procurement contracts. They direct and coordinate the activities of workers engaged in formulating bid proposals, and administer, extend, terminate and renegotiate contracts.

Outside Property Agents

Outside Property Agents locate and arrange for the purchase or rental of props specified for use in motion pictures when such props are not in studio stock and cannot be constructed by studio personnel.

Procurement Engineers

Procurement Engineers develop specifications and performance test requirements to facilitate the procurement of parts and equipment for aeronautical and aerospace products. They investigate potential suppliers and recommend those who are most desirable.

Procurement Services Managers

Procurement Services Managers direct and coordinate the activities of personnel who are engaged in purchasing and distributing raw materials, equipment, machinery and supplies in industrial plants, public utilities and other organizations.

Purchase-Price Analysts

Purchase-Price Analysts compile and analyze statistical data to determine how practical it would be to buy certain products and establish price objectives for contract transactions.

Promotion Managers

Promotion Managers plan and administer sales policies and programs to foster and promote hotel patronage. They consult newspapers, trade journals and other publications to learn about planned conventions and social functions.

Commissary Superintendents

Commissary Superintendents manage the commissary department of companies that operate sea-going vessels and process requests for supplies and equipment from vessels. They represent the company in contract disputes with the unions, and negotiate contracts with supply houses, manufacturers and wholesalers for equipment, supplies and furnishings.

WORK ENVIRONMENT

Immediate Physical Environment

Purchasing agents alternate between office settings and on-site visits with suppliers. They also frequently attend large conferences and trade shows.

Transferable Skills and Abilities

Communication Skills
- Persuading others
- Speaking effectively
- Writing concisely

Interpersonal/Social Skills
- Cooperating with others
- Working as a member of a team

Organization & Management Skills
- Coordinating tasks
- Following instructions
- Making decisions
- Managing people/groups

Research & Planning Skills
- Using logical reasoning

Technical Skills
- Performing scientific, mathematical and technical work

Plant Environment

Purchasing agents may travel to factories or plants to inspect a supplier's manufacturing processes or to examine their products.

Human Environment

Peer-to-peer and customer-client interaction is the hallmark of the purchasing industry. Purchasing agents are traditionally skilled conversationalists with strong negotiating skills.

Technological Environment

Purchasing agents utilize technologies ranging from telephone conferencing, e-mail, and video-conferencing software to financial analysis tools.

EDUCATION, TRAINING, AND ADVANCEMENT

High School/Secondary

High school students can best prepare for a career as a purchasing agent with course work in algebra, calculus, economics, finance, and introductory computer science. Gaining some hands-on business experience though internships, volunteer programs, or participation in school-run fundraisers or entrepreneurial programs can benefit those who are interested in a career in purchasing. Classes in rhetorical communication and participation in debate and forensic clubs can help students hone their negotiation tactics and strategies, which can be useful in the occupation.

Suggested High School Subjects
- Accounting
- Business
- Business Data Processing
- College Preparatory
- Economics
- English
- Keyboarding
- Mathematics
- Merchandising
- Social Studies

Related Career Pathways/Majors

Agriculture, Food & Natural Resources Cluster
- Agribusiness Systems Pathway
- Animal Systems Pathway
- Food Products & Processing Systems Pathway

Architecture & Construction Cluster
- Construction Pathway

Business, Management & Administration Cluster
- Management Pathway

Manufacturing Cluster
- Manufacturing Production Process Development Pathway

Marketing, Sales & Service Cluster
- Buying & Merchandising Pathway
- Management & Entrepreneurship Pathway

Postsecondary

Postsecondary education has not historically been a requirement for entry-level positions in purchasing due to the extensive on-the-job training new employees receive. However, recent trends indicate that candidates benefit from having completed postsecondary course work in engineering, business management, economics, or applied science. Undergraduate students interested in pursuing a career in purchasing should explore courses in retailing, advertising, supply-chain management, or international business.

Related College Majors
- Agricultural Supplies Retailing & Wholesaling
- General Retailing & Wholesaling Operations & Skills
- Hotel/Motel & Restaurant Management
- Institutional Food Workers & Administration, General

Adult Job Seekers

Seasoned purchasing agents are customarily those who have been fortunate enough to accrue several years of professional experience. As such, purchasing is not traditionally a field of professional transition or temporary employment for adult job seekers. That said, professionals with extensive corporate experience may be able to transition to the field with relative ease. Purchasing can require extensive travel and time away from home, which may make the job difficult for individuals interested in maintaining a clear work-life balance.

Professional Certification and Licensure

No specific certification or licensure is required to be a purchasing agent, although professional certification will give a purchasing agent a competitive advantage in the field. Organizations such as the American Purchasing Society, the Association for Operations Management, and the National Institute of Governmental Purchasing offer professional credentials to purchasing agents who have completed several years of professional experience and successfully passed the necessary exams. Certain permissions may be required for purchasers working in specific industries involving chemicals, energy, and other controlled substances or goods.

Additional Requirements

Patience, amicability, and honesty are all important traits for a successful purchasing agent. Purchasing is primarily about establishing and maintaining relationships, and individuals who are at ease negotiating with both individuals and small groups are often those who forge the most successful careers.

Fun Fact

Gunpei Yokoi, the man who invented Game Boy, worked at Nintendo for many years...starting as a factory janitor.

Source: funfactz.com

EARNINGS AND ADVANCEMENT

Earnings depend on the size and geographic location of the employer and the employee's responsibilities and experience. Median annual earnings for purchasing agents were $61,862 in 2016. The lowest ten percent earned less than $36,157, and the highest ten percent earned more than $111,947.

Purchasing agents may receive paid vacations, holidays, and sick days; life and health insurance; and retirement benefits. These are usually paid by the employer. Retail buyers often earn cash bonuses based on their performance and may receive discounts on merchandise bought from the employer.

EMPLOYMENT AND OUTLOOK

There were approximately 365,000 purchasing agents employed nationally in 2010. Employment of purchasing agents is expected to grow slower than the average for all occupations through the year 2024, which means employment is projected to increase 3 percent to 9 percent. A trend toward large companies increasing the size of their purchasing departments and requiring their agents to procure more services than in the past will be somewhat offset by technological advances that allow supplies to be purchased online. The best opportunities will be available for persons with a master's degree in business or public administration. Graduates of bachelor degree programs in business should have the best chance of obtaining a job in wholesale or retail trade or within government.

Related Occupations
- Cost Estimator
- Fashion Coordinator
- Online Merchant
- Personal Financial Advisor
- Production Coordinator
- Wholesale & Retail Buyer
- Wholesale Sales Representative

Related Military Occupations
- Purchasing & Contracting Manager
- Supply & Warehousing Manager
- Supply & Warehousing Specialist

MORE INFORMATION

American Purchasing Society
North Island Center, Suite 203
8 East Galena Boulevard
Aurora, IL 60506
630.859.0250
propurch@propurch.com
www.american-purchasing.com

**APICS: The Association for
Operations Management**
8430 West Bryn Mawr Avenue
Suite 1000
Chicago, IL 60631
800.444.2742
www.apics.org

**Institute for Supply Management
Information Center**
P.O. Box 22160
Tempe, AZ 85285-2160
800.888.6276
bnawrocki@ism.ws
www.ism.ws

**International Purchasing and
Supply Chain Management
Institute**
16192 Coastal Highway
Lewes, DE 19985
206.203.4894
admin@ipscmi.org
www.ipscmi.org

**National Contract Management
Association**
21740 Beaumeade Circle, Suite 125
Ashburn, VA 20147
800.344.8096
wearelistening@ncmahq.org
www.ncmahq.org

**National Institute of
Governmental Purchasing**
151 Spring Street
Herndon, VA 20170-5223
800.367.6447
customercare@nigp.org
www.nigp.org

John Pritchard/Editor

Quality Control Inspector

Snapshot

Career Cluster(s): Government & Public Administration, Manufacturing, Transportation, Distribution & Logistics
Interests: Testing and inspecting, analysis, manufacturing processes, production processes, industrial engineering
Earnings (Yearly Average): $35,012
Employment & Outlook: Slower Than Average Growth Expected

OVERVIEW

Sphere of Work

Quality control inspectors evaluate products and materials for errors and defects to ensure that they meet the manufacturer's specifications. Quality inspectors play a crucial role in automated manufacturing systems, providing firsthand, human intervention in an otherwise highly mechanized process. In addition to removing all defective products prior to resale, quality control inspectors may also be responsible for recommending changes to

production processes in order to prevent further errors and disruptions to the work flow.

Work Environment

The majority of quality control inspectors work in manufacturing facilities. They test and inspect the parts that will be assembled into manufactured and salable items or the completed products themselves, depending on their particular industry of employment. For example, some inspectors may be responsible for evaluating materials such as lumber or petroleum products, while others may be responsible for testing electronic equipment, automobiles, or furniture prior to their sale. The mode of inspection varies from position to position as well. Some quality control inspectors may conduct stress tests or other analyses on the actual physical parts, while others may monitor various kinds of production data.

Profile

Interests: Data, Things
Working Conditions: Work Inside
Physical Strength: Light work
Education Needs: On-The-Job Training, High School Diploma or G.E.D., Junior/ Technical/Community College
Licensure/Certification: Required
Physical Abilities Not Required: Not Climb, Not Kneel
Opportunities For Experience: Part Time Work
Holland Interest Score*: REI

* See Appendix A

Occupation Interest

Quality control typically attracts individuals who thrive in tasks related to deductive reasoning and who are perceptive to errors and problems in continuity and production. Quality inspectors also possess a keen eye for detail and the ability to spot discrepancies in both the products and processes. The position of quality inspector attracts people of all ages and from a variety of professional and educational backgrounds.

A Day in the Life—Duties and Responsibilities

Quality control inspectors must be familiar with all aspects of the products and manufacturing processes they inspect. Some quality control inspectors travel between several different facilities, inspecting the same processes and goods on a rotating basis. Some quality control inspectors may be required to review new production specifications frequently, depending on how often their employing organization changes their product line or production methods.

Inspection of materials and goods is the main duty of quality control inspectors. Inspectors may either survey each manufactured item or take frequent samples of the manufactured goods to gauge the quality of its construction and adherence to specifications. Reoccurring errors on production lines are often the result of malfunctioning equipment.

Quality control inspectors have the final say in the rejection of items they deem to be poor quality or unsuitable for sale. Inspectors must record data to track how much inventory was lost and detail the cause.

Inspectors are customarily required to report their findings to other members of an organization's staff. The frequency and form of these presentations varies from industry to industry. Manufacturers of artisan and specialty products may review quality control findings for every single production run, while companies and factories that assemble or create a large volume of product may only require weekly to bimonthly reporting, depending on the frequency of errors.

Duties and Responsibilities

- Conducting visual and physical examinations of products
- Testing products and recording results
- Comparing results of tests and examinations to determine if the products meet the standards set by the manufacturer
- Making reports and recommendations based on test results

OCCUPATION SPECIALTIES

Quality Control Technicians

Quality Control Technicians test and inspect products at various stages of production to determine and maintain the quality of the products. They make recommendations for modifications to the products and set up destructive or nondestructive tests to measure the performance or life of a product.

General Inspectors

General Inspectors inspect materials and products, such as sheet stock, auto body or engine parts, dental instruments, machine shop parts and metal castings for conformance to specifications. They compare the product with a parts list or with a sample model of the product to insure that the piece was assembled correctly.

WORK ENVIRONMENT

Immediate Physical Environment

The work environment for quality control inspectors varies from industrial and manufacturing settings to administrative settings.

Plant Environment

Quality control inspectors work primarily in industrial settings, such as factories and production plants, where they can review the completed products as well as the equipment and processes used. Quality control inspectors employed by the pharmaceutical industry may also work in laboratory settings where they test and evaluate the safety of medications.

Transferable Skills and Abilities

Interpersonal/Social Skills
- Cooperating with others
- Working as a member of a team

Organization & Management Skills
- Paying attention to and handling details

Research & Planning Skills
- Analyzing information

Technical Skills
- Performing scientific, mathematical and technical work
- Understanding which technology is appropriate for a task
- Working with data or numbers

Work Environment Skills
- Working in a factory setting
- Working in a laboratory setting

Human Environment

Quality control inspectors do not typically interact with coworkers extensively on a daily basis, as their primary focus is placed on the production process and the systems related to it. Their occasional presentation of findings and suggestions for improvement do, however, require extensive and clear communication with plant managers and industrial engineers.

Technological Environment

Quality inspectors utilize a variety of different use technologies, ranging from data-tracking tools to desktop-publishing software. The production technologies and equipment used in the manufacturing process vary in complexity according to an inspector's realm of industry.

EDUCATION, TRAINING, AND ADVANCEMENT

High School/Secondary

High school students can prepare for a career as a quality control inspector with course work in engineering, algebra, calculus, geometry, physics, and introductory computer science. Drafting, mapping, and traditional art classes can also serve as important precursors for careers related to industrial design. English composition course work prepares students for many of the reporting elements of the role.

Suggested High School Subjects
- Applied Communication
- Applied Math
- Biology
- Business Law
- Business Math
- Computer Science
- English
- Foods & Nutrition
- Foreign Languages
- Geometry
- Government
- Trade/Industrial Education

Related Career Pathways/Majors

Government & Public Administration Cluster
- Regulation Pathway

Manufacturing Cluster
- Health, Safety & Environmental Assurance Pathway
- Logistics & Inventory Control Pathway
- Manufacturing Production Process Development Pathway
- Quality Assurance Pathway

Transportation, Distribution & Logistics Cluster
- Health, Safety & Environmental Management Pathway
- Transportation Systems/Infrastructure Planning, Management & Regulation Pathway

Postsecondary

Job openings for quality control inspectors in supply, mechanical, and manufacturing industries do not traditionally require postsecondary education. However, a college degree may be required for inspectors working in more complex industries such as medical and pharmaceutical labs, digital engineering, and food processing. While some colleges offer degree and certificate programs in quality control management, they are rare. Aspiring quality control inspectors interested in these fields should consider earning a degree in food sciences and technology or industrial engineering.

Related College Majors
- Food Sciences & Technology
- Industrial/Manufacturing Technology

Adult Job Seekers

Individuals with extensive professional experience can often transition to the field without difficulty, particularly since the intricacies of most quality control positions are learned through on-the-job training. Quality control inspectors traditionally work normal business hours, although those employed by large manufacturers who are in constant production may be required to work nights, weekends, and holidays.

Professional Certification and Licensure

State and national certification and licensure may be required of quality control inspectors depending on their particular industry or area of employment. Valid certification and licensure is typically required for individuals working in quality control in the food processing, pharmaceutical, and electronics industries, given the potential hazards of the components involved. Rules and regulations vary by state.

Additional Requirements

Successful quality control inspectors are self-motivated individuals who do not mind repetitive tasks. Inspectors are also detail-oriented problem-solvers who are able to actively monitor all aspects of the manufacturing process to spot errors or deficiencies and to recommend improvements.

EARNINGS AND ADVANCEMENT

The typical promotion of quality control inspectors is to a supervisory position. Education and continued training provides greater advancement opportunities. Earnings of quality control inspectors depend on the type and geographic location of the employer and the duties required of the employee. Median annual earnings of quality control inspectors were $35,012 in 2016. The lowest ten percent earned less than $21,342, and the highest ten percent earned more than $58,912.

Quality control inspectors may receive paid vacations, holidays, and sick days; life and health insurance; and retirement benefits. These are usually paid by the employer.

EMPLOYMENT AND OUTLOOK

Quality control inspectors held about 416,000 jobs nationally in 2010. Employment is expected to grow slower than the average for all occupations through the year 2024, which means employment is projected to increase 3 percent to 9 percent. This slower growth is primarily due to the increased use of automated inspections and the moving of quality control duties from inspectors to production workers

Related Occupations
- Construction & Building Inspector
- Inspector & Compliance Officer
- Inspector & Tester
- Nuclear Quality Control Inspector

Conversation With . . .
JOHN W. BLAKE

Services Quality Manager at Microsoft for EMEA
(Europe, Middle-East and Africa)
Munich, Germany
37 years in the tech sector

1. What was your individual career path in terms of education/training, entry-level job, or other significant opportunity?

I graduated from Rensselaer Polytechnic Institute with a bachelor's degree in physics. Back then, computers were not what they are today. After graduating, I got a job writing software with a tech start-up in the Boston area. They were looking for a quick learner, which can be typical with tech companies. They would give me a research paper and I would put it into the software language they had developed.

I had lived in Germany for a semester abroad as a college junior and decided to move there for graduate school. My girlfriend at the time lived in Germany, and another major motivating factor—graduate school was free for foreigners who met the German language proficiency requirements, which I did.

I graduated with the equivalent of a master's degree in mathematics from the Ludwig-Maximilian University in Munich. I worked as a freelance software consultant during my studies and kept this up for about 10 years until I joined a large U.S. IT multinational. After eight years they were bought by another U.S. company, so I helped integrate my team with the new organization and worked for them for another two years. Some friends and I then decided to startup an IT company in Berlin. That was around 2000, when the tech bubble burst, so we were not able to get enough venture capital funding to survive. I left in 2002 and joined General Electric, then moved to Microsoft.

Microsoft has a services group of about 40,000, which either supports our products or consults with customers to develop solutions that meet their specific needs. I focus on consulting, mostly on the large deals. I work with a team to ensure we can deliver what we are contracted to deliver and to minimize our risks. A $5 million deal in a stable country might be much less risky than a $100,000 deal in a developing country. Many projects are with large companies that want to use the latest technology to make them unique in their market. Other projects involve moving applications from the data center to the cloud, or are for governments that use technology to provide public services via the internet, such as registering a change of address.

2. What are the most important skills and/or qualities for someone in your profession, particularly someone who decides to work overseas?

Cultural sensitivity. Being able to know what you have to accept and where you have to stay strong. You need to know where your limits are, and how people operate. For instance, if you have a customer in Russia and he and his boss are in the same room, he won't tell you anything. He will defer to his boss. You need to be able to gain someone's trust.

For a lot of international jobs, U.S companies want people who can bridge both cultures. Being a native English speaker certainly was a plus for me.

3. What do you wish you had known before deciding to work abroad?

If you are working for a U.S. company and they send you overseas, you need to know: is there a relocation package and, if so, what does it look like? How do I get back? Is it a one-way ticket or not?

Every year that you spend overseas, you are investing in that country's health care and retirement systems. If you want to go back to the U.S., it's important to understand how you can get credit for whatever investments you've made into those systems. You also need to know the tax implications before you go. I'm lucky because there's a double-taxation treaty between the U.S. and Germany. So if I owe $40,000 in taxes to the U.S. and $50,000 to Germany, I can deduct my German taxes from the US taxes owed. On the other hand, Dubai, which has many ex-patriates because there is no income tax, isn't attractive for Americans because you still have to pay U.S. taxes on your worldwide income.

4. Are there many job opportunities overseas in your profession? In what specific geographic areas?

The tech sector offers a lot of opportunities. In the UK there's the M4, which is southwest of London. Paris and Munich are also booming. Berlin has a very, very vibrant startup scene. As with the U.S. startup scene, you need to be self-motivated, confident, flexible, and willing to take risks.

5. Will the need for professionals in your career to travel and live overseas change in the next five years? What role will technology play in those changes, and what skills will be required?

We are seeing a shift to a more multi-cultural career. You can be sitting in Detroit, your colleague is in Singapore or Beijing, and you work together remotely. Technology like Skype is really big. I have not had a work telephone for nine years. Collaboration tools are being widely used, like Microsoft Office. On a daily basis, I might be working on one chapter of a contract in Word and can see my colleague in Dubai concurrently working on another.

6. What do you enjoy most about your job? What do you enjoy least about your job?

I enjoy my diverse set of customers and projects. For instance, I have a couple of projects with football teams, who are now looking for technology to help them engage with their fans through the internet. We go to the stadium for meetings. Or I might work with a startup in Sweden, the government of South Africa, or a bank in Moscow.

I least enjoy that I am mostly supporting teams who are on the ground working directly with the customer on a daily basis; I'm typically called in to fix a problem.

7. Can you suggest a valuable "try this" for students considering a career overseas in your profession?

You've got to take initiative. Don't be afraid of failing. Startups pay you almost nothing but you get a lot of experience. In college, do a year abroad. Microsoft's MACH program signs up college graduates for a period of time and they'll ship you around the world. Join a high school foreign exchange program– and that's something that would look good on a resume.

MORE INFORMATION

American Society for Quality
P.O. Box 3005
Milwaukee, WI 53201-3005
800.248.1946
help@asq.org
www.asq.org

Society of Quality Assurance
154 Hansen Road, Suite 201
Charlottesville, VA 22911
434.297.4772
sqa@sqa.org
www.sqa.org

John Pritchard/Editor

Wholesale & Retail Buyer

Snapshot

Career Cluster(s): Agriculture, Food & Natural Resources, Business, Management & Administration, Human Services, Marketing, Sales & Service

Interests: Purchasing, sales negotiations, retail management, advertising, marketing

Earnings (Yearly Average): $52,629

Employment & Outlook: Slower Than Average Growth Expected

OVERVIEW

Sphere of Work

Wholesale and retail buyers select merchandise to be sold either to purchasers of wholesale items, such as large retailers, or to the public. They negotiate the purchase of goods directly from manufacturers or purchase items from wholesalers for retail purposes. Buyers arrange for transportation and delivery of goods, and they make purchasing decisions for clients based on customer feedback and industry trends.

Work Environment

Wholesale and retail buyers generally split their time between office or store environments—where they meet with management, manage online transactions, and attend meetings—and trade shows, conferences, markets, and manufacturing centers. Hours are often irregular and may include weekends and evenings.

Profile

Interests: Data, People, Things
Working Conditions: Work Inside
Physical Strength: Light Work,
Education Needs: On-The-Job Training, Junior/Technical/Community College
Licensure/Certification: Recommended
Physical Abilities Not Required: Not Climb, Not Kneel
Opportunities For Experience: Internship, Part Time Work
Holland Interest Score*: ESA

* See Appendix A

Occupation Interest

Individuals drawn to the profession enjoy working in fast-paced, competitive environments. They must be able to interact with many different types of people, and they are often required to negotiate sales in high-pressure situations. They should also enjoy identifying and following trends. Buyers must keep track of prices, sales records, and quality standards, and they often employ spreadsheet and retail-management software to do so. Buyers are often expected to train and mentor entry-level staff and should be comfortable supervising others.

A Day in the Life—Duties and Responsibilities

The daily duties of a wholesale or retail buyer vary according to the commodity or merchandise that he or she purchases. Buyers may visit factories and manufacturing facilities directly, review available products, and perform quality tests or review testing data. They then negotiate the price of merchandise and arrange the transportation of goods. Some buyers, particularly for retail establishments, conduct business at trade shows and markets or in one-on-one meetings with wholesalers. Buyers work closely with vendors and manufacturers to develop and purchase desirable products. They analyze market and industry data to anticipate customer needs and buying patterns, and they determine the quantity of goods needed. They are also sometimes required to work with point-of-sale and retail-management software, set prices and discount levels for goods, and provide inventory information.

Buyers work with manufacturers and vendors to develop quality standards and inspect and return merchandise if it fails to meet them. They introduce new merchandise to other sales staff and train them to sell it. Buyers also monitor competitors' activities by following advertising and sales information and keep abreast of industry and economic trends. Retail buyers may work for multiple independent businesses and meet with owners and managers to ascertain their needs. They may help marketing staff determine which products should be featured in advertisements and when. Seasonal fluctuations and sales can influence the pace of this work.

Duties and Responsibilities

- Supplying institutional buyers with commodities
- Consulting with a store or merchandise manager on a budget and items to be purchased
- Analyzing sales records to determine what products are currently in demand
- Selecting and ordering merchandise
- Inspecting, grading or appraising merchandise
- Visiting manufacturers' showrooms
- Assisting in establishing markup rates and prices of new merchandise
- Determining necessary markdowns to sell slow-moving merchandise
- Traveling throughout various market areas in the United States or foreign countries to examine and select merchandise

OCCUPATION SPECIALTIES

Assistant Buyers

Assistant Buyers authorize payment of invoices, approve advertising copy, inspect or sell merchandise and provide information for pricing.

Procurement Engineers

Procurement Engineers develop specifications and performance tests in order to get parts and equipment for aeronautical and aerospace products.

Purchasing Agents

Purchasing Agents obtain goods and services, such as raw materials, equipment, tools, parts, supplies, and advertising.

Contracts Managers

Contracts Managers negotiate contracts with representatives of oil products, refiners, and pipeline carriers for purchase, sale, or delivery of crude oil, petroleum, and natural gas.

Merchandise Managers

Merchandise Managers establish policies and coordinate merchandising activities, like mark-up and mark-down percentages, in wholesale and retail businesses.

WORK ENVIRONMENT

Immediate Physical Environment

Wholesale and retail buyers work in a variety of environments, depending on the merchandise or commodities they purchase. Most travel frequently and often work from off-site locations and hotels. They spend time inspecting goods in factories or attending large conferences and trade shows, where they may negotiate purchases with many vendors simultaneously.

Transferable Skills and Abilities

Communication Skills
- Persuading others
- Speaking effectively
- Writing concisely

Interpersonal/Social Skills
- Cooperating with others
- Working as a member of a team

Organization & Management Skills
- Coordinating tasks
- Making decisions
- Managing people/groups
- Managing time
- Meeting goals and deadlines
- Performing duties which change frequently

Research & Planning Skills
- Using logical reasoning

Technical Skills
- Performing scientific, mathematical and technical work

Work Environment Skills
- Traveling

Human Environment

As interacting with others is a crucial part of their job, wholesale and retail buyers must have excellent interpersonal skills. They must be energetic and persuasive negotiators to ensure the best pricing and quality for their clients. Buyers must have strong critical-thinking skills and be able to develop close professional relationships with vendors and clients alike. They often work on sales teams and collaborate with other staff within their organizations as well as with off-site colleagues.

Technological Environment

Wholesale and retail buyers must be comfortable with point-of-sale, inventory, and spreadsheet software. They travel frequently and often work remotely, so they must be able to manage the technology that makes this possible. Buyers often use planning and management programs as well as presentation and word processing software.

EDUCATION, TRAINING, AND ADVANCEMENT

High School/Secondary

Students interested in the position of wholesale or retail buyer should work to develop strong speaking and writing skills. They should take courses in business management, if available, and in English and math. Entry-level retail experience is also helpful.

Suggested High School Subjects
- Applied Communication
- Arts
- Bookkeeping
- Business
- Business Data Processing
- Business Law
- Clothing & Textiles
- College Preparatory
- Economics
- English
- Mathematics
- Merchandising
- Psychology
- Speech

Related Career Pathways/Majors

Agriculture, Food & Natural Resources Cluster
- Agribusiness Systems Pathway

Business, Management & Administration Cluster
- Marketing Pathway

Human Services Cluster
- Consumer Services Pathway

Marketing, Sales & Service Cluster
- Buying & Merchandising Pathway
- Professional Sales & Marketing Pathway

Postsecondary

Wholesale and retail buyers are typically required to have completed some postsecondary study, though requirements vary from employer to employer. Large firms often require at least a two-year degree and two to five years of work experience. Some firms require a bachelor's degree in a business-related field. Manufacturing buyers may need degrees in engineering or applied sciences to understand the needs of their clients fully. Sales and marketing degrees are available from both two- and four-year programs, and internships in this field are virtually mandatory. Most companies have comprehensive training programs for new employees and require a significant training and trial period.

Related College Majors
- Agricultural Supplies Retailing & Wholesaling
- Business
- Clothing, Apparel & Textile Technology & Management
- General Retailing & Wholesaling Operations & Skills
- Home Furnishings & Equipment Installation & Consultants
- International Business
- Marketing Management & Research
- Purchasing, Procurement & Contracts Management

Adult Job Seekers

Adults interested in the wholesale or retail buying field should investigate internship opportunities, which may be available for adult job seekers as well as college students and young professionals. In addition, they may benefit from gaining retail sales experience, which can be readily obtained and allows workers to explore the field. The most important characteristics of a successful buyer are negotiating ability, high energy, and a willingness to work hard. Internal training programs ensure that candidates from various backgrounds are given an equal start.

Professional Certification and Licensure

Certification and licensure are generally not required but may be preferred by some employers. The Institute for Supply Management offers various certifications to wholesale and retail buyers, including the Accredited Purchasing Practitioner (APP) and Certified Purchasing Manager (CPM) certifications. The American Purchasing Society grants Certified Purchasing Professional (CPP) and Certified Professional Purchasing Manager (CPPM) designations. Governmental supply purchasers are awarded other designations through written and oral examinations. Professional development is very important in the field, and buyers participate regularly in training sessions and seminars offered by industry trade associations.

Additional Requirements

Wholesale and retail buyers work in a fast-paced, competitive field that is stimulating for high-energy individuals who enjoy negotiating and travel. Buyers must demonstrate leadership and ethical behavior, since they often train and supervise assistants and trainees and also represent the company in meetings with outside vendors and suppliers.

Fun Fact

One in 10 Europeans is conceived in an Ikea bed, and 94 percent of the world's population recognizes Coca Cola's red and white logo.

Source: Buzzfeed

EARNINGS AND ADVANCEMENT

Earnings depend on the size and geographic location and the experience of the employee. Median annual earnings of wholesale and retail buyers were $52,629 in 2016.

Wholesale and retail buyers may receive paid vacations, holidays, and sick days; life and health insurance; and retirement benefits. These are usually paid by the employer. Wholesale and retail buyers may also receive employee discounts on merchandise.

EMPLOYMENT AND OUTLOOK

There were approximately 122,000 wholesale and retail buyers employed nationally in 2010. Employment of wholesale and retail buyers is expected to grow slower than the average for all occupations through the year 2024, which means employment is projected to increase 3 percent to 9 percent. Most job opportunities will result from the need to replace workers who leave the work force or transfer to other occupations.

Related Occupations
- Online Merchant
- Purchasing Agent
- Retail Salesperson
- Retail Store Sales Manager
- Wholesale Sales Representative

MORE INFORMATION

American Purchasing Society
North Island Center, Suite 203
8 East Galena Boulevard
Aurora, IL 60506
630.859.0250
propurch@propurch.com
www.american-purchasing.com

**Institute for Supply Management
Information Center**
P.O. Box 22160
Tempe, AZ 85285-2160
800.888.6276
bnawrocki@ism.ws
www.ism.ws

**National Institute of
Governmental Purchasing**
151 Spring Street
Herndon, VA 20170-5223
800.367.6447
www.nigp.org

National Retail Federation
325 7th Street NW, Suite 1100
Washington, DC 20004
800.673.4692
www.nrf.com

Bethany Groff/Editor

GLOBALIZING EDUCATION

The long history of teaching abroad has its roots in the colonial era when missionaries began establishing schools in third world countries with the goal of spreading Christianity to societies typically perceived of as primitive. As early as the 1600s, there were British missionary schools active in India with the goal of bringing Western philosophy, and religion, to the native Hindu population. Over the years, the idea that foreign peoples should be "civilized" by introducing western European ideals, knowledge, and Christianity, fell out of favor, but the activity of teaching abroad endured and evolved.

In the 21st century, there are many different ways for a person from the U.S., or many other nations, to travel internationally as a teacher or other educational professional. In some cases, teaching abroad positions are part of humanitarian missions that place teachers in poor, underserved areas, while other international teaching positions are offered by more profit-oriented educational institutions and are aimed at more affluent populations. International teaching programs fill a needed niche in many nations and create opportunities for students and teachers to broaden their horizons and knowledge of foreign cultures. The international exchange in education now fosters closer connections between cultures and helps prepare future generations for an increasingly globalized professional and social environment.

Exporting English

Among the most familiar ways for students and professionals to teach abroad is through the many numerous companies and educational programs providing English language instruction for children and adult in numerous foreign countries. Historically known as English as a Second Language (ESL), programs in this vein are now more commonly known as Teaching English as a Foreign Language (TEFL).

The economic dominance of the United States and other English-speaking nations, has created a pressing need for foreign English instruction and has, likewise, created demand for native English speakers with a grasp of other internationally widespread languages, like Spanish, Japanese, and Chinese. Programs that send instructors to foreign nations to teach English help fill both of these demands, by spreading English to students and adults in foreign nations, while allowing instructors to deepen their fluency with foreign languages as well, potentially returning to their native nations and participating in programs that teach Chinese, Spanish, or other languages to native English speakers.

The International TEFL Academy, a leading company sending U.S. students abroad, advertised in 2017 for English teachers interested in traveling to South Korea, China, Japan, Vietnam, and several nations in the Gulf Arab States. The academy offers reimbursement for travel expenses, furnished, paid housing for participants, and pays as much as $600 to more than $4000 per month after expenses. Companies like the International TEFL Academy also facilitate the relocation and licensing process, helping participants to obtain insurance and licenses/permits and other documentation required for their stay, with contracts ranging from one to several years.

Western Education Abroad

While teaching English overseas is the most familiar avenue into international education, there are many other ways for U.S. residents to find work as educators overseas. For one, many American colleges and universities maintain international campus locations where students enrolled in the U.S. can travel for a semester or academic year abroad. For instance, Webster University, a liberal arts institution based in Webster Groves, Missouri, has extension campuses in Switzerland, Austria, Greece, the Netherlands, Thailand, China, and Ghana. Each year, Webster University brings teachers, administrators, and students who want to teach or learn overseas and hosts programs and classes specific to the regions in which the university has campuses.

Outside of opportunities through international campuses, U.S. students and teachers, can apply for enrollment or positions at foreign learning institutions. Students and professionals from the United States are more likely to qualify for enrollment or positions at English speaking universities, though students and teachers with foreign language experience might also have options for employment in areas where English is not the primary educational language. According to the website *Collegechoice.com*, the most popular international school for U.S. students in 2017 was the London School of Economic and Political Science, which hosts 6,583 international students, comprising some 70 percent of the student body. Similarly, the University of Salamanca, in Madrid, Spain, has 9,200 international students, 25 percent of the student body.

Teachers, in a variety of fields, can also find opportunities for overseas work through international schools, which are institution founded, at least in part, by U.S. educators or administrators, but operating entirely in a foreign nation. International schools are often established to serve the needs of U.S. residents living abroad, such as the families of diplomats and other governmental personnel, but many international schools are also open to native students as well as students from other international locations. The U.S. Department of State's Office of Overseas Schools provides funding to support associated institutions and helps to regulate the industry. International schools vary in scope and size, from small schools like the American International School of Algiers, which serves 17 students annually, to larger schools like the Singapore American School, which hosts a student population of over 4000.

To provide an example of the scope of international schooling, in 2017 the State Department listed 41 international schools in Africa, employing 903 U.S.-born teachers, as well as 507 native teachers and 890 from another nation other than the U.S. or the host nation. The 41 international schools collectively hosted 3,617 U.S. citizen students, 3,927 students from host nations, and 8,897 from other foreign nations. The State Department also listed 39 schools in the Americas, 25 in East Asia, 67 in Europe, and 21 in the Near East.

Sensitivity and Preparedness

In the past, international education was based on prejudiced nationalism and the belief that the American, or at least Western European, approach to education, religion, and culture was in some way superior to practices and customs in many other parts of the world. Such Western-centric views have largely fallen out of favor and those participating in Western education abroad should be sensitive to the cultural practices and traditions in their host nations. Institutions and companies hiring U.S. educators for overseas positions now search for individuals who have an earnest and genuine interest in spreading the benefits of quality multi-cultural education and who are equally interested in learning about the culture in their host nation. Additionally, while some view teaching abroad programs as a chance for recreation and tourism, many foreign teaching programs require difficult and demanding work and applicants should be prepared to meet these challenges before enrolling in a program or applying for overseas positions. For those interested in a challenging and enriching experience, however, teaching abroad is one of the best ways to gain international experience while also participating in a time-honored exchange of ideas and culture that has helped to foster closer and more cooperative ties between the world's nations.

Fun Fact

Eighty-three percent of Americans agree that the U.S. is better off when more of its students are internationally educated and understand other cultures and languages.
Source: nafsa.orgs

Works Used

Thanasoulas, Dimitrios. "History of English Language Teaching." *Englishclub*. English Club. 2017. 4 Aug 2017.

Turner, Gerrilynn. "The 50 Most Popular International Universities for U.S. Students Getting a Global Education." *Collegechoice.net*. College Choice. 2017. Web. 3 Aug 2017.

"Worldwide Fact Sheet 2016-2017." *State*. Department of State. American-Sponsored Elementary and Secondary Schools Overseas. 2016. Web. 21 Jul 2017

Librarian

Snapshot

Career Cluster(s): Education & Training, Health Science
Interests: Reading, research, arranging information, communicating with others, helping others
Earnings (Yearly Average): $57,770
Employment & Outlook: Slower Than Average Growth Expected

OVERVIEW

Sphere of Work

A librarian is an information specialist who helps patrons locate various kinds of information quickly and effectively within a library setting. He or she is responsible for the selection, organization, and circulation of library materials, including print media, books, magazines and periodicals, and digital and electronic media. A librarian also manages non-print materials, including films, tapes, CDs, maps, and microfiche. He or she generally performs administrative, technical, and customer service tasks.

Work Environment

A librarian assists patrons in finding and reaching books and information sources. A librarian usually works in a public or academic library, as well as in a school library media center or special library. In all cases, a librarian works in a pleasant, comfortable environment, either independently or under the supervision of a library director. A librarian generally works a standard thirty-five to forty-hour workweek and may be required to work during the evenings or on weekends.

Profile

Interests: Data, People
Working Conditions: Work Inside
Physical Strength: Light work
Education Needs: Bachelor's Degree, Master's Degree, Doctoral Degree
Licensure/Certification: Required
Physical Abilities Not Required: Not Climb, Not Kneel
Opportunities For Experience: Internship, Volunteer Work, Part Time Work
Holland Interest Score*: SAI

* See Appendix A

Occupation Interest

People looking to become librarians should find satisfaction in learning about the ways in which ideas and information are communicated within modern society. They should be passionate about working with people and helping them locate and obtain various kinds of information effectively and accurately. Librarians often work alone or with a small staff and must be comfortable managing and overseeing all aspects of a public or private library. Aspiring librarians should be extremely organized, with a passion for cataloging and arranging information systematically.

A Day in the Life—Duties and Responsibilities

Librarians primarily manage the day-to-day operations of the libraries in which they work. Most librarians select and procure print, audiovisual, and electronic information sources for the various sections of the library. They organize, classify, and maintain library materials according to physical or electronic catalogs and databases. They assist library patrons and respond to any reference questions patrons may have. In smaller libraries, librarians are responsible for checking out and receiving materials.

Librarians often act as teachers, transferring library skills to customers or groups of customers. They sometimes hold regular tutoring sessions, which orient new patrons to the library. Some librarians schedule a daily or weekly storytelling or literacy meeting to read aloud to groups of small children visiting the library. In larger libraries, librarians specialize in a specific subject area and must coordinate with other librarians and library staff to make sure each section or department runs smoothly. Librarians also take on various administrative tasks, such as preparing budgets and other reports and maintaining employee and circulation records. In many cases, librarians hire, train, and supervise other library personnel.

In recent years, technology has begun to decrease the public's reliance on print and hardcopy materials. As a result, librarians are now responsible for remote and electronic databases, Internet research and cataloging, and web content management. They also instruct patrons on the use of various electronic library systems.

Duties and Responsibilities

- Maintaining the library's collection of print and non-print materials
- Selecting, ordering, cataloging and classifying materials
- Assisting patrons in obtaining library services and materials
- Utilizing the Internet and electronic databases

OCCUPATION SPECIALTIES

Branch or Department Chief Librarians

Branch or Department Chief Librarians coordinate the activities of a library branch or department; train, assign duties and supervise staff; and perform librarian duties.

Reference Librarians

Reference Librarians assist groups and individuals in locating and obtaining library materials.

Children's Librarians

Children's Librarians manage library programs for children and select books and other materials of interest to children for the library to acquire. They plan and conduct programs for children to encourage reading, viewing, listening and using of library materials and facilities.

Acquisitions Librarians

Acquisitions Librarians select and order books, periodicals, articles and audiovisual materials on particular subjects.

Special Collections Librarians

Special Collections Librarians collect and organize materials on select subjects used for research.

Bibliographers

Bibliographers work in research libraries and compile lists of books, periodicals, articles and audiovisual materials on particular subjects.

Classifiers

Classifiers classify materials by subject.

Catalogers

Catalogers describe books and other library materials.

Information Scientists

Information Scientists design systems for storage and retrieval of information and develop procedures for collecting, organizing, interpreting and classifying information.

WORK ENVIRONMENT

Transferable Skills and Abilities

Communication Skills
- Expressing thoughts and ideas
- Speaking effectively
- Writing concisely

Interpersonal/Social Skills
- Cooperating with others
- Working as a member of a team

Organization & Management Skills
- Coordinating tasks
- Making decisions
- Managing people/groups
- Paying attention to and handling details
- Performing duties which change frequently

Research & Planning Skills
- Developing evaluation strategies

Immediate Physical Environment

Most librarians work in clean, quiet, and well-ventilated library spaces. They maintain a library's level of calm and serenity by monitoring patrons' behavior to ensure their compliance with library rules and regulations.

Human Environment

Librarians regularly interact with library patrons, including young children, adolescents, college students, teachers, and members of community organizations. They report to a library supervisor or director and often manage library assistants, technicians, administrative staff members, and janitorial personnel.

Technological Environment

Librarians use a wide variety of tools and equipment to help them organize information. They regularly work with paper and electronic card catalogs, microforms, the Internet and e-mail, and computer programs. They also use projection equipment, audiovisual devices, and fax machines.

EDUCATION, TRAINING, AND ADVANCEMENT

High School/Secondary

High school students who wish to become librarians should focus on college preparatory courses that deal with business, communications, language and literature, technology, and public speaking. Students may also benefit from studying at least one foreign language. Interested students should spend time in their high school and local libraries, familiarizing themselves with current information systems and cataloging procedures as well as the structure of a library.

Suggested High School Subjects
- Arts
- Audio-Visual
- Business
- Business Data Processing
- College Preparatory
- Composition
- Crafts
- English
- Foreign Languages
- Government
- History
- Humanities
- Keyboarding
- Literature
- Mathematics
- Photography
- Political Science

- Science
- Social Studies
- Speech

Related Career Pathways/Majors

Education & Training Cluster
- Professional Support Services Pathway

Health Science Cluster
- Health Informatics Pathway

Postsecondary

After high school, prospective librarians must obtain a bachelor's degree, preferably in library science. Employers generally give preference to students who graduate from American Library Association (ALA)-accredited schools. At the college level, students should prepare for a career in library science by studying librarianship, children's and adult literature, archival methods, humanities, science and technology, and subject reference and bibliography, among other subjects.

In order for a librarian to work in a public, academic, or special library, he or she must obtain a master's degree in library science (MLS) after completing an undergraduate degree. Graduate programs in library science usually cover the foundations of information science, censorship, user services, and automated circulation systems, in addition to other supplemental and elective courses. Though not required, some librarians choose to obtain a doctorate in library and information science.

Related College Majors

- Library Assistant Training
- Pre-Law Studies

Adult Job Seekers

Many aspiring librarians begin by volunteering or working part-time in local libraries. Those enrolled in an undergraduate or graduate program may also be able to participate in a work-study program or internship with a participating library. Prospective librarians can apply for employment directly with a library, through library associations, or through school placement services.

Experienced librarians may advance to supervisory or teaching positions. These positions may require more budgetary, administrative, and managerial skills and duties. Advancement is often dependent on seniority, education, and library size.

Professional Certification and Licensure

Librarians who work in public schools or local libraries are usually required to be certified. Certification and licensure requirements vary by state. Many states also require librarians to acquire teacher certifications, and some states require librarians to pass a comprehensive examination. Interested individuals should research and fulfill the education and certification requirements of their home state.

Librarians who specialize in certain subject areas, such as law, medicine, or the sciences, may also need to earn an advanced degree in their desired subject. For example, twenty states require school librarians to have an advanced degree in library science or education.

Additional Requirements

Librarians are responsible for maintaining large databases of information and must therefore be extremely organized and detail-oriented. They must also be passionate about information systems and interested in the changing trends in and improvements to those systems. They should enjoy continually learning about new research methods and classification technology.

EARNINGS AND ADVANCEMENT

Earnings of librarians depend on the individual's qualifications and the type, size and geographic location of the library. Median annual earnings of librarians were $57,770 in 2012. The lowest ten percent earned less than $35,605, and the highest ten percent earned more than $88,521.

Librarians may receive paid vacations, holidays, and sick days; life and health insurance; and retirement benefits. These are usually paid by the employer.

EMPLOYMENT AND OUTLOOK

There were approximately 156,000 librarians employed nationally in 2010. About one-fourth worked part-time. Employment is expected to grow slower than the average for all occupations through the year 2020, which means employment is projected to increase 3 percent to 9 percent. Offsetting the need for librarians are government budget cuts and the increasing use of computerized information storage and retrieval systems in libraries that allow users to bypass librarians and conduct research on their own.

Related Occupations
- Archivist and Curator
- Computer & Information Systems Manager
- Library Technician
- Media Specialist
- Research Assistant

MORE INFORMATION

American Association of Law Libraries
105 W. Adams Street, Suite 3300
Chicago, IL 60603-6225
312.939.4764
support@aall.org
www.aallnet.org

American Association of School Librarians
50 E. Huron Street
Chicago, IL 60611
800.545.2433
aasl@ala.org
www.aasl.org

American Library Association
50 E. Huron Street
Chicago, IL 60611
800.545.2433
aasl@ala.org
www.ala.org

American Society for Information Society & Technology
1320 Fenwick Lane, Suite 510
Silver Spring, MD 20910
301.495.0900
asis@asis.org
www.asis.org

Library of Congress
101 Independence Avenue SE
Washington, DC 20540
202.707.5000
www.loc.gov

Medical Library Association
65 E. Wacker Place, Suite 1900
Chicago, IL 60601-7298
312.419.9094
info@mlahq.org
www.mlanet.org

Special Libraries Association
331 South Patrick Street
Alexandria, VA 22314-3501
703.647.4900
www.sla.org

Briana Nadeau/Editor

Archivist and Curator

Snapshot

Career Cluster(s): Arts, A/V Technology & Communications, Hospitality & Tourism

Interests: History, culture, art, preserving documents, organizing information, research, communication

Earnings (Yearly Average): $49,635

Employment & Outlook: Faster Than Average Growth Expected

OVERVIEW

Sphere of Work

Archivists and curators are preservationists of human culture and history and the natural world. They collect, appraise, organize, and preserve documents, artwork, specimens, ephemera, films, and many other objects for historical and educational purposes. Archivists usually handle documents and records that are of historical value. Curators are more likely to manage cultural or biological items, such as artwork or nature collections.

Work Environment

Archivists work in libraries, government depositories, universities, and historical museums, while curators are more often employed in art museums, zoos, nature centers, and other cultural or scientific institutions. Each typically divides the workweek between independent projects and interaction with other staff and outsiders, such as dealers, researchers, and the public.

Profile

Interests: Data, People
Working Conditions: Work Inside
Physical Strength: Light work
Education Needs: Master's Degree, Doctoral Degree
Licensure/Certification: Usually Not Required equired
Physical Abilities Not Required: Not Climb, Not Kneel, Not Hear and/or Talk
Opportunities For Experience: Internship, Apprenticeship, Volunteer Work, Part Time Work
Holland Interest Score*: AES, IRS

* See Appendix A

Occupation Interest

People interested in archivist or curator positions value the contributions of humans or the natural world and realize their importance in research. They are scholars who possess good organizational skills and a knack for handling irreplaceable items that are often fragile and extremely valuable. They need to be both detail-oriented and aware of larger cultural, scientific, and/or historical contexts. Other important traits include critical thinking, leadership ability, oral and written communication skills, and a high level of integrity.

A Day in the Life—Duties and Responsibilities

Archivists and curators build on their institution's collections by purchasing items or receiving them as gifts, often the result of bequests. A collection donated by a celebrated author might consist of boxes of unpublished manuscripts and drafts, personal correspondence, publishing contracts, and other printed matter. A collection obtained from a philatelist might include rare postal stamps, philatelic books and journals, microscopes, antique magnifying glasses, and other materials.

The archivist or curator is usually responsible for deciding what items to keep based on physical condition, financial, historical, and cultural value, and relevance to the institution's mission or purpose. While assessing each item, he or she authenticates its provenance (date and origin) and researches the item for any additional relevant information. The archivist or curator also determines how best to preserve and store items. For example, special cabinets may have to be ordered or an item may be given to a conservator for repairs.

Next, the archivist or curator catalogues or classifies items in a database so scholars can access the information. These databases also allow archivists or curators to keep track of their collections, provide reference service, and plan exhibits. Many different classification systems are used, although the most common one in the United States is the Library of Congress Classification System. Some items may be given a taxonomic classification as well as a call number.

Curators and archivists have other tasks in addition to their preservation work. Curators and archivists often write articles, grant proposals, and annual reports. Depending on their work environment, they may give tours and presentations to the public. Curators and archivists may also take care of other administrative duties or oversee assistants who handle some of these responsibilities, or they may do everything themselves.

Duties and Responsibilities

- Analyzing and appraising the value of documents, such as government records, minutes, meetings, letters and charters of institutions
- Selecting and editing documents for publication and display
- Preparing budgets, maintaining inventories, representing the institution at meetings and soliciting financial support
- Planning and designing exhibits
- Writing for technical publications
- Setting up educational displays at a muse

OCCUPATION SPECIALTIES

Museum Technicians

Museum Technicians prepare specimens for museum collections
and exhibits. They preserve and restore specimens by reassembling
fragmented pieces and creating substitute pieces.

Art Conservators

Art Conservators coordinate the examination, repair and conservation
of art objects.

Historic-Site Administrators

Historic-Site Administrators manage the overall operations of an
historic structure or site.

Museum Registrars

Museum Registrars maintain records of the condition and location of
objects in museum collections and oversee the movement of objects to
other locations.

WORK ENVIRONMENT

Immediate Physical Environment

Archivists and curators tend to work at least part of the time in
climate-controlled storage facilities. They may have to wear white
gloves or masks to protect items from human contamination. They
sometimes deal with dust, mold, and insect infestations. Fieldwork
may include visits to off-site locations such as auctions, schools, and
private residences.

Transferable Skills and Abilities

Communication Skills
- Speaking effectively
- Writing concisely

Organization & Management Skills
- Coordinating tasks
- Making decisions
- Managing people/groups
- Paying attention to and handling details

Research & Planning Skills
- Analyzing information
- Creating ideas
- Developing evaluation strategies
- Using logical reasoning

Technical Skills
- Performing scientific, mathematical and technical work

Human Environment

Archivists and curators usually report to a director and may supervise assistants, volunteers, or interns. In some cases, the curator is the director and reports to a board of administrators. Archivists and curators also interact with clerical staff and fellow preservation professionals, such as librarians, conservators, or museum technicians. They also work with researchers and other members of the public who use their facilities.

Technological Environment

Archivists and curators rely heavily on computers for research, database management, file sharing, and communication. They also use a variety of digitization equipment for preservation purposes, including digital photography and video cameras. Microscopes are often used for detail work. In many cases, they must be familiar with radio-frequency identifications (RFIDs) and other inventory control and anti-theft systems.

EDUCATION, TRAINING, AND ADVANCEMENT

High School/Secondary

Archivist and curator positions require advanced education. A strong college preparatory program with electives in the areas of professional interest will provide the best foundation for postsecondary studies. History courses are especially important for aspiring archivists and curators. Students interested in becoming a curator of art should take art history and appreciation courses. Botany, zoology, and other natural sciences are important for curators of natural history. Students should also consider volunteering or working part-time in a library, museum, or other similar institution.

Suggested High School Subjects
- Algebra
- Arts
- Biology
- Chemistry
- College Preparatory
- Composition
- English
- Foreign Languages
- History
- Humanities
- Literature
- Social Studies

Related Career Pathways/Majors
Arts, A/V Technology & Communications Cluster
- Visual Arts Pathway

Hospitality & Tourism Cluster
- Recreation, Amusements & Attractions Pathway

Postsecondary

A bachelor's degree in history, art history, botany, political science, or other relevant discipline, with additional coursework in archival or museum studies, is the minimum requirement; however, most positions require a master's degree or doctorate in the specialized discipline or a master's degree in library science, archival studies, or museum studies. Business and public administration courses may also be useful. An internship or other work experience in a related institution is typically required for employment. Continuing education courses are expected as part of ongoing professional training.

Related College Majors
- American (U.S.) History
- Art History, Criticism & Conservation
- Art, General
- Historic Preservation/Conservation & Architectural History
- History
- Library Science/Librarianship
- Museology/Museum Studies
- Public History & Archival Administration

Adult Job Seekers

Adults who have experience working at a relevant institution, researching a particular type of collection, or writing grant proposals or fundraising have an advantage over inexperienced graduates, as maturity and experience are often desired in addition to education.

Advancement is highly dependent upon the size of the institution. In larger institutions, advancement usually takes the form of increasing responsibility, such as a supervisory or directorial position. In government positions, one can move into higher pay grades with proper experience and education. Consulting is also an option for experienced professionals.

Professional Certification and Licensure

Licensing is typically not necessary for archivists and curators, although some employers may require certification by a professional organization, such as the Academy of Certified Archivists (ACA). A master's degree and archival experience are necessary before one can take the ACA written exam for certification. Those interested in becoming certified should consult credible professional associations within the field and follow professional debate as to the relevancy and value of any certification program.

Additional Requirements

Physical strength is needed to lift heavy boxes or other items, and good eyesight is needed for detail work. Membership in professional archivist or curator associations may provide access to networking opportunities and professional development programs.

EARNINGS AND ADVANCEMENT

Earnings of archivists and curators vary greatly according to the individual's education and experience, the employer, geographic location and job specialty. The size and funds of a museum may also affect earnings. Salaries in the Federal government are generally higher than those in private organizations. Salaries of curators in large, well-funded museums may be several times higher than those in small ones.

Median annual earnings of archivists were $47,912 in 2012. The lowest ten percent earned less than $27,009, and the highest ten percent earned more than $85,489. Median annual earnings of curators were $51,357 in 2012. The lowest ten percent earned less than $29,298, and the highest ten percent earned more than $91,637.

The average annual salary for archivists in the federal government was $82,669 in 2012, while curators averaged $80,136 in 2012.

Archivists and curators may receive paid vacations, holidays, and sick days; life and health insurance; and retirement benefits. These are usually paid by the employer.

EMPLOYMENT AND OUTLOOK

There were approximately 18,000 archivists and curators employed nationally in 2010. They were employed in museums and historical sites; federal, state, and local governments; and public and private educational institutions, mainly college and university libraries. Employment of archivists and curators is expected to grow faster than the average for all occupations through the year 2020, which means employment is projected to increase 20 percent to 28 percent. Demand is expected to increase as public and private organizations emphasize establishing archives and organizing records, especially electronically. Museum and zoo attendance has been on the rise and is expected to continue increasing, which will generate demand for curators.

Related Occupations
- Anthropologist
- Librarian
- Media Specialist
- Research Assistant

MORE INFORMATION

Academy of Certified Archivists (ACA)
1450 Western Avenue, Suite 101
Albany, NY 12203
518.694.8471
ww.certifiedarchivists.org

Certifies archivists:
www.certifiedarchivists.org/get-certified/
application.html

American Association for State and Local History
1717 Church Street
Nashville, TN 37203-2991
615.320.3203
membership@aaslh.org
www.aaslh.org

American Association of Museums
Attn
Bookstore
1575 Eye Street NW, Suite 400
Washington, DC 20005
202.289.1818
bookstore@aam-us.org
www.aam-us.org

American Institute for Conservation of Historic & Artistic Works (AIC)
1156 15th Street NW, Suite 320
Washington, DC 20005
202.452.9545
info@conservation-us.org
www.conservation-us.org

Sponsors continuing education courses:
www.conservation-us.org/
index.cfm?fuseaction=Page.
viewPage&pageId=473

Sponsors scholarships and grants:
www.conservation-us.org/
index.cfm?fuseaction=Page.
viewPage&pageId=474

Association for Art Museum Curators (AAMC)
174 East 80th Street
New York, NY 10075
646.405.8065
www.artcurators.org

Provides grants for students and
professional development:
www.artcurators.org/?page=Grants

Association of Moving Image Archivists (AMIA)
1313 North Vine Street
Hollywood, CA 90028
323.463.1500
AMIA@amianet.org
www.amianet.org

Provides scholarships and fellowships:
www.amianet.org/events/scholarship.php

Offers the Silver Light Award for "career achievement in moving image archiving":
http://www.amianet.org/events/awardsilver.php

National Association of Government Archives and Records Administrators (NAGARA)
1450 Western Avenue, Suite 101
Albany, NY 12203
518.694.8472
nagara@caphill.com
www.nagara.org

National Council on Public History
327 Cavanaugh Hall - IUPUI
425 University Boulevard
Indianapolis, IN 46202
317.274.2716
ncph@iupui.edu
www.ncph.org

National Trust for Historic Preservation
1785 Massachusetts Avenue, NW
Washington, DC 20036-2117
202.588.6000
www.nthp.org

Organization of American Historians
112 N. Bryan Avenue, P.O. Box 5457
Bloomington, IN 47408-5457
812.855.7311
oah@oah.org
www.oah.org

Society for History in the Federal Government
P.O. Box 14139
Benjamin Franklin Station
Washington, DC 20044
www.shfg.org

Society of American Archivists (SAA)
17 North State Street, Suite 1425
Chicago, IL 60602-3315
866.722.7858
www2.archivists.org

Maintains a directory of postsecondary archival programs:
www2.archivists.org/dae

Sally Driscoll/Editor

College Faculty Member

OVERVIEW

Sphere of Work

A college faculty member is a professional instructor who teaches courses at a post-secondary institution. He or she has a master's or doctorate degree in a specific academic discipline and is considered qualified to teach within that discipline only. Faculty members design their own courses, plan discussion topics and reading and writing assignments, and plan and coordinate test and examination schedules. As they conduct their classes, faculty members lecture students, grade papers and exams, and advise students

on their major fields of study. A college faculty member will typically research and write scholarly books and articles on their particular field of expertise and, occasionally, present their individual works at relevant conferences.

Work Environment

A member of a college faculty typically manages his or her classes individually (although at larger universities, many professors delegate grading papers and exams or running student discussion groups to graduate students). Outside of the classroom, however, they often collaborate with fellow professors in writing and editing scholarly books and articles. Furthermore, as part of the faculty, they will meet frequently with their department colleagues to discuss departmental policies and other school news. A college faculty member's workload is therefore diverse, although not physically strenuous.

Profile

Interests: Data, People
Working Conditions: Work Inside
Physical Strength: Light work
Education Needs: Master's Degree, Doctoral Degree
Licensure/Certification: Usually Not Required equired
Physical Abilities Not Required: Not Climb, Not Kneel
Opportunities For Experience: Military Service, Part Time Work
Holland Interest Score*: ESI

* See Appendix A

Occupation Interest

Most people pursue careers in postsecondary institutions because they love to study a particular subject and share their insights with others. Aspiring college faculty members should also be interested in helping to shape young minds. College faculty members are, by nature, intellectuals willing to spend long hours researching, writing on, and teaching the many elements of their particular discipline.

College faculty members (often called professors) come from a wide range of backgrounds and demonstrate an equally broad range of perspectives, experience, and teaching styles. They are considered experts in their fields, having completed many years of study at the undergraduate and postgraduate levels.

A Day in the Life—Duties and Responsibilities

A member of a college faculty is primarily a teacher, using his or her past studies, research, and professional experience on a particular subject to help others learn more about it. He or she will select the required texts and articles for the course, design a course syllabus (an overview of the topics for discussion and required reading and homework for each scheduled class), prepare lectures and discussions for each class, lead effective class discussion, and issue and grade tests and student work. Depending on the nature and level of the course, the faculty member may simply lecture a class or provide a "seminar" approach in which students are expected to actively participate.

In addition to their responsibilities to the courses they teach, faculty members will also pursue their own projects, researching and writing scholarly works on topics within their discipline. Occasionally, when these works are published, professors will present these scholarly documents at regional, national, and international conferences. This individual research can help the faculty members continue to work at their respective colleges and even receive tenure (an agreement that the professor may stay on the faculty indefinitely).

College faculty members must also work with other members of their respective departments to shape departmental policies, activities, and courses. Periodically, these individuals may be selected to serve as department chairs, the senior-most position of a department's faculty.

Duties and Responsibilities

- Preparing and delivering lectures
- Compiling, administering and grading papers and examinations
- Supervising laboratory assignments, field work and independent study
- Directing research of others working for advanced degrees
- Advising students on academic and vocational curricula
- Participating in conferences
- Serving on faculty committees
- Conducting research and publishing findings in professional journals
- Providing consulting services to government and industry

WORK ENVIRONMENT

Immediate Physical Environment

A college faculty member works at buildings that are situated on a university campus. Their immediate physical environment includes classrooms, lecture halls, laboratories, and seminar rooms. They will also perform some of their duties in their offices, such as advising students, meeting with peers, and grading and preparing for classes.

Faculty members who teach engineering, chemistry, and other scientific or vocational courses work in a lab environment and are required to follow certain safety procedures. Faculty may be exposed to some dangerous equipment or chemicals and are responsible for educating students as to their proper handling.

Transferable Skills and Abilities

Communication Skills
- Expressing thoughts and ideas
- Persuading others
- Speaking effectively
- Writing concisely

Interpersonal/Social Skills
- Cooperating with others

Organization & Management Skills
- Coordinating tasks
- Making decisions
- Organizing information or materials

Research & Planning Skills
- Analyzing information
- Gathering information
- Using logical reasoning

Human Environment

While professors at smaller colleges and universities tend to manage their classes alone, faculty members at larger institutions will often call upon graduate students to assist them in preparing syllabi, grading papers, and lecturing. Professors also meet frequently with one another on departmental matters and collaborate on research projects.

Technological Environment

Faculty members typically use basic office technology and tools to aid them with lecturing, compiling research, organizing class materials, and in communicating with students. Professors working in scientific fields may use a number of other technologies that are relevant to their fields, such as particle accelerators, spectrometers, and engineering equipment.

EDUCATION, TRAINING, AND ADVANCEMENT

High School/Secondary

In addition to taking courses in the intellectual discipline in which they are interested, high school students who wish to become college faculty members are encouraged to take classes and participate in clubs that help them develop their research and communications skills, such as debate teams, writing courses, and extracurricular clubs that focus on the field in which they are interested.

Suggested High School Subjects
- Algebra
- Arts
- Audio-Visual
- Biology
- Bookkeeping
- Business
- Business & Computer Technology
- Business Math
- Chemistry
- College Preparatory
- Composition
- Computer Science
- Earth Science
- Economics
- English
- Entrepreneurship
- Foreign Languages
- Geography
- History
- Humanities
- Literature
- Mathematics
- Merchandising
- Physics
- Science
- Social Studies

- Sociology
- Speech
- Statistics

Related Career Pathways/Majors
- Education & Training Cluster
- Teaching/Training Pathway

Postsecondary

College faculty members develop their knowledge and experience over a period of many years at the undergraduate and postgraduate levels. Postsecondary students should continue to study all aspects of their chosen discipline at the undergraduate level. Many students choose to obtain an internship in their chosen field, studying this discipline outside of the college setting. Additionally, college professors are strongly encouraged to pursue master's and doctorate degrees in their chosen field, taking a wide range of courses at the graduate level and writing an extensive independent study known as a dissertation.

Related College Majors
- For this occupation, related college majors will vary, based on the area of faculty expertise.

Adult Job Seekers

College faculty positions are often difficult to obtain due to the large number of individuals with advanced degrees seeking jobs in higher education. Many adults who plan to become a full member of a faculty may start out as "adjunct" professors, teaching at an institution on a part-time basis. Many other people will attend conferences and similar events to meet and share their independent work with tenured professors and university officials to help secure a faculty position.

Professional Certification and Licensure

For most full-time college faculty members, a master's and doctorate degree are required. Some institutions are willing to allow people to join without a doctorate, provided that those candidates have extensive experience and expertise in their fields.

Additional Requirements

College faculty members find satisfaction in researching, learning, and sharing knowledge with others. They must be self-motivated and able to motivate others as well. In addition, they should be willing to handle multiple tasks, such as managing multiple classes, working with students, and conducting their own individual research.

Fun Fact

Sixty-one percent of the U.K.'s university-industry co-authored publications involve international businesses, a reflection of the universities' global engagement.

Source: universitiesuk.ac.uk

EARNINGS AND ADVANCEMENT

Earnings of college faculty members depend largely on the academic qualifications, academic specialty, academic rank and experience of each individual, and the type of institution. Generally, professors of medicine, dentistry, engineering and law receive higher salaries than professors in other fields. Faculty in four-year schools earned higher salaries, on the average, than those in two-year schools.

Full-time college faculty members usually work on a nine-month contract. Median annual earnings of college faculty members were $75,430 in 2016. The lowest ten percent earned less than $38,290, and the highest ten percent earned more than $168,270. Many faculty have additional earnings from research, consulting, writing and other employment opportunities.

College faculty members may receive paid vacations, holidays, and sick days; life and health insurance; and retirement benefits. These are usually paid by the employer.

EMPLOYMENT AND OUTLOOK

There were approximately 1.3 million college and university faculty members employed nationally in 2016. Employment is expected faster than average for all occupations through the year 2024, which means employment is projected to increase 13percent. This is due to the projected growth in college and university enrollment over the next decade from the expected increase in the population of 18 to 24 year olds.

Related Occupations
- Anthropologist
- Astronomer
- Biological Scientist
- Career & Technical Education Teacher
- Education Administrator
- Physicist
- Secondary & Middle School Teacher
- Social Scientis

Related Military Occupations
- Teacher & Instructor

MORE INFORMATION

Academic Keys, LLC
P.O. Box 162
Storrs, CT 06268
860.429.0218
www.academickeys.com

**American Association for
Employment in Education**
3040 Riverside Drive, Suite 125
Columbus, OH 43221
614.485.1111
execdir@aaee.org
www.aaee.org

American Federation of Teachers
Public Affairs Department
555 New Jersey Avenue, NW
Washington, DC 20001
202.879.4400
online@aft.org
www.aft.org

**National Teaching and Learning
Forum**
2203 Regent Street
Madison, WI 53726
www.ntlf.com/

Preparing Future Faculty
One Dupont Circle NW, Suite 230
Washington, DC 20036-1173
202.223.3791
www.preparing-faculty.org/

Michael Auerbach/Editor

Principal

Snapshot

Career Cluster(s): Education & Training
Interests: Education, management, school administration, budgeting, child development, resource planning
Earnings (Yearly Average): $90,410
Employment & Outlook: Average Growth Expected

OVERVIEW

Sphere of Work

Principals are educational administrators who manage elementary, middle, and secondary schools. Principals establish student and teacher performance goals, set school policies in accordance with the wishes of parents and teachers, hire and supervise school personnel, and enforce rules and discipline students as necessary. They manage the school's finances, make annual budgets, establish teacher and class schedules, and perform other administrative duties as necessary. Principals function as the school's representative within the community; they meet with vendors and

suppliers, organize fundraising activities, attend conferences, and issue statements to the press.

Work Environment

Principals work from offices located inside the schools they oversee. Although the principal has his or her own office, he or she spends much of the workday walking the halls of the school, meeting with teachers, students, facilities staff, administrative assistants, and others. Schools are crowded, energetic environments during school hours. Principals frequently respond to stressful situations, such as student fights, angry parents, disciplinary issues, or school-wide emergencies. They attend regular meetings of local government agencies, such as school committees and boards of selectmen or city councils. Principals typically work a forty-hour workweek, although they may work at the night for public meetings and student activities. There are significant differences in the job responsibilities of a principal depending on the ages of the students and the size and location of the school.

Profile

Interests: Data, People
Working Conditions: Work Inside
Physical Strength: Light work
Education Needs: Master's Degree
Licensure/Certification: Required
Physical Abilities Not Required: Not Climb, Not Kneel
Opportunities For Experience: Internship
Holland Interest Score*: SEI

* See Appendix A

Occupation Interest

Principals are highly educated individuals interested in school administration who find job satisfaction acting as managers and leaders within elementary, middle, and secondary schools. Principals perform a variety of activities and enjoy considerable authority within the school. They make final decisions regarding academic and disciplinary policies as well as staffing and scheduling needs. They should have strong communication skills as they frequently function in a public relations capacity during meetings with families and community leaders. Principals are financially well compensated for their years of education and the demands of the job.

A Day in the Life—Duties and Responsibilities

Students often view the principal mainly as an enforcer of the school's disciplinary and attendance rules, but in fact, his or her job duties comprise a wide range of tasks. The principal meets with families to discuss students' progress as well as relevant developments and policies at the school. The principal is responsible for hiring qualified faculty members and supervises teachers on new materials, educational goals, testing requirements, teaching methods, and classes. He or she sets performance standards for staff, evaluating their progress and meeting with them to discuss ways to improve. The principal ensures that the school and its staff act in compliance with government-imposed standards and monitors the effectiveness of those standards, reporting periodically to the school superintendent and local school committee. The principal works with school officials and teachers to develop and implement the school's curriculum, programs, and standards.

The principal acts as the chief administrator of the school. He or she must develop mission statements, strategic plans budgets, and other important documents. The principal sets daily schedules, establishes administrative systems and protocols, and approves orders for food, repair work, and supplies.

The principal also manages the school's public relations efforts. When an emergency occurs, the principal communicates with the media, school officials, families, and the public. He or she also assists in raising funds for the school from local businesses during times of economic difficulty.

All principals spend some time addressing students' emotional needs and family situations. To that end, they may implement daycare programs, gifted programs, school breakfast or lunch programs, parent-teacher conferences, learning disability programs, or anti-bullying policies. Principals at high schools must often address and develop strategies to cope with complex behavioral issues, such as substance abuse, teenage pregnancy, safety and security, and poor student attendance. Principals are obligated to take thoughtful teaching approaches and make every effort to improve the quality of education for their students.

Duties and Responsibilities

- Setting standards, policies and procedures
- Developing academic programs
- Training and motivating teachers and staff
- Advising and meeting with students and parents
- Preparing budgets and reports

WORK ENVIRONMENT

Immediate Physical Environment

Principals work in elementary, middle, and secondary schools. They work in offices, usually located within the school's main administrative area. Schools are very active and complex, with sometimes hundreds of students, teachers, and other school personnel in the building and grounds at once. Principals also visit other schools and school systems and, when called upon, attend school board and other meetings at town or city halls and other local government offices.

Human Environment

Principals work with a wide range of people within and outside of the school. Within the school, they work with teachers, administrators, assistants, custodial staff, cafeteria workers, librarians, coaches, and students. Outside of the school, principals work with school officials and elected officials, vendors and suppliers, consultants, accountants, and students' families.

Transferable Skills and Abilities

Interpersonal/Social Skills
- Being able to remain calm
- Cooperating with others
- Working as a member of a team

Organization & Management Skills
- Coordinating tasks
- Handling challenging situations
- Managing people/groups
- Managing time
- Organizing information or materials

Work Environment Skills
- Working in a fast-paced environment

Technological Environment

Principals must be familiar with public address systems and two-way radios. They must also have skills with computers and school administrative and office management software, such as school attendance databases, budgeting programs, and enterprise resource planning (ERP) software.

EDUCATION, TRAINING, AND ADVANCEMENT

High School/Secondary

High school students should take courses that will help them build a career as an educator. Coursework in mathematics, science, social studies, and English will prepare students for college-level studies. Interested students are also encouraged to take child growth and development classes as well as psychology courses.

Suggested High School Subjects
- Algebra
- Biology
- Business
- Business English
- Business Math
- Calculus
- Child Growth & Development
- College Preparatory
- English

- Foreign Languages
- Geometry
- Literature
- Physical Science
- Psychology
- Social Studies
- Sociology
- Statistics

Related Career Pathways/Majors
Education & Training Cluster

- Administration & Administrative Support Pathway

Postsecondary

Elementary, middle and secondary school principals need to earn
a master's or doctorate degree in education, psychology, education
administration, or a related field. Interested college students should
consider applying to graduate programs in education or education
administration as most principals begin their careers as teachers.

Related College Majors

- Education Administration & Supervision, General.

Adult Job Seekers

Qualified individuals seeking a job as a principal may apply directly to
the city or town in which an open position is located (or in the case of
private schools, directly to the school itself). They may also seek jobs
as assistant principals in order to gain more experience and exposure
as a potential principal.

A principal at a small school or an elementary school principal is often
viewed as being in the first years of school administration. Moving to
a larger school or one with older students and issues that are more
complex is usually considered an advancement opportunity.

Professional Certification and Licensure

Most states require that a principal receive a license as a professional school administrator. Licensure may require passing a training course and examination. A master's or doctorate degree in education or a related field may be sufficient for such certification. Private school principals do not fall under this requirement, although an advanced degree is a prerequisite for these positions as well.

Additional Requirements

Principals must be effective managers. They should be able to lead, inspire, communicate effectively, cope calmly with difficult or fast-paced situations, and set educational, staffing, and facilities-related goals. They should also be perceptive, able to understand the motives and perspectives of those with whom they interact. They must have exceptional judgment and decision-making abilities, as well as a solid understanding of government standards and performance expectations. Finally, principals must be skilled at working with children of different socioeconomic backgrounds and development levels.

EARNINGS AND ADVANCEMENT

Principals advance by moving up the administrative ladder or transferring to another school that might be larger or in a different system. Median annual earnings of principals were $92,510 in 2016. The lowest ten percent earned less than $59,910, and the highest ten percent earned more than $135,770.

Principals may receive paid vacations, holidays, and sick days; life and health insurance; and retirement benefits. These are usually paid by the employer.

EMPLOYMENT AND OUTLOOK

Principals held about 240,000 jobs nationally in 2014. Employment is expected to grow about as fast as the average for all occupations through the year 2024, which means employment is projected to increase 6 percent. As education and training take on greater importance in everyone's lives, the need for education administrators will grow. Job opportunities should also be excellent because a large number of education administrators are expected to retire over the next ten years. Enrollments of school-age children will also have an impact on the demand for education administrators. Enrollment of students in elementary and secondary schools is expected to grow slowly over the next decade; however, preschool and childcare center administrators are expected to experience substantial growth as enrollments in formal child care programs continue to expand as fewer private households care for young children.

Related Occupations
- Education Administrator
- Elementary School Teacher
- Secondary School Teacher

MORE INFORMATION

Administrative Leadership and Policy Studies Program
University of Colorado Denver
School of Education and Human
Development
1380 Lawrence Street
Denver, CO 80204
303.315.4985

Offers licensure for principals:
www.ucdenver.edu/academics/colleges/
SchoolOfEducation/Academics/
LicenseEndorsements/Licenses/Pages/
PrincipalLicense.aspx

American Association of School Administrators
801 N. Quincy Street, Suite 700
Arlington, VA 82203-1730
703.528.0700
info@aasa.org
www.aasa.org

American Federation of School Administrators
1101 17th Street, NW, Suite 408
Washington, DC 20036
202.986.4209
afsa@AFSAadmin.org
www.admin.org

Association for Supervision and Curriculum Development
1703 N. Beauregard Street
Alexandria, VA 22311-1714
800.933.2723
www.ascd.org

Sponsors professional development events:
www.ascd.org/professional-development.
aspx

National Association of Elementary School Principals
Educational Products Department
1615 Duke Street
Alexandria, VA 22314
800.386.2377
naesp@naesp.org
www.naesp.org

National Association of Secondary School Principals
1904 Association Drive
Reston, VA 20191-1537
703.860.0200
www.nassp.org

National Association of Student Personnel Administrators
111 K Street, NE, 10th Floor
Washington, DC 20002
202.265.7500
office@naspa.org
www.naspa.org

National Education Association
1201 16th Street, NW
Washington, DC 20036-3290
202.833.4000
www.nea.org

Technology Information Center for
Administrative Leadership
www.portical.org

Michael Auerbach/Editor

Secondary & Middle School Teacher

Snapshot

Career Cluster(s): Education & Training

Interests: Teaching, lesson planning, leading instructional activities, adolescent development, student safety, peer mentoring

Earnings (Yearly Average): $58,000

Employment & Outlook: Average Growth Expected

OVERVIEW

Sphere of Work

Secondary and Middle school teachers, also called middle and high school teachers, are teaching professionals that focus on the educational needs of adolescents. Secondary and Middle school teachers may be generalists with knowledge and talents in a wide range of subjects, or they may have an academic specialization, such as history, language arts, mathematics, physical educations, science, art, or music. Secondary and Middle school teachers work in both public and private school

settings. They may be assigned student and peer mentoring and administrative tasks in addition to their teaching responsibilities.

Work Environment

Secondary and Middle school teachers work in high schools and middle schools designed to meet the social and educational needs of adolescents. The amounts and types of resources in middle and high schools and middle and high school classrooms such as art supplies, music lessons, physical education facilities, fieldtrips, and assistant teachers, differ depending on the school's financial resources and the educational philosophy directing the curriculum. Middle and high schools may be private or public. They may be an independent entity or part of a larger school that encompasses more grade levels.

Profile

Interests: Data, People
Working Conditions: Work Inside
Physical Strength: Light work
Education Needs: Bachelor's Degree, Master's Degree
Licensure/Certification: Required
Physical Abilities Not Required: Not Climb, Not Kneel
Opportunities For Experience: Internship, Volunteer Work, Part Time Work
Holland Interest Score*: SAE

* See Appendix A

Occupation Interest

Individuals drawn to the profession of Secondary and Middle school teacher tend to be intelligent, creative, patient, and caring. Secondary and Middle school teachers, who instruct and nurture secondary and middle school students, should find satisfaction in spending long hours instructing and mentoring adolescents. Successful Secondary and Middle school teachers excel at long-term scheduling, lesson planning, communication, and problem solving.

A Day in the Life—Duties and Responsibilities

A Secondary and Middle school teacher's daily duties and responsibilities include planning, teaching, classroom preparation, student care, family outreach, school duties, and professional development.

Secondary and Middle school teachers plan and execute specific teaching plans and lessons. They may also be responsible for buying or securing donations for classroom or project supplies. They assign homework and projects, teach good study habits, grade student work, maintain accurate academic records for all students, and lead and administer activities such as lab sessions, reviews, exams, student clubs, and small group learning.

Classroom preparation and cleaning duties may include labeling materials, organizing desk and work areas, displaying student work on bulletin boards and display boards, and, depending on janitorial support, cleaning up and sanitizing spaces at the end of the school day.

Secondary and Middle school teachers greet students as they arrive in the classroom, promote a supportive learning environment, maintain student safety and health, provide appropriate levels of discipline in the classroom and school environment, build student cooperation and listening skills, and work to present lessons in multiple ways to accommodate diverse learning styles.

Some teachers may provide family outreach by greeting student families at school drop off and dismissal times and using a student school-family communication notebook when required. All teachers must communicate regularly with families regarding student academic performance.

Secondary and Middle school teachers must attend staff meetings, participate in peer mentoring, enforce school policies, and lead open houses for prospective families. Teachers may also be responsible for overseeing students in the school hallways and for supervising school fieldtrips. Their professional development duties include attendance at professional meetings, continued training, and recertification as needed.

Secondary and Middle school teachers must work on a daily basis to meet the needs of all students, families, fellow teachers, and school administrators.

Duties and Responsibilities

- Preparing lesson plans
- Guiding the learning activities of students
- Instructing students through demonstrations or lectures
- Evaluating students through daily work, tests and reports, or through a portfolio of the students' artwork or writing
- Computing and recording grades
- Maintaining discipline
- Counseling and referring students when academic or other problems arise
- Conferring with parents and staff
- Assisting with student clubs, teams, plays and other student activities
- Supplementing lecturing with audio-visual teaching aides

OCCUPATION SPECIALTIES

Resource Teachers

Resource Teachers teach basic academic subjects to students requiring remedial work using special help programs to improve scholastic levels.

WORK ENVIRONMENT

Immediate Physical Environment

A Secondary and Middle school teacher's immediate physical environment is the middle and high school classroom. Secondary and Middle school teachers tend to have a fair bit of autonomy in deciding classroom layout and curriculum. Secondary and Middle school teachers generally work forty-hour weeks and follow an annual academic schedule with ample winter, spring, and summer vacations. Summer teaching opportunities in summer school and summer camps are common.

Transferable Skills and Abilities

Communication Skills
- Expressing thoughts and ideas
- Persuading others
- Speaking effectively
- Writing concisely

Interpersonal/Social Skills
- Being patient
- Cooperating with others
- Working as a member of a team

Organization & Management Skills
- Coordinating tasks
- Making decisions
- Managing people/groups

Research & Planning Skills
- Creating ideas
- Using logical reasoning

Human Environment

Secondary and Middle school teachers are in constant contact with adolescents, student families, school administrators, and fellow teachers. Secondary and Middle school teachers may have students with physical and mental disabilities as well as students who are English language learners (ELL). Secondary and Middle school teachers must be comfortable working with people from a wide range of backgrounds and able to incorporate lessons on diversity into their teaching.

Technological Environment

Secondary and Middle school classrooms increasingly include computers for student use. Teachers should be comfortable using Internet communication tools and teaching adolescent students to use educational software. Teachers may also use computers to perform administrative tasks and record student progress. Secondary and Middle school teachers should be comfortable with standard office and audiovisual equipment.

EDUCATION, TRAINING, AND ADVANCEMENT

Middle and high school/Secondary and Middle

Middle and high school students interested in becoming Secondary and Middle school teachers should develop good study habits. Interested middle and high school students should take a broad range of courses in education, child development, science, mathematics, history, language arts, physical education, and the arts. Those interested in the field of education may benefit from seeking internships or volunteer/part-time work with children and teachers at camps and afterschool programs.

Suggested High School Subjects
- Algebra
- Arts
- Audio-Visual
- Biology
- Child Growth & Development
- College Preparatory
- Composition
- Computer Science
- English
- Foreign Languages
- Government
- Graphic Communications
- History
- Humanities
- Literature
- Mathematics
- Political Science
- Psychology
- Science
- Social Studies
- Sociology
- Speech
- Theatre & Drama

Related Career Pathways/Majors

Education & Training Cluster
- Teaching/Training Pathway

Postsecondary

College students interested in working towards a degree or career in Secondary and Middle education should consider majoring in education and earning initial teaching certification as part of their undergraduate education program. Aspiring teachers should complete coursework in education, child development, and psychology. Those interested in pursuing a career in secondary education often major in the subject area they wish to teach. Prior to graduation, college students intent on becoming Secondary and Middle school teachers should gain teaching experience through an internship or volunteer/part-time work; prospective teachers should also research master's of education programs and state teaching certification requirements.

Related College Majors
- Agricultural Teacher Education
- Art Teacher Education
- Bilingual/Bicultural Education
- Business Teacher Education (Vocational)
- Computer Teacher Education
- Education Admin & Supervision, General
- Education of the Blind & Visually Handicapped
- Education of the Deaf & Hearing Impaired
- Education of the Specific Learning Disabled
- Education of the Speech Impaired
- Elementary/Pre-Elem/Early Childhood/Kindergarten Teacher Education
- English Teacher Education
- Family & Consumer Science Education
- Foreign Languages Teacher Education
- Health & Physical Education, General
- Health Teacher Education
- Marketing Operations Teacher Education (Vocational)
- Mathematics Teacher Education
- Music Teacher Education
- Physical Education Teaching & Coaching
- Science Teacher Education, General

- Secondary and Middle/Jr. High/Middle School Teacher Education
- Special Education, General
- Speech Teacher Education
- Technology Teacher Education/Industrial Arts Teacher Education
- Trade & Industrial Teacher Education (Vocational)
- Vocational Teacher Education.

Adult Job Seekers

Adults seeking jobs as Secondary and Middle school teachers should research the education and certification requirements of their home states as well of the schools where they might seek employment. Adult job seekers in the education field may benefit from the employment workshops and job lists maintained by professional teaching associations, such as the American Federation of Teachers (AFT).

Professional Certification and Licensure

Professional certification and licensure requirements for Secondary and Middle school teachers vary between states and between schools. Secondary and Middle school teachers generally earn a master's in education, with a single-subject teaching concentration in language arts, history, science, political science, music, physical education, or art, and obtain a state teaching license for grades eight through twelve. Single-subject teaching licenses for Secondary and Middle school teachers require academic coursework, supervised student teaching, and successful completion of a general teaching exam. Background checks are also typically required. State departments of education offer state teaching licenses and require continuing education and recertification on a regular basis. Savvy and successful job seekers will find out the requirements that apply to them and satisfy the requirements prior to seeking employment.

Additional Requirements

Individuals who find satisfaction, success, and job security as Secondary and Middle school teachers will be knowledgeable about the profession's requirements, responsibilities, and opportunities. Successful Secondary and Middle school teachers engage in ongoing professional development. Secondary and Middle school teachers must have high levels of integrity and ethics as they work with adolescents and have access to the personal information of student families. Membership in professional teaching associations is encouraged among beginning and tenured Secondary and Middle school teachers as a means of building status in a professional community and networking.

EARNINGS AND ADVANCEMENT

Earnings of Secondary and Middle school teachers depend on their education and experience, and the size and location of the school district. Pay is usually higher in large, metropolitan areas. Secondary and Middle school teachers in private schools generally earn less than public Secondary and Middle school teachers.

Median annual earnings of Secondary and Middle school teachers were $58,030 in 2016. The lowest ten percent earned less than $38,180, and the highest ten percent earned more than $92,920. In some schools, Secondary and Middle school teachers receive extra pay for coaching sports and working with students in extracurricular activities. Some Secondary and Middle school teachers earn extra income during the summer working in the school system or in other jobs.

Secondary and Middle school teachers have vacation days when their school is closed, as in during the summer and over holidays. They may also receive life and health insurance and retirement benefits. These are usually paid by the employer.

EMPLOYMENT AND OUTLOOK

There were approximately 961,000 Secondary and Middle School teachers employed nationally in 2016. Employment is expected to grow about as fast as the average for all occupations through the year 2020, which means employment is projected to increase 6 percent. Most job openings will occur as a result of the expected retirement of a large number of teachers and will vary by area.

The supply of Secondary and Middle school teachers is likely to increase in response to growing student enrollment, improved job opportunities, more teacher involvement in school policy, greater public interest in education and higher salaries. Job prospects are greater in central cities and rural areas. However, job growth could be limited by state and local government budget deficits.

Related Occupations
- Career/Technology Education Teacher
- College Faculty Member
- Education Administrator
- Elementary School Teacher
- Principal
- Special Education Teacher
- Teacher Assistant

Conversation With . . .
MARÍA ELISA MORALES

Teacher
Taught English in Madrid and Bilbao, Spain
Taught abroad for two years

1. **What was your individual career path in terms of education/training, entry-level job, or other significant opportunity?**

   I went to the University of Vermont and graduated with a Bachelor of Science in neuroscience with plans to attend medical school after graduation. However, after graduating I quickly realized that I had a long road ahead of me and I really wanted to travel before getting into that. I've always been pretty horrible at saving money—which is very necessary for traveling—so I figured the easiest way to do it was to work abroad and travel in my free time. While there are many jobs abroad, being an English teacher is a quick way to get a visa without needing formal training. Luckily, I had a strong background in tutoring and peer mentoring, which made me a good candidate for teaching abroad. I'm also fluent in Spanish, but that wasn't a requirement. It's definitely helpful to speak the language of whatever country you're going to, but not necessary in most places—at least not in Europe. All you need to apply for a job that will give you a visa is a bachelor's degree in literally anything. The first year, I went through a teach-abroad program, the Council on International Educational Exchange (CIEE). The second year, I decided to do it through the Spanish Ministry of Education. I believe you can also teach in an academy by going directly through the academy, but it might be a little more difficult to get a visa.

2. **What are the most important skills and/or qualities for someone in your profession?**

   Aside from being a native English speaker, which is really what these employers look for, the job will be much easier with a lot of creativity, leadership/management skills and above all, loads and loads of patience.

3. **What do you wish you had known going into this profession?**

   Though I grew up in a bicultural household, there were still some differences one can't really be prepared for until experiencing it. I wish I had known the expectations in the behavior of students in other countries as well as the way government and bureaucracy works. We often complain about how these things are here, but we actually have it pretty good. Government bureaucracy abroad really is a pain. It's the kind of system where if you want to get anything done, you should expect to be on the phone for hours, getting transferred from one person to another. Or if you want to get something done in person, get ready to take the whole day off work. Most of this mattered when I had to do things like get my residency card or do banking. Things got really bad in my second year when, due to some kinks, I didn't get paid for three months.

4. Are there many job opportunities in your profession? In what specific areas?

Here in the U.S., we are luckier than we know to grow up speaking English. In some Western European and Asian countries, English is a priority, but most countries in the world are just starting to make English as a second language the norm. This means thousands of job opportunities as these countries seek native speakers to teach in schools and language academies.

5. How do you see your profession changing in the next five years? What role will technology play in those changes, and what skills will be required?

In two short years, I have already seen changes in the way things are done. The majority of popular media and entertainment in the world is in English, which is a huge driving force for people, especially children. Students are learning more English outside of school than ever before and that's thanks to technology. I expect this trend to continue and to actually make its way into the classroom now that personal tablets and computers are more accessible.

6. What do you enjoy most about your job? What do you enjoy least about your job?

What I loved most about my job was the students, of course. While they can be trying at times, they are so excited to learn. The U.S. has always been "as seen on TV" for them. They couldn't believe things like how many kinds of Oreos are available and that I actually went to that school dance called "prom." While the language can be difficult for them sometimes, the cultural side of it makes it worth it for them and I loved seeing them enthused about it.

The most difficult part of my job was probably some of the teachers I worked with. We all had different ideas about teaching and class management. While most of us were able to agree, sometimes you have to learn to work with people who are either unpleasant or fundamentally different than you are.

7. Can you suggest a valuable "try this" for students considering a career in your profession?

Make sure you like kids, and make sure you can transmit information in an effective way. Try babysitting and tutoring. Also, if you haven't already, try learning a new language and see what method works for you so that you can turn that around for students in the future.

MORE INFORMATION

American Association for Employment in Education
3040 Riverside Drive, Suite 125
Columbus, OH 43221
614.485.1111
execdir@aaee.org
www.aaee.org

American Association for Health Education
1900 Association Drive
Reston, VA 20191-1598
800.213.7193
www.aahperd.org/aahe

American Association of Colleges for Teacher Education
1307 New York Avenue, NW
Suite 300
Washington, DC 20005-4701
202.293.2450
aacte@aacte.org
www.aacte.org

American Federation of Teachers
Public Affairs Department
555 New Jersey Avenue, NW
Washington, DC 20001
202.879.4400
online@aft.org
www.aft.org

National Association for Sport and Physical Education
1900 Association Drive
Reston, VA 20191
800.213.7193
naspe@aahperd.org
www.aahperd.org/naspe

National Board for Professional Teaching Standards
1525 Wilson Boulevard, Suite 500
Arlington, VA 22209
800.228.3224
www.nbpts.org

National Council for Accreditation of Teacher Education
2010 Massachusetts Avenue, NW
Suite 500
Washington, DC 20036-1023
202.466.7496
ncate@ncate.org
www.ncate.org

National Council of Teachers of English
1111 W. Kenyon Road
Urbana, Illinois 61801-1096
877.369.6283
www.ncte.org/second

NCTE Distinguished Service Award:
www.ncte.org/awards/service/dsa

NCTE Middle and high school Teachers of Excellence Award:
www.ncte.org/second/awards/hste

National Council of Teachers of Mathematics
1906 Association Drive
Reston, VA 20191-1502
703.620.9840
nctm@nctm.org
www.nctm.org

National Education Association
1201 16th Street, NW
Washington, DC 20036-3290
202.833.4000
www.nea.org

National Science Teachers Association
1840 Wilson Boulevard
Arlington, VA 22201
703.243.7100
www.nsta.org

NSTA Distinguished Teaching Awards:
www.nsta.org/about/awards.aspx?lid=tnav

Publishes The Science Teacher for middle
and high school level science teachers:
www.nsta.org/highschool/

Simone Isadora Flynn/Editor

INTERNATIONAL ARTS AND CULTURE

In 1998, *Washington Post* writers Paul Farhi and Megan Rosenfeld argued that America's most important export was no longer agricultural or manufactured products, but had become, instead, the nation's pop culture. For decades, American entertainment, including music, film and television, literature, computer software, and other artistic products, have been among the nation's most lucrative exports. In 2013, a study from the U.S. Bureau of Economic Analysis and the National Endowment for the Arts estimated that creative arts and products contribute $504 billion to the nation's annual GDP and much of this revenue is derived from international sales and exports.

The massive and growing global demand for U.S. cultural products creates opportunities for artists and creative professionals willing to tour or live and work overseas and there are many opportunities for musicians, actors, dancers, choreographers, designers, models, and professional athletes to perform or sell their creative products to foreign consumers. In addition, some actors, musicians, and artists who might struggle in crowded U.S. markets have found greater success by relocating to foreign nations, where they can find larger audiences and so earn more from their artistic or cultural endeavors. Whether traveling on tour, or living permanently overseas, globalization and digital distribution of pop culture, has fueled the growth of an increasingly worldwide artistic industry and this has created new opportunities for independent artists and performers to profit from international audiences.

The Touring Phenomenon

Touring is a unique form of international artistic exhibition that involves traveling to a foreign nation for a limited stay, where an artist or group of artists give a series of performances before moving on to another location, or returning to their native nation. While musical tours are familiar around the world, many other types of artists also tour, including visual artists whose paintings, sculptures, or other works may be displayed in locations around the world, to dance and performance troupes, and professional athletes. For headlining bands, dance troupes, and performers, production and management companies typically facilitate the touring process, helping the artist with travel logistics and ensuring that the touring company adhered to licensing and other legal requirements. However, thanks to the ease of communicating internationally with cellular telephone and Internet communication, in the twenty-first century it is possible for independent artists to book their own international tours and international touring has therefore become more common for beginning and emerging artists.

Musicians

While musicians may earn revenue by selling recorded copies of their music, many artists earn far more each year through live performances. For instance, pop star Jay-Z, touring with other pop-hip-hop acts like Busta Rhymes and Missy Elliot, can earn as much as $100,000 per performance, a rate of approximately $1000 for every minute spent onstage, or $3.3 million for a summer touring season. Veteran rock band the Eagles also benefits from the demand for American entertainment abroad, earning $30 million annually from touring. While revenues on this scale are not the norm for touring performers, engaging in international tours can provide far more revenue than selling recordings and can also help performers to build a market for digital recordings of their work.

Artists

For independent artists looking to get involved in the touring market, it is important to have the tools and knowledge to promote and market one's performances. Websites (rather than Facebook or other social media pages) are important as they provide international booking agents with an easy way to get information about the artist. Using email and other digital media, artists can then contact appropriate venues, attempting to string performances together into a logical and cost effective sequence of locations. However, independently booking overseas work can be challenging, and those interested in doing so should take ample time to research the appropriate licenses and permits needed to perform abroad and to plan lodging, food, and other needs for themselves and other participants in the tour.

Fashion

In the fashion industry, touring to various fashion shows and gatherings to stage exhibitions has long been an essential feature of the industry and top level designers and models may tour each year to participate in trade exhibitions and display items from that year's collections. Another field that features international travel is professional athletics, especially in those sports that have a significant international following. For instance, many of the sports included in the International Olympic Games, draw audiences around the world and athletes in these sports, when not performing in the Olympics, might travel internationally for performances and tours. The annual Stars on Ice figure skating tour, for instance, invites professional figure skaters from various nations to participate in a tour of the United States, Europe, Canada, and Japan.

Working on Location

There are other artistic fields in which professionals are asked to travel not to find new audiences or to engage in international revenues, but to access key environments or events. Professional media and news agencies, for instance, sometimes hire journalists, photographers, and other news professionals to work in foreign locations where they can cover local events and bring international news to audiences in their native nation.

Some news outlets like NPR, CBS News, or the *New York Times*, divide reporters and support staff into "news bureaus" so that reporters and other staff can specialize in news coming from a certain region or nation. Traditionally, news bureaus would establish foreign offices or outlets overseas and would often station reporters overseas on a long term or indefinite basis so that the reporters focusing on a certain region would be on-location to cover any emerging news. Competition from digital news agencies has reduced funding for television and print news outlets and many have therefore cut funding for "foreign desk" reporting. In the twenty-first century, it is more common for news agencies to hire native reporters and staff native cover events in a certain region. This evolution provides advantages in that native reporters/ journalists are often able to provide a more nuanced view of emerging events. Despite an overall decline in the industry, news outlets continue to dispatch reporters around the world every year to cover developing news. Those interested in positions in international news and/or reporting may increase their chances of finding employment by studying foreign languages and international studies during their secondary and postsecondary education.

Another industry that commonly works "on-location" is film and television entertainment. Many movies, and a lesser number of television shows, film abroad to save money on production or to locate specific geographical or environmental features needed for a production. Filming in developing nations, for instance, costs little compared to filming in a town or city in the United States and production companies might also save by hiring native workers and laborers to assist with preparation, filming, and set management. In fact, a 2015 report on the film analysis site *Stephen Follows* indicated that only 48 percent of Hollywood films were filmed entirely in the United States, with 28 percent filmed entirely or primarily overseas and 24 percent being shot in both the United States *and* another nation.

In some cases, to enhance the realism of a production, film crews will choose to shoot in the same locations in which the story is supposed to be set while, in other cases, filmmakers may chose overseas locations to find an environment that matches or resembles the environment in which a story is set. For instance, a number of movies set in Vietnam during the Vietnam War, were filmed in the nation of Thailand, which has a similar environment and so provides a reasonable way to mimic the Vietnamese landscape. Many famous films have also used international locations to depict fantastic or imaginative worlds for fantasy fiction, though audiences are typically unaware of the real locations used for the shoot. For instance, the globally popular science fantasy epic *Star Wars*, used the desert African nation of Tunisia to film scenes set on the fictional desert planet Tatooine.

Works Used

Farhi, Paul and Rosenfeld, Megan. "American Pop Penetrates Worldwide." *Washington Post*. Oct 25 1998. Web. 22 Jul 2017.

"Hollywood, Creative Industries Add $504 Billion to U.S. GDP." *Hollywood Reporter*. Eldridge Industries. Dec 5 2013. Web. 22 Jul 2017.

Kafka, Peter. "Concert Tours Are Where the Real Money Is." *ABC News*. ABC. Jul 11 2017. Web. 22 Jul 2017.

"Where are the top Hollywood movie locations?" *Stephen Follows*. Feb 2 2015. Web. 22 Jul 2017.

Director/Producer

Snapshot

Career Cluster(s): Arts, A/V Technology & Communications, Information Technology
Interests: Theater, film, planning events, coordinating tasks
Earnings (Yearly Average): $128,290
Employment & Outlook: Average Growth Expected

OVERVIEW

Sphere of Work

Directors and producers oversee all aspects of a film or theatrical production. Directors plan, coordinate, and manage the creative aspects of the production, including interpreting scripts, casting talent, approving artistic designs, and directing the work of actors, cinematographers, set designers, wardrobe designers, and other members of the cast and crew. Producers plan, coordinate, and manage the business side of a production, which includes raising money, approving and developing

the script, and performing any related administrative tasks. In most cases, directors and producers must both report to the executive producer (usually the person or entity who finances the project), who must approve all final decisions.

Work Environment

Like actors, directors and producers must be willing to work an irregular schedule with long hours and evening and weekend work, punctuated by frequent periods of unemployment. Productions may last from one day to several months, and during that time, directors and producers are expected to be on call and available to solve problems that arise before, during, and after a production has finished. They may also be away from home, or "on location," for extended periods. The irregular hours and intense competition in these occupations can result in stress, fatigue, and frustration. Most directors and producers must work day jobs or other employment unrelated to entertainment.

Profile

Interests: People, Things
Working Conditions: Work Inside, Work Both Inside and Outside
Physical Strength: Light work
Education Needs: On-The-Job Training, Junior/Technical/Community College, Apprenticeship
Licensure/Certification: Usually Not Required
Physical Abilities Not Required: Not Climb, Not Kneel
Opportunities For Experience: Internship, Apprenticeship, Military Service, Volunteer Work, Part Time Work
Holland Interest Score*: ESA, SEC, SEI

* See Appendix A

Occupation Interest

Prospective directors should be highly creative, confident, and possess a strong desire to tell stories. They must be extremely organized, be natural leaders, and understand all aspects of coordinating a theatrical or film production, including the role that each cast and crew member plays in the successful completion of a production. Prospective producers should be detail-oriented people who have a desire to take on both small and large tasks. Producers should enjoy planning, coordinating, and organizing an event from start to finish and should be willing to handle and resolve any issues that arise.

A Day in the Life—Duties and Responsibilities

There are many different styles of directing films and plays, just as there are many different styles of acting. Directors are ultimately responsible for the appearance, stylistic and emotional tone, and aesthetic organization of a dramatic production. A film studio or independent producer normally hires a director through the director's agent or manager. Before production begins, a director auditions and chooses actors, holds rehearsals, and prepares the cast for production. He or she also consults with set designers, choreographers, cinematographers, music supervisors, and other creative personnel to plan and develop a successful production. During production, a director guides and oversees the entire creative execution of a project, often with help from assistant directors and production assistants. Once production is finished, a director oversees any postproduction responsibilities, such as video and sound editing, graphic design, and music selection.

Producers are responsible for handling the business aspects of a production. They secure funds, set budget limitations, coordinate schedules, and ensure smooth management of the whole project. Producers also work with directors to approve their decisions regarding talent, locations, and other creative choices, as well as to ensure that deadlines are met and money is spent according to financier instructions. Larger productions usually require the services of associate or line producers to assist the producer with his or her duties.

Duties and Responsibilities

- Judging and motivating acting talent
- Making artistic interpretations of scripts
- Making optimum use of taping and production equipment
- Working with union representatives
- Managing contractual obligations
- Maintaining strict production time schedules

OCCUPATION SPECIALTIES

Stage Directors

Stage Directors interpret scripts, direct technicians and conduct rehearsals to create stage presentations.

Motion Picture Directors

Motion Picture Directors read and interpret scripts, conduct rehearsals and direct the activities of cast and technical crews for motion picture films.

Television Directors

Television Directors interpret scripts, conduct rehearsals and direct television programs.

Radio Directors

Radio Directors direct radio rehearsals and broadcasts.

Casting Directors

Casting Directors audition and interview performers for specific parts.

Motion Picture Producers

Motion Picture Producers initiate and manage all the business needs of a motion picture production.

WORK ENVIRONMENT

Immediate Physical Environment

Most directors and producers work on set during the production of a theatrical project. Set locations vary greatly and may be indoors or outdoors in any weather conditions. Some productions are held in different locations across the country or around the world. Before production begins (during "preproduction") and after a production finishes (during "postproduction"), directors and producers may work from an office or home studio.

Transferable Skills and Abilities

Communication Skills
- Describing feelings
- Expressing thoughts and ideas

Interpersonal/Social Skills
- Asserting oneself
- Being sensitive to others
- Cooperating with others
- Working as a member of a team

Organization & Management Skills
- Managing conflict
- Managing time
- Organizing information or materials
- Paying attention to and handling details
- Performing duties which change frequently

Research & Planning Skills
- Creating ideas

Human Environment

Directors and producers constantly interact with other cast and crew members. Their coworkers typically include executive producers, actors, production staff, set designers, costume and makeup personnel, and assistants. Producers regularly work with external vendors, such as caterers, insurance representatives, and establishment owners.

Technological Environment

Directors and producers employ a wide variety of tools and equipment to assist them in the completion of their daily tasks. Directors use video cameras, lighting and sound equipment, two-way radios, cell phones, audiovisual editing equipment and software, and the Internet. Producers use schedules, budgets, contracts, e-mail and the Internet, laptops, cell phones, and other devices.

EDUCATION, TRAINING, AND ADVANCEMENT

High School/Secondary

High school students who wish to become directors or producers should have an inherent interest in the dramatic arts and should foster that interest by pursuing academic study in English literature, theater, public speaking, communications, and cinema. They should also learn as much as they can about management, business, and event planning. Involvement in school groups or extracurricular activities, such as drama clubs, plays, musical productions, dance performances, film clubs, and photography clubs, can provide a solid background in the arts. They should also enroll in a basic acting class to become familiar with the fundamentals of acting, dramatic literature, and theater production.

Suggested High School Subjects
- Accounting
- Arts
- Audio-Visual
- Business
- College Preparatory
- English
- Literature
- Mathematics
- Speech
- Theatre & Drama

Related Career Pathways/Majors
Arts, A/V Technology & Communications Cluster
- Performing Arts Pathway
Information Technology Cluster
- Interactive Media Pathway

Postsecondary

Although an undergraduate degree is rarely required in order for one to become a director or producer, many people consider it helpful to have received some formal training at the postsecondary level. Many universities and colleges offer bachelor's degree programs in the dramatic arts. Some directors find it beneficial to have studied directing, filmmaking, writing, acting, designing, radio broadcasting, film history, or public speech at the college level. Producers can benefit by taking undergraduate business courses in marketing, public relations, management, and finance.

After obtaining a bachelor's degree, some directors and producers earn a master of fine arts degree (MFA) in directing, producing, acting, or screenwriting. Some conservatories, like the American Film Institute (AFI) in Los Angeles, offer MFA programs that teach students the practical skills needed to start a career in filmmaking. Often, students are required to complete a thesis film as part of their coursework, designed to simulate a large-scale production. Producers and directors must raise money, find talent, and promote their thesis films.

Related College Majors
- Acting & Directing
- Drama/Theater Arts, General
- Film-Video Making/Cinema & Production
- Film/Cinema Studies
- Playwriting & Screenwriting
- Radio & Television Broadcasting .

Adult Job Seekers

Prospective directors and producers possess varying levels of experience. Those who attend conservatories often make valuable connections with faculty and other students, which eventually lead to production work. Others become apprentices, interns, or assistants for established directors or producers. Some job seekers begin by taking other employment positions in the entertainment industry and working their way up to director or producer positions through networking and industry contacts.

Many directors and producers are members of professional organizations, such as the Producers Guild of America and the Directors Guild of America, which protect the rights of the producers and provide networking opportunities.

Professional Certification and Licensure

Directors and producers are not required to receive any kind of professional certification or licensure in dramatic production. There is no official training for producers, but many directors train or take classes in directing and cinematography.

Additional Requirements

Directing and producing are highly competitive fields, and few people are able to achieve financial stability through these occupations. Candidates must be able to handle criticism well, demonstrate emotional and physical stamina, and remain incredibly driven to succeed. Being talented is not enough to make one successful in these fields—directors and producers must not give up easily, especially after experiencing rejection. They should be self-promoters who are passionate about their work and use every opportunity to meet potential investors, employers, and talent. Long hours and demanding or difficult employers or work conditions are common in these occupations.

EARNINGS AND ADVANCEMENT

Due to the entrepreneurial nature of directing and producing, earnings vary according to the success of the productions in progress. Earnings of directors and producers also vary greatly due to the type of production they are producing or directing, location, project budget, and personal reputation. Median annual earnings of directors and producers were $70,950 in 2016. The lowest ten percent earned less than $32,940, and the highest ten percent earned more than $189,870. Median annual earnings were $98,389 in motion picture and video industries and $58,260 in radio and television broadcasting.

Fringe benefits for directors are typically provided according to union guidelines, but vary according to the size and financial scope of a given production. Producers, being entrepreneurs, are responsible for their own fringe benefits.

EMPLOYMENT AND OUTLOOK

Directors and producers held about 122,600 jobs in motion pictures, stage plays, television and radio in 2014. Employment of directors and producers is expected to grow about as fast as the average for all occupations through the year 2020, which means employment is projected to increase 9 percent. Expanding cable and satellite television operations, increasing production and distribution of major studio and independent films, and continued growth and development of interactive media, online movies and mobile content for cell phones and other portable devices, should increase demand.

Related Occupations
- Actor
- Dancer/Choreographer

Related Military Occupations
- Audiovisual & Broadcast Director
- Audiovisual & Broadcast Technician

MORE INFORMATION

Actors' Equity Association
165 West 46th Street
New York, NY 10036
212.869.8530
www.actorsequity.org

American Film Institute
2021 North Western Avenue
Los Angeles, CA 90027-1657
323.856.7600
www.afi.com

Association of Independent Commercial Producers
3 West 18th Street, 5th Floor
New York, NY 10011
212.929.3000
www.aicp.com

Directors Guild of America
7920 Sunset Boulevard
Los Angeles, California 90046
310.289.2000
www.dga.org

National Association of Schools of Theatre
11250 Roger Bacon Drive, Suite 21
Reston, VA 20190-5248
703.437.0700
info@arts-accredit.org
nast.arts-accredit.org/index.jsp

Producers Guild of America
8530 Wilshire Boulevard, Suite 450
Beverly Hills, CA 90211
310.358.9020
www.producersguild.org

Briana Nadeau/Editor

Fashion Designer

Snapshot

Career Cluster(s): Arts, A/V Technology & Communications, Marketing, Sales & Service

Interests: Fashion, art, design, visual communications, marketing, trends, drawing

Earnings (Yearly Average): $63,670

Employment & Outlook: Slower Than Average Growth Expected

OVERVIEW

Sphere of Work

Fashion designers work in the fashion industry designing clothing, footwear, and accessories, such as belts, hats, and handbags. They usually specialize in one of these areas or in a more specific product line, such as children's wear, menswear, or sporting apparel.

Most job opportunities for fashion designers involve working for small to large apparel manufacturers whose garments are made for mass-market consumption through retail outlets, such

as department stores. At the top of the trade, fashion designers work for high fashion ("haute couture") labels. Some fashion designers may work as freelancers, designing custom-made apparel for private clients.

The clothing design process usually demands research into fashion trends, including styles, colors, and fabrics. As well as being able to sketch and draw apparel, fashion designers must also be skilled in garment construction techniques. Fashion designers are often expected to construct their own patterns and samples.

Work Environment

Working conditions and environments vary greatly. Most fashion designers work in an office or comfortable workshop environment. Self-employed fashion designers often work from home.

Full-time fashion designers generally work for apparel manufacturers. A full-time employee can expect to work forty hours per week during normal office hours. They may be required to work longer hours as needed.

Job opportunities for fashion designers are concentrated in regions where there are a high number of apparel manufacturers. In the United States, approximately two-thirds of fashion designers are employed in New York or California.

Profile

Interests: Data, Things
Working Conditions: Work Inside
Physical Strength: Light Work
Education Needs: Junior/Technical/Community College, Bachelor's Degree
Licensure/Certification: Usually Not Required
Physical Abilities Not Required: Not Climb, Not Kneel
Opportunities For Experience: Apprenticeship
Holland Interest Score*: ASR

* See Appendix A

Occupation Interest

Fashion design attracts graduates and professionals who have a strong interest in fashion, art, design, and visual communication. This occupation suits people with an awareness of fashion trends and a creative flair for capturing personal expression, moods, styles, values, and attitudes through apparel.

Fashion designers are good at pencil sketching and drawing. They usually have a strong interest in color theory and an understanding of fabrics and textiles. It also helps if they have knowledge about different fashion markets, retail segments, budgets, and buying trends.

A Day in the Life—Duties and Responsibilities

The fashion designer's day is characterized by periods of independent and collaborative work. Some fashion designers are responsible for the entire design process. Design activities may include researching a fashion or trend; sketching designs, making patterns, and sewing prototypes; selecting, testing, and costing materials and construction; ordering fabrics and textiles; and liaising with manufacturing production teams.

Fashion designers with experience may supervise other employees. They may provide design leadership and technical guidance to a number of people. Junior fashion designers typically have less responsibility. Prior research, costing, and fabric selections may already have been completed, and the junior fashion designer may be required to work within these parameters. In large organizations, sample makers and patternmakers may assist the fashion designers. Fashion designers must also perform administrative tasks. Some may contribute to business development, marketing, and promotional activities. This may involve working with marketing and branding agencies, wholesalers, distributors, event coordinators, photographers, and graphic designers.

Outside of the office, fashion designers keep their fashion knowledge current by attending fashion shows and trade shows, reading fashion magazines, and browsing stores where apparel is sold.

Duties and Responsibilities

- Making original sketches of apparel
- Dictating the fabric and colors that are to be used in each design
- Studying fashion trends
- Determining material costs and likely effects on the production and sale of the apparel
- Researching designs by attending fashion shows and shops that sell high quality clothing

WORK ENVIRONMENT

Immediate Physical Environment

Well-lit, comfortable office settings predominate. Full-time fashion designers generally work for small to large apparel manufacturers. Self-employed fashion designers may work from home.

Transferable Skills and Abilities

Communication Skills
- Speaking effectively

Creative/Artistic Skills
- Being skilled in art, music or dance

Interpersonal/Social Skills
- Being able to work independently
- Being objective

Organization & Management Skills
- Making decisions
- Paying attention to and handling details

Research & Planning Skills
- Creating ideas

Technical Skills
- Performing scientific, mathematical and technical work

Plant Environment

Some fashion designers may find that they work in an environment co-located with an apparel manufacturing facility. With the increasing trend toward outsourcing clothes manufacturing to countries with lower labor costs, however, domestic manufacturing facilities are becoming less common.

Human Environment

Fashion design demands strong collaborative skills. Fashion designers interact with a broad range of creative and business specialists. They must possess strong communication and negotiation skills to work with and manage multiple people and agencies to achieve a coordinated outcome. Due to globalization and increased outsourcing, many fashion designers work in cross-cultural settings.

Technological Environment

Fashion designers use technologies that range from telephone, e-mail, and the Internet to standard office software and computer-aided design software. Fashion designers usually complement digital design skills with advanced artistic skills, such as pencil sketching.

EDUCATION, TRAINING, AND ADVANCEMENT

High School/Secondary

High school students can best prepare for a career in fashion design by taking courses in art, visual communication, graphic design, clothing construction, merchandising, and textiles. Subjects such as business studies, entrepreneurship, mathematics, computing studies, and computer-aided design may also assist in preparing candidates for the business and technical demands of fashion design. English, social and cultural studies, history, psychology, and foreign languages may also provide students with an understanding of the place of fashion in the broader cultural context.

Becoming involved in extracurricular school activities that develop art, design, fashion, and business competencies can also provide students with an opportunity to develop relevant skills and learn from others prior to graduation. Such activities might include entering art and design competitions or participating in business incubation projects.

Suggested High School Subjects
- Applied Math
- Arts
- Clothing & Textiles
- English
- Family & Consumer Sciences
- Graphic Communications
- Merchandising

Related Career Pathways/Majors
Arts, A/V Technology & Communications Cluster
- Performing Arts Pathway
- Visual Arts Pathway

Marketing, Sales & Service Cluster
- Professional Sales & Marketing Pathway

Postsecondary

The most common pathway to a career in fashion design is by obtaining an associate's or bachelor's degree in fashion design. A large number of colleges and universities offer fashion design as a major, minor, or course electives within other degree programs, such as fine arts. Interested postsecondary students should study related subjects like sewing, fashion, technology, mathematics, and anatomy. Aspiring fashion designers can gain design, sales, and marketing experience through internships or by working in retail settings.

Employers expect candidates to have appropriate educational qualifications and possess a design portfolio that demonstrates the quality and range of their work. The portfolio may include design sketches, photographs, advertisements, and fashion spreads of the fashion designer's work.

Related College Majors
- Fashion & Fabric Consulting
- Fashion Design & Illustration.

Adult Job Seekers

Adults seeking to enter the job market in fashion design are advised to have some educational background in the field, a portfolio of design work, and an updated resume. It is important for the portfolio to demonstrate a current understanding of fashion trends, fabrics and textiles, colors, garment construction techniques, and different fashion market segments.

Networking is extremely important in the apparel industry as many job openings are filled without being formally advertised. Professional associations may provide inquirers with a list of their members, a daily job alert service for subscribers, and professional development or continuing education seminars.

Professional Certification and Licensure

There are no formal professional certifications or licensing requirements for fashion design.

Additional Requirements

Fashion design is a highly competitive industry, with many talented designers vying for limited opportunities. Beyond excellent fashion sense and design expertise, success in this career demands hard work, commitment, persistence, and the ability to continually expand one's skills and design ethic.

EARNINGS AND ADVANCEMENT

Advancement of fashion designers often involves changing firms. More experienced fashion designers may be promoted to chief designers, design department heads, or other supervisory positions. Other fashion designers choose to begin their own firms. Salaries usually vary for fashion designers depending on their skill and creativity.

Median annual earnings of fashion designers were $65,170 in 2016. Those in management positions had a median salary of $76,300. The lowest ten percent earned less than $33,740, and the highest ten percent earned more than $130,050. Top fashion designers earned well into the hundreds of thousands to millions of dollars.

Fashion designers may receive paid vacations, holidays, and sick days; life and health insurance; and retirement benefits. These are usually paid by the employer. Self-employed fashion designers must provide these benefits on their own.

EMPLOYMENT AND OUTLOOK

Fashion designers held about 23,100 jobs nationally in 2014. Employment of fashion designers tends to be concentrated in region fashion centers, like New York or California. Employment is expected to grow slower than the average for all occupations through the year 2020, which means employment is projected to increase 3 percent to 9 percent. Although consumers continue to seek new, fashionable clothing, declines in the apparel manufacturing industry will contribute to an overall slowing of job growth in this field. Fashion designers can expect to face stiff competition throughout their careers due to an abundant supply of workers in the field. Individuals with the proper training, excellent skills, creativity and perseverance will succeed. Turnover at the top level is low due to high pay and prestige.

Related Occupations
- Designer
- Interior Designer

MORE INFORMATION

American Apparel & Footwear Association
1601 N. Kent Street, Suite 1200
Arlington, VA 22209
800.520.2262
alengels@apparelandfootwear.org
apparelandfootwear.org

Council of Fashion Designers of America
1412 Broadway, Suite 2006
New York, NY 10018
Info@cfda.com
www.cfda.com

CFDA Fashion Awards
www.cfda.com/category/fashion-awards/

CFDA Scholarship Program:
www.cfda.com/scholarship-program/

Fashion Group International, Inc.
8 West 40th Street, 7th Floor
New York, NY 10018
212.302.5511
cheryl@fgi.org
newyork.fgi.or

Kylie Hughes/Editor

Journalist

Snapshot

Career Cluster(s): Arts, A/V Technology & Communications
Interests: Writing, story-telling, research, solving problems, communicating with others
Earnings (Yearly Average): $38,870
Employment & Outlook: Decline Expected

OVERVIEW

Sphere of Work

The field of journalism involves reporting news, events, and ideas to a wide audience through various media, including print (newspapers and magazines), broadcasting (television and radio), or the Internet (news websites and blogs). Journalists usually start out as reporters, covering anything from sports and weather to business, crime, politics, and consumer affairs. Later, they may become editors, helping to direct the process of gathering and presenting stories.

Journalists can operate on many different levels local,

regional, national, or international. It is common for a journalist to start out working on the local or regional level and then move up the ladder as his or her career progresses. Journalists spend the bulk of their time investigating and composing stories, observing events, interviewing people, taking notes, taking photographs, shooting videos, and preparing their material for publication or broadcast. This work can happen in a matter of minutes, or it can take days or weeks to gather information and build a story.

Work Environment

A journalist's work environment is fast-paced and competitive, subject to tight and changing deadlines, irregular work hours, and pressure to get breaking news on the air or on-line before other news organizations. Journalists covering "hard news"—current events that directly affect people's lives, such as crime, politics, or natural disasters—typically work with stories that are moving and changing constantly; their challenge is to present as much relevant and verifiable information as possible under the circumstances. Journalists covering less pressing subjects, like economic and social trends, popular culture, or "human interest" stories, are subject to less immediate time pressures, but are under no less of an obligation to get their facts straight.

Journalists must therefore be able to adapt to unfamiliar places and a variety of people. They must be accustomed to interruptions and have the ability to pick up and process new information at all times.

Profile

Interests: People, Things
Working Conditions: Work Both Inside and Outside
Physical Strength: Light work
Education Needs: Bachelor's Degree, Master's Degree
Licensure/Certification: Usually Not Required
Physical Abilities Not Required: Not Climb, Not Kneel
Opportunities For Experience: Internship, Apprenticeship, Military Service, Volunteer Work, Part Time Work
Holland Interest Score*: EAS

* See Appendix A

Occupation Interest

Successful journalists are curious by nature and can work comfortably with a wide variety of subjects. They enjoy writing and presenting stories, and they have a great respect for principals that define a free society. These principals include the public's right to know and to question government, business, and social institutions. They also respect an individual's desire to feel connected to what is going on in society. Journalists have to be adept at dealing with people, and successful journalists often have a competitive nature that drives them to try to get the "scoop" before other journalists.

Journalism can be multifaceted work—it can be a low-key, local position for a community newspaper, or it can involve travel and a myriad of settings. Reporting can be a fast-paced in- or out-of-office experience driven by publication editors or broadcast producers.

Finally, journalists have to exhibit tenacity and a tough skin, able to pursue a story to its natural end with a commitment to fair and accurate reporting, even when dealing controversial topics or evasive interview subjects.

A Day in the Life—Duties and Responsibilities

On any given day, journalists are researching and developing story ideas, checking facts, writing articles for publication, all on a tight deadline. Journalists uncover news, information, statistics, and trends that they incorporate into news stories, broadcasts, feature stories, and editorials. They meet regularly with editors and get assignments based on the day's or week's happenings. Depending where a journalist works, a typical day can vary.

Daily newspapers and newswire services, with very short lead times, have journalists working at all times, around the clock, following ongoing news stories. Weekly newspapers, and weekly and monthly magazines, have longer lead times, and so deadlines are less frequent.

Some journalists work in the field as correspondents, perhaps traveling with a camera crew and conducting "man-on-the-street" interviews, or gathering information about rapidly developing events, which they then submit electronically to newspaper editors or radio or television producers. Since the rise of the Internet, the distinction between print and broadcast journalism has become less sharp: newspaper websites today often include video feeds, and television news stations have websites where their stories appear in text form.

The most important part of a journalist's job is making sure that the stories he or she presents are based on solid, verifiable facts, rather than rumors or misinformation. Inaccuracies can creep into news stories in many ways honest mistakes, the reporter's own conscious or unconscious biases, and sources attempting to deceive the public are just a few. For this reason, journalists must invest a good deal of time in making sure their stories are correct before they reach the public.

Duties and Responsibilities

- Researching public records
- Interviewing people
- Writing stories on computer relay terminals
- Specializing in one or more fields of news
- Covering news in a particular location
- Taking photographs
- Writing headlines
- Laying out pages
- Editing wire service copy
- Writing editorials
- Investigating leads and news tips

OCCUPATION SPECIALTIES

News Writers

News Writers write news stories from notes recorded by reporters after evaluating and verifying the information, supplementing it with other material and organizing stories to fit formats.

Reporters and Correspondents

Reporters and Correspondents gather and assess information, organize it and write news stories in prescribed style and format. They may also take photographs for stories and give broadcast reports, or report live from the site of events.

Columnists

Columnists analyze news and write columns or commentaries based on personal knowledge and experience with the subject matter. They gather information through research, interviews, experience, and attendance at functions such as political conventions, news meetings, sporting events, and social activities.

Critics

Critics write critical reviews of literary, musical, or artistic works and performances.

Editorial Writers

Editorial Writers write comments on topics of reader interest to stimulate or mold public opinion in accordance with the viewpoints and policies of publications.

WORK ENVIRONMENT

Immediate Physical Environment

A journalist's work environment can be anywhere, from a crime scene to a press conference to a desk in an office. News outlets usually house journalists in large, well-lit rooms filled with work stations, computer equipment, and the sounds of keyboards and printers. "Boots-on-the-ground" reporting can take a journalist anywhere, though: embedded war correspondents may travel with a military unit right into battle; a journalist reporting on the fishing industry may spend several days on a fishing boat at sea; the next week, that same journalist may tour a farm or a factory or a school to get the next story.

Human Environment

Journalists deal with people. They are constantly interviewing people and collecting and analyzing information; therefore, they can usually be found speaking with anyone who has something to do with the story at hand, be it politicians, company officials, protesters, or an average person.

Transferable Skills and Abilities

Communication Skills
- Speaking effectively
- Writing concisely

Interpersonal/Social Skills
- Asserting oneself
- Being flexible
- Being persistent
- Cooperating with others
- Working as a member of a team

Organization & Management Skills
- Managing time
- Meeting goals and deadlines
- Paying attention to and handling details

Research & Planning Skills
- Analyzing information
- Gathering information
- Solving problems

Unclassified Skills
- Discovering unusual aspects of stories

Technological Environment

Today, journalists submit their stories electronically and can therefore be anywhere in the world, collecting information. They often carry their technology on their back, with just a laptop computer and camera, or travel with a crew of broadcast professionals who can put the journalist on the air live at any time.

EDUCATION, TRAINING, AND ADVANCEMENT

High School/Secondary

High school students can prepare to be a journalist by working for the school newspaper or yearbook, volunteering with local broadcasting stations, and participating in internships with news organizations. Coursework should include a strong focus on writing and communication, through classes such as English, social studies, political science, history, and psychology. Knowledge of foreign languages can also be highly useful in many journalism jobs.

Practical experience is highly valued and can be found through part-time or summer jobs, summer journalism camps, work at college broadcasting stations, and professional organizations. Work in these areas can help in obtaining scholarships, fellowships, and assistantships for college journalism majors.

Local television stations and newspapers often offer internship opportunities for up-and-coming journalists to improve their craft by reporting on town hall meetings or writing obituaries and human-interest stories.

Suggested High School Subjects
- Business
- College Preparatory
- Composition
- Computer Science
- Economics
- English
- Government
- Journalism
- Keyboarding
- Literature
- Photography
- Political Science
- Social Studies
- Speech

Related Career Pathways/Majors
Arts, A/V Technology & Communications Cluster
- Journalism & Broadcasting Pathway

Postsecondary

Most, but not all, journalists have a bachelor's degree in journalism, English, or another liberal arts-related field. There are many journalism schools within colleges and universities across the country. Many schools also offer master's and doctoral degrees, which are especially useful for those interested in journalistic research and teaching.

Bachelor degree program coursework should include broad liberal arts subjects, a general overview of journalism, and then specialty courses that correspond with the highly important requirements for good writing and communication. These can include classes in social media, broadcast writing, news editorial writing, magazine writing, copy editing, interviewing, media ethics, blogging, feature writing, news reporting, and news photography.

All college and university students should make the effort to use career centers, academic counselors, and professors when seeking opportunities for advancement through volunteering or interning.

Related College Majors
- Broadcast Journalism
- Journalism

Adult Job Seekers

Almost anyone can become a journalist if they can find a local newspaper willing to let them try writing a story. Adults can seek continuing journalism education and ongoing opportunities to volunteer in various capacities, perhaps by writing guest newspaper columns, or helping produce a local newsletter, or writing for a blog. These options mean it is entirely viable to seek journalism jobs after having been out of the workplace for a while. Prospective journalists will need to have updated resumes, preferably with portfolios showing relevant work.

More experience leads to more specialized and challenging assignments. Large publications and news stations prefer journalists with several years of experience. With more experience, journalists can advance to become columnists, correspondents, announcers, reporters, or publishing industry managers.

Becoming adept at freelancing—where reporters work independently by selling stories to any interested media outlet—is another way to stay involved in the journalism field.

Professional Certification and Licensure

In the United States, professional certification is not necessary to be a journalist; however, involvement in the Society of Professional Journalists or other professional organizations can help journalists network and raise their profile.

Additional Requirements

It is extremely useful for journalists to have experience with computer graphics and desktop skills, as well as proficiency in all forms of multimedia. Familiarity with databases and knowledge of news photography is an added plus.

EARNINGS AND ADVANCEMENT

Median annual earnings of journalists were $37,820in 2016. The lowest ten percent earned less than $22,120, and the highest ten percent earned more than $86,610.

Journalists may receive paid vacations, holidays, and sick days; life and health insurance; and retirement benefits. These are usually paid by the employer.

EMPLOYMENT AND OUTLOOK

Journalists held about 54,400 jobs nationally in 2014. About one-half worked for newspaper, magazine and book publishers, and another one-fourth worked in radio and television broadcasting. About one-fourth were self-employed. Employment of journalists is expected to decline 9 percent through the year 2024. Many factors will contribute to the limited job growth in this occupation. Consolidation and convergence should continue in the publishing and broadcasting industries. As a result, companies will be better able to allocate their journalists to cover news stories. Constantly improving technology also is allowing workers to do their jobs more efficiently, another factor that will limit the number of workers needed to cover a story or certain type of news. However, the continued demand for news will create some job opportunities. For example, some job growth is expected in new media areas, such as online newspapers and magazines. There is high turnover in this field, as the work is hectic and stressful. Talented writers who can handle highly specialized scientific or technical subjects will be at an advantage in the job market.

Related Occupations
- Copywriter
- Radio/TV Announcer and Newscaster
- Technical Writer
- Writer & Editor

Conversation With . . .
BEN ABRAMSON

Deputy Managing Editor, Travel
USA Today, Venice, FL
Journalist, 25 years

1. **What was your individual career path in terms of education/training, entry-level job, or other significant opportunity?**

I was a history major at George Washington University, and always had great curiosity about the world, both as an avid traveler and academically. I also loved the written word. I took an entry-level position in the *Washington Post* newsroom, and worked a hybrid admin/journalism job for several years after college. I was immediately captivated working in a newsroom, which are often filled with interesting, worldly characters. The commercial Internet didn't even exist when I was a student in the 1980s, so like most prospective journalists at that time I assumed my career would be for a newspaper or magazine. My newsroom career started with seeking any opportunities to write, primarily in local news.

Then *The Post* launched its first online product, a dial-up service called *Digital Ink*, where I was hired as an editor. The service was a precursor to one of the first major newspaper websites, washingtonpost.com, for which I was part of the launch team. Working for the launch team presented a wealth of new options. I presented a plan to launch a Travel section and local Washington visitors guide, and that path has led to a job I love.

Travel is an interesting topic to cover because it's something many people do for leisure and adventure, while others must take less glamorous trips for business. So an editor is always looking for a mix of content that inspires and entertains on the one hand, and helps consumers stay safe and save money on the other. Coming up with story ideas and working with reporters, photographers and videographers to put out a newspaper section, website and mobile apps is demanding but rewarding.

2. **What are the most important skills and/or qualities for someone in your profession, particularly someone who decides to work overseas?**

Journalists should always be curious. Talk to people, study history and culture, seek immersive experiences. Speaking a foreign language fluently can be a great competitive advantage. Also, news media relies on accuracy and timeliness; your professional conduct should mirror that.

3. What do you wish you had known before deciding to work abroad?

Generally speaking, I've seen too many people try to land full-time jobs from their home base. That puts you in competition with everyone who can see a job listing. Go directly to the destination where you wish to work, and learn about it. Being on the ground will give you opportunities you wouldn't have had from home.

4. Are there many job opportunities overseas in your profession? In what specific geographic areas?

Journalism has a strange paradox; more great content is produced and consumed than ever, but many media companies are struggling and have minimal budgets. So as you search for good paying gigs, think creatively—YouTube, obscure outlets, even consumer brands.

For geography, choose a good strategic base. Tens of thousands of young Americans will try to make it in London each year. You could end up with a better story to tell if you find a more unique location, especially if it's in an area of the world that's newsworthy.

5. Will the willingness of professionals in your career to travel and live overseas change in the next five years? What role will technology play in those changes, and what skills will be required?

Journalism is largely self-selected for people who are willing to travel, and go to great lengths in general, for a story. But technology has been a great boon, allowing reporters to live in far-flung locations and still have all the tools and access of an office job.

You should give yourself the broadest range of media skills. Any reporting assignment could come with a request for video hosting, or a social media campaign, and you should have basic abilities in as many current tools and methods as possible. Note also that this is an ongoing process, you need to be on top of popular new forms of media throughout your career.

6. What do you enjoy most about your job? What do you enjoy least about your job?

Working as a travel editor exposes me daily to things I'm passionate about. A work day filled with art, architecture, culture and food, and an occasional geography lesson is generally a good one. On the negative end, with an endless news cycle, all journalists, no matter their specialty, are always on call all the time.

7. **Can you suggest a valuable "try this" for students considering a career overseas in your profession?**

Give yourself a news assignment—pick an interesting topic/venue, interview primary sources, take photos and shoot videos. Post it yourself, or seek a university or local outlet to publish. You should enjoy the experience, because it's something you'll repeat many times over the course of a journalism career.

MORE INFORMATION

Accred. Council on Education in Journalism & Mass Comm.
University of Kansas
Stauffer-Flint Hall
1435 Jayhawk Boulevard
Lawrence, KS 66045-7575
785.864.3973
www2.ku.edu/~acejmc

Association for Women in Communications
3337 Duke Street
Alexandria, VA 22314
703.370.7436
info@womcom.org
www.womcom.org

Dow Jones Newspaper Fund, Inc.
P.O. Box 300
Princeton, NJ 08543-0300
609.452.2820
djnf@dowjones.com
www.newsfund.org

Association of Broadcasters
1771 N Street NW
Washington, DC 20036
202.429.5300
nab@nab.org
www.nab.org

National Federation of Press Women
P.O. Box 34798
Alexandria, VA 22334-0798
800.780.2715
presswomen@aol.com
www.nfpw.org

National Newspaper Association
P.O. Box 7540
Columbia, MO 65205-7540
800.829.4662
briansteffens@nna.org
www.nnaweb.org

National Press Club
529 14th Street NW, 13th Floor
Washington, DC 20045
202.662.7500
www.press.org

Newspaper Association of America
4401 Wilson Boulevard, Suite 900
Arlington, VA 22203-1867
571.366.1000
membsvc@naa.org
www.naa.org

Newspaper Guild, CWA
Research and Information
Department
501 Third Street NW, 6th Floor
Washington, DC 20001-2797
202.434.7177
guild@cwa-union.org
www.newsguild.org

Poynter Institute
801 3rd Street S.
St. Petersburg, FL 33701
727.821.9494
www.poynter.org

Society of Professional Journalists
Eugene S. Pulliam National Journalism Center
3909 N. Meridian Street
Indianapolis, IN 46208
317.927.8000
cvachon@spj.org
www.spj.org

Model

Snapshot

Career Cluster(s): Business, Management & Administration
Marketing, Sales & Service
Interests: Fashion, Advertising, Fashion Design, Fitness,
Entertainment
Earnings (Yearly Average): $29,931
Employment & Outlook: Average Growth Expected

OVERVIEW

Sphere of Work

Models work in the fashion and advertising industries, helping
to promote a wide variety of products or campaigns by posing for
photographs, artwork,
and other mediums, and
by modeling apparel and
accessories on fashion
runways. Models generally
appear in print and online
advertisements, television
commercials, and in front
of live audiences in order to
demonstrate the merits of
a particular product, style,
or campaign. Most models
work with modeling agencies,

fashion designers, photographers, and directors, and must adhere to the physical requirements set forth by their employers.

Work Environment

Models work in a variety of settings and are required to work in numerous locations. Many models work in indoor studios under strong lights, and must stand, pose, or walk for extended periods of time. They also work outdoors, often in extreme weather conditions, including cold water, snow, and extreme heat. Elite models are usually required to travel extensively, often to international and remote locations. They rarely follow a normal schedule, and regularly work weekends, evenings, and additional hours during seasonal peaks such as spring and fall.

Profile

Interests: People, Things
Working Conditions: Work Both Inside and Outside
Physical Strength: Light work
Education Needs: On-The-Job Training
Licensure/Certification: Usually Not Required
Physical Abilities Not Required: Not Climb, Not Hear and/or Talk
Opportunities For Experience: Volunteer Work, Part Time Work
Holland Interest Score*: EAS

* See Appendix A

Occupation Interest

A model's physical appearance is of the utmost importance. Generally speaking, models must maintain their weight, be physically attractive, possess healthy hair and skin, and in most cases, meet certain height requirements. (For specific models, such as a hand model, the value lies in the appearance and health of the hand.) Those interested in pursuing a career in modeling must also be familiar with and passionate about the latest trends in fashion, photography, and the beauty care industry. Models must also demonstrate a positive, "can-do" attitude, and must be willing to spend extended periods of time away from home.

A Day in the Life—Duties and Responsibilities

Most models sign with modeling agencies. These agencies promote models and help them find employment in exchange for a percentage of earnings made. In order to be hired for fashion shows, photography shoots, or any other projects, models generally must audition, or attend "go-sees," where prospective employers will evaluate their physical appearance, movement, and past modeling experience. Models are expected to handle and maintain a photographic portfolio, current headshots, composite cards, and current measurements. Once chosen for a project, a model will learn about the details and duration of the project from his or her agent.

Models usually accept a combination of commercial, editorial, and catalog work. Before a photo shoot, models are styled by makeup, hair, and clothing artists. When working in a studio or at an outdoor location, models may be required to use facial expressions and bodily movements to convey different emotions. Models take direction from photographers or directors, and are expected to quickly and flawlessly change and alter their poses and expressions when asked to do so. During fashion shows, models walk, pose, and exhibit clothing in front of a live audience. Models who pose for painters, artists, or sculptors usually work in a private, more intimate setting.

To prepare for a photo shoot or other job, successful models find it beneficial to research and understand the company, brand, and or product(s) they will represent. On a typical day, most models travel to far more "go-sees" and auditions than paid jobs. Building a beginning career as a model takes persistence, an unflappable demeanor, and lots of energy—many days can be longer than the typical eight hour work day, and a positive attitude helps models secure future employment and develop industry contacts.

Duties and Responsibilities

- Standing, turning, sitting, rising and walking to display garment features to observers
- Moving or posing as directed
- Holding one pose and remaining practically motionless for long periods of time
- Occasionally working with animals or unfamiliar products

WORK ENVIRONMENT

Immediate Physical Environment

Modeling is a career with a demanding schedule, irregular hours, and work in a variety of locations. Work environments vary from extremely comfortable to difficult, stressful, and sometimes glamorous.

Transferable Skills and Abilities

Interpersonal/Social Skills
- Asserting oneself
- Cooperating with others
- Working as a member of a team

Organization & Management Skills
- Following instructions
- Performing routine work

Human Environment

Models work with a number of different people and must easily adapt to diverse personalities and attitudes. They regularly interact with other models, agents, photographers, designers, project directors and producers, makeup artists, and other stylists.

Technological Environment

Models must be comfortable using equipment related to their craft, including makeup kits, digital and print portfolios, cumbersome clothing and accessories, hair styling tools, sewing accessories, and telecommunication tools. Models must be extremely comfortable in front of a camera or multiple cameras.

EDUCATION, TRAINING, AND ADVANCEMENT

High School/Secondary

There are no formal educational requirements for people looking to pursue a career in modeling. High school students who wish to pursue modeling after graduation should study communications, fashion, public speaking, photography, digital video, and other general arts courses. They should also practice posing, moving, and expressing themselves in front of a camera. Aspiring models find it helpful to obtain professional photographs, which they can then submit to modeling agencies.

Suggested High School Subjects
- Arts
- Clothing & Textiles
- Cosmetology
- English
- Physical Education
- Speech
- Theatre & Drama

Related Career Pathways/Majors

Business, Marketing & Administration Cluster
- Marketing Pathway

Marketing, Sales & Service Cluster
- Professional Sales & Marketing Pathway

Postsecondary

Many prospective models attend modeling schools which offer practical training in vocational areas such as makeup application, photo posing techniques, still photo shooting, image analysis, posture language, wardrobe, and runway movement. Modeling agencies regularly send representatives to look for and discover new talent at modeling schools. The majority of aspiring models, however, move to an urban center after high school to pursue job opportunities and apprenticeships, and to gain modeling experience.

Postsecondary training in acting, dance, and voice can also be beneficial to aspiring models, since models are frequently asked to produce bold movements and intense facial expressions when being photographed and displaying clothes for an audience or a prospective employer.

Adult Job Seekers

Many potential models attend local "open call" auditions for modeling agencies. Though this process is extremely competitive, most professional models are discovered through "open call" auditions, where they have a chance to meet with agents in person and where they can relay their interest and experience in the field. Once signed by an agency, a model is advised on what to wear, how to manage a portfolio, and how to handle designer "go sees" and bookings. Aspiring models can also apply directly with an art school or studio looking to hire models for sculpture and art classes.

Professional Certification and Licensure

Models are not required to receive any kind of formal or professional certification or licensure in their field. They should always have an up-to-date, valid passport, as extensive international travel may be required.

Additional Requirements

Ultimately, a professional model must have an engaging personality and be extremely photogenic. It is crucial that aspiring models not only look pretty in photographs, but natural as well. Because a model plays a large role in the sale and promotion of particular merchandise, he or she must be able to immediately capture and express a certain look or tone when asked. Above all else, a model must always look healthy, fresh, and naturally beautiful. To achieve this, a model must pay strict attention to diet, exercise, and his or her overall personal appearance. The modeling world is a highly competitive one, and prospective models must be thick-skinned, unfazed by constant rejection, and driven to succeed.

EARNINGS AND ADVANCEMENT

Earnings depend on the model's experience and popularity as well as the type of modeling and the number and length of assignments. Earnings also are affected by whether a model freelances or is employed by one firm. Models working through an agency have irregular earnings because they are paid only when their agency books them for a job.

Median annual earnings of models were $34,902 in 2016. The lowest ten percent earned less than $21,012, and the highest ten percent earned more than $63,631. Earnings can be quite high for supermodels, but most models do not have work every day, and jobs may only last a few hours.

Full-time models for garment manufacturers and retailers may receive paid vacations, holidays, and sick days; life and health insurance; and retirement benefits. These are usually paid by the employer. Some employers may also provide discounts on merchandise and services.

EMPLOYMENT AND OUTLOOK

Nationally, there were approximately 5,800 models employed in 2014. Little or no change is expected from 2014 to 2024. Applicants are likely to face strong competition, and becoming a highly paid professional model is very difficult.

Related Occupations
- Actor
- Dancer/Choreographer

MORE INFORMATION

American Federation of Television and Radio Artists
260 Madison Avenue, 7th Floor
New York, NY 10016
212.532.0800
www.aftra.org

International Modeling and Talent Association
www.imta.com

Modeling Association of America International, Inc.
350 East 54th Street
New York, NY 10022
212.753.1555

World Model Association
www.worldmodel.org

Briana Nadeau/Editor

Musician and Composer

Snapshot

Career Cluster(s): Arts, A/V Technology & Communications
Interests: Music, musical instruments, entertaining and performing, composing or arranging music, recording, promotion
Earnings (Yearly Average): $46,647
Employment & Outlook: Average Growth Expected

OVERVIEW

Sphere of Work

Musicians and composers, considered entertainers regardless of their genre or stature, express themselves through the use of instruments and/or voice. While many musicians write their own music, recognition as a composer is usually reserved for those who compose original works meant to be performed by other musicians. They each tend to specialize in a particular musical genre, although crossovers are common. In addition to contemporary compositions, musicians and composers are

able to draw on a vast collection of music in the public domain for new arrangements and interpretations.

Work Environment

Musicians compose and practice in studios, often located in their homes, and perform in diverse environments, from cruise ships, nightclubs, and churches to large concert halls and stadiums. Some perform outdoors when weather permits. Performance makes up only a fraction of the musician's workweek, with the bulk of their time taken up by practice, rehearsals, composing, travel, and other responsibilities, including recording, if they are a recording artist. With the exception of orchestra members, church organists, and a few others, most musicians and composers are self-employed. Musicians have the highest chance of succeeding professionally if they live near major cities, where the greatest number of employment opportunities can be found.

Profile

Interests: Data, People
Working Conditions: Work Inside
Physical Strength: Light work
Education Needs: High School Diploma or G.E.D., Junior/Technical/Community College, Bachelor's Degree
Licensure/Certification: Usually Not Required
Physical Abilities Not Required: Not Climb, Not Kneel
Opportunities For Experience: Apprenticeship, Military Service, Volunteer Work, Part Time Work
Holland Interest Score*: ASE, ASI

* See Appendix A

Occupation Interest

Most people who choose to become a professional musician or composer do so after becoming proficient at one or more instruments. They enjoy expressing themselves creatively in this "nonverbal language," and, in the case of musicians, enjoy performing for an audience. While they have certainly learned that practice is the key to success, they demonstrate other necessary qualities as well, including creativity, stamina, confidence, and the ability to cooperate with other musicians.

A Day in the Life—Duties and Responsibilities

Musicians divide much of their time between practice and rehearsals, performing, and any related travel, and, in many cases, recording and promotion. A practice session normally involves an individual musician learning a brand new piece, polishing a technique, or gaining proficiency on a new instrument, whereas rehearsal involves the whole band or ensemble, if there is one, practicing a complete piece of music for performance. Established musicians with a degree of professional recognition may have a manager to handle the details of promotion, scheduling, recording, and production, while those who are just starting out may have to do everything themselves.

A successful professional composer may be offered commissions to write advertising jingles, film scores, orchestral works, or other types of music. Some composers are also hired to arrange music— that is, take an existing work and have it performed in a novel way. For example, a composer might take a pop song and turn it into an orchestral work. When not busy with their creative work, composers meet with clients and spend time promoting their talents.

Musicians may also set aside time for composing music or writing songs. They also listen to recordings by other musicians and keep abreast of new equipment and technologies. Because the field is so competitive, making a living as a full-time musician or composer is difficult. Therefore, many musicians and composers also hold day jobs that divide their attentions even further.

Duties and Responsibilities

- Playing one or more musical instruments
- Studying and rehearsing scores
- Playing from memory or by following a score
- Composing or arranging music
- Improving and transposing music

OCCUPATION SPECIALTIES

Instrumental Musicians

Instrumental Musicians play musical instruments as soloists or as members of a musical group, such as an orchestra or band, to entertain audiences.

Choral Directors

Choral Directors conduct vocal music groups, such as choirs and glee clubs.

Orchestra Conductors

Orchestra Conductors lead instrumental music groups, such as orchestras and dance bands.

Musical Directors

Musical Directors plan and direct the activities of personnel in studio music departments and conduct studio orchestras.

Singers

Singers entertain by singing songs on stage, radio, and television or in nightclubs.

Arrangers

Arrangers transcribe musical compositions or melodic lines to adapt them to or create a particular style.

Orchestrators

Orchestrators write musical scores for orchestras, bands, choral groups or individuals.

WORK ENVIRONMENT

Immediate Physical Environment

Musicians play in a variety of settings, ranging from elegant concert halls to smoky bars to weddings and other private events. Depending on the type and size of venue as well as the type of music they play, musicians need to pay attention to the effect of the performance environment on their instruments and especially on their bodies, as they can be at risk for ailments such as hearing loss and repetitive motion injuries.

Transferable Skills and Abilities

Communication Skills
- Expressing thoughts and ideas

Creative/Artistic Skills
- Being skilled in art, music or dance

Research & Planning Skills
- Analyzing information

Research & Planning Skills
- Creating ideas

Human Environment

Musicians interact with many different people, most notably their audiences and other musicians or singers. A session musician will also work closely with studio technicians, a touring artist may travel with his staff and stage crew, and a church organist will collaborate with the music director and minister. Composers often work closely with a film director, advertising team, choreographer, and other professionals.

Technological Environment

Musicians playing instruments that are not electric or electronic, including string, wind, and other traditional instruments, are concerned mainly with the operation and maintenance of those instruments, although any performing artist typically needs to also work with microphones, amplifiers, and other electrical equipment. Additional musical technologies are involved in working with electric guitars, keyboards, and the like, and for recording artists there is a world of sound recording technology with which to become familiar.

EDUCATION, TRAINING, AND ADVANCEMENT

High School/Secondary

Musicians today generally need at least a high school diploma. Most will want to pursue a strong college preparatory program, with electives in music and courses specific to their interests, such as creative writing, electronics, or film studies. Private lessons, summer music camps, and extracurricular performance opportunities are extremely important. Proficiency on one or more instruments will be required for admission to a college music program or conservatory.

Suggested High School Subjects
- Arts
- English
- Foreign Languages
- Humanities
- Instrumental & Vocal Music
- Mathematics

Related Career Pathways/Majors

Arts, A/V Technology & Communications Cluster
- Performing Arts Pathway

Postsecondary

In general, musicians must find the balance of formal and informal education that best meets their needs. An unusually talented musician may choose to forego college and move directly into their performing career. On the other hand, some musicians benefit from at least a bachelor's degree in music. Music programs include courses in theory, composition, arranging, and performance. Instead of music, one might consider majoring in music education, audio engineering, or even double majoring in music and business. Continuing education courses in piano tuning, instrument repair and construction, or other related courses might be good choices as well.

Related College Majors
- Music Conducting
- Music General Performance
- Music History & Literature
- Music Piano & Organ Performance
- Music Theory & Composition
- Music Voice & Choral/Opera Performance
- Music, General

Adult Job Seekers

Adults who take up an instrument later in life face stiff competition; however, it is common for a musician to become a composer later in adulthood, and for musicians to switch instruments later in life. Although musicians can work part time, the hours, and often the pay, are not always conducive to parenting and other adult responsibilities.

Advancement opportunities are limited and, in most cases, highly dependent on one's level of success. They include chaired positions or opportunities for solos, more lucrative recording contracts, performance fees, or commissions, and/or the ability to hire a manager to take care of business responsibilities, thus opening up more time for creative pursuits. Only a very small percentage of musicians and composers reach celebrity status.

Job seeks might consider joining professional organizations such as the American Federation of Musicians, considered to be the largest such organization dedicated to furthering the careers of professional musicians, to seek career advancement opportunities.

Professional Certification and Licensure

There are no certificates or licenses needed for most performers or composers, although a few organizations offer certification that may be required for jobs in that specialty, such as the American Guild of Organists.

Additional Requirements

Musicians are usually artists with a passion for their craft, but forging a professional career in this field is no easy task. Aspiring professional musicians need to be prepared for all the financial hazards of freelance work, including an inconsistent income (or backup income from another source) that needs to be spread over periods of no musical work. As with any fine arts career, passion and persistence are often the most important qualifications.

Fun Fact

She may be a Material Girl, but it's not likely we'll see Madonna doing a commercial anytime soon. Yet she's one of a long list of American stars who have done commercials overseas, typically for generous compensation. Among the others: George Clooney, Jodi Foster, and Leonardo DiCaprio.

Source: Business Insider

EARNINGS AND ADVANCEMENT

Earnings and Advancement of professional musicians are influenced by specialization, steadiness of work, demand for the instrument played, place of employment, location, personal ability and professional reputation. Median annual earnings of musicians were $50,110 in 2016. The lowest ten percent earned less than $20,820, and the highest ten percent earned more than $132,332.

Musicians and composers who belong to a union may receive life and health insurance, and retirement benefits.

EMPLOYMENT AND OUTLOOK

There were approximately 82,100 musicians and composers employed nationally in 2014. Around one-half worked part-time, and about another half were self-employed. Musicians, singers, and related workers are employed in a variety of settings, such as religious, civic, professional or other similar organizations; professional orchestras, small chamber music groups, opera companies, musical theater companies, and ballet troupes. Musicians and singers also perform in nightclubs and restaurants and for weddings and other events. Well-known musicians and groups may perform in concerts, appear on radio and television broadcasts, and make recordings and music videos. The Armed Forces also offer careers in their bands and smaller musical groups.

Employment of musicians and composers is expected to grow slower than average for all occupations through the year 2024, which means employment is projected to increase 3 percent. Increased attendance at musical performances will create job demand. In addition, singers will be needed to make musical recordings for films television and commercials. The Internet and other new forms of media may provide independent musicians and singers alternative methods to distribute music. Strong competition for jobs in this field is expected to continue.

Related Occupations
- Actor
- Dancer/Choreographer
- Sound Engineer

Related Military Occupations
- Music Director
- Musician

MORE INFORMATION

**American Federation of
Musicians (AFM)**
1501 Broadway, Suite 600
New York, NY 10036
212.869.1330
www.afm.org

Lists a variety of scholarships:
www.afm.org/young-musicians/
scholarships

American Guild of Musical Artists
1430 Broadway, 14th Floor
New York, NY 10018
212.265.3687
agma@musicalartists.org
www.musicalartists.org

American Guild of Organists
475 Riverside Drive, Suite 1260
New York, NY 10115
212.870.2310
info@agohq.org
www.agohq.org

American Guild of Variety Artists
363 7th Avenue, 17th Floor
New York, NY 10001-3904
212.675.1003
agva@agvausa.com
www.agvausa.com

American Music Center
322 8th Avenue, Suite 1401
New York, NY 10001
212.366.5260
allison@amc.net
www.amc.net

**American Society of Composers,
Authors, and Publishers (ASCAP)**
1 Lincoln Plaza
New York, NY 10023
800.952.7227
www.ascap.com

**American Society of Music
Arrangers and Composers
(ASMAC)**
5903 Noble Avenue
Van Nuys, California 91411
www.asmac.org

Sponsors scholarships:
www.asmac.org/478590

Offers masterclasses:
www.asmac.org/478577

The ASCAP Foundation
1 Lincoln Plaza
New York, NY 10023-7142
212.621.6219
www.ascapfoundation.org

Sponsors dozens of scholarships (and
professional awards):
www.ascapfoundation.org/scholarships.
html

League of American Orchestras
33 West 60th Street, 5th Floor
New York, NY 10023
212.262.5161
www.americanorchestras.org

MENC
The National Association for Music
Education
1806 Robert Fulton Drive
Reston, VA 20191
800.336.3768
www.menc.org

Sponsors the Tri-M Music Honor Society
for secondary students:
www.menc.org/resources/view/tri-m-
music-honor-society

Presents information about music careers:
www.menc.org/careers

**Music Publishers Association of
the United States**
243 5th Avenue, Suite 236
New York, NY 10016
212.327.4044
admin@mpa.org
www.mpa.org

**National Association of Schools of
Music**
11250 Roger Bacon Drive, Suite 21
Reston, VA 20190-5248
703.437.0700
info@arts-accredit.org
nasm.arts-accredit.org/index.jsp

Sally Driscoll/Editor

Professional Athlete

Snapshot

Career Cluster(s): Hospitality & Tourism

Interests: Exercising, training, leading and motivating, strategizing, physical education

Earnings (Yearly Average): $44,196

Employment & Outlook: Faster Than Average Growth Expected

OVERVIEW

Sphere of Work

A professional athlete is a paid sports competitor who participates in official athletic events in front of small or large live audiences.

Professional athletes are generally self-employed or work for athletic clubs or organizations. They are physically fit and fully understand the strategy behind the sport they play. More successful athletes often benefit from product endorsement deals.

The career of a professional athlete can be short, as

athletes are vulnerable to a wide variety of physical injuries related to their occupation. Further, professional athletes should know that professional sports is a fickle, dog-eat-dog industry. Athletes are only as good as their last performance, and there are always younger and more talented replacements waiting to take an athlete's place in the lineup. It is critical that athletes understand and prepare for the end of their career by paying close attention to issues such as contracts, financial planning, and life after professional athletics.

Work Environment

The work environment of a professional athlete depends on the sport in which they participate. Athletes spend much of their working time training and practicing, either indoors in training facilities or outdoors on athletic fields. Most athletes spend a good deal of time traveling to and from sporting events. (At the highest level of professional sports, athletes will travel by plane, while at the lower levels, such as minor league hockey or baseball, travel by bus is the norm.) During competitive seasons, athletes can work up to seven days a week. When they are not competing, athletes usually enjoy extended periods of time off and/or training.

Profile

Interests: Data, People
Working Conditions: Work Outside Work Both Inside and Outside
Physical Strength: Medium Work
Education Needs: On-The-Job Training, High School Diploma or GED
Licensure/Certification: Usually Not Required
Opportunities For Experience: Military Service, Volunteer Work, Part Time Work
Holland Interest Score*: SRC

* See Appendix A

Occupation Interest

Professional athletes are expected to maintain an excellent physique and should take pride in exercising, training, and challenging themselves mentally and physically. People interested in becoming professional athletes should exhibit a natural talent in their designated sport and a willingness to devote their personal time and energy towards improving their personal performance and developing those skills that might benefit their respective teams. They should be able to lead and motivate a group of people, as well as take instruction from a coach or supervisor.

A Day in the Life—Duties and Responsibilities

Throughout the year, professional athletes spend time training, competing, and resting. Prior to the start of the season, professional athletes exercise and train their bodies on their own and/or under the direction of their coaches and along with other teammates. Most athletes regularly consult with nutritionists who advise them on healthy eating habits and diet restrictions. Athletes also work with physical therapists, strength trainers, massage therapists, and chiropractors (before the season begins as well as during the season) to monitor and maintain muscular dexterity and physical fitness.

During the training season, professional athletes meet daily with their team members and coaches to exercise and practice. Many athletes review footage of prior games and competitions to improve their skills, evaluate those of their opponents, and to break down strategies and plays.

During the competitive season, athletes spend days or hours resting, eating properly, and preparing mentally for the series of games ahead. Many athletes play back-to-back games (meaning they have competitions daily, often in different locations), and because of this, must demonstrate excellent physical and mental endurance and stamina. They usually try to rest and relax between games in order to restore energy. Before competitions, athletes usually arrive two to three hours early, review strategy, stretch and warm up, and perform any practice routines designated by the coach. During the competitive season, athletes usually spend a great deal of time away from home, traveling across the country and to international destinations (thus ensuring the need for a professional athlete visa) to compete.

Duties and Responsibilities

- Playing the game or sport according to established rules
- Performing against competition
- Training for the sport by physical exercise and practice, usually under the direction of a trainer or coach

WORK ENVIRONMENT

Immediate Physical Environment

Most professional athletes train and compete in environments similar to those of their designated sports. Some athletes spend the majority of their time indoors, while others spend their time outdoors, sometimes in cold weather. Those athletes competing in well-funded sports, like pro football, have access to top-notch facilities, equipment, personnel, and support. For those athletes competing in those sports that do not generate the revenues that organizations like the National Football League does, facilities, equipment, and access to training professionals may be much more limited.

Transferable Skills and Abilities

Communication Skills
- Speaking effectively
- Writing concisely

Interpersonal/Social Skills
- Asserting oneself
- Cooperating with others
- Working as a member of a team

Organization & Management Skills
- Following instructions
- Making decisions
- Managing time
- Meeting goals and deadlines
- Paying attention to and handling details

Technical Skills
- Performing scientific, mathematical and technical work

Human Environment

Professional athletes work closely with other athletes (especially their teammates), as well as coaches, assistant coaches, sports managers, and agents throughout the year. When competing, athletes interact with referees, sports therapists, athletic supervisors, and fans. The professional sports industry is not without its theatrics. Those athletes hoping to reap significant financial rewards will understand that public persona and showmanship garner attention from fans and those industries seeking product endorsements.

Technological Environment

All athletes must use specified training equipment related to the sport they play. They must also be comfortable using common gym equipment such as free weights, strength training aids, and cardiovascular machines. They must utilize digital technology to break down past games and plays, and should be comfortable using walkie-talkies and similar communication devices. They should expect to wear a team uniform and/or company logo during all sports competitions, and to comply with other dress code regulations in accordance with the policy of the team they represent.

EDUCATION, TRAINING, AND ADVANCEMENT

High School/Secondary

High school students who wish to become professional athletes should maintain a grade point average that allows them to continue to participate and compete in school athletics. Most schools will not let athletes with poor grades participate in sports, so it is incumbent upon all students to organize their time to allow for study and practice. Athletes benefit from study in subjects such as biology, nutrition, health, communications, anatomy, physical education, and other sciences. They should join a sports team or enroll in a club sport. Students who wish to pursue a specific sport should work to excel at that sport by practicing or taking lessons during non-school hours as well in school (if the desired sport is offered). Reading about specific sports techniques and keeping up with the latest trends and technologies in different sports is also helpful.

Suggested High School Subjects
- Biology
- English
- Health Science Technology
- Physical Education
- Science

Related Career Pathways/Majors

Hospitality & Tourism Cluster

• Recreation, Amusements & Attractions Pathway

Postsecondary

Though professional athletes are not required to have earned an undergraduate degree, many prospective professional athletes (especially those who play a team sport) compete in their desired sport at the collegiate level as a way to develop their talents and hone their skills. Some colleges and universities offer sports scholarships to students who are extremely accomplished in their athletic areas. These students are usually required to maintain a certain academic grade point average in addition to joining the university's team or individual sports roster. A small number of them are discovered by athletic scouts or sports agents who see them compete at large events or who invite them to seasonal recruitment sessions.

Related College Majors

• Health & Physical Education, General
• Physical Education Teaching & Coaching
• Sports Medicine & Athletic Training

Adult Job Seekers

The odds of a talented athlete becoming a professional athlete are slim. Because their bodies are in peak physical shape early in their careers, most professional athletes usually only enjoy a few years of successful competition. Prospective athletes should make contact with local coaches, sports agents, or sports scouts to inquire about tryouts or recruitment processes. Athletes who have finished the competitive portion of their career frequently transition to second careers as sports commentators or coaches, partly through the contacts they make and relationships they form during their early career.

Professional Certification and Licensure

For the most part, the requirement of a license or certification for participation in a professional sport varies by the sport itself. For example, certain drivers in professional racing need to be licensed in order to compete in certain events and competitions. Generally, a professional athlete's participation in their respective sport is controlled by the governing board of that sport. Usually, the governing board can suspend or revoke a professional athlete's license based on inappropriate or illegal behavior, ethical violations, or the inability to meet specific performance, education, or training requirements.

Additional Requirements

Professional athletes must be in peak physical condition and demonstrate an inherent passion and talent for their particular sport. They must also possess excellent communication skills and the capacity to motivate, inspire, and lead teammates and other athletes. They must be willing to endure difficult schedules and sustain physical injuries for the good of their team and sport. Because professional athletes inspire and entertain the audiences for whom they are playing, they must work well under pressure and be able to do so in front of a crowd. Finally, some athletes must work well with others as part of a collaborative effort to succeed; if they cannot do so, the team's performance suffers. Drug testing has also become paramount in many professional leagues, and professional athletes should be prepared to undergo routine and/or random drug testing.

Fun Fact

Some 29 former college basketball stars with dreams of making it to the NBA are playing in war-torn Iraq's Superleague, where they're sought after and admired for their flashy style of play.

Source: Washington Post

EARNINGS AND ADVANCEMENT

Earnings of professional athletes are most directly related to individual performance. Minimum salaries are often governed by agreements between team owners and players' unions or associations. In some sports, such as tennis and golf, earnings depend more heavily on the success of the individual than they do in such sports as baseball and football where players are guaranteed salaries. In addition to salaries or winnings, some professional athletes receive cash bonuses, cars, a percentage of ticket sales or of closed-circuit TV sales or other income supplements. Some earn extra money by playing in play-off and championship games, endorsing products in print or on radio or TV, telling their life stories to magazine reporters and making personal appearances.

Salaries of professional athletes are different for each sport. Median annual earnings of professional athletes were $47,710 in 2016. The lowest ten percent earned less than $19,540, and the highest ten percent earned more than $208,000. However, the highest paid professional athletes earn salaries much more.

Excellent pension systems are available for major league baseball, hockey, football and basketball players. Professional athletes may have to purchase and maintain their own sports equipment.

EMPLOYMENT AND OUTLOOK

There were about 13,700 professional athletes employed nationally in 2014. Employment of professional athletes is expected to about as fast as average for all occupations through the year 2024. Competition for professional athlete jobs will continue to be extremely intense. Opportunities to make a living as a professional in individual sports such as golf or tennis may grow as new tournaments are established and prize money distributed to participants increases.

Most professional athletes' careers last only several years due to debilitating injuries and age, so a large proportion of the athletes in these jobs is replaced every year, creating some job opportunities. However, a far greater number of talented young men and women dream of becoming a sports superstar and will be competing for a very limited number of job openings.

Related Occupations
- Athletic Director
- Fitness Trainer and Aerobics Instructor
- Health Club Manager
- Radio/TV Announcer and Newscaster
- Recreation Worker
- Sports Instructor/Coach

Related Military Occupations
- Teacher & Instructor
- Training Specialist & Instructor

Conversation With . . .
SHEYLANI PEDDY

Point Guard
TTT Riga Women's Basketball, Latvia
Professional basketball player, 6 years

1. What was your individual career path in terms of education/training, entry-level job, or other significant opportunity?

When I was younger I thought I was a mind reader. My family at times led me to believe that I was. So, as I grew older I became more confident in my "ability." Hence I decided that I would best serve as a psychologist, which is what I majored in at Temple University in Philadelphia.

I've been playing basketball pretty much since I was a toddler. My mom said I always wanted to play with a basketball and never left the house without it. You know how some babies are attached to a blanket or teddy bear? I was attached to a basketball. I went to Melrose High School in Melrose, MA, where I hold the scoring record for both men's and women's basketball. I played two years at Wright State University in Dayton, Ohio, before finishing out my college career at Temple University, where I majored in psychology. Because of basketball, I got full scholarships.

I always knew I wanted to play professionally. I would watch the WNBA games and knew I wanted to play amongst the best players in the U.S. I was lucky enough to get drafted to the WNBA by Chicago Sky in 2012, but unfortunately, I didn't make the team. Although I was disappointed, I hired an agent and was able to play professionally in Israel. I am entering my sixth season as a professional. After Israel, I played in Austria one season, then in Germany from 2104 to 2017 and now Latvia.

I was player of the year at Temple as well in Austria and Germany for three consecutive years. Basically, that means I was the best player of the league, equivalent to MVP.

This whole experience is allowing me to grow as a person and keeps me grounded and thankful—to family and friends for always supporting me and encouraging me to take basketball seriously and to all the coaches who helped me develop my skills and turn my dreams to a reality.

I have been lucky enough to travel and play in about 15 different countries. I turned something that I did mostly for fun into a job that I love. I truly believe I have one of the best jobs ever.

2. What are the most important skills and/or qualities for someone in your profession, particularly someone who decides to work overseas?

You definitely have to able and willing to adapt to the culture of the country you're in. You always have to conduct yourself in a professional manner on and off the court and be willing to learn new things. Having a great personality helps a lot. Learning the language is the hardest part and at times the only words I retained pertained to work. I struggled to learn German and was only able to learn basics like hi, bye, excuse me, yes/no. Fortunately for me, almost everyone spoke or understood English.

3. What do you wish you had known before deciding to work abroad?

The decision to work abroad really didn't come by foresight, as I thought I would be working in the U.S. When the opportunity to work abroad presented itself, it became more about working harder, taking care of business on the court, and maintaining a positive attitude with hopes of still playing in the states. Quite frankly, in my opinion, the less you know, the more accepting you are when you arrive in a new country.

4. Are there many job opportunities overseas in your profession? In what areas, both in terms of geography and subject matter?

Upwards of 50 countries have professional women's basketball teams. The interest in women's basketball has grown immensely. But there are many more women than there are jobs, both abroad and in the states. However, there are other job opportunities if you choose to be a coach at any level or an official or to work behind the scenes. I've learned that it's essential to network and be professional with everyone, because you never know who knows whom.

5. How do you see the importance of international experience in your profession changing in the next five years? What role will technology play in those changes, and what skills will be required?

I believe that the dynamics of teams will change, along with the pay scale. Teams consist of 6 or 7 players, usually from that country, but they're starting to hire the better players from wherever. As for technology, streaming of more games will pique the interest of more potential players.

6. **What do you enjoy most about your job? What do you enjoy least about your job?**

I enjoy traveling all over the world and experiencing different cultures. I really enjoy meeting people of different cultures and appreciate the knowledge they share with me. I enjoy being able to showcase my talent while doing what I love.

What I don't enjoy is leaving my family for months at a time and being unable to communicate with them as much as I would like due to the time differences.

7. **Can you suggest a valuable "try this" for students considering a career overseas in your profession?**

Growing up, I always played on an Amateur Athletic Union (AAU) team. This allowed me to measure my talent against players across the country. Find a similar league that will get you to the next level. If you can't find a team, look for someone in your area who's willing to help you develop. The important thing for the athlete to know is that your desire and determination is your destiny in whatever you choose.

MORE INFORMATION

Ladies Professional Golf Association
100 International Golf Drive
Daytona Beach, FL 32124-1092
386.274.6200
www.lpga.com

Major League Baseball Players Association
12 East 49th Street, 24th Floor
New York, NY 10017
212.826.0808
www. mlbplayers.mlb.com

National Basketball Players Association
310 Lenox Avenue
New York, NY 10027
212.655.0880
www.nbpa.org

National Football League Players Association
2021 L Street NW, Suite 600
Washington, DC 20036
800.372.2000
www.nflpa.org

National Hockey League Players' Association
20 Bay Street Suite 1700
Toronto, ON
M5J 2N8
www.nhlpa.com

The PGA of America
100 Avenue of the Champions
Palm Beach Gardens, FL 33410
561-624-8400
www.pga.com

Women's National Basketball Association
Olympic Tower, 645 5th Avenue
New York, NY 10022
212.688.9622
www.wnba.com

Briana Nadeau/Editor

GOVERNMENT AND SECURITY

Government and Security

A nation's foreign affairs consists of the various policies and activities that a government uses to promote and protect the nation's interests and to form constructive relations with other nations around the world. In the United States, hundreds of thousands of Americans are employed in overseas locations working on a wide variety of projects that play a role in the nation's foreign affairs policies and projects. This includes more than 15,000 Americans working in U.S. diplomatic and foreign service offices, as well as the thousands of employees of the nation's intelligence agencies, and the millions working in the nation's military service branches. There are a variety of careers in foreign affairs, each of which requires specific preparation, training, and skills, and many of which offer professionals the opportunity to travel and live abroad for extended periods, learning about foreign cultures while also serving as representatives of their native nation.

Diplomacy and the Foreign Service

Historians have traced the history of Western diplomacy back to the Byzantine Empire (330 to 1450 CE). Following the 476 CE collapse of Rome, the Byzantine Empire established the world's first known "diplomatic corps," a group of professionals whose role was to promote the interests of the empire by establishing and developing relations with foreign government. The globalization of the world's economies and increasing interdependence between nations towards the goal of preventing international conflict and protecting diminishing natural resources fundamentally changed diplomacy around the world. Since World War II, international consultation and cooperation has become a more common and familiar part of governance and this has increased the demand for governmental representatives skilled and trained to represent the nation overseas.

In the United States, individuals who work as diplomats or ambassadors are part of what's called the U.S. Foreign Service, a branch of the U.S. Department of State. Diplomates typically work at one of the nation's 270 embassies or consulates. An embassy is a foreign office led by the nation's official ambassador to the foreign nation. As the U.S. assigns only one official ambassador to each nation, each nation also has only one embassy, but may have other diplomatic offices in the same nation known as consulates.

Most U.S. diplomats are more specifically known as Foreign Service Officers (FSOs) and obtain their positions by participating in a program through the U.S. Department of State. Applicants must pass a written exam, complete a comprehensive interview, and participate in training through the National Foreign Affairs Training Center. Following this, successful applicants may bid for one of many international assignments, though more desirable postings may be reserved for senior diplomats.

In addition to foreign service officers and ambassadors, there are many other types of positions available in foreign relations and foreign service. Embassies, consulates, and other foreign mission offices also often employ translators and interpreters and so those with fluency in foreign languages might look to foreign affairs as a possible career path. There are many other support personnel who may work at foreign missions, such as secretarial and logistics assistants, economic and budget specialists, drivers, cooks and hospitality professionals, and security agents. There are also opportunities for those interested in the foreign service to learn about the field through internships and student diplomatic programs offered through the Department of State in conjunction with learning institutions offering education in history, foreign service, foreign affairs, or international studies.

Fun Fact

The process of becoming a Foreign Service Officer is intense, with essays, a day-long oral assessment, and a 60-question exam. Twenty of them can be found at: www.csmonitor.com/World/2011/0127/Are-you-smarter-than-a-US-diplomat-Take-our-Foreign-Service-Exam/US-History.

Conversation With . . .
KARA C. McDONALD

Consul General
United States Foreign Service, Strasbourg, France
Foreign Service, 20 years

1. What was your individual career path in terms of education/training, entry-level job, or other significant opportunity?

Growing up in the Midwest of the United States, I had little exposure to, but a great interest in, foreign settings and affairs. At the age of 13, I began participating in volunteer trips to the Caribbean and spent summers during college interning at the International Labor Office in Geneva and volunteering with a non-governmental organization in Burkina Faso in West Africa. I majored in French and Comparative Literature at the University of Michigan. It was only after graduating that I decided to pursue international relations and applied to the Fletcher School of Law and Diplomacy at Tufts University, which launched my career.

2. What are the most important skills and/or qualities for someone in your profession, particularly someone who decides to work overseas?

Adaptability. The Foreign Service tests the flexibility of every part of your being, both professional and personal. Living in another culture certainly requires adaptability. Interacting with diplomats, officials, and citizens with a different cultural anchor requires patience, good humor, and humility. So does the lifestyle of moving every few years. It can be challenging to personal stability—relationships, schools, community ties, etc. I find that colleagues who thrive most in the Foreign Service are those with deep curiosity and the courage to keep exploring.

3. What do you wish you had known before going into your professional, and, specifically, before moving abroad?

I wish I had understood how tough it would be on my family. I joined the Foreign Service as an unmarried officer. My now husband is in the same general profession, and even so, it is hard to overstate the challenges that constant uprooting poses. As children age too, it becomes more and more difficult to find assignments that match the complex issues we face as a family. At the same time, the needs of the service have also transitioned to require even more flexibility of individuals and families. It feels like we have more unaccompanied positions—such as war zones or other designated danger zones, where family may not be able to accompany you—than ever before. We demand service in hardship and conflict. There seems to be greater stress on the corps and their families. And family structures are changing significantly—long gone are the days of only nuclear families with a one-career spouse. But the diversity of our corps is a strength, even if it's not always obvious how to manage and support that diversity within the demands of a Foreign Service career.

4. Are there many job opportunities overseas in your profession? In what areas, both in terms of geography and subject matter?

One of the great advantages of a career in the Foreign Service is its diverse array of jobs. I always tell those contemplating the Foreign Service Officer Test that getting into the Foreign Service is really an opportunity to apply for a vast array of public service jobs in foreign affairs that are not open to the general public. There are no two jobs alike in the Foreign Service, and because we move around every couple of years, it is impossible for one to become bored or stagnant. You can spend a year learning a language for your next position; helping American citizens abroad; reporting on economic issues in a country; managing a bilateral relationship with another country; running exchange programs; overseeing building maintenance and motor pools; or advancing a high-level official visit—there is something for everyone.

5. How do you see the importance of international experience in your profession changing in the next five years? What role will technology play in those changes, and what skills will be required?

The globalization of international affairs has seen a proliferation of actors in international diplomacy. International experience will continue to be a benefit because of the skills and capacities that it exercises. Technological skills will continue to be highly sought, of course, but even more so will be interpersonal or people-to-people skills, I believe. I am continually surprised by how in demand the latter are. There are a lot of smart, even brilliant, people in this business, and what sets apart those colleagues whom I most admire is the ability to work effectively and generously with and through others to accomplish goals as a team.

6. What do you enjoy most about your job? What do you enjoy least about your job?

I most enjoy the variety of what I do year to year and the amazing opportunities the Foreign Service affords. It is, of course, an honor to serve one's country, and I am extremely grateful for the jobs I have held in the Foreign Service. I also have enjoyed and benefited from the chance to learn languages. There are few careers that value language-learning like the Foreign Service. I speak and/or have studied French, Romanian, and Russian.

7. Can you suggest a valuable "try this" for students considering a career overseas in your profession?

Any immersion in a country—an internship, study abroad, volunteer work, or professional opportunities abroad—helps provide a glimpse of Foreign Service life. Many who enter the Foreign Service came out of the Peace Corps. While I did not, I do believe that it presents a unique view on cultural immersion and adaptability that prepares a person well for a life in the Foreign Service.

Military and Security Overseas

The United States military includes five major branches, the Army, Navy, Air Force, Marines, and Coast Guard, with 1,281,900 active duty personnel and an additional 801,200 members in reserve units. In 2017, 199,485 service members (approximately 35.8 percent) were deployed overseas at one of more than 800 international bases located in 70 nations. Those stationed at overseas military bases and temporary camps may participate in a variety of activities, from training local military and/or police, to helping with construction or infrastructure projects, to serving as security personnel for diplomatic or consular personnel.

Finding work with the military, or more specifically, working with the military overseas, typically requires specialized training and/or experience. While some branches of the U.S. military accept students with a secondary education, many positions require a bachelor's or higher level degree. Those entering into a military contract with previous international experience or knowledge of foreign languages will have a better chance of being selected for international postings.

The U.S. intelligence community, which consists of 17 separate civilian and military agencies is another branch of the government that regularly conducts work overseas. With a wide variety of agencies handling specialized intelligence activities, the nation's intelligence community provides employment opportunities to individuals from divergent backgrounds and with different skills, education, and training. For instance, the Department of the Treasury's Office of Intelligence and Analysis works to prevent economic terrorism, money laundering, and black market activity and typically seeks to hire individuals with previous experience in accounting, budget analysis, and other financial fields.

The intelligence community as a whole can be divided into two basic types of agencies, civilian and military. Each branch of the U.S. military has its own intelligence division, while the Defense Intelligence Agency, headquartered in the Pentagon, is the leading agency for all military intelligence, and collects data from the other military intelligence offices. The civilian agencies include the most familiar intelligence groups, like the Central Intelligence Agency and the Federal Bureau of Investigation. While some individuals employed in intelligence function as "operatives" or "agents," filling the "spy" role depicted in popular culture, most of those employed by intelligence agencies work in a supportive capacity, performing clerical or logistics work or conducting research. The nation's 17 intelligence agencies employ tens of thousands of Americans in a variety of positions in postings both domestic and abroad. Those interested in a career in intelligence gathering, research, or support can seek out information from the United States Intelligence Community (IC) official offices in Washington, D.C.

For those with experience in security and logistics, there are also private security companies that hire agents and other personnel for international assignments. Many security agencies hiring for postings overseas prefer applicants who have previous military, intelligence, or police training, but may also hire a variety of support personnel to work in assistive positions overseas. To give one of many examples, the controversial Blackwater USA company, now going by the name ACADEMI, hired ex-military and other security experts to supplement security for federal, state, and other governmental officials working in areas with security concerns. ACADEMI not only provides security services directly, but also provides security training for individuals and groups, including canine training and various security consultation services.

From the foreign service to private security contractors, there are many different options for those interested in foreign affairs to live and work overseas. Those interested in foreign affairs might therefore approach the career path from a variety of different starting points. For students interested in the field, whether planning on joining the military, working in governmental intelligence, or pursuing a career as a diplomat, students who focus on foreign languages and/or international relations.

Conversation With . . .
GREGORY B. STARR

Retired Assistant Secretary of State for Diplomatic Security
U.S. Department of State
International Security Expert, 37 years

1. What was your individual career path in terms of education/training, entry-level job, or other significant opportunity?

When I was in college, I did a year abroad in Paris. A friend's father, a Foreign Service Officer, was visiting the U.S. embassy. We had dinner and I met the senior security officer for the embassy and that's how I learned about jobs in international security. I got my undergraduate degree in political science and a master's in forensic science, both from George Washington University. I was hired as a special agent for the U.S. Department of State in 1980. When I retired in 2009, I was the Director of Diplomatic Security. I then went to work for the U.N. for four years as Undersecretary General for Security, but was recalled to the Department of State after Benghazi. As Assistant Secretary of State for Diplomatic Security, I've been a political appointee for the last four years. I left on Jan. 20, 2017.

Over the course of my career, we did two years in the Congo, three years in Senegal, three years in Tunisia, and three years in Israel — and when I say we, that's the entire family.

2. What are the most important skills and/or qualities for someone in your profession, particularly someone who decides to work overseas?

First is a willingness to relocate often. You're going to be working in very different cultures with different people. Flexibility is perhaps the single best trait to have. Because you're security—and in many cases, security and law enforcement—integrity and judgment are the two next things. The ability to communicate is critical. Having either foreign language skills or the ability to learn foreign languages is incredibly important. French is my other language. I worked in Africa quite a bit and French was a predominant language there.

3. What do you wish you had known before going into your profession, and, specifically, before moving abroad?

Looking back, we didn't understand how hard it would be for my wife Carla to have a career, and that's very difficult. I'm not sure we clearly understood the amount of travel and how much time I would spend away from the family. There are great opportunities when you're in the Foreign Service—you live in very different places and see many different things—but the moving can be difficult. In many ways, this has got to be a family decision.

4. Are there many job opportunities overseas in your profession? In what areas, both in terms of geography and subject matter?

Within the U.S. government, the State Department has the most overseas jobs, although other agencies have positions in embassies abroad. There are a lot of security jobs in Latin America and South America and in the Middle East for private companies. And then there's the United Nations, which has a presence in about 180 countries and rather large security programs. Regretably, since 1975, the international security situation, particularly for Americans and tourists abroad, has become significantly more difficult and that's why the security industry has grown.

5. How do you see the importance of international experience in your profession changing in the next five years? What role will technology play, and what skills will be required?

I see the security industry staying robust globally, due to the much greater need for continued diplomacy in many places around the world; the globalization of private industry and the globalization of media, with people learning things and understanding different cultures and understanding that they can move around easier; and the need for humanitarian operations and humanitarian aid, which comes with a huge security portfolio.

People talk about cyber security but in reality, efforts have not really matured yet. This is a very big growing industry.

6. What do you enjoy most about your job? What do you enjoy least about your job?

The thing I enjoyed most is that I felt I was doing something worthwhile. As security officers working in hard, difficult places, we ensured that diplomats could continue to do their jobs. I consider the continuation of diplomacy a crucial international factor, rather than breaking down into war or conflict. I felt every day that what we were doing—protecting our people and our families—was important. You're faced with many situations and some of them are critical: terrorism or civil unrest or evacuations. All of the things we did—procedural security, cyber security, personal security, physical security, and mobility security—helped diplomacy and humanitarian operations proceed under very difficult conditions. And if we hadn't had the right security programs, neither the diplomacy nor the humanitarian operations could have succeeded.

The worst part is having to work through difficult bureaucracies and, in many cases, find the funding for security programs. In the humanitarian world, every dollar that you have to spend on security is a dollar that you're not spending on aid, be it supplying food or medicine or teaching agriculture. So it's difficult to work through making sure you have adequate funding to do security. But the world has gotten so violent in many places where diplomats and humanitarians and companies need to do their work that security is a necessity.

7. **Can you suggest a valuable "try this" for students considering a career overseas in your profession?**

Most everybody thinks, "Oh, this is glamorous and I'll live in Paris or London," but the reality is most of our work has to get done in tough places: Afghanistan and Iraq and Sudan and Angola and Libya or Chad.

Before you decide on this career, the most helpful thing may be to experience living and working abroad to see whether you find enough joy and satisfaction to put up with hardships, because quite frankly, living in some of these countries, there are quite a few hardships. And also, if you're serious about this career path, determine whether you have the capacity to learn foreign languages.

Works Used

Agrawal, Nina. "There's more than the CIA and FBI: The 17 agencies that make up the U.S. intelligence community." *Latimes*. Los Angeles Times. Jan 17 2017. Web. 22 Jul 2017.

Desjardins, Jeff. "Nearly 200,000 US Troops are Currently Deployed Around the World—here's where." *Business Insider*. Business Insider, Inc. Mar 20 2017. Web. 22 Jul 2017.

Glaser, John. "Why We Should Close America's Overseas Military Bases." *Time*. Time Inc. Oct 7 2016. Web. 22 Jul 2017.

"How do you become a diplomat?" *Diplomacy.state.gov*. U.S. State Department. Discover Diplomacy. 2016. Web. 22 Jul 2017.

Customs Inspector

Snapshot

Career Cluster(s): Government & Public Administration, Law, Public Safety & Security

Interests: Current events, paying attention to detail, making decisions, dealing with crises

Earnings (Yearly Average): $61,600

Employment & Outlook: Slower than average growth expected

OVERVIEW

Sphere of Work

Customs inspectors are federal law enforcement agents who uphold the laws and regulations governing imports and exports. Working under the umbrella of the U.S. Customs and Border Protection department, customs inspectors perform thorough checks of commercial trucks, ships, trains, and cargo planes to ensure that all incoming and outgoing shipments are accounted for and present no danger, and to determine the duties or taxes that must be paid on incoming cargo. They also

inspect international travelers' passports and visas, search for drugs and other contraband in baggage and clothing, and detain potentially dangerous individuals. Customs inspectors collaborate with other law enforcement officials as well as private shipping and logistics companies to facilitate compliance with federal laws.

Work Environment

Customs inspectors work in shipyards, commercial and private airfields and airports, rail yards, border stations, and other locations where international travel and shipping occur. These venues are busy, with many people and packages passing through every day. Some customs inspectors must work outside for most of the day, in all types of weather. Most work standard forty-hour weeks; however, customs inspectors may work late-night, weekend, and holiday shifts, as the work they perform is required twenty-four hours a day year-round. Coping with uncooperative travelers or shippers can add stress to the job.

Profile

Interests: Data
Working Conditions: Work Inside
Physical Strength: Light Work
Education Needs: On-The-Job Training, High School Diploma or G.E.D
Licensure/Certification: Required
Physical Abilities Not Required:
Not Climb,Not Kneel
Opportunities For Experience: Part Time Work
Holland Interest Score*: CEI

* See Appendix A

Occupation Interest

Customs inspectors safeguard the country's borders and ports of entry from international terrorism, drug trafficking, and other kinds of smuggling, and they collect revenue for the government in the form of duties and taxes from commercial shippers. Therefore, prospective customs inspectors must have keen judgment, strong observational and decision-making skills, and personal integrity. They should also be extroverted, communicate effectively, and thrive under pressure. Demand for qualified customs inspectors remains high, which means jobs are available in a wide range of locations.

A Day in the Life—Duties and Responsibilities

The daily responsibilities of customs inspectors vary based on their work setting. For example, inspectors who work in airports meet individual travelers, check their identification and other documentation, inspect luggage and cargo, and interview travelers as they enter the airport. On occasion, they may also perform pat-downs to check for drugs, weapons, or other contraband. Airport customs inspectors also supervise the loading and unloading of cargo, checking manifests, and weighing and measuring boxes and materials. They must keep thorough records of all passenger interactions and inspected cargo and luggage.

Customs inspectors working in other areas, such as at border stations and at ports of entry, perform additional tasks. At ports of entry, customs inspectors board incoming ships to inspect cargo and ensure that all documentation is accurate. They also seize any illegal materials or undeclared goods, including shipments from countries whose exports are forbidden in the United States under federal boycotts. Port customs officials may even impound ships or have them stay offshore pending a thorough investigation. Border station–based customs inspectors, meanwhile, halt vehicles along the US borders with Canada and Mexico. These officials check passports and visas of travelers, board and search trailers, interview suspicious individuals, and verify vehicle documentation. In many cases, customs inspectors become specialists in one particular area, such as narcotics, antiques, agriculture, exotic animals, or machinery.

Some customs inspectors have the authority to carry firearms, issue warrants, and make arrests in relation to customs law violations. They may testify in court proceedings related to seized goods.

Duties and Responsibilities

- Examining, counting, weighing, gauging, measuring, and sampling commercial and noncommercial cargo
- Insuring cargo is properly described
- Inspecting baggage and articles worn by passengers and crew members
- Insuring all property complies with entrance and clearance requirements
- Insuring all merchandise is declared and proper duties are paid
- Intercepting all contraband

WORK ENVIRONMENT

Immediate Physical Environment

Customs inspectors work in well-lit and well-ventilated airports, shipping ports, border stations, and other ports of entry. These locations also experience heavy traffic, with many travelers and/or shipments passing through each day. Many venues are outdoors and require inspectors to work in all weather conditions, day or night. Due to the nature of their work, customs inspectors risk exposure to dangerous substances, such as explosives, drugs, and toxic chemicals.

Transferable Skills and Abilities

Communication Skills
- Speaking effectively
- Writing concisely

Interpersonal/Social Skills
- Being patient

Organization & Management Skills
- Demonstrating leadership
- Paying attention to and handling details

Unclassified Skills
- Keeping a neat appearance

Human Environment

Customs inspectors work with a wide range of individuals, which may include international travelers, commercial ship crews, forklift operators, dockworkers, airline and airport staff, truck drivers, and members of federal, state, and local law enforcement. During the course of their work, customs inspectors must deal calmly and firmly with travelers and shippers.

Technological Environment

As federal agents, customs inspectors must have training in the use of lethal and nonlethal weapons, including handguns and pepper spray. In the inspection process, they use radiation and weapons detection equipment, such as explosives detectors, radioisotope detection devices, and x-ray and gamma-ray imaging machinery. They must use computer systems that link them with international and national law enforcement resources, such as the National Crime Information Center (NCIC) database. Customs inspectors should also be familiar with basic word processing and spreadsheet software, as they must record daily interactions and transactions.

EDUCATION, TRAINING, AND ADVANCEMENT

High School/Secondary

High school students interested in becoming customs inspectors are encouraged to take courses in social studies, government, and history. Psychology and sociology courses are also useful, as is English, which promotes communication skills. Additionally, foreign language training is highly beneficial for aspiring customs inspectors.

Suggested High School Subjects
- English
- Foreign Languages
- Government
- Humanities
- Psychology
- Social Studies
- Sociology

Related Career Pathways/Majors
Government & Public Administration Cluster
- Regulation Pathway

Law, Public Safety & Security Cluster
- Law Enforcement Services Pathway

Postsecondary

Customs inspectors are encouraged to pursue an undergraduate degree in law enforcement, criminal justice, or a related field, although three or more years of direct experience in customs inspection may serve as an alternative to a postsecondary degree. Candidates must enter and complete a fifteen-week training course at the Customs Border Protection Academy in Artesia, New Mexico. Requirements may vary between work settings and specialties. Interested individuals should research the requirements of the agency and/or specialty in which they wish to work.

Related College Majors
- Law Enforcement/Police Science
- Security & Loss Prevention Services

Adult Job Seekers

Qualified customs inspectors may find positions on the federal government's employment website or by applying directly to positions offered by the Department of Homeland Security, US Customs and Border Protection, or US Immigration and Customs Enforcement. They may also obtain job placement upon completion of the Customs Border Protection Academy. Bilingual applicants with college degrees may find employment as customs inspectors more easily.

Professional Certification and Licensure

Customs inspectors must be trained and licensed to carry a firearm. They must also pass a civil service examination and have a valid US driver's license.

Additional Requirements

Customs inspectors must be citizens of the United States who are over the age of twenty-one. They should be physically fit, able to work on their feet for long periods in all weather conditions. Customs inspectors are required to undergo a comprehensive background check, as well as frequent medical checkups and drug tests. Prior military or law enforcement experience is also useful for many positions. Fluency in a foreign language is highly useful for all customs inspectors and is required for US Border Patrol positions.

Fun Fact

Think of canine patrols and you probably envision a German Shepherd. But for detecting forgotten or smuggled fruit and potential pests in airport luggage, U.S. Customs & Border Protection prefers a Beagle or Beagle mix, thanks to their keen sense of smell, non-threatening size and gentle manner with the traveling public.
Source: U.S. Customs & Border Protection

EARNINGS AND ADVANCEMENT

According to the Bureau of Labor Statistics (BLS), law enforcement officers had an annual average salary of $61,600 in 2016, though individuals in the criminal investigation field, including customs inspectors, had median salaries of closer to $78,120. Customs inspectors employed by federal, state, and local governments and large firms may receive paid vacations, holidays, and sick days; life and health insurance; and retirement benefits, with benefits typically paid for by the employer.

EMPLOYMENT AND OUTLOOK

Overall, job opportunities for inspectors and investigators were expected to increase by 4 percent between 2014 and 2024, marking slower than average growth in comparison to the 6-7 percent estimated for all U.S. occupations during the same period. Due to slower than average growth, applicants with higher level degrees will have an advantage on the job market. The growth of government agent and inspector positions is closely tied to government budgets and spending and the industry therefore grows during times of governmental surplus.

Related Occupations
- Construction & Building Inspector
- Federal Law Enforcement Agent
- Fish & Game Warden
- Inspector & Compliance Officer
- Security & Fire Alarm System Installer

Conversation With . . .
JAMES CASEY

Canine Enforcement Officer
U.S. Customs and Border Protection
Department of Homeland Security, Boston
Customs Officer, 16 years

1. What was your individual career path in terms of education/training, entry-level job, or other significant opportunity?

My career path began when I enlisted in the U.S. Army after I graduated from high school. Upon my return from serving in the Army, I started working as a letter carrier with the U.S. Postal Service while going to school at night to earn my bachelor's degree in criminal justice from Western New England College satellite campuses. My first entry-level job in law enforcement was as a uniformed police officer for the US Postal Inspection Services. I became a U.S. Customs Officer for U.S. Customs and Border Protection (CBP) in 2001 and became a K-9 officer in 2003.

Being a K-9 officer is competitive. I've been doing it 14 years. My partner is a Belgian Malinois named IMMI. He lives in a commercial kennel when he's not working. I'm assigned to a special team, CBP's Anti-Terrorism Contraband Enforcement Team (ATCET) based out of the Conley Carrier Terminal at the Seaport, but I also cover Logan International Airport.

I've accumulated 32 years of time working for the United States government, between my time in the Army, being a letter carrier and 16 years of being in law enforcement.

2. What are the most important skills and/or qualities for someone in your profession?

The two most important skills as a K-9 Officer are observation and the ability to listen. Every day when I'm working with my K-9 partner, I am observing him to see if he "alerts"—that is, changes in his behavior—when he's searching. I am also listening to and observing all of the passengers in the luggage area while my K-9 is searching.

3. What do you wish you had known going into this profession?

I wish that I had started my law enforcement career earlier, right when I completed my military duty. I really enjoy the work. It's much more fulfilling than my work with the U.S. Postal Service.

4. Are there many job opportunities overseas in your profession? In what areas, both in terms of geography and subject matter?

There are numerous opportunities overseas for Customs Border Protection officers, wherever CBP has pre-clearance locations, such as at airports, seaports, border crossings and along U.S. borders. There are many overseas locations. These opportunities are in cargo screening—which could be luggage or cargo on ships and trucks and so on—as well as individual admissibility, which involves screening people.

5. How do you see your profession changing in the next five years? What role will technology play in those changes, and what skills will be required?

I don't see the K-9 officer profession changing that much over the next five years. The only aspect of the job that will probably change will be training dogs to detect additional types of drugs, like Fentanyl, which we've seen much more of with the current opioid crisis. The opioid epidemic has already caused the law enforcement community to make many changes in policies. For instance, to deal with the multiple overdoses, Customs Agents now carry Narcan, which is used to revive people who have overdosed on opioids.

6. What do you enjoy most about your job? What do you enjoy least about your job?

I enjoy working with my canine partner. The most enjoyable part of my job is having him at the end of my leash and watching him work. There's no better feeling than watching him alert to one of his odors and then having a confirmed find of narcotics or concealed humans. We could be searching luggage, mail packages or vehicles.

The thing that I enjoy the least about my job is having to do computer work like reports.

7. Can you suggest a valuable "try this" for students considering a career overseas in your profession?

I would suggest enlisting in the Armed Services if college is not a priority. The military will provide you with a good basis for a law enforcement career. And apply to take all of the available federal entrance exams. Check out www.usajobs.gov.

MORE INFORMATION

U.S. Customs and Border Protection
1300 Pennsylvania Avenue NW
Washington, DC 20229
877.227.5511
www.cbp.gov

Provides training at the US Customs and Border Protection Academy
www.cbp.gov/xp/cgov/careers/customs_careers/border_careers/cbp_bp_academy.xml

U.S. Department of Homeland Security
245 Murray Lane SW
Washington, DC 20528
202.282.8000
www.dhs.gov

Sponsors the DHS Scholarship Program:
www.dhs.gov/xabout/careers/gc_1292310525588.shtm

U.S. Immigration and Customs Enforcement
500 12th Street SW
Washington, DC 20536
202.732.4242
www.ice.gov

Offers internships for students interested in law enforcement careers:
www.ice.gov/careers/internships/#scep

Michael Auerbach/Editor,
updated by Micah Issitt

Interpreter and Translator

Snapshot

Career Cluster(s): Business, Management & Administration, Hospitality & Tourism

Interests: Languages, foreign cultures, writing, working with people, communicating with others

Earnings (Yearly Average): $46,120

Employment & Outlook: Much faster than average growth expected

OVERVIEW

Sphere of Work

Interpreters and translators facilitate communication between people who speak different languages or hearing and deaf people. While the terms are commonly thought to be interchangeable, translators and interpreters work in different media. A translator translates written materials, usually into his or her native language, while an interpreter translates oral communication and may switch between languages. Many professionals in the field work as both translators and interpreters. Among the most

popular languages being translated into English today are Spanish, Arabic, Chinese, and American Sign Language (ASL).

Work Environment

Translators often work by themselves at home, where they receive assignments via the Internet or mail. Interpreters work in a variety of settings, such as hospitals, courtrooms, schools, airports, and government offices. Interpreters and translators may work alone with just their clients or with partners or might work in an office environment surrounded by other professionals. In some cases, a translator or interpreter might work the night shift or odd hours, especially when communicating with people who live and work in other time zones. Globalization has dramatically increased the demand for interpreters willing to live and work overseas assisting in meetings and negotiations for governmental and corporate clients operating in foreign nations.

Profile

Interests: Data, People
Working Conditions: Work Inside
Physical Strength: Light Work
Education Needs: Bachelor's Degree, Master's Degree
Licensure/Certification: Recommended
Physical Abilities Not Require: Not Climb, Not Kneel
Opportunities For Experience: Military Service, Volunteer Work
Holland Interest Score*: ESA, ISC, SCE

* See Appendix A

Occupation Interest

Interpreting and translating attract those who are linguistically gifted and enjoy foreign cultures. Individuals who enjoy working alone and are proficient in reading and writing might choose translation, while individuals who enjoy being around people and engaging in social activities might be more drawn to work as interpreters. Translators are often expected to manage deadlines while interpreters comply with variable schedules and may need to be "on-call" and willing to work irregular hours. In either case, the work demands strong cognitive skills and a sharp memory. Sign language interpreters also need excellent hand dexterity.

A Day in the Life—Duties and Responsibilities

A translator spends most of his or her day translating documents at a computer. A job might be as simple as a few paragraphs in a blog, to a book or transcript hundreds of pages long. The translator takes time to reflect on what he or she reads and then tries to communicate the message with as much of its natural rhythm and nuances intact as possible. Such work requires full knowledge of each language, including slang, subject-specific jargon, and colloquialisms and so translators also need to have specialized knowledge of the native culture of the languages with which they work. Translators spend much of their time using specialized reference materials to ensure that their punctuation and grammar is correct.

Interpreters work closely with their clients, in person or via phone, videophone, or microphone. Simultaneous interpreting involves listening to a speaker and translating orally, or signing, at the same time that the speaker in speaking, while consecutive interpreting involves listening to a speaker complete a few words or a sentence and then translating it orally during a break in conversation or speech. Depending on the speaker's pace, the interpreter might have time to consider various interpretations of a word or phrase while, in other situations, the interpreter will need to work quickly to stay apace with the speaker.

Interpreters at United Nations conventions or other types of conferences often sit in the audience and whisper their translations into a microphone. Sign language interpreters sometimes use videophones and a computer to communicate with the deaf. Self-employed translators and interpreters might also spend part of the day keeping up with marketing, billing, and other administrative tasks to promote their services and might also spend time networking to find new clients.

Duties and Responsibilities

- Listening through earphones to what is being said
- Taking notes on what is being said
- Translating orally, possibly using a microphone
- Preparing written translations
- Editing translations for correctness of grammar and punctuation
- Reviewing finished translations for accuracy and completeness
- Reading a document in one language and then rewriting it into another following rules of grammar and punctuation

OCCUPATION SPECIALTIES

Deaf Interpreters

Deaf Interpreters translate spoken material into sign language for the understanding of those individuals who are deaf. They also interpret sign language of the deaf into oral or written language for hearing individuals.

WORK ENVIRONMENT

Immediate Physical Environment

Interpreters tend to work in diverse interior and exterior environmental conditions, including potentially dangerous or unhealthy job sites. Interpreters often travel and there are many opportunities for interpreters willing to live and work overseas for extended periods. Translators, on the other hand, work in offices with less variable conditions or may work out of their home. While much of a translator's work can be done via long distances, companies or agencies operating in foreign countries might hire on-site translators or might prefer a professional who can function as both a translator and interpreter.

Transferable Skills and Abilities

Communication Skills
- Expressing thoughts and ideas
- Speaking effectively
- Writing concisely

Interpersonal/Social Skills
- Cooperating with others
- Working as a member of a team

Organization & Management Skills
- Making decisions

Research & Planning Skills
- Creating ideas
- Developing evaluation strategies
- Using logical reasoning

Human Environment

Unless self-employed, translators and interpreters report to supervisors or directors and usually interact with various office staff and professionals. Interpreters interact directly with their clients and are also frequently involved in social, public environments while completing their work.

Technological Environment

Translators may utilize digital tools, including automated translation software, to complete their work and some use transcription machines to increase the speed of their translations. Interpreters might need to utilize digital software, including translation software, and mobile devices to communicate with clients and to quickly find information to enhance a interpretation. In many cases, interpreters learn to use microphones and listening devices to listen to conversation and deliver interpretations to an audience. Some sign language interpreters use a videophone along with a video relay service (VRS) or video interpreting service.

EDUCATION, TRAINING, AND ADVANCEMENT

High School/Secondary

Achieving proficiency in a foreign language takes many years. A college-preparatory program with four years of at least one foreign language, along with courses in English, speech, and the social sciences (political science, anthropology, and world cultures), will provide the best foundation for a career in interpretation or translation. Those students interested in translating technical material should consider additional courses in favored technical fields, such as science, technology, business, or law. Foreign exchange programs and travel, volunteer work with ethnic organizations, and other independent educational experiences can prove invaluable to those seeking future work as translators or interpreters and there are many study abroad and volunteer programs aimed at individuals seeking to improve fluency in a language or to add cultural knowledge to their linguistic training.

Suggested High School Subjects
- College Preparatory
- Composition
- English
- Foreign Languages
- Literature
- Speech

Related Career Pathways/Majors
Business, Management & Administration Cluster
- Human Resources Pathway

Hospitality & Tourism Cluster
- Travel & Tourism Pathway

Postsecondary

While a bachelor's degree is the minimum requirement for most jobs, the selection of a major is a personal decision based on the type of work desired. Students might consider double majoring in a foreign language and in another subject, such as computer science, English literature, engineering, nursing, or pre-law, or in two foreign languages, such as Spanish and French. Some translators and interpreters need an advanced degree to translate subject-specific concepts and vocabulary and many companies hiring interpreters/ translators, prefer professionals with some level of education in a specific field other than languages. Study abroad programs, foreign travel, and participation in international clubs are some ways to gain important hands-on experience for postsecondary students.

Related College Majors
- Communication Disorders, General
- Foreign Languages Teacher Education
- Linguistics
- Sign Language Interpretation

Adult Job Seekers

Bilingual adults should be able to transition well into an interpreting or translating career, especially with relevant experience. For example, a bilingual nurse would have an advantage translating or interpreting in a medical setting and might therefore be eligible for hospital or medical-center-based interpreter positions. Continuing education courses can refresh or teach new skills and might help a bilingual individual to qualify for translation/interpretation jobs in specific fields. For instance, an individual trained in English and Spanish might attend continuing education classes in pre-law to qualify for work with bilingual law-firms or legal aid organizations. Prospective interpreters and translators should expect to be tested in their language abilities as a prerequisite for employment.

Advancement is highly dependent on experience and those with significant work experience can advance within a company or can use their experience to attract higher-paying clientele. Advancement opportunities might include better work hours, higher pay, or more interesting assignments. Those with experience may also consider moving into editorial positions or starting their own translation companies.

Professional Certification and Licensure

In the United States, interpreters and translators are not required to obtain professional licenses or certifications, though available certification programs may provide an advantage when seeking employment. Professional associations, such as the American Translators Association and the International Association of Conference Interpreters, offer certification programs in a variety of sub-specializations and such certification programs can provide useful experience and qualifications for professionals in the field. To obtain certification, translators and interpreters typically must pass a written test and to perform work under the guidance of specialist educators.

Additional Requirements

Interpreters and translators who wish to work for government agencies must pass a civil service exam while freelancers need good business skills as well as experience in the field. Interpreters and translators should consider membership in professional associations, which often provide opportunities for networking and professional development. Work experience or certification is required for membership in some organizations. For those looking to work as translators or interpreters overseas, interest in travel and exploring foreign cultures is important and translators/interpreters who succeed in the field often spend time developing detailed knowledge of foreign customs and culture.

EARNINGS AND ADVANCEMENT

Earnings of interpreters and translators depend on the type of work done and the language spoken, as well as the education, experience, and skill of the individual. Median annual earnings of interpreters and translators were $46,120 in 2016, with those at the lowest ten percent earning less than $25,000, while those at the upper end of the spectrum might earn more than $83,000.

Full-time interpreters and translators employed by multinational companies may receive paid vacations, holidays, and sick days; life and health insurance; and retirement benefits. These are usually paid by the employer. Interpreters working for the United Nations earn tax-free salaries. In addition, international organizations often pay supplementary living and family allowances to interpreters/translators working and living abroad.

EMPLOYMENT AND OUTLOOK

Globalization has had a dramatic effect on the interpreter/translator industry, with the Bureau of Labor Statistics (BLS) estimating as much as 29 percent growth in the industry between 2014 and 2024, which is far faster than average in comparison to the 6-7 percent growth expected for all U.S. industries during this same period. In 2016, about 20 percent of 61,000 translators and/or interpreters in the United States were self-employed. Professional and scientific companies and organizations employed roughly 29 percent of the remaining professionals in the field, while educational institutions employed 26 percent, healthcare organizations employed 16 percent, and 7 percent were employed by governmental organizations.

The rapid growth in the industry is the result of two continuing trends; an increase in the number of non-English and/or bilingual individuals living and working in the United States and the increasing interconnectedness of global educational, business, and governmental environments. As more and more U.S. companies do business overseas there is an increasing demand for bilingual individuals to work in the corporate and hospitality industries. International businesses, tourism companies, and a variety of other organizations and corporations frequently use the services of interpreters to facilitate their activities overseas. Demand is expected to remain especially strong for translators of the languages referred to as PFIGS - Portuguese, French, Italian, German, and Spanish (and the principal Asian languages - Chinese, Japanese, and Korean). In addition, current events and changing political environments, often difficult to foresee, will increase the need for persons who can work with other languages. For example, homeland security needs are expected to drive increasing demand for interpreters and translators of Arabic and other Middle Eastern languages, primarily in Federal Government agencies. In addition, demand for American Sign Language interpreters will grow due to the increasing use of video relay services that provide video calls using a sign language interpreter over an Internet connection.

Related Occupations
- Intelligence Officer
- Interpreter & Translator
- Radio Intelligence Officer

MORE INFORMATION

American Association of Language Specialists
P.O. Box 27306
Washington, DC 20038
www.taals.net

American Translators Association
225 Reinekers Lane, Suite 590
Alexandria, VA 22314
703.683.6100
ata@atanet.org
www.atanet.org

Certifies translators
www.atanet.org/certification/
aboutcert_overview.php

Offers honors and awards:
www.atanet.org/membership/
honorsandawards.php

National Security Education Program
P.O. Box 20010
Arlington, VA 22219
703.696.1991
nsep@nsep.gov
www.nsep.gov

Sponsors scholarships and fellowships
www.nsep.gov/initiatives

Registry of Interpreters for the Deaf
333 Commerce Street
Alexandria, VA 22314
703.838.0030
www.rid.org

Sponsors sign language interpreter
scholarships and awards:
www.rid.org/aboutRID/schol_awards/
index.cfm

Offers sign language certification and
professional development:
www.rid.org/education/overview/index.cfm

Sally Driscoll/Editor,
updated by Micah Issitt

Surveyor and Cartographer

Snapshot

Career Cluster(s): Agriculture, Food & Natural Resources, Architecture & Construction, Science, Technology, Engineering & Mathematics

Interests: Geography, maps and map-making, engineering, spatial data, demographics, mathematics

Earnings (Yearly Average): $59,390

Employment & Outlook: Decline in growth expected

OVERVIEW

Sphere of Work

Surveyors measure, record, and interpret features on and above the surface of the earth using specialized equipment. Cartographers are mapmakers who use survey data, photographs, and satellite images to create digital or graphical maps and charts of geographical and demographic information. Government agencies, utility companies, architectural and engineering firms, publishers, and other employers hire surveyors and cartographers to provide information necessary to their business operations or sales. The work that surveyors and cartographers produce leads to defining the earth's

surface and position and to locating boundaries of countries, states, and properties. In many cases, cartographers and surveyors will travel for their work and, in some cases, companies and organizations hiring translators and surveyors may need professionals willing to live and work in foreign locations for extended periods.

Work Environment

Surveyors and cartographers typically work forty hours or more each week, both at the field sites and in the office. Cartographers tend to do more solitary, sedentary office work than fieldwork. Field measurements are often taken by groups working together to adjust and operate surveying equipment. Travel to remote field sites may be required. Fieldwork can be physically demanding, requiring long periods of standing, walking long distances, and climbing with heavy loads of survey instruments.

Profile

Interests: Data
Working Conditions: Work Outside, Work Both Inside and Outside
Physical Strength: Medium Work
Education Needs: Bachelor's Degree
Licensure/Certification: Required
Physical Abilities Not Require: Not Climb, Not Kneel
Opportunities For Experience: Apprenticeship, Military Service, Part Time Work
Holland Interest Score*: IER, IRE

* See Appendix A

Occupation Interest

Individuals interested in becoming surveyors and cartographers are usually detail-oriented, fascinated by geography, and interested in maps and map-making. Prospective surveyors and cartographers tend to be adept at understanding spatial information, demonstrate an ease with numbers and mathematical functions, and enjoy the outdoors. Surveyors and cartographers have a great deal of responsibility as they provide critical geographical data for defense, first responders, and government agencies at all levels. Prospective professionals in the field should invest time in maintaining physical fitness in order to cope with the physical strain of hiking and walking long distance, sometimes burdened by heavy equipment, when working on a project. For those interested in overseas work, becoming a cartographer or surveyor can lead to many opportunities for short and long-term international work.

A Day in the Life—Duties and Responsibilities

Surveyors research land, air, and water features, primarily in the field but also in office settings. In the field, surveyors use a wide variety of tools to measure and record spatial information, such as latitude, longitude, elevation, position, and contour, among other physical characteristics. At the office, they analyze the collected data to write descriptions and reports and to create maps, charts, and other graphical representations. Since survey data is often used in legal documents and proceedings, surveyors or their work may occasionally be called upon in court or to give reports at governmental meetings. Surveyors may also research existing survey records, deeds, and boundaries to check their validity or gather information prior to conducting a new survey of an area. Experienced surveyors often focus on a single type of surveying, such as marine surveying or geodetic surveying, and supervise the work of technicians, apprentices, or assistants.

Cartographers make new maps and update old ones. They use aerial photography, satellite imagery, ground survey data, and GIS technology to compile data, which is often stored in databases. Computer-aided design (CAD) programs, mathematical formulas, and analytical processes help them produce graphical and digital charts, maps, and graphs. They also analyze and interpret non-spatial data about land-use, climate patterns, population density, and political, social, and economic demographics, and are responsible for determining a map's aesthetic presentation. Cartographers proofread their work before publication and revise existing maps as needed. In some cases, cartographers may also work with and troubleshoot photographic materials and processes in the course of drafting and replicating maps. Experienced cartographers may train and oversee less experienced cartographers.

Duties and Responsibilities

- Studying physical evidence, notes, maps, deeds or other records
- Checking the accuracy of the information gathered using complex mathematical computations
- Adjusting instruments to maintain accuracy
- Keeping notes and preparing sketches, maps, reports and legal descriptions of the survey
- Coordinating results with the work of engineering and architectural personnel, clients and others
- Calculating and adjusting survey data and planning survey systems

OCCUPATION SPECIALTIES

Geodetic Surveyors

Geodetic Surveyors plan, direct and conduct surveys of large areas of land such as states and counties.

Mine Surveyors

Mine Surveyors make surface and underground surveys for mine locations, tunnels, subways and underground storage facilities.

Marine Surveyors

Marine Surveyors make surveys of harbors, rivers and other bodies of water to determine shore lines, topography of bottom or other features to determine navigable channels.

Land Surveyors

Land Surveyors establish official land and water boundaries, write descriptions of land for deeds, leases and other legal documents, and measure construction and mineral sites.

Field-Map Editors

Field-Map Editors prepare maps using data provided by geodetic surveys, aerial photographs and satellite data.

WORK ENVIRONMENT

Transferable Skills and Abilities

Interpersonal/Social Skills
- Working as a member of a team

Organization & Management Skills
- Coordinating tasks
- Following instructions
- Managing people/groups

Organization & Management Skills
- Organizing information or materials
- Paying attention to and handling details

Research & Planning Skills
- Using logical reasoning

Technical Skills
- Performing scientific, mathematical and technical work
- Working with machines, tools or other objects
- Working with your hands

Work Environment Skills
- Working outdoors

Immediate Physical Environment

Surveyors spend a great deal of time outdoors, in all types of weather conditions and across all kinds of terrain. Cartographers work mostly indoors in an office sitting in front of a computer, but fieldwork may also be required.

Human Environment

Surveyors must have strong communication skills as they often work in a team called a "survey party" and must be able to communicate effectively with other professionals and, in some cases, to manage technicians and other assistants. Cartographers work with survey parties as well as independently and so also need sufficient communication skills to work with clients and other professionals. Among other professionals, surveyors typically work with survey technicians, assistants or apprentices, survey party chiefs, cartographic drafters, and supervisors.

Technological Environment

Surveyors and cartographers use a vast range of equipment and digital tools and technology are increasingly essential in the field, including mobile smartphone and tablet devices. Among other specialized equipment, surveyors and cartographers often use global positioning system (GPS) instruments to locate various distance segments as well as to measure and record angles and distances. Geographic information systems (GIS) allow surveyors and cartographers to collate, analyze, and store data in a digital platform so that the data they produce can be accessed from a variety of locations. Light-imaging detection and ranging (LIDAR) helps gather accurate spatial data, usually from aircraft, and is an essential tool for many types of cartography applications. Cartographers also use CAD and imaging software, databases, film processors, copy cameras, and photographs to complete their work.

EDUCATION, TRAINING, AND ADVANCEMENT

High School/Secondary

High school students interested in pursuing a career in surveying and cartography should prepare themselves by studying mathematics, technical drawing, and the sciences, including a focus on computer science and technology. Extracurricular activities that familiarize students with these subjects are also useful and there are many amateur cartography clubs where future professionals can meet others in their field and can gain experience working with professionals tools. While in high school, there may be opportunities to become an apprentice or assistant to a surveyor or cartographer to get work experience; however, postsecondary school training is usually required for professional positions.

Suggested High School Subjects
- Algebra
- Applied Math
- Calculus
- College Preparatory
- English
- Geography
- Geometry
- Mechanical Drawing
- Physical Science
- Statistics
- Trigonometry

Related Career Pathways/Majors

Agriculture, Food & Natural Resources Cluster
- Environmental Service Systems Pathway
- Natural Resources Systems Pathway

Architecture & Construction Cluster
- Design/Pre-Construction Pathway

Science, Technology, Engineering & Mathematics Cluster
- Engineering & Technology Pathway
- Science & Mathematics Pathway

Postsecondary

Those looking to become a cartographer or surveyor in the United States must adhere to state-specific employment guidelines and most states require professionals in both fields to obtain a bachelor's degree from an Accreditation Board for Engineering and Technology (ABET) accredited school. Many colleges and universities have both surveying and cartography degree programs. Most aspiring surveyors and cartographers study surveying, cartography, or a related field such as geography, engineering, or forestry during their postsecondary education, and professionals are also encouraged to seek out experience or classes in CAD, earth sciences, and geography. While some surveyors and cartographers work only in the United States, those interested in foreign work and/or travel are also encouraged to pursue education in foreign language/culture.

Related College Majors
- Geography
- Surveying

Adult Job Seekers

Adults seeking surveying and cartography jobs are generally required to obtain a related bachelor's degree, though there are other ways to enter the field. Individuals in the armed forces or who volunteer with a survey crew can work their way towards professional positions through job experience. Many surveyors begin their careers as surveyor technicians or assistants while completing their education or may spend enough time working in assistant positions to qualify for senior surveyor positions. It may be useful to contact professional associations for networking, apprenticeships, continuing education opportunities, and to learn about specific licensing requirements within each state.

Professional Certification and Licensure

All surveyors and some cartographers in the United States must obtain licensure from the National Council of Examiners for Engineering and Surveying (NCEES), which involves passing two written examinations taken four years apart. Between the two exams, candidates work under experienced surveyors. In addition, most states require surveyors to pass a state licensing board exam. Education prerequisites and continuing education requirements for renewal vary from state to state. For those looking to work overseas, requirements for legal employment may vary by country. Employers hiring cartographers or surveyors for overseas work may provide information on necessary certificates and licenses, while professional organizations might also be helpful in finding information about how to work as a surveyor or cartographer in a variety of overseas locations.

Additional Requirements

Visualization, accuracy, physical fitness and stamina, keen analytical abilities, and strong collaborative skills are essential qualities in surveyors and cartographers. Familiarity with computer technology and a college degree can provide a competitive edge in the field. For those working overseas, knowledge of foreign languages and customs can be invaluable and cartographers/surveyors who are bilingual will have an advantage when seeking overseas employment.

Fun Fact

Accurately depicting the spherical Earth on a flat map isn't easy. The AuthaGraph World Map developed in Japan in 1999, but not included in textbooks until 2015, is considered one of the most accurate. One problem with many other maps: European countries appear larger than they are.

Source: Popular Science

EARNINGS AND ADVANCEMENT

According to the Bureau of Labor Statistics (BLS), annual earnings of surveyors and cartographers were $59,390 in 2016, with those at the lower end of the spectrum earning less than $33,000, while those at the upper end could earn more than $98,000 per year. Depending on the employer, surveyors and cartographers may receive paid vacations, holidays, and sick days; life and health insurance; and retirement benefits. Surveyors and cartographers may also receive reimbursement for business-related travel expenses, but may be required to purchase their own uniforms and other work-related equipment.

EMPLOYMENT AND OUTLOOK

The Bureau of Labor Statistics estimates that opportunities for cartographers and surveyors will decline by approximately 2 percent between 2014 and 2024, largely due to the continuing impact of automation and technological enhancements that limit the number of professionals needed for even large surveying/cartography projects. With opportunities declining in the United States, there may be more opportunities for those with relevant experience and expertise to work in foreign locations where companies are exploring for resources or establishing construction projects for international business ventures.

Related Occupations
- Architect
- Civil Engineer
- Engineering Technician
- Geologist & Geophysicist
- Mathematician
- Mining & Geological Engineer

Related Occupations
- Surveying & Mapping Manager
- Surveying, Mapping & Drafting Technician

Conversation With . . .
GERALDINE SARMIENTO

Cartographer
Mapzen, San Francisco
Cartographer, 9 years

1. **What was your individual career path in terms of education/training, entry-level job, or other significant opportunity?**

I went to art school at Cooper Union in New York, which was a dream come true. I learned as many mediums as I could, from printmaking to typography to painting and photography, but always focusing on graphic design. It was a wonderful time.

My very first job was as a junior designer at a firm that specialized in annual reports, followed by a job with a small design studio that specialized in books. After a year of working in New York, I went home to the Philippines. That was around 1998. The world wide web was new. I had a taste of HTML at Cooper but really got into the web when I got back to Manila. I started experimenting and eventually was building websites for clients with a friend. I drew one of my very first maps then, of Boracay island. Little did I know that cartography would be my path.

When I returned to the U.S. in 1999, I worked as a web designer at Fodors.com, the well-known brand of travel books, which was part of Random House. So began my exposure to places, maps, design and technology. I worked there until the dot-com bubble burst in 2000. I felt right at home at Random House and eventually returned there, designing books while continuing to freelance on websites.

Despite my love of books and the fact that I was working with an amazing design team, I found myself looking at NASA earth observatory images every day and getting very excited about the work going on at the Media Lab at the Massachusetts Institute of Technology (MIT). I entered the Interactive Telecommunications Program (ITP) at NYU, where I could study both art and code. The graduate program was open to people without programming experience and highly encouraged art and technology collaborations.

In 2007 my husband and I moved to the West Coast to be closer to family. In San Francisco, I discovered Stamen Design, which was doing exciting work with data visualization. I decided I must visit and introduce myself. It was the first time I ever found a job this way, but it worked. Stamen had a fun atmosphere that really encouraged the play of art and technology. I was the sole designer and learned to work fast and move from one project to another. This was where I started to practice cartography. One of my very first projects was designing a map for the London 2012 Olympics. Many maps followed: for the ACLU, Chesapeake Bay Program, City of Copenhagen, Climate Central, *Esquire*, Google, Microsoft, Nike, *Popular Mechanics*, SmugMug, Trip Advisor, and others. Eventually, I found myself wanting to spend all my time doing cartography. I jumped into it without any training. Everything I learned, I learned by doing.

After five years, I joined Apple's cartography team, which I consider my true cartographic education. We would sit and look at maps every day, dissecting, deconstructing, and discussing. I would draw the same map over and over again and contemplate the meaning of every line, every symbol and every label. I was around the best cartographers.

I now work at Mapzen as a cartographer. It's a dream job. Every day, I get to draw maps and to help make the tools to generate them.

2. What are the most important skills and/or qualities for someone in your profession?

A good eye. Visual intelligence should not be underestimated. Images speak louder than words. After years in tech, I feel that design is undervalued.

You also have to work well with others because making maps is collaborative, with various areas of expertise. Cartography is a special medium where art and science meet.

3. What do you wish you had known going into this profession?

I was pleasantly surprised to discover that cartography brought all of my interests together into one medium. It brings together art, science and technology as well as my love of learning about places, language and culture, and my love of drawing, form and symbols. The act of cartography itself is the creation of a visual language, bringing together symbols and forms into the abstract representation of place.

4. Are there many job opportunities overseas in your profession? In what areas?

Yes, there are lots of opportunities. With current technologies, maps have become a major part of our lives. With daily exposure to maps and satellite imagery, we have become visually literate in the language of maps. It is far easier with the current technologies to work all over the world.

I have worked in Manila, but my type of cartographic work doesn't require me to travel, though it would be great to travel to every place I mapped! But lots of cartographers travel for work. For example, if you're collecting data for unmapped areas in the world, or mapping disaster areas after a hurricane or earthquake, you may need to travel.

5. How do you see the importance of international experience changing in the next five years? What role will technology play in those changes?

My father always told me that travel is the best education. I believe that's true. We must learn other ways of seeing. Every place, culture and language provides a unique perspective. It's important to step outside of our comfort zones and learn other ways of being.

It's good to be fluent at learning. Stay curious. There will always be some new technology to learn, but it's good to know that these are just tools. Don't get caught up with the technology itself.

6. What do you enjoy most about your job? What do you enjoy least about your job?

Thinking about drawing. I love thinking of the many ways I can draw a form. And contemplating the mark itself. What is the mark and its connection to place?

What I least enjoy is sitting in front of a computer. The body has its own intelligence. We need to use our bodies to reach the mind's full potential.

7. Can you suggest a valuable "try this" for students considering a career in your profession?

Whatever it is you would like to pursue, always practice and do.

Explore. Go on tangents. I've gone on many tangents that at the time seemed to lead nowhere. But these are not wasted moments. Everyday we're exposed to messages of productivity; our culture is obsessed with producing more and more. Let's not forget the playfulness of exploration.

MORE INFORMATION

American Society for Photogrammetry and Remote Sensing
5410 Grosvenor Lane, Suite 210
Bethesda, MD 20814-2160
301.493.0290
asprs@asprs.org
www.asprs.org

National Council of Examiners for Engineering and Surveying
280 Seneca Creek Road
Seneca, SC 29678
800.250.3196
www.ncees.org

National Society of Professional Surveyors
6 Montgomery Village Avenue
Suite 403
Gaithersburg, MD 20879
240.632.9716
www.nspsmo.org

Susan Williams/Editor,
updated by Micah Issitt

ENERGY AND RESOURCE EXPLORATION

Every nation around the world has a unique set of natural resources, whether in the form of minerals and precious metals, water, lumber, or deposits of fossil fuels like coal, natural gas, and petroleum. Every nation also has material needs that sometimes necessitate locating and harvesting resources outside of national boundaries. The search for resources has been a fundamental and transformative force in history, motivating mass migrations, wars, and some of the earliest diplomacy and trade agreements. The effort to locate, manage, and exploit natural resources remains a cornerstone of international diplomacy and military development. The United States, for instance, has been committed to nation building efforts in the Middle East since the end of World War II and this effort has been partially motivated by U.S. interests in the regions fossil fuels. The deployment of American military and diplomatic corps, in fact, follows trade routes used to supply U.S. citizens with resources not found, or not as easily or affordably found, within U.S. boundaries.

While resource exploration can be a lucrative career option, it is important to note that the future of the industry is in question. Over the past half century, scientists have demonstrated, incontrovertibly, that harvesting and utilizing natural resources to create energy is changing the global climate. Climate change has increased the frequency and severity of natural disasters, has created food and water shortages around the world, has led to the extinction of many plant and animal species and left thousands of other species on the brink of extinction, and has increased the potential for international conflict. For instance, the ongoing war in South Sudan (the world's longest continuous war) has been linked to global warming, which has reduced the availability of water, thus bringing native pastoralist and agricultural communities into conflict as they compete for remaining resources.

Concerned for their future, energy companies have invested billions of dollars to purchase the support of politicians and to hire lobbyists to promote the idea that climate change is not occurring or is not connected to resource exploitation. These efforts have been successful in preventing stronger environmental laws and thus have enabled energy companies to continue expanding despite global consequences. Despite this effort, awareness of climate change is growing and this has fueled rapid growth of an emerging alternative energy industry around the world. In 2017, for instance, the solar energy industry in the United States was growing 12 times faster than the US economy as a whole. If these trends continue, renewable and alternative energy companies may increasingly offer both domestic and international job opportunities in the future, as traditional energy exploration continues to decline in both profit and the potential for growth.

The Petroleum Industry

The petroleum industry, or "oil industry," involves the exploration, extraction, processing and refinement, and transport of petroleum products, of which the most common are gasoline and fuel oil. According to the U.S. Energy Information Administration (EIA), total consumption of fossil fuels in the United States averages

19.9 million barrels per day and will brow by 360,000 barrels per day over the coming year. To meet this demand, U.S. corporations have operations around the world, looking for new petroleum deposits, harvesting existing deposits, and purchasing/exporting petroleum harvested by foreign corporations.

Oil and Natural gas companies employ a wide variety of professionals to assist in the process of locating and harvesting petroleum products. For instance, companies may hire geographers and oceanographers to help map and evaluate oceanic and terrestrial environments while looking for new sources of petroleum. Teams involved in drilling oil wells and extracting the resulting products may include petroleum engineers, pump and drill operators, and various categories of laborers working on the offshore or terrestrial sites. For some positions, petroleum companies may offer training programs for those with no prior experience, while other positions may require specific qualifications. For those interested, the best way to learn about job opportunities is to contact companies involved in international exploration, such as Hess Oil and Gas or Transocean, which specializes in oceanic drilling operations.

Mineral Resources

Mining and mineral excavation companies also offer opportunities for overseas employment. For instance, Freeport McMoRan Copper & Gold, a mining company headquartered in Phoenix, Arizona, has ongoing mining operations in South America, Africa, and Indonesia. The company harvests more than 4.1 billion pounds of copper each year, in addition to vast quantities of gold and the mineral molybdenum, with annual profits of over $18 billion. While overseas mining companies tend to use local labor, to save on costs, U.S.-natives are often recruited for management, technical, and executive positions in the company's overseas operations.

The mining industry, as a whole, is in a state of flux and the outlook for various companies depends largely on the types of minerals that a company is harvesting. The domestic coal mining industry in the United States, for instance, has been in a state of decline since the 1980s and industry experts reports that the industry will inevitably continue to decline. Increasingly, as the cost of domestic mining increases, corporations turn to international operations in developing nations where a lack of worker's rights protections allows companies to pay laborers less for their work and where a lack of environmental regulation allows companies to avoid the cost of operating so as to conserve ecosystems. Mineral companies hire geological scientists to locate and evaluate potential resource deposits, as well as laborers, managers, and technical engineers involved in the mining process itself or in managing and using mining equipment. Companies may also hire clerical and support personnel for their overseas offices.

Agriculture and Forestry

Agriculture is a field that exists at the overlap between environmental protection and exploitation. One example, on the boundary between conservation and resource exploration, is the United States Department of Agriculture's Foreign Agricultural Service (FAS), which analyzes global agricultural production and markets and plays a role in establishing trade agreements and treaties. The FAS occasionally hires U.S. native agricultural scientists, engineers, and other specialists for international appointments. The FAS is active in South America and Africa and often works with developing nations, helping local communities to develop agricultural programs to reduce hunger and build local revenue opportunities, with the ultimate goal of protecting U.S. imports and exports.

Forestry is another international field that involves both the harvest of resources, like lumber and the process of conserving and sustaining forest resources. Most companies and organizations involved in forestry operate domestically, though there are some logging and forestry companies that operate internationally. Most positions in forestry require specialized training and experience, though logging companies may hire individuals without prior experience and/or provide on-the-job training. Those working in conservation or environmental remediation, may have more opportunities for working overseas as there are many private organizations working to protect international forests and other natural resources. The USDA Forest Service International can provide information for students and professionals interested in the field, especially those with academic training and/or experience in forestry, land management, or sustainable development.

Works Used

"International." *Fs.fed.us*. US Forest Service. 2016. Web. 6 Aug 2017.

"Oil and Gas Extraction: NAICS 211." *BLS.gov*. Bureau of Labor Statistics. 2016. Web. 6 Aug 2017.

"Resources that Fuel Global Growth." *FCX.com*. Freeport-McMoRan. 2017. Web. 23 Jul 2017.

"Short Term Energy Outlook." *EIA.gov*. U.S. Energy Information Administration. Jul 11 2017. Web. 7 Aug 2017.

Varinsky, Dana. "Solar-energy jobs are growing 12 times as fast as the US economy." *Businessinsider*. Business Insider, Inc. Jan 26 2017. Web. 6 Aug 2017.

Anthropologist

Snapshot

Career Cluster(s): Science, Technology, Engineering & Mathematics

Interests: History, gathering information, scientific discovery, cultural exploration

Earnings (Yearly Average): $63,190

Employment & Outlook: Slower than average growth expected

OVERVIEW

Sphere of Work

Anthropologists study human cultures, both past and present, investigating the way that cultures develop norms, values, beliefs, practices, and roles for individuals living within the society. As the general anthropology field covers a wide spectrum, most professionals in the field specialize in a subset of anthropology, such as cultural anthropology, linguistic anthropology, historical anthropology, forensic anthropology, economic anthropology, physical anthropology, and/or archaeology. Most anthropologists and archaeologists work for educational

institutions, though there are applied anthropologists who work for governmental or private organizations.

Work Environment

Anthropologists working in academic settings such as colleges and universities generally spend the majority of their work time in classrooms, libraries, and offices. Department interaction and meetings are frequent and professional anthropologists may spend much of their time interacting with students at various levels. Academic anthropologists usually perform research, including library research and ethnographic or archaeological fieldwork, as a requirement of their employment and eventual tenure. Applied anthropologists working in non-academic settings, such as government agencies, foundations, museums, or non-government organizations (NGOs), spend more of their time in the field where they interact with clients, patients, vendors, or community stakeholders. Both academic and applied anthropologists typically work full-time, though academic anthropologists may observe scheduled breaks in the academic year.

Profile

Interests: Data
Working Conditions: Work Inside
Physical Strength: Light Work
Education Needs: Bachelor's Degree, Master's Degree, Doctoral Degree
Licensure/Certification: Usually Not Required
Physical Abilities Not Require: Not Climb, Not Kneel, Not Hear and/or Talk
Opportunities For Experience: Internship
Holland Interest Score*: IRE

* See Appendix A

Occupation Interest

Individuals drawn to anthropology tend to be intellectually curious and should have the ability to gather information through research and synthesize their findings into scientific hypotheses and theories. Professional anthropologists are typically required to obtain advanced degrees and those pursuing work in the field should have a strong interest in academic study. In addition, anthropology is typically a collaborative field and individuals who thrive as professionals should enjoy or be comfortable with collaboration and interacting with other researchers and professionals. Individuals who succeed in the field of anthropology typically display traits such as leadership, initiative, scientific reasoning, project management, and an appreciation for cultural differences.

A Day in the Life—Duties and Responsibilities

The occupational duties and responsibilities of anthropologists may include teaching; lecturing; gathering and analyzing data; performing archaeological or ethnographic fieldwork; conducting interviews; curating museum exhibits; preparing press releases or meeting with media; grant writing; preparing manuscripts for publication; and meeting with students, colleagues, clients, or stakeholders. An anthropologist's specific daily duties and responsibilities vary based on specialty and employer.

Academic anthropologists typically spend much of their time teaching or managing students and this may include lecture and test preparation, course development, grading, and maintaining office hours to meet with students and colleagues. Departmental responsibilities and research and publishing obligations are also ever-present in the lives of academic anthropologists, who spend much of their time analyzing and synthesizing research data.

Applied anthropologists working for government agencies, non-governmental organizations, or businesses tend to have more direct daily supervision than academic anthropologists. The daily responsibilities of applied anthropologists are not fixed or regular. For instance, an applied anthropologist could work for an electric company in Brazil studying the human impact of a hydroelectric dam project or for the United States government gathering data about voting practices in new democracies. Anthropologists work in a number of fields outside of government, including archaeology, medicine, parks, museums, non-governmental agencies, and social services. Government agencies employing anthropologists include the Department of Defense, the Department of Justice, the Department of Health and Human Services, the Department of State, and the Department of Homeland Security.

As anthropologists study cultures around the world, there are many opportunities for U.S.-native or U.S.-trained professional anthropologists to live and work overseas. Academic anthropologists may spend time abroad each year conducting field studies and collecting data, while many applied anthropologists may be stationed abroad for extended periods or even indefinitely depending on the nature of his or her position.

Duties and Responsibilities

- Studying ancient cultures through examining artifacts and other remains excavated from the ground or ocean floor
- Dating and analyzing findings through scientific means
- Studying the role of language in different cultures
- Studying the evolution of humans, animals and plant life to try to determine the earliest forms of life

OCCUPATION SPECIALTIES

Ethnologists

Ethnologists live in primitive villages or urban societies to learn about how people live.

WORK ENVIRONMENT

Immediate Physical Environment

Anthropologists working in academic settings generally work full-time hours teaching and attending to departmental responsibilities such as grading and mentoring students. Fieldwork may take academic anthropologists to foreign locations with significant cultural, language, and environmental differences and challenges. Applied anthropologists working in non-academic settings, such as government offices, social service agencies, foundations, museums, non-governmental organizations, and businesses, generally work full-time hours and may work in a variety of international locations for extended periods.

Transferable Skills and Abilities

Communication Skills

- Reading well
- Speaking effectively
- Writing concisely

Organization & Management Skills

- Organizing information or materials

Research & Planning Skills

- Analyzing information
- Gathering information

Human Environment

Like most scientific fields, anthropology is highly collaborative and discoveries in the field build upon the work of other contemporary and historic researchers and academic specialists. In the academic environment, anthropologists interact with other teachers, students, assistants, and academic supervisors, while, in the field, anthropologists might interact with a wide range of individuals from different backgrounds. Anthropologists are trained in the practice of participant observation and must develop an ability to observe without prejudice or judgment, as anthropologists attempt to report on cultural developments without bias. Anthropologists need to have excellent communication skills and knowledge of foreign culture and customs is necessary for many types of applied anthropology and field work.

Technological Environment

Anthropologists typically use computers and telecommunication tools during their academic training and eventual employment. Some anthropological sub-specialties, such as archaeology and economic anthropology, will require specialized technological training and may use unique software programs or other digital tools. For instance, archeologists are trained to use specific preservation and excavation techniques to protect the objects they uncover during field excursions, while economic anthropologists often need to use statistical analysis software. Technological aptitude and the types of tools used will depend heavily on an individual's specific field.

EDUCATION, TRAINING, AND ADVANCEMENT

High School/Secondary

High school students interested in pursuing a career in anthropology should prepare themselves by developing good study habits. The study of foreign languages, sociology, anthropology, history, geography, and political science will provide a strong foundation for college-level work in anthropology, while additional experience with geology, earth sciences, physics, and environmental science will benefit those looking to work in archaeology. Due to the diversity of anthropological specialties, high school students interested in this career path will benefit from seeking internships or part-time work through local or national anthropological organizations or associations.

Suggested High School Subjects
- Algebra
- Calculus
- Composition
- Computer Science
- English
- Foreign Languages
- Geography
- History
- Humanities
- Photography
- Science
- Social Studies
- Sociology

Related Career Pathways/Majors
Science, Technology, Engineering & Mathematics Cluster
- Science & Mathematics Pathway

Postsecondary

Postsecondary students interested in pursuing a career in anthropology will benefit from taking courses in anthropology, foreign languages, sociology, history, geography, political science, behavioral science, and statistics. Internships and part-time work can offer postsecondary students the opportunity to learn more about anthropological specialties prior to entering graduate school, but most professional positions will require an advanced degree and students at the postsecondary level are therefore advised to prepare for applying to graduate level programs.

Related College Majors
- Anthropology
- Archeology
- International Relations & Affairs
- Sociology

Adult Job Seekers

Adults seeking jobs in anthropology will generally have earned a master's or doctoral degree in anthropology or a sub-specialty. Professional anthropological foundations, associations, and organizations can be helpful in searching for employment providing networking opportunities and linking candidates with potential positions in the field. The American Anthropological Association offers workshops in various anthropological subjects and maintain lists and forums of available jobs for new graduates and professionals looking for employment. Academic anthropologists beginning their careers may benefit from taking post-doctoral fellowships for one to four years to gain teaching experience while working on revising and publishing their doctoral research.

Professional Certification and Licensure

There are no professional certificates or licenses required for general anthropological practice in the United States, though some sub-specialties within anthropology prefer or require professionals to obtain training and certification in the use of certain tools or techniques. For instance, the American Board of Forensic Anthropology offers an exam-based forensic anthropology certification course that introduces trained anthropologists in the use of forensic science techniques in anthropological research. Professionals considering certification programs should consult with other professionals through academic or professional associations before beginning a certification program.

Additional Requirements

Successful anthropologists engage in ongoing development of their research and analytical skills. Written and verbal communication skills are essential skills and anthropologists should be comfortable with high-level collaboration. Collecting anthropological data may involve asking participants in various studies to disclose personal information or many require spending extended periods living and working with individuals in various communities. Anthropologists must therefore observe standards of professional ethnics and integrity in their work. Both junior and senior anthropologists are encouraged to take part in professional communities and associations in order to network and to keep abreast of new developments in the field. Anthropological field work often involves interacting with or spending extended periods within foreign cultures and anthropologists should be comfortable communicating and interacting across cultural and linguistic lines.

Fun Fact

They've been called "Underground Astronauts"—an all-female team of six highly educated paleontologists and archaeologists who were able to squeeze through a 7-inch opening in a South African cave to uncover 15 skeletons—all members of a previously unknown human ancestor.

Source: www.ewn.co.za

EARNINGS AND ADVANCEMENT

As of May 2016, the median annual salary for anthropologists and archaeologists was $63,190, with those at the lower end of the income spectrum earning less than $36,000 and those at the higher end of the spectrum earning closer to $99,000. Anthropologists entering careers in higher education may receive benefits such as summer research money, computer access, and student research assistants. Benefits available to applied anthropologists may include paid leave, holidays, sick days, and retirement benefits, typically at the discretion of a specific employer.

EMPLOYMENT AND OUTLOOK

According to the Bureau of Labor Statistics (BLS), the anthropological field is expected to grow by 4 percent between 2014 and 2024, which is slower than the 6-7 percent estimated for all U.S. occupations. Globalization, and the increasing tendency for U.S. businesses and organizations to operate internationally, may create new opportunities for applied anthropologists, while slow growth in U.S. academia overall will limit opportunities for academic professionals. Due to high competition for available positions, individuals with higher level degrees and higher levels of professional experience will have a distinct advantage when seeking employment. Individuals who are bilingual or who have advanced knowledge of foreign cultures and languages may also have a distinct advantage in seeking employment.

Related Occupations
- Archivist & Curator
- College Faculty Member
- Social Scientist
- Sociologist

Conversation With . . .
K. LINDSAY HUNTER

Program Manager/Facilitator
National Geographic "Umsuka" Public Paleoanthropology Project
Johannesburg, South Africa
Anthropologist, 13 years

1. **What was your individual career path in terms of education/training, entry-level job, or other significant opportunity?**

   I grew up in St. Louis, MO, and am a Midwesterner through and through! I followed the normal route of master's to PhD in biological anthropology/palaeoanthropology at the University of Iowa but languished in the "ABD"—all but dissertation—stage following lack of support from my primary supervisors. After taking part in the National Geographic 2013 Rising Star Expedition that excavated the first remains of the previously unknown human ancestor, Homo naledi, I took stock of my career and changed its trajectory. I am now pursuing a PhD at the University of the Witwatersrand in Johannesburg, working on an archaeology project that is less influenced by others' expectations and driven by my own interests and passions. I've been fortunate to do research on five continents in a multitude of countries, including Israel, Czech Republic, Croatia, Germany, France, United Kingdom, South Africa, Chile, and prestigious East Coast museums in the States. Neandertal researchers such as myself jokingly lament the dearth of Caribbean material, but the truth is the places we study are strikingly beautiful in their own ways. I have lived in South Africa since 2015.

2. **What are the most important skills and/or qualities for someone in your profession, particularly someone who decides to work overseas?**

   A somewhat extroverted personality with a deep interest in people will ease your path in anthropology (or indeed, any field). You need to be willing to step out of your comfort zone and stay there.

3. **What do you wish you had known before going into your professional, and, specifically, before moving abroad?**

   I wish I had understood that people who study the long dead don't tend to be "people persons" in a way that is pleasant to work with, and often are detached from their emotions in order to do their work.

As for working and living abroad, there will be no end to tedious paperwork. Documents you have accumulated in your own country—bank accounts, tax numbers, and drivers' license—will need to be recreated, and this in addition to the visa process.

Do your research regarding discomforts you are likely to encounter in your new home: if there is a significant difference in the wealth and culture, take a hard inventory as to whether you are prepared to meet these challenges. Stop yourself whenever you find yourself wanting to say something like, "In the States, we do X or have X to make things easier." You're not in Kansas anymore and the sooner you adapt to your new surroundings and stop clinging to the way you've always done things, the better.

4. Are there many job opportunities overseas in your profession? In what areas, both in terms of geography and subject matter?

Opportunities for a secure job in academia are relatively few and far between anywhere in the world. One of the great strengths of anthropology, as taught in the U.S., is its holism. An education in socio-cultural, linguistic, and biological anthropology, as well as archaeology, can assist you in marketing yourself no matter your specialization. Don't mistake this for an argument for a liberal arts education, though, as you learn very specific and specialized skills in anthropology, in addition to benefiting from a broad education.

The majority of early human history lies overseas, making international work and travel natural for palaeolithic archaeologists and palaeoanthropologists. Some anthropologists working internationally find themselves working for humanitarian projects, perhaps as Peace Corps staffers, or identifying remains from mass gravesites in war-torn areas. Ethnographers and linguists require long-term communication and relationships and often choose to work outside the cultures of their birth.

5. How do you see the importance of international experience in your profession changing in the next five years? What role will technology play in those changes, and what skills will be required?

I fervently believe that the value of international experience in any career will only increase as transnational collaboration becomes expected. The ability to communicate well and succinctly will be valuable, as will a tendency towards auto-didacticism, or being self-taught. All careers will depend more upon the ability to innovate and find the information you need, and anthropology will be no different. Many anthropologists find themselves in unconventional careers, even as successful entrepreneurs, simply because they never lose sight of the human element and ultimately, that is what drives economies.

6. What do you enjoy most about your job? What do you enjoy least about your job?

The things I enjoy most are traveling, meeting new people, and making connections. Seeing behind the scenes at museums and their collections is also pretty cool. I really dislike traditional excavations and number-based data collection, though many anthropologists thrive on these things. I greatly prefer working with words and archives. I am naturally more of a social scientist and philosopher and enjoy thinking about how knowledge is constructed and how culture and social milieu affect our interpretations of the same fossils. Find out which kind of anthropologist you are early on and don't let others convince you that one way or another is "better" or "more scientific": there is room for all. Do what you are good at and can stomach doing for the next 40 to 50 years (or whenever you reach retirement).

7. **Can you suggest a valuable "try this" for students considering a career overseas in your profession?**

If you like acting or, when reading, imagining yourself in different roles or living different lives, you might enjoy anthropology. If you are flexible and adaptable, you have a better than average shot of being a successful anthropologist.

A book that helped me determine if I could handle living in a different culture was an ethnography, *Never in Anger: Portrait of an Eskimo Family*, by Jean L. Briggs, who was very frank about her struggles in conducting research in the far north. I credit this book with really bringing home to me the concept of the anthropologist or scientist as the instrument or lens used to study a subject. If you are dealing with inner turmoil, it is difficult not to project that into your work. Science as a pursuit may be objective but the people that practice it often are not.

MORE INFORMATION

American Anthropological Association
2200 Wilson Boulevard, Suite 600
Arlington, VA 22201
703.528.1902
ksharp@aaanet.org
www.aaanet.org

AAA Fellowships and Support
www.aaanet.org/profdev/fellowships/

AAA Prizes and Awards
www.aaanet.org/about/prizes-awards/

Archaeological Institute of America
Boston University
656 Beacon Street, 6th Floor
Boston, MA 02215-2006
617.353.6550
aia@aia.bu.edu
www.archaeological.org

Consortium of Social Science Associations
1701 K Street NW, Suite 1150
Washington, DC 20006
202.842.3525
cossa@cossa.org
www.cossa.org

National Social Science Association
2020 Hills Lake Drive
El Cajon, CA 92020
619.448.4709
natsocsci@aol.com
www.nssa.us

Society for American Archaeology
1111 14th Street NW, Suite 800
Washington, DC 20005
202.789.8200
headquarters@saa.org
www.saa.org

Society for Applied Anthropology
PO Box 2436
Oklahoma City, OK 73101-2436
www.sfaa.net

Simone Isadora Flynn/Editor,
updated by Micah Issitt

Environmental Engineer

Snapshot

Career Cluster(s): Agriculture, Food & Natural Resources, Manufacturing, Science, Technology, Engineering & Mathematics
Interests: Science, mathematics, environmental issues, research, data analysis
Earnings (Yearly Average): $84,890
Employment & Outlook: Faster Than Average Growth Expected

OVERVIEW

Sphere of Work

Environmental engineers use the chemical, biological, and mechanical sciences to quantify, analyze, and mitigate pollution and other dangers to the natural environment. Environmental engineers design, implement, and supervise the operation of environmental systems used to address environmental pollution and health hazards and help mediate the environmental impact of human activities. On a typical day, an environmental engineer might investigate cases of pollution, write

environmental impact assessments, or provide technical expertise and advice on environmental cleanup projects to legislators, corporate managers, and other professionals. Environmental engineers usually specialize in one area of the field, such as water pollution or solid waste management.

Work Environment

Environmental engineers perform a great deal of their work in the field, visiting construction areas, pollution cleanup sites, reservoirs and water supply pipelines, forests, waste storage facilities and landfills, or any other area in which an environmental threat has been reported or suspected. Environmental engineers travel regularly to conduct research and investigations and, depending on the engineer's specific field, may have the opportunity to travel abroad for extended periods. Engineers working in the field risk exposure to toxic chemicals and pollutants and must observe safety guidelines when conducting their work. Other engineers work primarily indoors in engineering and industrial plants, laboratories, government agencies, or architectural firms. Environmental engineers usually work a regular forty-hour week, although they may work additional hours in the case of a professional emergency or when working under tight deadlines.

Profile

Interests: Data, Things
Working Conditions: Work Both Inside and Outside
Physical Strength: Light Work
Education Needs: Bachelor's Degree, Master's Degree, Doctoral Degree
Licensure/Certification: Required
Physical Abilities Not Require: Not Climb, Not Kneel
Opportunities For Experience: Internship
Holland Interest Score*: IRC

* See Appendix A

Occupation Interest

Environmental engineers are integral figures in the effort to protect the environment, natural resources, and wildlife from the threat of pollution and toxic substances and, as scientists, engineers rely on measurement and data (rather than political rhetoric or personal opinion) when they report on environmental issues. Data collected over the past thirty years demonstrating that human-mediated climate change has accelerated environmental degradation has increased demand for environmental engineers and prospective professionals should have a strong interest in environmental protection and remediation. Environmental engineers are an important resource in the growing effort to limit ecological damage and work in the cutting edge of green and renewable technology.

A Day in the Life—Duties and Responsibilities

Environmental engineers examine industrial and municipal sites to ensure compliance with environmental regulations as well as to estimate the efficiency and potential hazards of various types of environmental equipment. Engineers test emissions and waste to ensure that the environment is not exposed to excessive amounts of toxic pollution and help make recommendations to protect ecological areas and workers who are potentially exposed to pollutants. Environmental engineers also help design wastewater filtration, recycling, waste containment, air quality, and municipal water programs in cities and towns around the world, helping to balance the needs of the populace with the effort to limit pollution.

Environmental engineers also conduct research on the impact of industrial processes on the environment, and may study phenomena like acid rain, global climate change, air pollution, water quality, deforestation, loss of wildlife, and a variety of other environmental issues. In many cases, academic engineers write scholarly papers on various environmental issues, while others working in corporate or governmental fields may author environmental impact assessments and reports for corporate leaders or legislators to use in assessing various programs. Many environmental engineers help lawmakers and government officials craft environmental policies and regulations and conduct research on the effectiveness of such policies.

As with all true sciences, environmental engineering is a collaborative field and engineers frequently work with other scientists, legislators and community leaders, and corporate representatives when conducting their work. As environmental engineering is increasingly an essential part of development and construction projects, engineers are also involved with programs to expand housing and utilities, build roads and bridges, and a variety of other residential and commercial expansion projects. They may be asked to develop and maintain plans, obtain permits, and implement operating procedures to ensure that construction and engineering projects are handled safely and with limited environmental impact.

Duties and Responsibilities

- Designing and developing systems and equipment that comply with environmental standards
- Consulting with environmental scientists, hazardous waste technicians and other engineers and specialists
- Inspecting facilities to ensure observance with environmental regulations
- Educating organizations and government agencies on the necessary steps to clean up a contaminated site
- Creating and updating environmental investigation and recommendation reports
- Securing and maintaining necessary plans and permits for development of systems and equipment
- Overseeing the progress of environmental improvement programs

WORK ENVIRONMENT

Immediate Physical Environment

Environmental engineers conduct part of their work indoors, in office environments, and part of their work on-site at various facilities, projects, or environmental areas. When working in the field, engineers may be exposed to dirty, uncomfortable, or potentially hazardous conditions. The amount of time spent in the field varies depending on the engineer's specialization, employer, and field.

Human Environment

Environmental engineers interact with other professionals regularly, including government officials, environmentalists and environmental scientists, laboratory technicians, construction managers and

Transferable Skills and Abilities

Communication Skills

- Speaking effectively
- Writing concisely

Interpersonal/Social Skills

- Being able to work independently
- Working as a member of a team
- Having good judgment

Organization & Management Skills

- Initiating new ideas
- Paying attention to and handling details
- Managing time
- Promoting change
- Making decisions
- Meeting goals and deadlines
- Performing duties which change frequently

Research & Planning Skills

- Creating ideas
- Identifying problems
- Determining alternatives
- Identifying resources
- Solving problems
- Developing evaluation strategies
- Using logical reasoning

Technical Skills

- Performing scientific, mathematical and technical work
- Working with data or numbers

Unclassified Skills

- Using set methods and standards in your work

contractors, and architects. In many cases, engineers may be asked to speak at meetings or assemblies or may give reports to community or corporate leaders on various environmental issues.

Technological Environment

Environmental engineers use a wide range of tools and technologies in their work, including specialized measurement tools like air velocity and temperature monitors, spectrometers, and photometers. Engineers might also use a variety of hand and power tools when conducting work in the field. In the laboratory or office, environmental engineers use computers and other digital tools, including a variety computer modeling and design software, including computer-aided design (CAD) and photo-imaging software, to design plans and maps of sites or projects. Engineers also regularly utilize basic office programs and tools, like work processing, spreadsheet, and presentation software, as well as email and other digital communication programs.

EDUCATION, TRAINING, AND ADVANCEMENT

High School/Secondary

High school students interested in environmental engineering should study a wide range of natural sciences, such as biology, chemistry, physics, and earth sciences, as well as engineering and mathematics, including algebra, geometry, calculus, and trigonometry. Classes in social studies, political science, history, and other humanities can provide a deeper understanding of the intersection between public and environmental welfare and foreign language courses are helpful for those considering working overseas. Computer science and drafting classes are also highly beneficial and students should develop strong writing skills by taking English or composition classes.

Suggested High School Subjects
- Agricultural Education
- Algebra
- Applied Biology/Chemistry
- Applied Communication
- Applied Math
- Applied Physics
- Biology
- Blueprint Reading
- Calculus
- Chemistry
- College Preparatory
- Computer Science
- Drafting
- Earth Science
- English
- Forestry
- Geometry
- Humanities
- Mathematics
- Physical Science

- Physics
- Science
- Social Studies
- Trigonometry

Related Career Pathways/Majors

Agriculture, Food & Natural Resources Cluster
- Environmental Service Systems Pathway

Manufacturing Cluster
- Manufacturing Production Process Development Pathway

Science, Technology, Engineering & Mathematics Cluster
- Engineering & Technology Pathway

Postsecondary

Most environmental engineers earn postsecondary degrees in engineering, with a secondary specialization in environmental science. Engineers may improve their career prospects by obtaining advanced degrees in engineering with focus on an environmental field and many high-level environmental engineers obtain master's or doctorate level degrees in the field. At the post-graduate level, some universities offer environmental engineering programs or programs focusing specifically on a sub-field of environmental engineering, such as soil engineering or waste management.

Related College Majors

- Engineering, General
- Environmental & Pollution Control Technology
- Environmental Health
- Environmental Science/Studies
- Environmental/Environmental Health Engineering

Adult Job Seekers

Qualified environmental engineers may apply directly to firms and government agencies that have openings. Job fairs, Internet job boards, government employment web pages, and professional placement agencies may also be able to help qualified engineers find employment in their field. Additionally, prospective engineers may join professional organizations, such as the American Academy of Environmental Engineers, in order to network and potentially find new job opportunities.

Professional Certification and Licensure

In the United States, environmental engineers must obtain a
Professional Engineer (PE) license from the state or states in which
they work. This process entails passing a state examination as well
as meeting educational and work experience requirements. Because
the field of environmental engineering is broad, engineers may obtain
training and certification in specialized fields offered through various
engineering associations and organizations. Licensing and certification
requirements for engineers working abroad vary according to national
or regional laws and engineers planning on working abroad should
research the legal requirements of working abroad before applying for
open positions.

Additional Requirements

Engineering is a scientific field most suited to
individuals who are inquisitive and enjoy investigation
and solving problems. Environmental engineers must
be attentive to detail, able to research and understand
complex systems, and must be able to adhere to set procedures and
scientific standards. Engineers should demonstrate strong research,
writing, and analytical skills as well as the ability to use a wide range
of technologies, including computer software and technical tools
specific to their field. Federal government-employed environmental
engineers must be US citizens, and some must receive additional
government security clearance as part of the hiring process.

EARNINGS AND ADVANCEMENT

In 2016, the median annual wage for environmental engineers in the United States was $84,890 per year, with those at the lowest ten percent earning less than $49,000, while the highest paid engineers might earn over $130,000. Pay for engineers working abroad may vary considerably according to their employer and the nature of their job. In many cases, environmental engineers receive paid vacations, holidays and sick days; life and health insurance; and retirement benefits through their employer. Advancing in the field may involve seeking employment in higher-paid or more prestigious positions or advancing within an organization to become a senior engineer or project manager in charge of a team of engineers and other technical personnel.

EMPLOYMENT AND OUTLOOK

The Bureau of Labor Statistics (BLS) estimates that the environmental engineering field will grow by more than 12 percent between 2014 and 2024, which is faster than the average of 6-7 percent predicted for all U.S. occupations. Growth in the industry has been driven by the evolving environmental consciousness of the global population as decades of research have demonstrated the increasingly destructive impact of human culture on the world's environment and natural resources. In an effort to limit environmental destruction, reduce the risk of pollution-related injury or illness, and to preserve remaining natural resources, more and more companies and governmental organizations make use of environmental engineers and this has created an increasing demand for trained professionals.

In addition, as environmental engineers are important to commercial and residential expansion, the rapid growth of the human population also serves to increase demand for environmental engineers around the world. While there are many domestic opportunities for trained engineers, there are also numerous opportunities for engineers willing to travel abroad to conduct environmental studies and help mediate the environmental impact of various programs and projects. Environmental threats like climate change and water pollution are worldwide issues and so engineers involved in research may need to travel internationally to collect data.

Related Occupations	*Related Military Occupations*
• Agricultural Engineer • Biological Scientist • Chemical Engineer • Chemist • Energy Engineer • Environmental Science Technician • Forester & Conservation Scientist • Hazardous Waste Manager • Petroleum Engineer • Water & Wastewater Engineer • Wind Energy Engineer	• Environmental Health & Safety Officer • Environmental Health & Safety Specialist

> # *Conversation With . . .*
> # *JAN VERTEFEUILLE*
> Senior Director, World Wildlife Fund
> Advocacy, 15 years

1. What was your individual career path in terms of education/training, entry-level job, or other significant opportunity?

I transitioned into international advocacy for conservation after working at newspapers and loving it. But after a decade, I started thinking about what else I could do with my strongest skills: researching, writing, delivering work on deadline and drawing stories and information out of people.

I went to work for a nonprofit in D.C. called Environmental Media Services, which was run by a bunch of former reporters who educated journalists about environmental issues and worked to generate media coverage of issues like environmental health and genetically engineered food. I worked there for four years before learning of a communications job at World Wildlife Fund. Since my passion was wildlife, it seemed a great fit.

My job focuses on figuring out advocacy strategies to achieve a specific wildlife conservation goal, like trying to reduce illegal ivory sales in a particular country to reduce elephant poaching. We might launch a campaign that includes policy advocacy (i.e. lobbying), media outreach to raise public awareness, and direct public engagement, like asking citizens to pledge not to buy ivory or sign a petition to their government. Then we look at who might be influential with the decision-makers in that country. Would diplomatic pressure help? Would a celebrity or influential business leader take up the cause?

2. What are the most important skills and/or qualities for someone in your profession, particularly someone who decides to work overseas?

People think of advocacy as lobbying legislators and government officials to get a law passed, and that's part of it. But to be successful, you need to really understand the players you're trying to influence and what tactics will be successful and what ones might actually hurt your efforts.

Professional training and a degree is less important than innate skills, which can be cultivated and improved through practice: creativity, curiosity, strategic thinking, flexibility, persuasion and the ability to work with a cross-cultural team. And by that last one I mean the ability to really listen to members of your team from other cultures and draw out their ideas. During a brainstorming discussion, for instance, Americans tend to be forthright with their ideas and have no problem sharing ideas. Colleagues from other cultures may be more reluctant to speak up. I've learned the hard way that some people I work with find it very rude to tell me my idea is a bad one even when they know it won't work, so I now ask a lot of questions and listen carefully to the answers. I then offer ideas in ways that can be rejected by someone without the fear of being rude.

3. What do you wish you had known before deciding to work abroad?

I wish I'd known how fulfilling international work is—I would have started sooner! I love working with people all over the world even though it means holding conference calls at crazy hours, so that team members in Asia and North America can talk to each other. I also wish Americans were better informed about issues outside the U.S. There is a whole big fascinating world full of people who are just as smart, well-educated, compassionate and creative, and they're working just as hard to protect the environment where they live and improve their quality of life. It seems obvious, but it's worth stating explicitly.

4. Are there many job opportunities overseas in your profession? In what specific geographic areas?

As the population hurtles close to 9 billion people on the planet, there will be a surge in need for people interested in advocating for change internationally, whether it's figuring out how to feed all those people while protecting the environment, mitigating climate change before our coasts are swamped, ensuring elephants and tigers continue to roam in the wild, or improving the way we build cities. Nonprofit organizations and governments in wealthy countries like the U.S. that have a long history of international charitable giving will be doing a lot of the hiring.

5. Will the need for professionals in your career to travel and live overseas change in the next five years? What role will technology play in those changes, and what skills will be required?

Advances in video conferencing and communication apps like Skype, Webex, Whatsapp and Line have provided huge benefits in being able to keep in touch with colleagues all over the world at all hours of the day. That has cut down on the need for some international travel. But there is really no substitute for face-to- face interaction with colleagues, so I think some international travel will always be a part of jobs like mine.

Social media and platforms like change.org, Avaaz and other petition sites have increased opportunities to bring global attention to a problem. A great example is when WWF launched a campaign to press the president of Mexico to take more action to save the world's most endangered marine mammal, the tiny vaquita porpoise that's found only in Mexico's Gulf of California. We generated hundreds of thousands of emails to his office and launched a social media effort that Leo DiCaprio joined on Twitter. The president of Mexico, WWF and DiCaprio started a public dialogue on Twitter about the vaquita and the president and DiCaprio ended up signing a formal agreement to work together to save this critically endangered species.

6. What do you enjoy most about your job? What do you enjoy least about your job?

I enjoy being part of a global organization with such a diverse number of issues to work on (endangered species, climate change, fresh water, forests and oceans) and with team members all over the world to learn from.

My least favorite part of the job is dealing with budgets. Funding and tracking spending is important, but not something I enjoy.

7. Can you suggest a valuable "try this" for students considering a career overseas in your profession?

Start by writing a letter to the editor of your local paper or emailing the appropriate decision-makers about an issue you care about (school funding, lack of bike lanes in town, not enough recycling in the parks). Be constructive (criticizing people immediately makes them less likely to listen to you) and consider the issue from their perspective so you can be persuasive, and propose a solution. Will it require a new rule, for instance, to stop selling plastic water bottles at park concessions? What can you suggest to make that feasible?

MORE INFORMATION

Air and Waste Management Association
1 Gateway Center, 3rd Floor
420 Fort Duquesne Boulevard
Pittsburgh, PA 15222-1435
800.270.3444
www.awma.org

American Academy of Environmental Engineers
130 Holiday Court, Suite 100
Annapolis, MD 21401
410.266.3311
info@aaee.net
www.aaee.net

Association of Environmental & Engineering Geologists
P.O. Box 460518
Denver, CO 80246
303.757.2926
www.aegweb.org

Institute of Professional Environmental Practice
600 Forbes Avenue
339 Fisher Hall
Pittsburgh, PA 15282
412.396.1703
www.ipep.org

Solid Waste Association of North America
1100 Wayne Avenue, Suite 700
Silver Spring, MD 20910
800.467.9262
www.swana.org

U.S. Army Corps of Engineers Research and Development Center
3909 Halls Ferry Road
Vicksburg, MS 39180-6199
866.373.2872
www.erdc.usace.army.mil

Michael Auerbacht/Editor

Geologist and Geophysicist

Snapshot

Career Cluster(s): Agriculture, Food & Natural Resources, Science, Technology, Engineering & Mathematics

Interests: Seismology, hydrology, earth science, helping others

Earnings (Yearly Average): $89,780

Employment & Outlook: Faster Than Average Growth Expected

OVERVIEW

Sphere of Work

Geoscientists, including geologists and geophysicists, study the composition, natural history, and other aspects of the earth. Geologists are specialists in the history and chemistry of soil and rocks, and they analyze and investigate various types of rock, metallic ore, and precious stone deposits, and search for and study plant and animal fossils. Geophysicists use physics, chemistry, mathematics, and geology to study the earth's magnetic fields, oceans,

composition, seismic forces, and other geological forces and processes. Most geologists and geophysicists specialize in sub-fields such as mineralogy, hydrology, paleontology, seismology, and geochemistry. While many geoscientists work in academia, and many work for government agencies, universities, and museums, there are also many opportunities for geoscientists in the private sector. For instance, petroleum companies hire geologists and geophysicists to help locate and evaluate new petroleum deposits.

Work Environment

Most geologists and geophysicists spend a significant portion of their time in the field conducting research. Fieldwork often involves traveling great distances into remote, rugged environments and, depending on the specifics of a geoscientist's employment, professionals in the field might spend weeks, months, or years living and working in areas close to a specific research site. Geologists and geophysicists must also work in all weather conditions and are often exposed to adverse and potentially dangerous environmental hazards. When performing field research, geologists and geophysicists typically work long and irregular hours. When not conducting fieldwork, geologists and geophysicists are at work in offices and laboratories, studying samples, writing papers, and analyzing and interpreting data. There are many opportunities for geoscientists to work abroad or to travel internationally when conducting research. U.S.-trained paleontologists, for instance, may join research programs around the world, helping to study the ancient extinct fauna and flora of prehistoric environments.

Profile

Interests: Data, Things
Working Conditions: Work Both Inside and Outside
Physical Strength: Light Work, Medium Work
Education Needs: Master's Degree, Doctoral Degree
Licensure/Certification: Required
Physical Abilities Not Require: Not Hear and/or Talk
Opportunities For Experience: Military Service, Part Time Work
Holland Interest Score*: IRE, IRS

* See Appendix A

Occupation Interest

Geophysicists and geologists play an important role in protecting people from natural disasters – their work in seismology, hydrology, and other fields can help communities to avoid flood damage, prepare for seismic activity, or escape the impending volcanic disasters. Geoscientists also help businesses, universities, and government agencies locate safe locations for construction, find dinosaur remains, and identify new areas in which to dig for oil, metals, or precious stones. The work performed by geophysicists and geologists changes frequently, and new research contributes to a growing body of knowledge about the history and characteristics of the earth. Given the diversity of opportunities in the field, geoscientists might approach their work from a variety of different basic interest and motivations. Some prospective geoscientists might be motivated by an interest in environmental protection and conservation, while others may be interested in helping people and communities to avoid environmental dangers, and others might approach their field from a perspective of personal gain, such as by helping petroleum companies to exploit natural resources or searching for valuable geological deposits in the form of precious metals or stones.

A Day in the Life—Duties and Responsibilities

The work performed by geologists and geophysicists varies based on their area of expertise. For example, some mineralogists prepare cross-sectional diagrams and geographic surveys of areas from which precious stones and metals may be located and extracted. Others set up and maintain seismic monitors in and around active volcanic areas. Some geophysicists and geologists spend a great deal of time in the laboratory, while others spend the vast majority of time in the field. When choosing an area of specialization within the geosciences, therefore, prospective professionals can attempt to choose a subfield that matches aligning with a preferred lifestyle.

In the field, geologists and geophysicists plan and conduct geological surveys and other technical analyses of geological deposits or regions. Such studies often involve taking samples of stones, soil, and sediment, or usin sensory equipment to sample magnetic waves, tremors, and subterranean water flows. Using these samples and data, geologists and geophysicists compile technical reports, academic papers, charts, maps, and policy recommendations. Geologists and geophysicists rely on computer modeling software, sensory data recorders, and other pieces of hardware and software to organize and analyze their data and to prepare models and reports. Scientists who study the compositions of rocks, minerals, and other resources must also conduct laboratory experiments using chemicals and other specialized analytical tools.

Geologists and geophysicists employed by educational institutions may also need to spend time writing research proposals and grant applications in addition to performing their own research. Some geologists and geophysicists are also university professors who are responsible for teaching and mentoring students at various levels of their education. Many geoscientists divide their time between the classroom and the field and may also utilize students in conducting research and field investigations.

Duties and Responsibilities

- Examining rocks, minerals and fossil remains
- Determining and explaining the sequence of the earth's development
- Interpreting research data
- Recommending specific studies or actions
- Preparing reports and maps
- Managing and cleaning up toxic waste

OCCUPATION SPECIALTIES

Petroleum Geologists

Petroleum Geologists study the earth's surface and subsurface to locate gas and oil deposits and help develop extraction processes.

Mineralogists

Mineralogists examine, analyze and classify minerals, gems and precious stones and study their occurrence and chemistry.

Paleontologists

Paleontologists study the fossilized remains of plants and animals to determine the development of past life and history of the earth.

Hydrologists

Hydrologists study the distribution and development of water in land areas and evaluate findings in reference to such problems as flood and drought, soil and water conservation and inland irrigation.

Geological Oceanographers

Geological Oceanographers study the ocean bottom.

Physical Oceanographers

Physical Oceanographers study the physical aspects of oceans such as currents and their interaction with the atmosphere.

Seismologists

Seismologists interpret data from seismographs and other instruments to locate earthquakes and earthquake faults.

Stratigraphers

Stratigraphers study the distribution and arrangement of sedimentary rock layers by examining their contents.

WORK ENVIRONMENT

Immediate Physical Environment

Geologists and geophysicists spend much of their time in the field and fieldwork may involve traveling to remote areas and across rugged terrain. Geoscientists working in the field might be exposed to a variety of weather and environmental conditions and are sometimes exposed to potentially dangerous environmental hazards. When not working in the field, geologists and geophysicists typically work in offices, laboratories, and classrooms.

Transferable Skills and Abilities

Comunication Skills
- Editing written information
- Writing concisely

Interpersonal/Social Skills
- Cooperating with others
- Working as a member of a team

Organization & Management Skills
- Paying attention to and handling details

Research & Planning Skills
- Analyzing information
- Creating ideas
- Gathering information
- Solving problems

Technical Skills
- Applying the technology to a task
- Performing scientific, mathematical and technical work
- Working with machines, tools or other objects

Work Environment Skills
- Working outdoors

Human Environment

Depending on their area of specialty, geologists and geophysicists work with a variety of other scientists, engineers, students, research assistants, and corporate/governmental representatives. Geoscience is a collaborative discipline and professionals will typically need to work with other professionals and specialists to conduct research and prepare various reports and studies. Those working in corporate or governmental environments may report to company leaders or to legislators and other governmental representatives on various geological issues and projects.

Technological Environment

Geologists and geophysicists need to use a wide range of technology to complete their work. Geological compasses, electromagnetic instruments, water flow measurement instruments, soil core sampling tools, sonar, magnetic field measurement devices, geographic information systems software (GIS), global positioning systems (GPS), map creation programs, and scientific databases are only some of the tools and technologies used by individuals in this field. In addition, geoscientists must be competent with basic computing and digital technology and many also utilize basic office tools such as word processing, spreadsheet, and presentation software. In many cases, geoscientists also make extensive use of photographic equipment and many also use photo and video editing software when preparing models or reports.

EDUCATION, TRAINING, AND ADVANCEMENT

High School/Secondary

High school students interested in the geoscientists should attempt to utilize their secondary school education to gain a strong background in physics and the sciences. Classes in chemistry, physics, environmental science, biology, geology, meteorology, algebra, geometry, and trigonometry will be helpful for future professionals in the field. History, computer science, geography, English, foreign language, and photography courses can also useful for certain aspects of many geoscience specialties. Because professional geoscientists typically obtain advanced degrees in their field, secondary students should also focus on preparing for a future college or university-level education.

Suggested High School Subjects
- Algebra
- Applied Math
- Chemistry
- College Preparatory
- Earth Science
- English
- Geography
- Geometry
- History
- Photography
- Physical Science
- Science
- Trigonometry
- Foreign languages

Related Career Pathways/Majors
Agriculture, Food & Natural Resources Cluster
- Environmental Service Systems Pathway
- Natural Resources Systems Pathway

Science, Technology, Engineering & Mathematics Cluster
- Science & Mathematics Pathway

Postsecondary

Geologists and geophysicists generally need a master's degree in geology, paleontology, mineralogy, or a related geoscience field to qualify for entry-level jobs. Those who wish to pursue a senior-level research position or employment at an educational institution will need to obtain a doctorate. At the postsecondary level, many institutions offer undergraduate degrees in geoscience, geology, or physics that can provide the basic preparation for graduate level studies in a specific field. Classes in foreign language and culture will provide an advantage for those hoping to work or conduct research abroad. In addition, basic training in technical writing, computer science, sociology, anthropology, and archaeology provide a strong foundation for future study.

Related College Majors
- Anthropology
- Geography
- Geological Engineering
- Geology
- Geophysical Engineering
- Geophysics & Seismology
- Ocean Engineering
- Oceanography

Adult Job Seekers

Qualified geologists and geophysicists may apply directly to postings by government agencies, private corporations, or any of a variety of educational institutions. Geoscience journals frequently post job openings and professional geology and geophysics societies and associations help professionals to network and find job opportunities.

Professional Certification and Licensure

In the United States, licensing and certification requirements vary by state. In states that require licensing, professionals must typically provide proof of academic experience and pass a test before receiving a license. Geologists and geophysicists may also choose to pursue voluntary certification in specialized areas of expertise, typically offered through professional associations and organizations, as a way of enhancing their prospects for employment in a specific subfield.

Licensing requirements for geoscientists working overseas vary according to national laws and standards and professionals should research professional requirements before applying for positions in foreign countries. In many cases, companies hiring professionals can provide information about required certifications and licenses to prospective employees.

Additional Requirements

Geologists and geophysicists should be reasonably physically fit, as they frequently work in remote areas and are often required to engage in strenuous activities. Individuals who are interested in working outdoors and exploring nature may therefore be suited for geoscience fields that involve considerable field work and travel. Strong communication and interpersonal skills, writing abilities, and a sense of teamwork are also important for geologists and geophysicists as professionals in the field frequently collaborate with other specialists, scientists, and professionals when conducting their work.

EARNINGS AND ADVANCEMENT

Earnings depend on the individual's particular position, occupational specialty, amount of experience and level of education. According to the Bureau of Labor Statistics (BLS), the median annual wage for geoscientists working in the United States was $89,780 in 2016, with those at the lowest ten percent earning less than $47,000, while those at the upper end of the spectrum could earn more than $189,000 per year. Higher salaries are typically available to geoscientists who work in the petroleum, mineral, and mining industries, though fluctuations in oil, gas, and other precious geological materials can lead to reduced job security for those working in the corporate side of the field. Despite higher earnings, geoscientists with interest in environmental conservation and protection may be reluctant to work in corporate geoscience as corporate geological activities are inherently destructive to the environment and to animal/human populations. In many cases, geoscientists may receive paid vacations, holidays, and sick days; life and health insurance; and retirement benefits. Advancing in the field may involve applying for more prestigious or higher paid positions or advancing within an organization or institution, in some cases taking on managerial or supervisory roles.

EMPLOYMENT AND OUTLOOK

The BLS estimates that the geosciences field in the United States will grow by 10 percent between 2014 and 2024, which is faster than the 6-7 percent predicted for all occupations in the nation. Growth in the industry has been fueled by increasing environmental concern around the world, motivating more aggressive efforts to study and preserve the geophysical environment. In addition, growth in the geosciences field is related to dwindling natural resources with companies searching for new coal, natural gas, and petroleum deposits to meet global energy needs. Approximately 1/4th of all geoscientists were employed by companies involved in oil and gas extraction and exploration and the advent of new technologies, like hydraulic fracturing for oil, has created new opportunities in the corporate environment. For those motivated by environmental protection, geoscientists are also in demand for work in alternative energy, helping to design and implement wind, solar, and geothermal energy systems to reduce dependence on destructive resource exploration. Geoscientists who are willing to work abroad, and/or who have experience with foreign languages and cultures, will have a distinct advantage when searching for employment as many of the companies, institutions, and organizations hiring researchers or applied geoscientists increasingly conduct projects overseas. In some cases, foreign companies may be willing to hire U.S.-trained or native geoscientists for permanent or long-term work overseas, and those with previous experience in foreign languages or international travel will have an advantage when applying for such positions.

Related Occupations

- Geographer
- Hazardous Waste Manager
- Metallurgical/Materials Engineer
- Mining & Geological Engineer
- Oceanographer
- Petroleum Engineer
- Surveyor & Cartographer

Related Military Occupations

- Oceanographer

Conversation With . . .
Dr. JEROME E. "JERRY" DOBSON

Professor Emeritus, University of Kansas
President, American Geographical Society
Geographer, 48 years

1. What was your individual career path in terms of education/training, entry-level job, or other significant opportunity?

I was in my junior year, in a major with which I was not happy. One afternoon my roommate came home and said he'd decided to change his major to geography. I got up the next day and switched to geography. I knew it was for me. I'd had one geography course before and loved it. Even as a child, I liked to work with maps and plan our family's vacations. I got my undergraduate degree from the University of Georgia and went straight into a Master's program there, then went to the University of Tennessee for my PhD. My specialty was rural settlement, how people occupy rural lands. My first job was at Oak Ridge National Laboratory, right out of my PhD program, for 26 years before coming to the University of Kansas. Oak Ridge is a highly technical laboratory. If people have the misconception that geography is just about making maps or knowing their states and capitals, they have to reevaluate. Typically, they wonder what the lab can possibly do with geographers alongside physicists, chemists, and economists. At one time we had 41 geographers there.

Geography is to space what history is to time. The beauty of geography is that it has utility in so many applications. I've worked on continental drift. I led the LandScan Global Population project which developed the global population database that for a decade and a half has been the world standard for estimating at-risk populations. Later, at KU, I led the development of a new world standard for cartographic representation of land mines, mine fields, and mine action. My funded research now is studying factors that promote instability or stability and resilience among indigenous communities in Central America.

2. What are the most important skills and/or qualities for someone in your profession?

Think spatially. Be able to analyze patterns and connections and understand how everything flows and interacts. If a person likes maps, he or she likely will have those other skills; the map is not the skill, the skill is understanding what the map is showing.

3. **What do you wish you had known going into this profession?**

   I wish I had taken more computer science early in my career. GIS is the marriage of computer science and geography. I have heard people in computer science say it is easier to train a geographer in computer science than vice versa.

4. **Are there many job opportunities in your profession? In what specific areas?**

   Geography has one of the highest average salaries and lowest unemployment rates and is one of the fastest-growing job-creating industries. Whatever you do, whether it's human geography or physical geography, make sure you have GIS. That's what will get you the job.

5. **How do you see your profession changing in the next five years, what role will technology play in those changes, and what skills will be required?**

   The biggest change we're seeing in geography is a shift from commercial GIS to more friendly and cheaper "popular geographics." It's booming.

6. **What do you enjoy most about your job? What do you enjoy least about your job?**

   I enjoy travel, anywhere in the world. I tend to go places that are a little more on the edge, such as Honduras, Eritrea, and the Balkans. Liberia was a failed state when I spent five weeks there in 1981. Now it's in a health crisis, but I would go back in a heartbeat.

   Also, there are many circumstances in which I get to meet famous, accomplished people through the America Geographical Society's Flyer's and Explorer's Globe. We've had it since the 1920s, and it was signed by almost every famous explorer and record-breaking aviator of the 20th Century. Since 2000, I have presided over half a dozen ceremonies when, for instance, Neil Armstrong — the first person on the Moon — and Valentina Tereshkova — the first woman in space — signed. In 2012, my wife and were I invited to the annual meeting of the Board of Trustees of the Russian Geographic Society with Vladimir Putin presiding. Also present were the presidents of BP and BP Russia, chancellors of universities and heads of national academies. I was there because geography, in general, is appreciated far more in other countries than it is in the U.S. My AGS counterpart in Russia? His day job is Secretary of Defense.

   What I like least is America's great folly of rejecting geography. I'm talking about the education and academic system. Universities have been killing off geography departments regularly since 1948. Or, they rename departments so they are no longer called geography. Or they add something like "geography and atmospheric science" which implies that the earth's atmosphere is not part of the earth's geography. Geography is the most integrated of all disciplines. A 2012 survey polled the U. S. public on their knowledge of and values toward geography and found that they love it.

7. **Can you suggest a valuable "try this" for students considering a career in your profession?**

   If you want to experiment, see if you can create something that's worth posting on mapstory.com.*

   [*This interview was conducted in 2014. Web site may no longer be active.]

MORE INFORMATION

American Association of Petroleum Geologists
P.O. Box 979
Tulsa, OK 74101-0979
800.364.2274
www.aapg.org

American Geological Institute
4220 King Street
Alexandria, VA 22302-1502
703.379.2480
aeb@agiweb.org
www.agiweb.org

Environmental and Engineering Geophysical Society
1720 South Bellaire, Suite 110
Denver, CO 80222-4303
303.531.7517
www.eegs.org

Geological Society of America
P.O. Box 9140
Boulder, CO 80301-9140
303.357.1000
www.geosociety.org

Paleontological Society
P.O. Box 9044
Boulder, CO 80301
855.357.1032
www.paleosoc.org

Seismological Society of America
201 Plaza Professional Building
El Cerrito, CA 94530
510.525.5474
www.seismosoc.org

Society of Exploration Geophysicists
P.O. Box 702740
Tulsa, OK 74170-2740
918.497.5500
www.seg.org

United States Geological Survey
12201 Sunrise Valley Drive
Reston, VA 20192
703.648.5953
www.usgs.gov

Michael Auerbach/Editor,
updated by Micah Issitt

Oceanographer

Snapshot

Career Cluster(s): Agriculture, Food & Natural Resources, Science, Technology, Engineering & Mathematics

Interests: Marine life, natural science, oceanography, geology, ecology

Earnings (Yearly Average): $112,106

Employment & Outlook: Faster Than Average Growth Expected

OVERVIEW

Sphere of Work

Oceanographers are part of an interdisciplinary field that uses chemistry, geology, biology, and physics to study many different aspects of the earth's oceans and seas. They tend to focus on one of four main areas: physical, chemical, geological, and biological oceanography. Oceanographers study water currents and circulation, chemical composition, animal and plant life, and geological formations. Oceanographers often study oceanic weather patterns, environmental issues and pollution, and fossils. They are also hired

to help locate new mineral deposits, deep-sea oil reserves, new fishing locations, and alternative energy sources. Universities, government agencies at all levels, and private businesses and organizations employ oceanographers.

Work Environment

Oceanographers work for federal agencies such as the National Oceanic and Atmospheric Administration (NOAA), as well as colleges and universities, ecological and environmental organizations, and private industry. Some oceanographers conduct the majority of their research aboard offshore research vessels. Others perform office or laboratory work. On land, oceanographers work standard forty-hour weeks, during which they conduct laboratory experiments, examine and record data, and write academic papers. At sea, they may experience extreme weather conditions, rough seas, and cramped living conditions. While conducting research at sea, oceanographers frequently work much longer hours.

Profile

Interests: Data, Things
Working Conditions: Work Outside
  Work Both Inside & Outside
Physical Strength: Light Work
Education Needs: Bachelor's Degree,
  Master's Degree
Licensure/Certification: Usually Not
  Required
Physical Abilities Not Require: Not
  Climb, Not Kneel
Opportunities For Experience:
  Internship
Holland Interest Score*: IRE

* See Appendix A

Occupation Interest

Oceanographers often spend a great deal of time at sea, an aspect of the job that may appeal to those who love nature and enjoy working outdoors. They study firsthand the wide array of animal and plant life, geological formations, weather conditions, and other interesting aspects of the oceans. Oceanographers are respected for their expertise and can influence policymaking related to the environment. Vast stretches of ocean remain unexplored, meaning there is always a possibility of discovering new species or formulating new theories. As an interdisciplinary field, oceanography offers many areas of specialization from which scientists may choose.

A Day in the Life—Duties and Responsibilities

Oceanographers' duties and responsibilities vary based on the subfields in which they work. Physical oceanographers use models and databases to study changes in ocean temperature and salinity, currents, waves, and tidal patterns. Physical oceanographers and meteorologists work together to better understand the relationship between the ocean and climate. Chemical oceanographers take surface water and deepwater samples and use analytical equipment to study the natural and synthetic chemical compounds in those samples. They often seek to understand the impact of pollutants and observe interactions between bodies of water and the atmosphere. Geological oceanographers often use remote-controlled diving equipment to photograph and map deep-sea volcanoes, floor rock configurations, and other solid bodies. These oceanographers track and predict changes in the structure and mineral composition of the sea floor. Meanwhile, biological oceanographers, or marine biologists, locate, trap, tag, and release animal species to track their movement, feeding, mating, and other behavior patterns. Biological oceanographers study aquatic ecosystems and assist in developing techniques for sustainable resource harvesting.

Some of the most important work performed by oceanographers occurs on research vessels at sea. Such research can take place for extended periods, during which oceanographers compile soil and water samples, record temperatures and atmospheric conditions, take photographic images of geological formations and other subjects on the ocean floor, and capture live specimens of plants and wildlife. When they return to the laboratory, oceanographers compile data into databases, build models using computer software, and formulate theories. Using field data, samples, and models, oceanographers draft technical reports and assessments, author scholarly papers and articles, and submit policy recommendations to the government agencies, private businesses, and nonprofit organizations that employ them.

Many oceanographers are also university professors. In this capacity, they lead seminars, lectures, and laboratory sessions, advise students, and work with departmental peers. University-based oceanographers are able to pursue their independent research while teaching courses. They typically draft grant proposals to obtain government funding for their research.

Duties and Responsibilities

- Studying the links between the ocean and atmospheric changes
- Studying plant and animal life habits, growth and effects on the ocean and other marine life
- Determining what ecological changes occur as a result of the shifting of the sea floor
- Collecting and processing data used to help other scientists
- Analyzing the ocean's water, floor shifts, and composition

WORK ENVIRONMENT

Immediate Physical Environment

Oceanographers work at universities, private nonprofit organizations, corporations, and government offices and laboratories. The conditions at each of these venues are clean, bright, and well ventilated. When conducting research, they often travel for extended periods aboard research vessels. At sea, oceanographers are at risk of injury from dangerous weather, sea conditions, heavy lifting, malfunctioning equipment, and/or animal attacks.

Human Environment

Depending on their areas of specialty, oceanographers interact and collaborate with a wide range of scientists and professionals. They may work with marine biologists, laboratory technicians, interns and lab assistants, geologists, engineers, business executives, environmental scientists, ship crews, government officials, and university students and professors.

Transferable Skills and Abilities

Organization & Management Skills
- Making decisions
- Paying attention to and handling details

Research & Planning Skills
- Analyzing information

Technical Skills
- Performing scientific, mathematical and technical work

Work Environment Skills
- Working under different weather conditions
- Working with plants or animals

Technological Environment

Oceanographers use a number of pieces of equipment and technology to take samples and perform research at sea. They may capture animals with nets and snaring equipment, deploy scientific buoys to record measurements, or explore shallow areas with scuba equipment. Oceanographers also use submersible devices (both manned and remote-controlled) to travel to the ocean floor and take samples and photographs. In the laboratory, oceanographers rely on computer modeling, digital mapping, and database technologies to help formulate and validate theories.

EDUCATION, TRAINING, AND ADVANCEMENT

High School/Secondary

High school students should study biology, chemistry, physics, and other natural sciences. Mathematics, including algebra, geometry, and statistics, are important courses as well. Furthermore, high school students should take computer science courses and hone their writing and public speaking skills through English and communications classes.

Suggested High School Subjects
- Algebra
- Applied Math
- Applied Physics
- Biology

- Calculus
- Chemistry
- College Preparatory
- Computer Science
- Earth Science
- English
- Geography
- Geometry
- Mathematics
- Physics
- Science

Related Career Pathways/Majors

Agriculture, Food & Natural Resources Cluster
- Natural Resources Systems Pathway

Science, Technology, Engineering & Mathematics Cluster
- Science, Technology, Engineering & Mathematics Cluster

Postsecondary

Oceanographers must receive a bachelor's degree in a field related to oceanography, such as biology, chemistry, engineering, environmental science, and geology. Most oceanographers have at least a master's degree in one or more related scientific disciplines. Senior researchers and oceanography professors must have earned or be working toward a doctorate in an oceanography-related scientific field. Students can gain experience in the field through internships or research assistantships.

Related College Majors
- Geology
- Geophysics & Seismology
- Oceanography

Adult Job Seekers

Qualified oceanographers may apply directly to government agencies, universities, nonprofit organizations, or corporations with open positions. Many universities have placement programs that can help recent graduates find work. Additionally, oceanographers may join and network through professional and academic associations and societies such as the International Association for Biological Oceanography or the American Society of Limnology and Oceanography.

Professional Certification and Licensure

Oceanographers who also practice as engineers must be certified as professional engineers within the state in which they work.

Additional Requirements

Oceanographers should be able to analyze complex issues and concepts. They must demonstrate exceptional research and writing skills. Knowledge of and capability with mechanical devices greatly helps oceanographers as well. Furthermore, oceanographers should have strong computer skills, particularly with geographic information systems (GIS) and global positioning systems (GPS). Physical fitness and stamina are advantageous for fieldwork.

EARNINGS AND ADVANCEMENT

Oceanographers with experience may be promoted to teaching or high level research positions as well as administrative or supervisory positions. Graduate study and experience often expand employment opportunities. According to a salary survey by the National Association of Colleges and Employers, graduates with a bachelor's degree in geology and related sciences had average starting salaries of $55,764 in 2016.

Median annual earnings of oceanographers were $89,780 in 2016. The lowest ten percent earned less than $47,450, and the highest ten percent earned more than $189,020. In 2016, oceanographers employed by the federal government earned average annual salaries of 117,390.

Oceanographers may receive paid vacations, holidays, and sick days; life and health insurance; and retirement benefits. These are usually paid by the employer.

EMPLOYMENT AND OUTLOOK

Geoscientists and hydrologists, of whom oceanographers are a part, held about 36,400 jobs nationally in 2014. Many more individuals held geology, geophysics and oceanography faculty positions in colleges and universities. Most oceanographers are employed by the U.S. Geological Survey within the Department of the Interior and for the Department of Defense. Employment is expected to grow faster than the average for all occupations through the year 2024, which means employment is projected to increase 10 percent. Oceanographers, whose work is often research-oriented and dependent on grants from federal agencies, are expected to face strong competition. With more people graduating from oceanography programs than the field can absorb, those with advanced technical and research skills will be most desirable.

Related Occupations
- Biological Scientist
- Botanist
- Geographer
- Geologist & Geophysicist
- Marine Biologist
- Meteorologist
- Microbiologist

MORE INFORMATION

American Society of Limnology and Oceanography
5400 Bosque Blvd., Suite 680
Waco, TX 76710-4446
800.929.2756
business@aslo.org
www.aslo.org

Consortium for Ocean Leadership
1201 New York Avenue NW, 4th Floor
Washington, DC 20005
202.232.3900
www.oceanleadership.org

International Oceanographic Foundation
4600 Rickenbacker Causeway
Miami, FL 33149-1098
305.421.4000
barbgo@rsmas.miami.edu
www.rsmas.miami.edu

National Environmental Satellite, Data and Information Service
1335 East-West Highway
SSMC1, 8th Floor
Silver Spring, MD 20910
301.713.3578
answers@noaa.gov
www.nesdis.noaa.gov

National Oceanic and Atmospheric Administration (NOAA)
1401 Constitution Avenue NW
Washington, DC 20230
301.713.1203
www.noaa.gov

Oceanography Society
P.O. Box 1931
Rockville, MD 20849-1931
301.251.7708
www.tos.org

Woods Hole Oceanographic Institution
266 Woods Hole Road
Woods Hole, MA 02543
508.548.1400
www.whoi.edu

Michael Auerbach/Editor

Agricultural Scientist

Snapshot

Career Cluster(s): Agriculture, Food & Natural Resources, Manufacturing, Science, Technology, Engineering & Mathematics
Interests: Agricultural Science, Agronomy, Environmental Science, Biology, Chemistry, Research, Food Science
Earnings (Yearly Average): $62,920
Employment & Outlook: Average Growth Expected

OVERVIEW

Sphere of Work

Agricultural scientists study crops, farm animals, and other features of the agricultural industry in an effort to increase productivity and enhance the safety of agricultural workers. Agricultural scientists research ways to maximize crop yields, reduce pest infestations and weed growth, and the best ways to minimize the use of soil and water in the agricultural industry. Some agricultural scientists also study the impact of agriculture on the natural environment and work on programs designed to enhance environmental sustainability. Many

agricultural scientists are employed by agricultural companies, conducting research and development, while others provide consulting services, manage farms, conduct research at educational institutions, or work for government agencies.

Work Environment

Agricultural scientists typically divide their time between office and outdoor environments and the amount of time spent in each environment depends largely on a scientist's employer and specific field. In the field, agricultural scientists take samples and measurements from farms, agricultural plots, and natural areas abutting agricultural developments. Some scientists also spend time in laboratories conducting experiments or studying samples collected from the field. Many agricultural scientists conduct regular visits of dairies, feed lots, and other farming facilities and are often required to spend time in rural farming areas outside of major cities. When conducting field research, agricultural scientists may experience a variety of weather and environmental conditions and, in some cases, may be called upon to work in dangerous surroundings. While most U.S. trained agricultural scientists work domestically, there are opportunities for agricultural scientists around the world and some U.S. natives trained in the agricultural sciences can find work overseas, either with U.S. companies operating abroad, through non-governmental or governmental agricultural programs overseas, or by working for foreign companies directly.

Profile

Interests: Data, Things
Working Conditions: Work Both Inside & Outside
Physical Strength: Light Work
Education Needs: Bachelor's Degree, Master's Degree, Doctoral Degree
Licensure/Certification: Recommended
Physical Abilities Not Require: Not Climb, Not Kneel, Not Hear and/or Talk
Opportunities For Experience: Internship, Military Service, Part Time Work
Holland Interest Score*: IRS

* See Appendix A

Occupation Interest

Agricultural scientists fulfill a very important role because they help keep agricultural products safe, processing operations efficient, and output at maximum sustainable levels, while also helping to further the cause of environmental protection and management. Prospective professionals should have a strong interest in environmental science, agriculture, farming, and spending time outdoors, but should also have an interest in research and analysis as much of an agricultural scientist's work involves analyzing data and synthesizing reports.

A Day in the Life—Duties and Responsibilities

The daily responsibilities and duties of agricultural scientists vary significantly based on their area of expertise and employer. For example, soil scientists analyze soil in which crops are grown, while biotechnology specialists study ways to increase crop yields by altering strains of certain crops. Agricultural scientists working for government agencies frequently focus on sustainable development or environmental protection, while those working for private companies often place reduced emphasis on sustainability in favor of attempting to maximizing production and profit.

Agricultural scientists may spend part of a typical day visiting field sites, collecting samples, and/or analyzing data in a laboratory or office. In other cases, scientists may spend time meeting with clients to provide technical data on various agricultural projects. Agricultural scientists also provide public policy guidance for political leaders, sharing information on ways to safeguard the environment and ensure long-term soil fertility and sustainability. In some cases, agricultural scientists diagnose diseases and nutrient problems among animals and crops, assess the severity of insect infestations, track breeding trends, monitor weed growth, and examine the effectiveness of new farming techniques and technologies. Many agricultural scientists conduct controlled experiments in laboratories when developing techniques or new crop strains for production.

Individuals who advance to become senior agricultural scientists may also responsible for managerial tasks, including training technicians and other research assistants. In academic and research environments, agricultural scientists may write grant proposals and manage teams of researchers working on a specific project. Scientists in academia are also typically expected to teach and may spend time working with undergraduate and graduate students in addition to conducting and managing research programs.

Duties and Responsibilities

- Studying crop production to discover the best methods of planting and harvesting
- Determining feed requirements of animals
- Controlling breeding practices to improve strains of animals
- Managing marketing or production operations in companies that produce food products or agricultural supplies and machinery

OCCUPATION SPECIALTIES

Agronomists

Agronomists study how field crops such as corn, wheat and cotton grow. They improve their quality and yield by developing new growth methods and by controlling diseases, pests and weeds.

Animal Scientists

Animal Scientists conduct research on the selection, breeding, feeding, management and health of domestic farm animals.

Dairy Scientists

Dairy Scientists, along with Poultry Scientists. Food Technologists study the chemical, physical and biological nature of food to learn how to safely process, preserve, package, distribute and store it.

Horticulturists

Horticulturists work with fruit, vegetable, greenhouse and nursery crops and ornamental plants. They seek improved quality, yield and methods to resist crop diseases.

Animal Breeders

Animal Breeders, along with Plant Breeders. Entomologists study insects and their relationship to plant and animal life.

WORK ENVIRONMENT

Transferable Skills and Abilities

Communication Skills
- Speaking effectively
- Writing concisely

Interpersonal/Social Skills
- Being able to work independently
- Working as a member of a team

Organization & Management Skills
- Paying attention to and handling details

Research & Planning Skills
- Solving problems

Technical Skills
- Performing scientific, mathematical and technical work

Work Environment Skills
- Working in a laboratory setting
- Working outdoors

Immediate Physical Environment

Agricultural scientists spend part of their time working in office or laboratory environments, but many also spend a significant amount of time traveling and working outdoors when visiting various agricultural sites or projects. Some subfields of agricultural science require frequent outdoor work and activity while scientists in other fields may spend most of their time in offices or laboratories.

Human Environment

Depending on their areas of specialty, agricultural scientists interact and collaborate with a wide range of individuals, including government officials, agricultural technicians, farmers, environmental scientists, business executives, and food scientists. Agricultural science is a collaborative field in which scientists and private or public-sector specialists work together to accomplish shared goals. While some agricultural scientists may conduct much of their work independently, other specialists spend much of their time collaborating, working with teams, or managing assistants, students, and technicians.

Technological Environment

Agricultural scientists work with a wide array of technologies in the field, in the laboratory, and at the office. In the laboratory, agricultural scientists use chemical tools and measurement devices like spectrometers and photometers to study soil and other agricultural materials. In the field, scientists may use soil and water sampling equipment as well as a variety of field measurement and data recording devices. In the office, agricultural scientists frequently use computers and digital tools, utilizing both specialized scientific software and common office software, like word processors, spreadsheet, and presentation programs to work with various types of agricultural data.

EDUCATION, TRAINING, AND ADVANCEMENT

High School/Secondary

High school students interested in a career in science should prepare for higher education and should also take as many classes as possible in the natural sciences. Courses in biology, chemistry, physics, geology, geography, and other sciences will be helpful for future agricultural scientists as well as a strong background in basic mathematics and business/technical writing. With a variety of agricultural science positions available in international locations, experience with foreign language and culture can help prepare for agricultural science careers abroad. Secondary students should also consider part-time or seasonal work and internship opportunities with agricultural companies or, if possible, in an environmental or agricultural science program.

Suggested High School Subjects
- Agricultural Education
- Agricultural Mechanization
- Algebra
- Applied Biology/Chemistry

- Applied Math
- Biology
- Chemistry
- College Preparatory
- English
- Forestry
- Landscaping
- Physics

Related Career Pathways/Majors

Agriculture, Food & Natural Resources Cluster
- Animal Systems Pathway
- Food Products & Processing Systems Pathway
- Plant Systems Pathway

Manufacturing Cluster
- Health, Safety & Environmental Assurance Pathway

Science, Technology, Engineering & Mathematics Cluster
- Science & Mathematics Pathway

Postsecondary

There are many different options for postsecondary students seeking to become agricultural scientists, though most positions in the field require a graduate degree in a related field. Students can pursue agricultural science by specializing in biology, animal sciences, entomology, horticulture, or by applying for programs specifically covering agriculture or agricultural science. In the United States, each state has at least one agricultural education institution, known as "land grant" colleges, that offer education in agricultural science, while many other institutions offer related degrees or courses. While completing a degree, students might also consider applying for internships with agricultural science organizations, academic departments, or businesses to gain on-the-job experience in the field. After completing a bachelor's degree, students may apply for graduate programs in agriculture or a related field and such postgraduate programs can help students gain experience in important topics utilized in agricultural science, such as genetics, biotechnology, and technological design.

Related College Majors
- Agriculture/Agricultural Sciences, General
- Agronomy & Crop Science
- Animal Sciences, General
- Dairy Science
- Entomology
- Food Sciences & Technology
- Foods & Nutrition Science
- Foods & Nutrition Studies, General
- Horticulture Science
- International Agriculture
- Plant Sciences, General
- Poultry Science
- Soil Sciences
- Zoology, General

Adult Job Seekers

Qualified agricultural scientists may apply directly to government agencies, businesses, or educational institutions with open positions. Trained professionals are also advised to join professional organizations, like the American Society of Agronomy or the Soil Science Society of America, which can provide opportunities for networking, learning about new advancements in the field, and can help link professionals with employment opportunities.

Professional Certification and Licensure

In the United States, many states require some types of agricultural scientists to obtain licenses from state-approved boards. Licensure typically involves obtaining an undergraduate degree, gaining supervised experience in the field, and passing a written exam. Although professional certification may not be required to work in many agricultural science fields, such certifications may enhance a candidate's credentials and improve employment opportunities. Many certification programs are offered through professional organizations, like the American Society for Agronomy, which offers certification for agronomists and crop advisors, and The National Association of Animal Breeders, which offers voluntary certification for professional animal husbandry workers. Each nation has its own laws regarding licensing for agricultural scientists and individuals seeking to work abroad should take time to research relevant employment requirements for any area in which he or she might apply for open positions.

Additional Requirements

Agricultural scientists must demonstrate exceptional communications skills as well as research and analytical capabilities. Strong knowledge of computer software is useful for agricultural scientists, as well as excellent writing and speaking skills. As most agricultural science positions involve a considerable amount of outdoor activity and field work, prospective agricultural scientists should be comfortable working outdoors and in close proximity to livestock and other animals, and should be prepared to work under varying weather conditions.

EARNINGS AND ADVANCEMENT

Earnings and Advancement of agricultural scientists depend upon such factors as education, professional experience, individual ability and type of employment. According to the Bureau of Labor Statistics (BLS), agricultural scientists earned a median annual wage of $62,920 in 2016, with those at the lowest end of the spectrum earning less than $37,000, while those at the upper end could earn over $116,000. In many cases, agricultural scientists may receive paid vacations, holidays, and sick days; life and health insurance; and retirement benefits, supplemented by his or her employer. Agricultural scientists working overseas may have widely variable wages depending on the nature of the position and employer. In some cases, agricultural scientists willing to live and work overseas may receive assistance with the logistics of travel and/or assistance with living expenses while staying or living abroad.

EMPLOYMENT AND OUTLOOK

Employment of agricultural and food scientists is expected to grow by 5 percent between 2014 and 2024, which is considered average growth in comparison to the 6-7 percent estimated for all U.S. occupations during the same period. Population growth, dwindling natural resources, and the continuing and deepening environmental degradation brought about by human-mediated climate change has created increased demand for trained agricultural scientists to protect remaining resources and meet increasing demand for agricultural products. There is also increasing demand for agricultural workers willing to work with any of the large number of governmental and non-governmental food and agricultural programs aimed at helping at risk populations. Given the current trends in environmental awareness and public interest, there will also likely be increasing demand for agricultural specialists with knowledge of sustainable practices and the use of alternative energy in agriculture.

Related Occupations
- Agricultural Engineer
- Biological Scientist
- Biomedical Engineer
- Botanist
- Farm & Home Management Advisor
- Fish & Game Warden
- Forester & Conservation Scientist
- Range Manager
- Science Technician
- Soil Scientist

Related Military Occupations
- Environmental Health & Safety Officer
- Life Scientist

MORE INFORMATION

American Society for Horticultural Science
1018 Duke Street
Alexandria, VA 22314-2851
703.836.4606
webmaster@ashs.org
www.ashs.org

American Society of Agronomy
Career Development & Placement Services
5585 Guilford Road
Madison, WI 53711
608.273.8080
ipopkewitz@sciencesocieties.org
www.agronomy.org

Council for Agricultural Science and Technology
4420 W. Lincoln Way
Ames, IA 50014-3447
515.292.2125
www.cast-science.org

Institute of Food and Agricultural Sciences
P.O. Box 110180
Gainesville, FL 32611-0180
352.392.1971
www.ifas.ufl.edu

Soil and Water Conservation Society
945 SW Ankeny Road
Ankeny, IA 50021
515.289.2331
swcs@swcs.org
www.swcs.org

U.S. Department of Agriculture
Natural Resources Conservation Service
14th and Independence Avenue SW
Washington, DC 20250
202.720.3210
www.nrcs.usda.gov

Micah Issitt/Editor

INTERNATIONAL HUMANITARIANISM

For those interested in working abroad who also have an interest in working with and helping people, there are a wide variety of governmental and non-governmental organizations headquartered in the United States that operate around the world providing outreach and services to communities in need. Working in humanitarianism is typically a moral, ethical choice as much as it is a career path and many who take part in humanitarian work do so as volunteers, or accept lower paying positions than might be possible through profit-driven organizations or corporations, sacrificing personal gain for the opportunity to help others or to perform work that benefits humanity.

NGOs (non-governmental organizations) are independent organizations operating outside of governmental divisions or administrations. The term emerged at the end of World War II, and was used primarily to describe the many secular organizations engaged in humanitarian services and outreach. From antiquity, there have been organizations, primarily religious, that traveled to underserved communities to provide food, assistance, medicine, or other services. Likewise, such organizations have long been essential in civil rights efforts around the world. There are more than 20,000 international NGOs operating in 2016/17, ranging in size from small organizations with a handful of employees to massive international organizations like the International Co-Operative Alliance, which has more than a billion volunteers and employees involved connected member organizations around the world.

Fun Fact

More than 12 million people around the world need humanitarian assistance. At least 64 million of them have been forced to flee their homes.
Source: one.org

Working with NGOs and other Humanitarian Organizations

For those interested in working with an international NGO, the first step is to identify an organization or field of interest. NGOs can be broadly divided into different fields, such as education, anti-war, technology, development, human rights, refugee and medical services, environmental action, children and youth services, housing and shelter, and legal aid. With NGOs active in so many different fields, there are opportunities for professionals, students, and volunteers from many different backgrounds and with different skills and levels of education.

Individuals with skill in manual labor, for instance, might seek to work for an organization that performs manual labor, like Habitat for Humanity, which was founded in 1976 and is headquartered in Georgia. Habitat for Humanity specializes in building houses for individuals and families in need. Among other locations, the organization builds homes in Africa, the Middle East, Asia, Europe, Latin America, and the Caribbean. Though Habitat for Humanity needs laborers to participate in their many construction projects, the organization also needs help from individuals with a host of other skills, from business and financial specialists to childcare service experts, linguists and translators, and security and logistics personnel.

While there are many NGOs headquartered in the United States, U.S. residents interested in NGO work can also seek employment through one of the many thousands of other NGOs headquartered in other nations. For instance, the Bangladeshi-based organization BRAC (Building Resources and Communities), the world's largest development-based NGO, employs 115,000 people from around the world and recruits international interns, volunteers, and students to assist with the organization's various projects. Similarly, the Danish Refugee Council, an anti-poverty organization headquartered in Denmark that has provided aid to more than 1 million individuals, has employees and volunteers from across Europe and overseas.

Individuals interested in working with an NGO should research organizations involved in various types of activities. For instance, in the field of development, BRAC, the Acumen Fund, and the Mercy Corps are the three leading organizations worldwide. For those interested in working for human rights, Amnesty International, Human Rights Watch, and Landsea, are the world's three leading NGOs in that category. For those interested in exploring the field, many NGOs offer volunteer programs that allow individuals to explore the field before committing to a professional position. Additionally, many NGOs host seminars, workshops, and orientation programs in the United States for potential employees and volunteers to gain an introduction to the type of work the organization provides and to learn about opportunities for volunteer and paid positions.

The United States Agency for International Development (USAID), created by President John F. Kennedy in a 1961 executive order, is the U.S. government's primary organization for collecting, managing, and distributing international humanitarian aid and services. USAID works directly with a number of NGOs, providing funding and assistance to support their work and has international bureaus and offices around the world. Each regional branch employs professionals from a variety of fields, including administrators, managers, public policy experts, clerical and support staff, financial experts, security guards, human resources experts, and social workers. USAID can also help to connect those interested in international work with volunteer or employment opportunities through USAID itself or through one of the organization's NGO partners.

Conversation With . . .
SHEREEN TEWFIK

Program Manager, Global Leadership Programs
Vital Voices Global Partnership
Washington, DC
International programs manager, 5 ½ years

1. What was your individual career path in terms of education/training, entry-level job, or other significant opportunity?

I grew up in Manhattan with an Egyptian father and a Polish-American mother, so I was exposed to different cultures and foods, and I went to museums regularly. From a very young age, I wanted to learn about different cultures and travel the world.

When it came time to go to college, I didn't know what I wanted to study but chose a liberal arts school because it exposes you to a variety of subjects. At Franklin & Marshall College in Pennsylvania, I started by taking courses that interested me, which led me to major in women and gender studies, and sociology. I worked on the executive board of the college's Alice Drum Women's Center, where we put on programs such as those during the first few months of college—called the Red Zone—when students, particularly freshmen, are most susceptible to assault. I realized I was passionate about service.

After graduation, I thought I wanted to go into social work. I worked at the Green Door Clubhouse in Washington, DC. It was a chance to manage a caseload, do a variety of programming, and teach. I realized I liked building programs.

I returned to New York thinking I would teach. But, after substitute teaching at a preschool and running after-school programs for middle schools, I realized I liked creating programs more than teaching. It was the economic downturn of the late 2000s, so pursuing the job I wanted was tough. I'd always thought about joining the Peace Corps, but was afraid I wouldn't make it since I'm a New York City gal. I applied, was accepted, and in 2011, went to Guatemala as a youth development specialist in the town of Cantel for two years. I taught life skills to middle school students, worked with teachers to help them improve their teaching skills, and ran workshops for parents to help them understand how to support their children during that rocky period of adolescence. I organized their first-ever career fairs and did summer camps.

Now I manage a mentorship program for Vital Voices that pairs international women at the crossroads of their leadership paths with top American female executives. It's called the Fortune-U.S. Department of State Global Women's Mentoring Partnership. Women leaders from other countries come to the U.S. for a month every year and spend two weeks at a mentor company. Then we go to a particular region every year in a follow-up program that works with previous participants to strengthen their business and leadership skills. I've done programs in Jordan, Poland and Nepal and, this year, Ghana.

2. What are the most important skills and/or qualities for someone in your profession, particularly someone who decides to work overseas?

You need to be a big-picture thinker as well as someone who can see the nitty-gritty. Organizational and interpersonal skills are crucial.

3. What do you wish you had known before deciding to work abroad?

That culture rules. You don't realize how much cultural norms dictate behavior until you're in a situation that's totally different. You need to be conscious of the way you are perceived. Also, Murphy's Law: what can go wrong, will. You need to be flexible and resourceful.

4. Are there many job opportunities overseas in your profession? In what specific geographic areas?

Everywhere. It just depends on your interest. For example, if you want to do renewable energy programs, Africa is a good place to go. There are international development programs in every corner of the globe.

5. Will the willingness of professionals in your career to travel and live overseas change in the next five years?

Organizations like the Peace Corps are adjusting to the fact that we are so interconnected. People aren't as willing to live in rural communities as they used to be. People are also concerned with how a move like that serves their career. The private sector is increasingly looking to have a social impact through technology. In addition, we are working with a lot more platforms for things such as webinars. Even people in the most remote areas have a cell phone; unfortunately, we also see women who don't have strong enough internet to stream our webinars.

6. **What do you enjoy most about your job, and what do you enjoy least about your job.**

I most enjoy creating program agendas; it's like a puzzle. I love meeting and learning about our women. I get so inspired. I also enjoy the opportunity to meet our mentors, who are senior-level executives.

I least enjoy the logistics, such as booking flights or negotiating with vendors. That said, anyone thinking about getting into program management will start as a program assistant and will be doing that. It's a foundational building block for this field.

7. **Can you suggest a valuable "try this" for students considering a career overseas in your profession?**

Consider doing an internship because it gives you the opportunity to work in a professional setting. You make inroads at an organization, so you'll not only get the skills you need, but you'll be making connections. Also consider temporary positions. A lot of organizations need someone for a month or two.

Humanitarian Medicine

Doctors Without Borders (Médicins Sans Frontières) is a global, non-profit medical and medical news organization that sends physicians and other health professionals around the world to serve needy populations. The organization was established in 1971 by medical journalists from the French journal *Tonus*, who had been covering a violent military conflict in Biafra, Southern Nigeria and realized there was a need for medical volunteers and specialists willing to travel to areas affected by war and natural disasters. Among their earliest programs, Doctors Without Borders staged a relief effort in Managua, Nicaragua after a 1972 earthquake killed over 30,000 and the organization was also at the center of a 1975 relief effort for victims of the political violence of Cambodia's Pol Pot dictatorship. Operating in 28 nations, Doctors Without Borders employs more than 30,000 physicians and other staff and has served more than 100 million patients since its founding.

Doctors Without Borders was a pioneer in humanitarian medicine, but is now only one of many such organizations operating in the United States and abroad. In addition to physicians in various specialties and fields, humanitarian medical organizations also hire nurses, medical assistants, researchers, technicians, administrators, and a variety of other support personnel in addition to the many thousands of volunteers and interns working for international medical NGOs. Most organizations in the field provide logistical assistance for new employees and volunteers, helping them to obtain the necessary inoculations, arrange travel and accommodations, and to obtain needed licenses and permission to work internationally. Those interested might begin by contacting the World Health Organization (WHO), a branch of the United Nations focused on international healthcare and medicine that has connections to numerous NGOs across the world. The WHO can help connect volunteers and professional employees with humanitarian medical organizations and can also provide information about the many global health and medical crises facing needy populations.

Fun Fact

Average life expectancy in much of the world has increased due to the development of public health systems that bring health education and vaccinations to the general public.
Source: onlinemastersinpublichealth.org.org

Works Used

Davies, Thomas. "NGOs: A Long and Turbulent History." *Theglobaljournal*. The Global Journal. Jan 24 2013. Web. 23 Jul 2017.

Singh, Jerome Amir. "Humanitarian Medicine and Ethics." *Doctorswithoutborders*. MSF USA. 2007. Web. 31 Jul 2017.

"USAID History." *Usaid.gov*. USAID. 2017. Web. 6 Aug 2017.

World Health Organization. *Who.int/en*. 2017. Web. 31 Jul 2017.

Physician

Snapshot

Career Cluster(s): Health Science

Interests: Biology, physiology, chemistry, working with the sick or injured, making decisions quickly, communicating with others

Earnings (Yearly Average): $240-400,000

Employment & Outlook: Much faster than average growth expected

OVERVIEW

Sphere of Work

Physicians, generally called "doctors," care for sick and injured people and research methods to address disease and injury. In the United States, physicians can be divided into two broad specialties: medical doctors (MDs), who use pharmaceutical and surgical methods to treat patients, and doctors of osteopathic medicine (DOs), who use similar procedures and also incorporate preventative techniques and holistic

medical care. Physicians are among the highest paid professionals in the United States and the U.S. medical education industry is among the best in the world, attracting medical students from many foreign nations each year. Because the US medical education system enjoys a strong global reputation, US-trained doctors and surgeons are not limited to domestic employment opportunities and can often find positions living and working abroad. Those willing to sacrifice earning potential for humanitarian reasons can also find opportunities to work with one of many US and foreign humanitarian medical programs operating in at-need communities around the world.

Work Environment

Physicians typically work in medical office settings and in hospitals. Depending on experience and area of specialization, physicians may divide their time between treating patients, conducting medical research, and offering educational instruction to medical students in classroom, hospital, and laboratory settings. The location in which a physician works varies based on whether he or she has a private medical practice, is a researcher or physicians at a hospital or a university, or is employed by a pharmaceutical or health organization. Specialists in humanitarian medicine or emergency triage may travel extensively in their work, treating injuries or illnesses in the field. Some organizations bring physicians to areas in which the population is threatened by violent political unrest and physicians working for these organizations are often required to work in unusual and potentially dangerous environments.

Profile

Interests: Data, People, Things
Working Conditions: Work Inside
Physical Strength: Light Work
Education Needs: Doctoral Degree
Licensure/Certification: Required
Physical Abilities Not Require: Not Climb
Opportunities For Experience: Military Service, Volunteer Work
Holland Interest Score*: ISR

* See Appendix A

Occupation Interest

Becoming a physician in the United States is a long, laborious process that involves completing an undergraduate degree, a four to six-year medical education, and a medical residency and/or fellowship program. Physicians therefore typically spend more than a decade training before beginning their careers as full professionals. Individuals may be attracted to medicine because of the potential for high earnings or may be more motivated by the desire to help people and serve a positive humanitarian purpose. In either case, prospective physicians should have strong interest in the biological sciences and should be able to excel in research and academic pursuits.

A Day in the Life—Duties and Responsibilities

The day-to-day duties of physicians vary depending on their employers and medical specialties. Physicians who operate their own private medical practices spend their days visiting with patients to diagnose and treat illness and injuries. Private physicians instruct patients on strategies to prevent disease by leading healthier lives and prescribe medicines both to treat illness and disease and to prevent future disease.

Physicians employed in the field of medical research spend their days evaluating new treatments, primarily in a laboratory setting. Medical research involves both clinical investigation of the effects of medical treatment on humans over time and investigation of trends in sickness and disease through extensive evaluation of public-health records.

Hospital- and university-employed physicians divide their time between treating patients and instructing medical students while also making occasional forays into medical research. Unlike private practices, in which physicians are also charged with overseeing the administrative and financial aspects of their operations, hospitals and universities offer physicians the assistance of large administrative bodies comprising both medical health professionals and medical students.

Physicians may also choose to work in the field, either through outreach medical institutions or programs or through the military. Humanitarian medical programs bring physicians to a variety of international locations where physicians can bring modern medicine to underserved communities. In some cases, humanitarian medical organizations operate in war zones or areas plagued by frequent violence and physicians in such positions might spend much of their time practicing in makeshift medical structures or outdoors. Military physicians and medics similarly work in unusual conditions and may be subject to dangerous environments in the course of their work.

Duties and Responsibilities

- **Examining patients**
- **Ordering or performing various tests, analyses and x-rays**
- **Prescribing and administering drugs and treatments**
- **Conducting research**
- **Educating students and managing residents**
- **Meeting with clients and their families**

OCCUPATION SPECIALTIES

General Practitioners

General Practitioners diagnose and treat a variety of diseases and injuries in general practice. They order or execute various tests to obtain information on the patient's condition. They analyze the findings and prescribe drugs and other treatments. They make house or emergency calls, refer patients to specialized physicians and perform minor surgery.

Osteopathic Physicians

Osteopathic Physicians diagnose and treat diseases and injuries of the human body, and examine patients to determine symptoms attributable to impairments of the musculoskeletal system. They treat disorders of bones, muscles, nerves and other body systems through surgical procedures or manipulative therapy.

Surgeons

Surgeons perform operations to correct deformities, repair injuries, prevent diseases and improve body functions in patients.

Pediatricians

Pediatricians specialize in the diagnosis and treatment of children's diseases and in preventive medicine for children from birth through adolescence.

Obstetricians

Obstetricians and Gynecologists

Cardiologists

Cardiologists diagnose and treat diseases of the heart.

Psychiatrists

Psychiatrists study, diagnose and treat mental, emotional and behavioral disorders.

Podiatrists

Podiatrists diagnose and treat disorders and diseases of the foot and lower leg.

Radiologists

Radiologists use x-ray and radioactive substances to diagnose and treat diseases of the human body.

Anesthesiologists

Anesthesiologists administer anesthetics to render patients insensible to pain during surgical, obstetrical, and other medical procedures.

Ophthalmologists

Ophthalmologists diagnose and treat diseases and injuries of the eye.

Dermatologists

Dermatologists diagnose and treat diseases of the human skin.

Neurologists

Neurologists diagnose and treat organic diseases and disorders of the human nervous system.

Internists

Internists diagnose and treat diseases and injuries of human internal organ systems.

Family Practitioners

Family Practitioners provide comprehensive medical services for all members of a family, regardless of age or sex, on a continuing basis.

WORK ENVIRONMENT

Transferable Skills and Abilities

Communication Skills
- Speaking effectively
- Writing concisely

Interpersonal/Social Skills
- Being able to remain calm
- Being able to work independently
- Cooperating with others
- Providing support to others
- Working as a member of a team

Organization & Management Skills
- Handling challenging situations
- Making decisions
- Managing people/groups
- Paying attention to and handling details
- Performing duties which change frequently

Research & Planning Skills
- Developing evaluation strategies
- Using logical reasoning

Technical Skills
- Performing scientific, mathematical and technical work

Immediate Physical Environment

Physicians work in a wide variety of academic and medical settings, including laboratories, hospitals, and university classrooms. In some cases, physicians may work outdoors or in medical tents, traveling medical units, or in makeshift triage centers.

Human Environment

Physicians must be excellent interpersonal communicators possessing the capability to explain intricate medical concepts in an understandable manner. As physicians must often discuss sensitive topics with patients, they must be capable of exhibiting compassion and must be capable of diplomacy and tact when meeting with patients and their families. Medicine is a collaborative profession, and physicians are also responsible for working alongside medical assistants, technicians, nurses, orderlies, researchers, and other physicians. In hospital settings, physicians are typically answerable to hospital administrators while, in private practices, physicians might be responsible for managing other personnel.

Technological Environment

Physicians use a vast array of traditional and contemporary medical devices and diagnostic technology, ranging from complex computer software to highly specialized instruments. Various medical specialties have unique manual and computerized tools and software systems and physicians must typically spend years learning to utilize various types of tools and technology in their work. In addition, because medical technology develops and changes rapidly, physicians must continually learn about new software systems, administrative programs, and emerging medical tools entering the field.

EDUCATION, TRAINING, AND ADVANCEMENT

High School/Secondary

High school students can best prepare to enter the medical field by taking high-level courses in algebra, calculus, geometry, biology, chemistry, and physics. Students who become medical doctors usually demonstrate high levels of achievement in academic subjects and participation in extracurricular science and medical programs is an advantage to those applying for acceptance to medical education programs. Volunteerism and charitable work also help high school students attain and hone the interpersonal communication skills relevant to the career and training in foreign culture and language can provide an essential advantage both to physicians who plan to practice in the United States and for those who plan on working overseas.

Suggested High School Subjects

- Algebra
- Biology

- Chemistry
- College Preparatory
- English
- Geometry
- Health Science Technology
- Humanities
- Mathematics
- Physical Education
- Physics
- Physiology
- Psychology
- Science
- Sociology
- Statistics
- Trigonometry

Related Career Pathways/Majors
Health Science Cluster
- Therapeutic Services Pathway

Postsecondary

Medical education is one of the longest and most demanding academic pursuits in the US education system. Aspiring physicians first complete four years of premedicine collegiate courses and must successfully complete collegiate-level courses in organic chemistry, physics, and biology. Such coursework involves investigations into complex topics such as cell biology, genetics, and biochemistry. Students at this level are encouraged to take classes in computer science, language, composition and technical writing, and communication in addition to studying science and mathematics.

Upon the completion of premed studies, aspiring physicians are required to apply and be accepted to a four-year program at one of numerous accredited medical schools. In medical school, students spend time working in a variety of medical fields, such anatomy, internal medicine, and general surgery, and gradually focus on a specific area of interest through internships and intensive study.

Those pursuing a dual MD/PhD program will also need to satisfy the requirements of a doctoral education and may therefore spend six or more years working to complete the dual requirements. MD/PhD programs are aimed at individuals who plan to enter medical research or who plan to focus on medical education in their careers.

Aspiring physicians must then successfully complete a three- to six-year residency program in which they investigate the historical development of and contemporary issues related to their particular realm of medical expertise. Specific medical fields pursued by medical students may include pathology, radiology, clinical medicine, surgery, pediatrics, geriatrics, and neurophysiology. To further specialize in a specific field, such as neurosurgery or emergency pediatrics, a physician might complete a medical fellowship in which he or she will typically work at a hospital overseeing residents and students while working under the supervision of one or more attending physicians and professional specialists.

Related College Majors
- Anatomy
- Human & Animal Physiology
- Medicine (M.D.)
- Osteopathic Medicine
- Pre-Medicine Studies

Adult Job Seekers

The enormous educational commitment required to become a physician makes adult job seekers who have dedicated a significant portion of their careers to other disciplines a rarity in medicine. Medical students often rely on the contacts and professional networks they construct during their lengthy period of education to lay the groundwork for future professional opportunities. There remain several medicine-centric avenues for adult job seekers to begin new careers in the medical field, particular in the realms of nursing, research analytics, and record keeping. Trained physicians interested in international work can begin by utilizing professional physicians' associations in their area or by researching overseas work opportunities through job boards and postings in medical journals and publications. Those interested in humanitarian medicine can apply for positions or internships with humanitarian medical organizations, like

Doctors Without Borders, or a variety of international organizations that provide humanitarian medical services around the world.

Professional Certification or Licensure

In the United States, all physicians must hold and subsequently renew a state medical license, which grants them the right to practice medicine in that state. Medical license applications are reviewed annually by state medical boards. Licensing and certification requirements are specific to each nation and those working internationally may need to satisfy other requirements from national or regional medical organizations or governmental bodies. Typically, physicians hired to work and live abroad receive assistance from their employer in satisfying local licensing requirements.

Additional Requirements

Prospective physicians need to demonstrate dedication to academics and perseverance in the face of challenging coursework. In addition to the desire to help others, aspiring physicians must also be patient communicators who possess the ability to motivate themselves and those around them in the face of adversity. The personal, communicative, and technical skills needed to succeed as a physician also differ according to specialty. A pediatric physician might therefore need skill in communicating with and working with children and their families, while a field like neurosurgery might require far less skill in interpersonal communication. Medical researchers who spend most of their time working in a laboratory with other professionals might only rarely interact with patients or the public in the course of their work, while private practitioners and hospital doctors frequently and continually spend time interacting with patients and family members.

EARNINGS AND ADVANCEMENT

In the United States, wages for physicians are among the highest of all occupations. In 2016, the median salary for physicians ranged from just over $200,000 to more than $400,000 depending on specialization and experience. Anesthesiology is one of the highest paid professions in the United States, with an average salary of $443,853 in 2014, while individuals in family practice earned close to $221,419. Some physicians choose to sacrifice personal earnings to work in fields that provide humanitarian services. There are a variety of outreach medical organizations in the United States that serve underserved and needy communities as well as hundreds of international hospitals and medical programs where U.S. trained physicians can use their education for humanitarian purposes. Earnings vary widely for physicians employed overseas, though there are international hospitals and medical centers that pay competitive or higher wages than might be found in the United States. Physicians may receive paid vacations, holidays, and sick days; life and health insurance; and retirement benefits supplemented by their employer while those in private practice must manage their own insurance, retirement, and leave.

EMPLOYMENT AND OUTLOOK

The aging patterns of the U.S. population has created increasing demand for trained physicians and other medical professionals and the Bureau of Labor Statistics (BLS) estimates that employment in the field will grow by more than 14 percent between 2014 and 2024, which is far faster than the 6-7 percent predicted for all U.S. occupations. Changes in the domestic medical insurance industry play a major role in determining the level of demand for physicians. Individuals with more varied experience and who have trained in more prestigious institutions generally command higher salaries and enjoy a significant advantage in employment in general. Increasing international demand for physicians also means that physicians are not limited to local or national opportunities but can also find fulfilling, gainful employment internationally. Physicians with travel and/or linguistic experience will have a distinct advantage when seeking international employment though such skills are not required for many positions.

Related Occupations
- Allergist & Immunologist
- Anesthesiologist
- Cardiologist
- Chiropractor
- Dentist
- Medical & Health Services Manager
- Medical Scientist
- Neurologist
- Neuropsychologist
- Ophthalmologist
- Optometrist
- Pediatrician
- Physician Assistant
- Podiatrist
- Psychiatrist
- Radiologist
- Surgeon

Related Military Occupations
- Physician & Surgeon

MORE INFORMATION

American Medical Association
515 N State Street
Chicago, IL 60654
800.621.8335
www.ama-assn.org

American Medical Women's Association
Attn: Career Information
100 North 20th Street, 4th Floor
Philadelphia, PA 19103
215.320.3716
info@amwa-doc.org
www.amwa-doc.org

American Osteopathic Association
Public Relations Department
142 East Ontario Street
Chicago, IL 60611
800.621.1773
www.aoa-net.org

American Podiatric Medical Association
9312 Old Georgetown Road
Bethesda, MD 20814
301.581.9200
askapma@apma.org
www.apma.org

Association of American Medical Colleges
2450 N Street, NW
Washington, DC 20037-1126
202.828.0400
amcas@aamc.org
www.aamc.org

National Medical Association
8403 Colesville Road, Suite 920
Silver Spring, MD 20910
202.347.1895
www.nmanet.org

John Pritchard/Editor,
updated by Micah Issitt

Registered Nurse (RN)

Snapshot

Career Cluster(s): Health Science

Interests: Medicine, anatomy, biology, patient care, physiology, psychology

Earnings (Yearly Average): $68,450

Employment & Outlook: Much Faster Than Average Growth Expected

OVERVIEW

Sphere of Work

Registered nurses (RNs) assist physicians in the diagnosis and treatment of various medical conditions and diseases and work with patients in medical centers, offices, and hospitals. Their job largely consists of catering to the physical, mental, and emotional needs of patients, educating patients and their families on proper post-treatment care and pain management, and encouraging wellness and preventive health care

measures. Registered nurses can specialize in a type of treatment, medical condition, organ or body system, patient population, or work setting and nurses specializing in various fields may perform unique tasks specific to their chosen focus.

Work Environment

Most registered nurses work in health care facilities, offices, or hospitals, while home health and private duty nurses work in a variety of settings, often traveling to the homes of individual patients. Some nurses provide public health services to schools, nursing homes, or other community centers. Registered nurses are generally subject to irregular schedules, often working shifts of eight to twelve hours at night, on the weekends, and during holidays; some nurses are even on call to assist patients who need round-the-clock care. Head nurses or supervisor nurses also manage teams of nurses and other medical assistants.

Profile

Interests: Data, People, Things
Working Conditions: Work Inside
Physical Strength: Medium Work
Education Needs: Junior/Technical/Community College, Bachelor's Degree
Licensure/Certification: Required
Physical Abilities Not Require: Not Kneel
Opportunities For Experience: Military Service, Volunteer Work, Part Time Work
Holland Interest Score*: SIE

* See Appendix A

Occupation Interest

Those who succeed in nursing typically have a strong and enduring interest in interacting with and helping other people. Prospective nurses should be empathetic, kind, reassuring, and committed to helping those in physical, mental, and emotional need. Effective communication, physical and emotional endurance, and a sense of discretion are also helpful. Nursing involves difficult interactions and tasks and nurses need to be comfortable with the human body and its functions and able to comfortably handle working with patients who have a variety of disorders or illnesses and often represent diverse backgrounds and cultures.

A Day in the Life—Duties and Responsibilities

Registered nurses juggle many responsibilities during each shift. They may be responsible for a single patient or several patients at a time and may spend time evaluating record patients' symptoms and vital signs and interacting with patients and their families. When necessary, nurses are responsible for ordering diagnostic tests, preparing patients for procedures, conducting laboratory tests, and assessing test results. Registered nurses prescribe and administer treatments according to the patient's plan of care, which may involve tasks as simple as giving a patient antibiotic medication or as complex as providing life support to trauma patients. They also educate patients and family members on post-hospital care, disease prevention, plans of care, and health improvement methods. In many cases, registered nurses take on managerial roles and must perform various administrative tasks, such as budget planning, inventory maintenance, and staff scheduling.

Often, registered nurses must supervise a specific unit or department, which involves overseeing and instructing other nurses and health care professionals. They consult with physicians on treatments and plans of care for patients and assist physicians with patient examinations, treatments, and surgeries, for which they may be required to prepare examination rooms and organize medical equipment. Nurses often follow up with patients more often than physicians, providing continued support and altering plans of care when necessary. Many registered nurses also perform medical research, studying changes in the field of nursing. Public health nurses focus heavily on the educational aspect of the work and design prevention and wellness programs.

There are many opportunities for qualified nurses to travel or live overseas by working for one of many international hospitals, medical centers, or specialized medical programs. Those interested in humanitarian work, for instance, may be able to find work or volunteer opportunities with one of the many international humanitarian medical programs active around the world that

Duties and Responsibilities

- Greeting and familiarizing new patients with hospital routines
- Determining nursing and health needs of patients
- Tending to wounds and injuries
- Preparing patients for surgery
- Aiding the physician during examination and treatment
- Assisting with operations and deliveries by preparing rooms, equipment and supplies and assisting the physician
- Administering prescribed drugs, injections and treatments
- Observing and recording the condition of patients
- Directing and supervising less skilled nursing personnel
- Teaching and counseling patients and their families
- Helping people to improve or maintain their health

OCCUPATION SPECIALTIES

typically focus on providing medical care in at-need or underserved communities.

General Duty Nurses

General Duty Nurses, those who work in hospitals or institutions, provide general or specialized nursing care to patients in hospitals, long-term care facilities or similar institutions.

Occupational Health Nurses

Occupational Health Nurses provide nursing service and first aid to employees or persons who become ill or injured on the premises of department stores, industrial plants or other establishments. They also develop employee programs such as health education and accident prevention.

Office Nurses

Office Nurses care for and treat patients in medical offices as directed by physicians.

Private Duty Nurses

Private Duty Nurses provide constant bedside care to one patient either in a hospital or at the patient's home.

Community Health Nurses

Community Health Nurses instruct individuals and families in health education and disease prevention in community health agencies.

Head Nurses

WORK ENVIRONMENT

Head Nurses supervise and coordinate nursing activities in hospital units. They assign duties and coordinate services.

Immediate Physical Environment

Most nurses work at hospitals, clinics, private homes, and community centers. All nursing work environments must be organized and sanitary; however, private duty, home health, and public health nurses may have less control over the condition of the physical environments in which they work. Nurses constantly bend, walk, and stand and must be physically fit to avoid injury from repetitive motion and strain. Nurses must learn about and follow strict safety protocols to avoid contracting infectious diseases, being exposed to toxins or radiation, and incurring work-related injuries.

Human Environment

Registered nurses regularly work with a diverse staff of other professionals, including doctors, other nurses, physician assistants, administrative personnel, and other hospital or clinic staff. Nurses also frequently interact with patients as well as patients' friends and family members. Registered nurses usually report to a head nurse, supervisor, or physician, while those who advance to head nurse positions might also spend time managing a staff of medical assistants and nurses.

Transferable Skills and Abilities

Communication Skills
- Speaking effectively
- Writing concisely

Interpersonal/Social Skills
- Cooperating with others
- Working as a member of a team

Organization & Management Skills
- Coordinating tasks
- Following instructions
- Making decisions
- Managing people/groups
- Paying attention to and handling details

Technical Skills
- Performing scientific, mathematical and technical work

Technological Environment

Registered nurses use a wide array of technical equipment to aid them in their daily tasks and the types of tools and technology used vary according to the nurse's role and area of specialization. Nurses commonly use manual and computerized medical tools such as stethoscopes, electronic blood pressure monitors, and oxygen masks. As for digital resources, they may use medical reference databases, medical software, and the Internet in their work. While training to become professional nurses, nursing students learn to use a variety of specialized tools and software programs and must continue to learn about emerging technologies and programs as they become available.

EDUCATION, TRAINING, AND ADVANCEMENT

High School/Secondary

High school students who wish to pursue a career in nursing should start by taking courses in the sciences, sociology, psychology, social work, health and nutrition, English, and technology. Preparatory courses in mathematics, physical education, and communications are also beneficial for the prospective nursing student. During the summer months or during school vacations, students can volunteer at or tour local hospitals, clinics, nursing homes, or community centers where they can provide assistance to patients in need. Through these experiences, students can also become familiar with the various responsibilities of a registered nurse. Training in foreign languages and culture is increasingly important for nurses working in multicultural communities in the United States and will provide a distinct advantage to nurses interested in traveling or living abroad as professionals.

Suggested High School Subjects

- Algebra
- Applied Biology/Chemistry
- Applied Communication
- Applied Math
- Biology
- Chemistry
- Child Growth & Development
- College Preparatory
- English
- First Aid Training
- Foods & Nutrition
- Health Science Technology
- Medical Assisting
- Nurse Assisting
- Physical Science
- Physics
- Physiology
- Psychology
- Science
- Social Studies

Related Career Pathways/Majors

Health Science Cluster

- Therapeutic Services Pathway

Postsecondary

After high school, students can enroll in one of three programs to obtain a postsecondary degree in registered nursing. They can earn a bachelor's degree in nursing (BSN), an associate's degree in nursing (ADN), or a three-year diploma from a hospital or medical center. Educational programs in nursing involve coursework in biology, chemistry, anatomy, nutrition, physiology, psychology, psychiatry, human development, pharmacology, and patient care and there are extended education programs aimed at introducing nurses to the specific skills, technologies, and practices of various specialty fields, such as pediatrics, emergency, or transplant surgery. Nursing programs also provide practical clinical experience by placing nurses in health care facilities or hospitals where they can train under the supervision of professional nurses and physicians. Those who wish to specialize in advanced areas of practice or find employment in administration or education must pursue a master's degree in nursing (MSN). An MSN may take two to four years to complete, depending on whether the applicant already holds a BSN degree.

Related College Majors
- Anatomy
- Human & Animal Physiology
- Nursing (L.P.N.)
- Nursing (R.N.)
- Nursing Anesthetist
- Nursing Midwifery

Adult Job Seekers

After obtaining a nursing degree, registered nurses can enter the workforce as staff nurses or private nurses. Many educational institutions help link nurses with potential employers as well as providing links to internships and apprenticeships at hospitals or health centers.

Those who enter nursing through a two-year or associate degree program may have a disadvantage in comparison to nurses who complete a bachelor's degree program. Those who complete the requirements to obtain a master's degree in nursing stand to earn higher salaries and will have an advantage when seeking employment. Many working registered nurses with an ADN or diploma can complete an RN-to-BSN program through a hospital or health care facility. Accelerated one-year BSN or two-year MSN programs are available to individuals who have already earned a bachelor's degree in another field and some employers offer tuition reimbursement for nurses who pursue further education to advance in their field.

Professional Certification and Licensure

In the United States, all nurses must obtain and maintain licenses offered through state nursing or medical boards. To obtain professional licensure, registered nurses must complete an approved nursing program and successfully pass the National Council Licensure Examination (NCLEX-RN). Licensure requirements vary by state, so applicants should consult the National Council of State Boards of Nursing for specific details. Voluntary professional certification is available in certain nursing specialties and may be a requirement for employment or promotion. Continuing education may also be required for ongoing licensure or certification. Requirements for licensing for nurses working in other nations vary according to national and regional laws, and nurses applying for overseas positions need to research relevant legal and administrative procedures needed to meet national legal requirements for their field.

Additional Requirements

Registered nurses must always follow and adapt to changes in the medical field. As new trends and recommendations surface, registered nurses should actively seek to understand and learn more about them. Because the field of medicine is vast and the number of illnesses and disorders is so high, registered nurses must seek to evaluate, diagnose, and treat patients with the greatest degree of accuracy possible. They must also remain calm and clear-headed during emergencies and crises, be able to think on their feet, and make quick executive decisions.

EARNINGS AND ADVANCEMENT

Earnings depend on the type of institution (hospital, medical school, doctor's office or medical center), the geographic location and the employee's education, experience and position. According to the Bureau of Labor Statistics (BLS), registered nurses working in the United States have a median salary of $68,450, with those at the lower end of the spectrum earning less than $47,000, while the highest paid nurses may earn over $100,000 annually. Nurses employed by the government or in hospitals earn higher salaries, on average, than nurses employed in private care or in private practice. Earnings for those working abroad may vary significantly. In countries that have a shortage of trained nurses, nurses may stand to earn more than in the United States while nurses focusing on international humanitarian services may earn lower salaries than possible in the United States.

EMPLOYMENT AND OUTLOOK

The aging of the US population has created an increased demand for trained nurses and other medical professionals and the BLS estimates that employment for registered nurses will grow by 16 percent between 2014 and 2024, which is much faster than the average of 6-7 percent predicted for all US occupations during the same period. Despite growth, high paid nursing positions remain competitive and nurses who have earned advanced degrees or have diverse experience will have an advantage when searching for employment.

- Surgical Technologist

Related Occupations
- Emergency Medical Technician
- Licensed Practical Nurse (L.P.N.)
- Nurse Anesthetist
- Nurse Midwife
- Nurse Practitioner
- Perfusionist
- Physician Assistant

Related Military Occupations
- Registered Nurse

MORE INFORMATION

American Association of Colleges of Nursing
1 Dupont Circle NW, Suite 530
Washington, DC 20036
202.463.6930
www.aacn.nche.edu

Sponsors scholarships for students in nursing programs:
www.aacn.nche.edu/Education/
scholarships.htm

American Nurses Association
8515 Georgia Avenue, Suite 400
Silver Spring, MD 20910-3492
800.274.4262
www.nursingworld.org

American Society of Registered Nurses
1001 Bridgeway, Suite 233
Sausalito, CA 94965
415.331.2700
www.asrn.org

National Council of State Boards of Nursing
111 E. Wacker Drive, Suite 2900
Chicago, IL 60601-4277
312.525.3600
www.ncsbn.org

National League for Nursing
61 Broadway
New York, NY 10006
800.669.1656
www.nln.org

National Student Nurses Association
45 Main Street, Suite 606
Brooklyn, NY 11201
718.210.0705
nsna@nsna.org
www.nsna.org

Briana Nadeau/Editor

Surgeon

Snapshot

Career Cluster(s): Health Science
Interests: Medicine, science, solving problems, analyzing information, detailed work, communicating with others
Earnings (Yearly Average): $252,910
Employment & Outlook: Much Faster Than Average Growth Expected

OVERVIEW

Sphere of Work

Surgeons are physicians specializing in utilizing surgery to treat illnesses and injuries. There are many different types of surgery designed to treat different types of ailments and involving specialized tools and techniques. Most surgeons specialize in a specific field, such as brain surgery, pediatric surgery, or cosmetic surgery, and spend years mastering the specific tools and techniques of their field. Surgeons also examine

patients, perform specific tests, research and evaluate medical records, and counsel patients and their families/friends.

Work Environment

Most surgeons work out of medical facilities, especially hospitals, where they are assisted by nurses and other personnel. While performing an operation, a surgeon typically stands for a long period of time and professionals in the field need to have dexterity, strength, and endurance. Many surgeons work irregular hours and often work more than forty hours per week and many surgeons work at more than one facility, traveling between hospitals or clinics to perform various procedures. Surgeons at times work on call and must be able to travel quickly to a hospital if there is an emergency. Surgeons also have opportunities to live and work abroad or to spend time utilizing their education in humanitarian medical programs and such individuals might be required to work in unusual surroundings and situations.

Profile

Interests: People, Things
Working Conditions: Work Inside
Physical Strength: Light Work
Education Needs: Doctoral Degree
Licensure/Certification: Required
Physical Abilities Not Require: Not Climb, Not Kneel
Opportunities For Experience: Military Service, Volunteer Work
Holland Interest Score*: IRA

* See Appendix A

Occupation Interest

Like most medical professionals, surgeons must undergo extensive education and training, and prospective surgeons should possess a strong interest in research and intellectual activity as well as an interest in physical challenges and manual work. Some surgeons, like other doctors, might be motivated in their careers by empathy and the desire to help others while other surgeons may choose their career solely or primarily based on personal gain and high earning potential. Surgery is detailed, demanding work and professionals should be comfortable handling new challenges and problems as they arise. Successful surgeons are also good communicators with the ability to work closely with other professionals in addition to working with patients and other clients directly.

A Day in the Life—Duties and Responsibilities

The primary duty of a surgeon is to perform operations on patients. In addition to the actual act of surgery, surgeons also examine patients and their medical histories, make diagnoses, and perform specialized tests. Depending on the specialization of the surgeon, the day-to-day activities can vary.

When a surgeon first meets a patient, he or she will analyze the patient's medical history, physical condition, allergies, and other physical aspects, and assess what type of surgery might be used to treat a patient's issues. Based on the examination and the patient's symptoms, the surgeon may call for further tests to be administered. Once the surgeon has determined the best surgical method to use, he or she will thoroughly explain what the procedure entails, its risks, and what the recovery will be like. Successful surgeons also help to make patients and their families/friends comfortable with the procedure that will be performed and to understand the requirements for extended care after an operation.

During the operation, nurses, anesthesiologists, residents, and other specialists aid the surgeon, who directs and manages those assisting. Surgical instruments and tools must be checked for sterility. In addition to a variety of small surgical instruments, modern surgeons use miniature cameras and powered tools.

In some cases, surgeons conduct research on surgical techniques and instruments that can help improve operating procedures and results. Many surgeons publish their research findings in medical journals and attend related conferences. In other cases, surgeons may dedicate some of their time to working in the field or in international medical programs based on serving needy or underserved communities. In such cases, the daily activities and routines can differ widely from standard practices in the United States.

Duties and Responsibilities

- **Conducting personal and medical interviews**
- **Evaluating medical test results and x-rays**
- **Examining surgical equipment to insure a sterile and safe environment**
- **Overseeing the work of numerous assistants and medical technicians**
- **Prescribing medication**

WORK ENVIRONMENT

Immediate Physical Environment

Surgeons work in various medical facilities, such as hospitals and surgical outpatient centers, as well as their own offices. Travel between hospitals and offices is common, especially for specialist surgeons who perform their work at multiple hospitals, clinics, and/or medical centers in a certain area.

Human Environment

Surgeons work alongside a variety of other individuals in the medical profession, including physicians, nurses, medical assistants, and other scientific specialists. Depending on a surgeon's area of expertise, the surgeon may also spend considerable time interacting with patients and their families/friends before and after performing an operation. Like most medical professions, surgery is a collaborative field and the best surgeons have skill in interpersonal communication and management.

Transferable Skills and Abilities

Communication Skills
- Speaking effectively
- Writing concisely

Interpersonal/Social Skills
- Being able to remain calm
- Being patient
- Working as a member of a team

Organization & Management Skills
- Following instructions
- Handling challenging situations
- Making decisions
- Managing people/groups
- Managing time
- Organizing information or materials
- Paying attention to and handling details

Research & Planning Skills
- Using logical reasoning

Technical Skills
- Performing scientific, mathematical and technical work
- Working with your hands

Work Environment Skills
- Working in a medical setting

Technological Environment

Surgeons use a wide range of specially designed instruments and tools, including scalpels, retractors that open tissue, clamps for blood vessels, tubes and needles for injecting fluids, fiber optic endoscopes, and different measuring devices. The types of tools typically used by a surgeon depend largely on the surgeon's specific field and area of specialization. Surgeons must typically spend years to use industry-specific tools and technological devices and must continue to learn about and learn to use new tools as they become available in the industry.

EDUCATION, TRAINING, AND ADVANCEMENT

High School/Secondary

The education and training requirements for surgeons are highly demanding. Surgeons must earn a bachelor's degree with a focus on pre-med education, followed by a medical school education, followed by an on-the-job internship and specialized apprenticeship known as a residency. High schools offer an assortment of basic and advanced courses that will be beneficial to a student interested in becoming a surgeon, including education in mathematics, physics, biology, chemistry, sociology, communications, languages, and computer technology.

Suggested High School Subjects

- Biology
- Chemistry
- College Preparatory
- Computer Science
- English
- Health Science Technology
- Physics
- Physiology
- Science

Related Career Pathways/Majors

Health Science Cluster

- Therapeutic Services Pathway

Postsecondary

Most surgeons complete at least four years of undergraduate studies and four years of medical school, though some medical school programs in the surgical field may require as many as six years of training. An undergraduate studying to be a surgeon should complete courses in biology, physics, chemistry, and mathematics and many colleges and universities offer specialized pre-med programs for those seeking to enter medical school. Learning to communicate well with others both orally and in written form is crucial, so students should also take English and humanities courses. Foreign languages are another area helpful for those working in the United States, or who might plan to spend time working abroad after completing their education. Students can volunteer at hospitals or outpatient clinics in order to gain experience and work alongside professionals.

To continue on to medical school, a student must typically hold a bachelor's or more advanced degree. Applicants must submit transcripts, letters of recommendation, and sometimes essays detailing why they believe they should be selected and must also successfully complete the Medical College Admission Test (MCAT). Gaining admission to medical school is a highly competitive process and students who excel academically and earn high scores on the MCAT examination will have an advantage when seeking employment. Some medical schools offer combined undergraduate and medical school programs that can last six to seven years.

The first two years of medical school are typically spent in a formal classroom and laboratory where students are instructed in anatomy, biochemistry, pathology, medical ethics, and a variety of related topics. Students acquire practical knowledge and skills, such as how to record a patient's medical history, examine patients, and make diagnoses. The last two years are spent working with patients in hospitals or clinics, where students learn about the procedures and techniques involved in surgery under the guidance of experienced professionals. After medical school, surgeons enter a rotating residency in which they acquire hands-on training in a hospital or other medical facility. Residencies can last anywhere from two to eight years and surgical residencies regularly last at least six years, depending on the surgeon's specialization.

Related College Majors
- Anatomy
- Human & Animal Physiology
- Medicine (M.D.)
- Osteopathic Medicine
- Pre-Medicine Studies

Adult Job Seekers

Trained surgeons can apply for open positions at hospitals, clinics, medical centers, teaching facilities, or can attempt to work privately by opening a private practice. Individuals rarely transition from another career to surgery during adulthood due to the extensive training and schooling required and the prohibitively high cost of medical education. Job postings for surgeons can be found through job centers at medical education institutions, through Internet job postings, and through posts in medical publications.

Professional Certification and Licensure

In the United States, surgeons, like other doctors, must be licensed by state medical boards. To obtain a license, a surgeon must graduate from an accredited medical school, pass an examination, and complete one to seven years of graduate medical education. Licenses earned in one state might, in some cases, qualify a surgeon to practice in other states as well. Requirements for surgeons looking to work overseas differ according to national and regional laws. In some nations, surgeons who have completed a US medical program might be immediately qualified to work while, in other nations, surgeons may have to take additional tests or complete a national or regional licensing program.

Additional Requirements

Surgeons must be detail oriented, persistent, and committed to their work. In many specialties, surgeons must also be able to work long, irregular hours and must be able to make decisions quickly during emergencies. Different types of surgeons have different requirements in terms of their interpersonal communication ability as some surgeons spend considerable time interacting with patients and other types of surgeons only rarely interact directly with patients or their families/friends. Different specializations within the surgical field might therefore appeal to individuals with different sets of skills, levels of physical ability, or comfort with communication, teaching, and management.

EARNINGS AND ADVANCEMENT

In the United States, general surgeons earn a median wage of over $200,000, while specialists in many surgical fields regularly earn over $400,000. Surgeons working for humanitarian outreach programs, either in the United States or elsewhere around the world, typically earn far lower salaries for their work and sacrifice personal gain in order to utilize their skills to help others in need. Advancement in surgery typically involves accruing work experience and a reputation in a specific field, which a surgeon can then use to raise rates for procedures or to seek work at more prestigious medical centers or hospitals. Earnings for surgeons typically depend largely on the surgeon's field and number of years in practice.

EMPLOYMENT AND OUTLOOK

According to the Bureau of Labor Statistics (BLS), employment of surgeons and physicians is expected to grow by more than 14 percent between 2014 and 2024, which is far faster than the average growth of 6-7 percent expected for all professions in the US. The increasing demand for medical professionals is a function of the aging of the US population, which has created dramatically increased need for medical professionals. Despite growth in the job market, competition is high for many surgical positions and applicants with diverse work experience and training at more prestigious institutions typically have an advantage in employment. Hospitals and medical education institutions typically assist graduates in finding work and networking through hospitals and other medical conferences, or through medical associations and organizations, is a good way to learn about and prepare for job opportunities as they appear. Surgeons trained in the United States also enjoy many different opportunities for international work, either through humanitarian governmental or non-governmental programs, or by applying for positions in international hospitals or other medical centers.

Related Occupations
- Allergist & Immunologist
- Anesthesiologist
- Cardiologist
- Dentist
- Medical Scientist
- Neurologist
- Ophthalmologist
- Pediatrician
- Physician
- Podiatrist
- Radiologist

Related Military Occupations
- Physician & Surgeon

MORE INFORMATION

American College of Surgeons
633 N Saint Clair Street
Chicago, IL 60611
312.202.5000
postmaster@facs.org
www.facs.org

American Medical Association
Attn: Undergraduate Medical
Education
515 N. State Street
Chicago, IL 60610
800.621.8335
www.ama-assn.org

**American Medical Women's
Association**
Attn: Career Information
100 North 20th Street, 4th Floor
Philadelphia, PA 19103
215.320.3716
info@amwa-doc.org
www.amwa-doc.org

**American Osteopathic
Association**
Public Relations Department
142 East Ontario Street
Chicago, IL 60611
800.621.1773
www.aoa-net.org

American Surgical Association
500 Cummings Center, Suite 4550
Beverly, MA 01915
978.927.8330
www.americansurgical.info

**Association of American Medical
Colleges**
2450 N Street, NW
Washington, DC 20037-1126
202.828.0400
amcas@aamc.org
www.aamc.org

Patrick Cooper/Editor, updated by Micah Issitt

Veterinarian

Snapshot

Career Cluster(s): Agriculture, Food & Natural Resources, Health Science

Interests: Medicine, Biology, Science, Animal Husbandry, Animal Care

Earnings (Yearly Average): $88,770

Employment & Outlook: Faster Than Average Growth Expecteded

OVERVIEW

Sphere of Work

A veterinarian is a physician specializing in the treatment of injuries and disease in non-human animals. In the United States, veterinarians are required to complete a specialized education program to become a Doctor of Veterinary Medicine (DVM). Although the majority of veterinarians work with household pets, some treat wild animals, livestock, and exotic animals in zoos or shelters. A few veterinarians specialize

in preventing the diseases spread by animals and others conduct research related to the medical science of animals. A subspecialty of veterinary medicine involves working with animals in-the field, treating diseases and disorders that affect wildlife or threaten wild populations.

Work Environment

Most veterinarians operate out of a private medical practice or clinic and specialize in one or two animal species. Veterinarians who work primarily with pets (such as cats, dogs, birds, ferrets, and reptiles) typically work more than forty hours per week. Their work environment, while indoors and private, is busy and noisy due to the constant animal traffic in their offices and noise from overnight boarding facilities Veterinarians who work with livestock or horses generally spend long hours outdoors and commute from their offices or homes to farms, barns, or ranches. Veterinarians whose jobs are research based or related to public health work in offices or laboratories and can expect to work regular hours. Field or wildlife veterinarians work in a variety of outdoor environments and in makeshift medical facilities erected in the field and may work variable hours and under a variety of environmental conditions. Depending on the nature of their practice or position, veterinarians may be expected to be "on-call" 24-hours-per-day to deal with emergencies.

Profile

Interests: Data, People, Things
Working Conditions: Work Inside, Work Both Inside and Outside
Physical Strength: Light Work, Medium Work
Education Needs: Doctoral Degree
Licensure/Certification: Required
Physical Abilities Not Require: Not Climb
Opportunities For Experience: Military Service, Volunteer Work, Part Time Work
Holland Interest Score*: IRS

* See Appendix A

Occupation Interest

Successful veterinarians have a genuine, strong interest in animal life and well-being and many are also strongly interested in science, investigation, and research. Though veterinary patients are non-human animals, veterinarians also work closely with animal owners and handlers and successful veterinarians have skill interacting with people as well as with non-human animals. Wildlife and field veterinarians also typically have a passion for conservation, environmental protection, and the preservation of animal species.

A Day in the Life—Duties and Responsibilities

Most veterinarians are general practitioners who work in private medical practices and diagnose and treat pets, including dogs, cats, birds, reptiles, rabbits, hamsters, and other small animals. These veterinarians often perform spaying and neutering operations, orthopedic procedures, animal dentistry, and trauma surgery, as well as euthanize animals they are unable to help. Some veterinarians specialize in livestock and farm animals, operating out of private practices or medical centers that treat cattle, horses, pigs, and other livestock. Livestock vets may spend part of their time working in an office or medical facility, but also typically travel to farms and ranches to diagnose and treat animals on site. A few veterinarians in private practice focus solely on a single type of animal. For instance, there are veterinarians who specialize entirely in the diagnosis and treatment of conditions occurring in equines (horses). Wildlife and field veterinarians, like livestock veterinarians, perform much of their work on-site and may travel extensive distances to reach patient populations. Wildlife vets protect the lives of threatened and endangered animals and prevent diseases from spreading from wild populations to domestic animals or livestock. In some cases, veterinarians specializing in exotic animals and wildlife might work in zoos or other wildlife facilities. Veterinarians in such practices must also know how to capture and subdue wild animals for treatment.

All veterinarians diagnose diseases, perform surgeries, vaccinate, euthanize, medicate, treat broken bones and open wounds, and counsel owners on the proper care, maintenance, and breeding of animals. All veterinarians also perform diagnostic tests, including ultrasounds, x-rays, and blood and stool tests. Some specialized veterinarians work with exotic and wild animals.

While most veterinarians practice medicine, either independently or in an animal clinic/hospital, others specialize in research, working in laboratories to investigate illnesses or other issues that affect certain types of animals. In some cases, veterinary research focuses on investigating diseases that could potentially affect human populations.

In addition to working with animals, veterinarians constantly interact with animal owners, animal handlers, ranchers, farmers, and other professionals who work with animals. Pet owners have increasingly shown a willingness to pay for more sophisticated health care procedures and treatments for their pets, and as pets' health care becomes more advanced, veterinarians must continue to learn new techniques and offer more choices to clients in order to remain financially competitive. In the United States, some veterinary specialists have moved into alternative practices, offering specialized services such as pet chiropractic care or holistic medicine programs for animals.

Duties and Responsibilities

- Treating animals by performing surgery, dressing wounds and setting bones
- Testing and vaccinating animals for disease
- Advising owners on care and breeding of animals
- Performing autopsies to determine the cause of an animal's death
- Inspecting animals to be used as food
- Performing research in areas of animal and human diseases

OCCUPATION SPECIALTIES

Public Health Veterinarians

Public Health Veterinarians control and prevent diseases which are transmitted from animals to humans. They inspect food and drug processing plants and livestock and provide information to the public.

Poultry Veterinarians

Poultry Veterinarians advise poultry raisers on problems, gather information from owners and inspect flocks, pens and housing.

Veterinary Livestock Inspectors

Veterinary Livestock Inspectors test animals for the presence of disease by performing standard clinical tests and submitting specimens of tissues and other parts for laboratory analysis.

Veterinary Virus-Serum Inspectors

Veterinary Virus-Serum Inspectors inspect establishments that manufacture serums, toxins and similar products used in the treatment of animals to enforce state or federal standards.

Veterinary Meat Inspectors

Veterinary Meat Inspectors inspect establishments engaged in slaughtering livestock and processing meat to detect evidence of disease or other conditions.

WORK ENVIRONMENT

Immediate Physical Environment

Most veterinarians in animal clinics, hospitals, or private practices work indoors in clean, well-ventilated clinical settings. Veterinarians who travel to farms or ranches, or who work with wildlife, work outdoors, often in inclement weather and, often, in unsanitary conditions. Veterinarians who perform research usually work in sterile, well-lit offices or laboratories.

Human Environment

All veterinarians must work and interact with numerous other individuals, including office personnel, veterinary technicians, interns, farm or ranch owners and employees, and pet owners.

Transferable Skills and Abilities

Communication Skills
- Speaking effectively
- Writing concisely

Interpersonal/Social Skills
- Cooperating with others
- Working as a member of a team

Organization & Management Skills
- Paying attention to and handling details
- Performing duties which change frequently

Technical Skills
- Performing scientific, mathematical and technical work

Work Environment Skills
- Working with plants or animals

Technological Environment

Veterinarians must be comfortable handling surgical instruments, hypodermic needles, medications, and diagnostic, radiographic, and ultrasound equipment. Veterinarians who primarily perform research must use complex laboratory equipment. As veterinary technology is constantly in a state of flux, with new tools, software programs, and techniques being developed, veterinarians must engage in continuing education to learn about new developments in their field.

EDUCATION, TRAINING, AND ADVANCEMENT

High School/Secondary

High school students who wish to become veterinarians should prepare by obtaining a strong foundation in mathematics and science, with classes in chemistry, biology, physiology, algebra, trigonometry, and physics, as well as environmental science. Future veterinarians also need training in English, health, technology, and communications to supplement their primary studies. Outside of school, students can gain valuable experience with animals by working or volunteering at a local animal shelter, grooming facility, farm, pet store, or general veterinary medical practice. For those interested in working with wildlife, zoos and wild animal shelters may also offer internships or volunteer opportunities for students at the secondary level. Training in foreign languages and culture is also helpful, both for veterinarians planning to work in the increasingly multicultural United States environment and for those seeking opportunities to travel or perform veterinary work abroad.

Suggested High School Subjects

- Algebra
- Biology
- Chemistry
- College Preparatory
- English
- Geometry
- Health Science Technology
- Physical Science
- Physics
- Physiology
- Science
- Social Studies
- Trigonometry

Related Career Pathways/Majors

Agriculture, Food & Natural Resources Cluster
- Animal Systems Pathway

Health Science Cluster
- Therapeutic Services Pathway

Postsecondary

In order to become a veterinarian in the United States, an individual must obtain a Doctor of Veterinary Medicine (DVM or VMD) degree by completing a four-year program in veterinary medicine from a college that has received accreditation by the Council on Education of the American Veterinary Medical Association (AVMA). Although most veterinary programs expect applicants to have earned a bachelor's degree, a few require applicants only to have completed a substantial number of undergraduate semester hours to gain acceptance. To prepare for veterinary training, undergraduate students should study courses like organic and inorganic chemistry, animal nutrition, zoology, cellular biology, business management, and mathematics.

Related College Majors
- Human & Animal Physiology
- Pre-Veterinary Studies
- Veterinary Medicine (D.V.M.)

Adult Job Seekers

Licensed veterinarians can begin to practice immediately; however, new veterinarians often choose to participate in internships at private medical practices. Internships usually last for one year and afford the new veterinarian excellent employment opportunities once finished. Those interested in research apply directly for research jobs with government agencies or private companies. Individuals interested in veterinary specialization, working with horses, livestock, or wildlife, might seek out intership or volunteer opportunities with organizations or specialist practitioners before beginning in private practice or applying for professional positions.

Professional Certification and Licensure

In the United States, veterinarians must be licensed through state veterinary boards and all licenses require veterinarians to obtain a DVM degree and to have successfully passed the North American Veterinary Licensing exam. In many states, veterinary candidates must complete additional testing, which may include a state examination and the evaluation of clinical competency. Some veterinarians choose to specialize in a specific area of medicine; these doctors must be board certified and have successfully completed a residency program in one of thirty-nine AVMA-recognized veterinary specialties. Requirements for veterinarians working abroad differ according to national and regional laws and veterinarians should research any and all legal work requirements before attempting to apply for international positions.

Additional Requirements

Most veterinarians have a general love for animal life and enjoy working with animals and animal owners/handlers. As the situation arises, veterinarians must be comfortable counseling difficult or upset pet owners, demonstrating patience, and offering sympathy and understanding. At the same time, they should be highly analytical and proficient in scientific investigation. Excellent vision, dexterity, and physical strength are important in veterinary practice, especially for those working with certain types of animals. Veterinarians in private practice must also be able to manage and maintain a successful business to which customers want to return, and this may involve marketing, advertising, and expertise in customer service and networking. Veterinarians who have a calm, collected demeanor are often more successful in working directly with animals.

EARNINGS AND ADVANCEMENT

According to the Bureau of Labor Statistics, veterinarians in the United States earn an average annual salary of $88,770, with those at the lower end of the spectrum earning just under $52,000, while those at the higher end of the income spectrum may earn over $160,000. Wages for veterinarians depend largely on the nature of the community in which a veterinarian works and whether or not the veterinarian provides specialized services. Local community veterinarians may therefore earn far less than those in affluent communities or who offer specialized veterinary care. Individuals specializing in animal surgery or in alternative treatments might therefore charge higher rates than general practitioners operating a private, community-based practice. Earnings for veterinarians working abroad or with wildlife and ecological programs, have variable incomes, but typically earn less than veterinarians catering to pets or working in the agricultural industry, and are typically motivated by genuine interest in certain types of animals rather than personal profit.

EMPLOYMENT AND OUTLOOK

The BLS estimates that employment of veterinarians in the United States will increase by approximately 9 percent between 2014 and 2024, which is faster than the average of 6-7 percent predicted for all US occupations during the same period. Despite strong job growth, many veterinary positions in hospitals and clinics, as well as internships with specialists, are highly competitive and individuals with advanced training and experience will have an advantage when seeking employment or advanced training opportunities. Positions working with pets and in high-income communities are more competitive and less abundant than positions working with livestock or in less-affluent areas. US trained veterinarians may be considered qualified for working in other countries as well, and some professionals may find increased opportunities in other regions of the world with a shortage of trained veterinary professionals. Experience with foreign languages and culture will be helpful for those interested in working or living abroad.

Related Occupations
- Microbiologist
- Veterinary Assistant/ Technician
- Wildlife Biologist

Related Military Occupations
- Life Scientist

MORE INFORMATION

American Holistic Veterinary Medical Association
P.O. Box 630
Abingdon, MD 21009-0630
410.569.0795
www.ahvma.org

American Veterinary Medical Association
1931 N. Meacham Road, Suite 100
Schaumburg, IL 60173-4360
800.248.2862
www.avma.org

American Veterinary Medical Foundation
1931 N. Meacham Road
Schaumburg, IL 60173
800.248.2862
www.avmf.org

Association of American Veterinary Medical Colleges
1101 Vermont Avenue, Suite 710
Washington, DC 20005-3521
202.371.9195
www.aavmc.org

National Association of Federal Veterinarians
1910 Sunderland Place, NW
Washington, DC 20036
202.223.4878
www.nafv.net

National Board of Veterinary Medical Examiners
P.O. Box 1356
Bismarck, ND 58502
701.224.0332
www.nbvme.org

U.S. Department of Agriculture
Agricultural Research Service
5601 Sunnyside Avenue, Room 4-1139
Beltsville, MD 20705-5100
301.504.1074
www.ars.usda.gov

GLOBAL RESEARCH AND SCIENTIFIC DISCOVERY

Since before recorded history, adventurous intellectuals have been traveling across national boundaries to explore new regions or to investigate intriguing puzzles of the natural world. By the 18th century, explorers from many European nations were beginning to organize international expeditions, not for the purposes of colonial expansion, but to engage in scientific discovery and inquiry. From the 1764 to 66 voyage of the *HMS Dolphin*, the first scientific voyage funded and organized by the British Royal Navy, more and more western intellectuals began setting off to study the flora, fauna, and natural history of the world.

Resource Conservation

Natural ecosystems do not adhere to national boundaries and the scientists and researchers who are involved in the effort to study biological and natural diversity therefore regularly conduct their research across international lines. Deforestation and other forms of activity that destroy and degrade natural ecosystems have created a global environmental crisis, with thousands of species nearing extinction due to human harvesting of natural resources. This has generated new impetus for scientific exploration and conservation and, in turn, has created many career opportunities for professionals interested in working abroad with expertise or interest in scientific research and the preservation of animal and plant species.

In many cases, careers in biological conservation and research require specialized academic training. Wildlife biologists, for instance, typically obtain a bachelor's or other postsecondary degree in biology or a related field and then go on to pursue a postgraduate degree in zoology or ecology. Those interested in careers in environmental protection and conservation are therefore advised to begin by pursuing higher education in the sciences as well as by seeking out volunteer, internship, or study opportunities in conservation or environmental science.

One of the most rapidly growing fields within conservation ecology is climate science, the study of the earth's climate and the way that the climate affects ecosystems. Climate science is a multidisciplinary field that includes oceanographers, geographers, geologists, marine and wildlife biologists, ecologists, forestry specialists, agricultural managers, atmospheric chemists, physicists, and many other scientific and conservation specialists. Climate scientists not only have opportunities for work through academic or professional organizations, but can also find work with corporations interested in climate management or companies working on products for the renewable and alternative energy industry.

Global Biodiversity

The Missouri Botanical Garden, a research institution in St. Louis, Missouri, funds and participates in dozens of international research programs around the world and researchers, research assistants, and other personnel working for the garden may spend weeks, months, or years living in and exploring botanical environments abroad, typically working alongside local researchers and institutions to broaden the scope of global botanical knowledge. The Missouri Botanical Garden is one of numerous institutions around the world that conduct research on biodiversity and ecology and also manage and fund conservation efforts worldwide.

Forging a career in the biological sciences typically requires specialized knowledge and education. Professional researchers typically obtain postgraduate degrees, though they may begin participating in international scientific studies while still completing their education. The University of California, Santa Barbara, for instance, hosts international research programs in marine biology, ecology, climate science, geology, and more, and facilitates participation for students and researchers at many different levels. Even for those who do not plan to pursue a career as a scientist, international research programs may hire individuals to serve in an assistive or logistical capacity. Students interested in studying biodiversity might begin by contacting the National Science Foundation (NSF), a U.S. governmental organization that has partnerships with numerous scientific research organizations and programs around the world and can help connect students and professionals with a variety of opportunities.

International History and Human Welfare

There are also fields of scientific research that focus on humanity, gathering data that helps to better understand the history of the species and can potentially be useful in improving the human condition in the future. Researchers and research assistants in fields like anthropology and archaeology also depend on international access to complete their research and research organizations in these fields therefore regularly fund and manage overseas research projects and offices.

Anthropologists are researchers who study human societies and so must travel to regions where their subject cultures exist, sometimes spending time living within those societies to better understand their culture and history. Archaeologists study the remnants of ancient societies, exhuming and studying artifacts and other evidence of human activity from history. Those interested in an international career investigating past and present human societies can focus on anthropology or archaeology as a field, or can apply for assistant or volunteer positions with organizations conducting research.

The New Age of Discovery and Collaboration

Over centuries of research, scientists working in many fields have helped to popularize the fact that the ecosystems (both human and non-human) of the world are intricately interconnected and this realization has helped to make scientific research a truly global and collaborative field, often transcending the political and economic competition between nations. While the governments of the United States and Russia have been in nearly constant conflict since the beginning of the Cold War, for instance, scientists from Russia and North American have readily worked together when the opportunity arises, recognizing that the global exchange of knowledge benefits all who participate. International cooperation in science has also become more and more important as the world faces global issues like climate change, disease epidemics, and hunger. Globalization, the processes driving closer economic, social, and cultural links between nations, is a phenomenon that has been viewed with skepticism and fear by those who believe the process has negatively impacted their nations or communities. In science, globalization is a positive and transformative process, helping to bridge gaps in knowledge and adding international data to the global understanding of the planet's evolution and potential futures. For this reason, professionals in scientific research may have the opportunity to live and work in regions or nations that do not as readily invite international participation in fields like finance, business, or resource exploration. Scientists and the professionals who assist in their research thereby demonstrate modes of cooperation and collaboration that might pave the way for governmental partnerships and programs with the potential to address global issues on a global scale.

Works Used

Farhi, Paul and Rosenfeld, Megan. "American Pop Penetrates Worldwide." *Washington Post*. Oct 25 1998. Web. 22 Jul 2017.

"Hollywood, Creative Industries Add $504 Billion to U.S. GDP." *Hollywood Reporter*. Eldridge Industries. Dec 5 2013. Web. 22 Jul 2017.

Physicist

Snapshot

Career Cluster(s): Science, Technology, Engineering & Mathematics

Interests: Science, mathematics, designing and performing experiments, data analysis, numerical data

Earnings (Yearly Average): $114,870

Employment & Outlook: Average Growth Expected

OVERVIEW

Sphere of Work

Physicists research and explore the scientific laws that govern the behavior of the physical world. They design and perform experiments to study matter, energy, and the interaction of physical forces and the scope of their inquiry ranges from the smallest subatomic particles to the basic forces governing all energy and development in the entire universe.

Physicists work for public and private research

institutions, including universities, national space and defense agencies, and corporations engaged in primary or applied physics research. Physicists also teach in high schools, colleges, and universities.

Work Environment

Physicists spend most of their working time in sterile, specialized laboratory environments with access to a variety of specific tools. Laboratories vary in size, ranging from small individual laboratories to large international research facilities, and physicists may travel between different facilities, either within a single country or internationally, to access different tools and to collaborate on projects. Certain types of tools, such as particle accelerators, are only available in a small number of specialized facilities and physicists may therefore travel to these locations when certain types of equipment are needed. Physicists also work in an office setting when writing about their research, applying for grants, or conducting academic activities such as mentoring or meeting with students at various levels. Physicists often work in teams that include specialists from other scientific disciplines, including engineers, astronomers, mathematicians, theoretical chemists, and many other types of scientists.

Profile

Interests: Data, People, Things
Working Conditions: Work Inside
Physical Strength: Light Work
Education Needs: Doctoral Degree
Licensure/Certification: Usually Not Required
Physical Abilities Not Require: Not Climb, Not Kneel, Not Hear and/or Talk
Opportunities For Experience: Military Service, Volunteer Work, Part Time Work
Holland Interest Score*: IRE

* See Appendix A

Occupation Interest

Physics appeals to individuals who like to design, build, and perform physical experiments and to individuals who have curious, inquisitive minds and a strong interest in the natural world. Physicists need to have imagination, creativity, and a high capacity for intellectual analysis and rigorous manipulation of complex mathematical data. Aspiring physicists should be prepared for a long academic career, including undergraduate, postgraduate, and doctoral work, as well as years of on-the-job training.

A Day in the Life—Duties and Responsibilities

The day-to-day work of a physicist typically involves conducting experiments and analyzing data. Physicists work regularly with other scientists, technicians, and engineers in the design and implementation of experiments. While some physics experiments employ simple designs, others involve complex computer models and extensive use of specialized scientific apparatuses. Once an experiment has been conducted, physicists perform data analysis, in which they and their colleagues pore over data generated by the experiment and attempt to interpret the results. While experiments take place in laboratories, data analysis is often conducted in an office environment.

Physicists in a high school or academic setting spend much of their time in classrooms, conducting lectures and monitoring student experiments. They also attend seminars and spend time grading student work. More experienced physicists spend some of their time conducting administrative tasks, including writing grant applications, academic articles, and research reports. Physicists involved in larger projects with teams of other researchers often travel to different locations around the world to conduct their work. However, some physics experiments can be conducted live or recorded on a digital feed, allowing the data to be analyzed and interpreted by scientists working in different locations and different time zones.

Physicists work in a variety of fields and specialties, including atomic physics, astronomy, astrophysics, biophysics, and mathematical physics. Other disciplines include nonlinear dynamics, quantum field theory, relativity, and cosmology.

Duties and Responsibilities

- Devising procedures for conducting research and physical testing of materials
- Determining physical properties of materials
- Relating and interpreting research
- Describing observations and conclusions in mathematical terms
- Developing theories/laws based on observation and experiments
- Developing mathematical tables and charts
- Supervising scientific activities in research

OCCUPATION SPECIALTIES

Electro-Optical Engineers

Electro-Optical Engineers conduct research and plan developments and the design of gas and solid state lasers and other light emitting and light sensitive devices.

Theoretical Physicists

Theoretical Physicists design, conceive and interpret experiments in physics and formulate theories consistent with obtained data. They analyze the results of experiments that are designed to detect and measure previously unobserved physical phenomena.

WORK ENVIRONMENT

Immediate Physical Environment

Physicists spend an equal amount of time in the laboratory and in the office, generally in urban or suburban environments. Those employed as teachers spend most of their time in schools and classrooms. Some academic positions may be located in rural settings. Research physicists and astrophysicists may travel frequently to collaborate with teams in other areas, or in foreign countries, and to access specialized equipment for certain experiments.

Transferable Skills and Abilities

Organization & Management Skills
- Coordinating tasks
- Managing people/groups
- Paying attention to and handling details
- Performing duties which change frequently

Research & Planning Skills
- Analyzing information
- Developing evaluation strategies

Technical Skills
- Performing scientific, mathematical and technical work
- Working with machines, tools or other objects

Human Environment

Physicists often work in teams with other scientists. They also interact with nonscientists, such as politicians and education administrators, in order to acquire funding for their work, so good interpersonal skills are invaluable.

Technological Environment

Physicists work with cutting-edge technology and physics research utilizes some of the most complex experimental devices ever invented. Because physics underlies all other scientific fields, physicists are often at the forefront of experimental design and research from physics is utilized by scientists around the world studying a variety of different disciplines. Physicists also use a variety of laboratory equipment, including telescopes, amplifiers, chemical processors, spectrometers, and video equipment. Physicists must also be able to use basic office technology, including personal computers and mobile digital tools, and should be familiar with office software, including word processing, spreadsheet, and presentation programs.

EDUCATION, TRAINING, AND ADVANCEMENT

High School/Secondary

Students interested in physics should focus their efforts at the secondary level on achieving a well-rounded basis in physical science and mathematics. Classes in physics, applied physics, chemistry, and electronics are essential, as are math classes such as algebra, applied mathematics, calculus, geometry, trigonometry, and statistics, and classes in computer science and technology, when available. If possible, students should enroll in advanced placement (AP) courses or should take part in academic programs for students with higher than average aptitude in mathematics and science. Writing and reading skills are also important, as physicists are routinely required to write reports, apply for funding, and communicate their findings. In addition to their course work, students interested in physics should consider attending science camps and participating in science and technological clubs in their area.

Suggested High School Subjects

- Algebra
- Applied Math
- Applied Physics
- Calculus
- Chemistry
- College Preparatory
- Computer Science
- Electricity & Electronics
- English
- Geometry
- Mathematics
- Physics
- Science
- Statistics
- Trigonometry

Related Career Pathways/Majors

Science, Technology, Engineering & Mathematics Cluster
- Science & Mathematics Pathway

Postsecondary

A person interested in a career as physicist should be prepared to pursue the field through the doctoral level. Though some research assistant/technician, or secondary level teaching positions may require only a bachelor's degree, those aspiring to become researchers must take their education further. Aspiring research physicists should begin by earning a bachelor's degree in physics or a related field, which will typically include training in key physical science subjects like quantum mechanics, thermodynamics, optics, and electromagnetism. A double major in mathematics can be helpful as physical science research depends heavily on mathematical calculation and the interpretation of numerical data.

Graduate students in physics usually specialize in specific subfield, such as particle physics, medical physics, or optical physics. A master's degree in physics can improve a candidate's eligibility for jobs in academia and a variety of positions in applied physics research and development in the corporate world. However, the successful completion of a doctoral program is required for those seeking to conduct research at the top level.

In the United States, there are approximately 190 universities and colleges with doctoral programs in physics. Doctoral students spend five to seven years doing course work and conducting research before earning a Ph.D. in physics. Typically, those who earn their Ph.D. spend two to three additional years training in a postdoctoral position, deepening their understanding of their specialty through work with senior physicists. There are also numerous educational institutions in Europe and Asia with well-respected physics departments and programs and students interested in international travel may therefore also apply for study abroad programs or directly to foreign institutions for acceptance as full students.

Related College Majors
- Anatomy
- Astrophysics

- Chemistry, General
- Earth & Planetary Sciences
- Engineering Physics
- Physics, General

Adult Job Seekers

Adult job seekers interested in physics should investigate undergraduate and graduate programs in a physics-related specialty. Newly trained physicists are encouraged to attended employer conferences and job seminars. The website for the Society of Physics maintains updated information about networking and employment opportunities in the field. Depending on their area of specialization, physicists can seek employment in engineering, science, and/or education.

Professional Certification and Licensure

Generally, physicists are not required to earn any special certificate or license. There are some exceptions for physicists employed in engineering jobs and, in some cases, physicists may need specialized training to learn how to operate complex experimental equipment or computer programs. As many physicists play a role in designing their own experiments, some study computer coding in order to modify or create programs to help in their research or analysis.

Additional Requirements

Physicists should enjoy both designing and performing experiments and have a solid understanding of mathematics. Physicists need to be comfortable working independently and spending long periods performing complex measurements, analyses, and experiments, but should also be willing and able to collaborate and work alongside other scientists, assistants, and students.

EARNINGS AND ADVANCEMENT

According to the Bureau of Labor Statistics (BLS), physicists working in the United States earned median annual salaries of approximately $114,870 in 2016. Wages vary considerably in the field, with those at the lower end earning less than $50,000, while those at the upper end of the spectrum, most of whom work for medical or applied research institutions, can earn over $160,000 per year. Physicists typically receive certain employer-supplemented benefits, such as retirement and insurance and paid leave and vacations. Like many other scientific researchers, physicists contribute to their own earnings by participating in applying for grants from scientific funding organizations and governmental agencies. Physicists able to earn larger sums in grants therefore stand to earn higher annual wages as well as having the ability to fund more complex and expensive research projects.

EMPLOYMENT AND OUTLOOK

According to the BLS, employment in physics and astronomy is expected to grow by approximately 7 percent between 2014 and 2024, which is average growth compared to the 6-7 percent growth expected for all US occupations during the same period. Most funding for physics research comes from federal government funding sources in the United States and so political and cultural interest in physics research and the potential applications of the physical sciences determines relative funding levels and so affects growth in the industry. Competition for higher paid and senior research positions is considerable and individuals with higher degrees and levels of experience will therefore have a considerable advantage when seeking employment.

Related Occupations
- Astronomer
- College Faculty Member
- Medical Scientist
- Meteorologist

Related Military Occupations
- Nuclear Engineer
- Physicist

MORE INFORMATION

American Association for the Advancement of Science
1200 New York Avenue NW
Washington, DC 20005
202.326.6400
webmaster@aaas.org
www.aaas.org

American Association of Physics Teachers
1 Physics Ellipse
College Park, MD 20740-3845
301.209.3311
webmaster@aapt.org
www.aapt.org

American Astronomical Society
2000 Florida Avenue, NW, Suite 400
Washington, DC 20009-1231
202.328.2010
www.aas.org

American Center for Physics
1 Physics Ellipse
College Park, MD 20740
301.209.3000
www.acp.org

American Institute of Physics
Education Division
One Physics Ellipse
College Park, MD 20740-3843
301.209.3100
www.aip.org

American Physical Society
Education Department
One Physics Ellipse
College Park, MD 20740-3844
301.209.3200
www.aps.org

Association for Women in Science
1442 Duke Street
Alexandria, VA 22314
703.372.4380
awis@awis.org
www.awis.org

National Aeronautics and Space Administration
Public Communications Office
Suite 5K39
NASA Headquarters
Washington, DC 20546-0000
202.358.0000
public-inquiries@hq.nasa.gov
www.nasa.gov

R. C. Lutz/Editor

Astronomer

Snapshot

Career Cluster(s): Science, Technology, Engineering & Mathematics

Interests: Mathematics, physics, chemistry, engineering, research, appreciation of the unknown

Earnings (Yearly Average): $104,740

Employment & Outlook: Average Growth Expected

OVERVIEW

Sphere of Work

An astronomer is a scientist who studies celestial objects like planets, moons, and stars, and natural space phenomena like black holes, sunspots, and quasars.

Astronomers also research interstellar mediums such as dust, gases, and cosmic rays and develop complex models to help understand the past, present, and future of cosmic evolution. Astronomers spend most of their time conducting research, using theoretical models and equipment such

as telescopes and radio observatories to gather and interpret data. Most professional astronomers also write and publish scholarly papers and present their findings at various governmental, academic, and scientific conferences.

Work Environment

Astronomical research often requires finding and utilizing specialized environments known as "dark sky locations," which are typically in remote locations far enough from nearby settlements to have low levels of light pollution. Astronomers actively conducting astronomical research may therefore need to travel frequently and spend long hours working in the field, locating and utilizing dark sky locations to observe various phenomena using telescopes and other observational tools. Astronomers conducting research may work irregular hours as they must schedule their observations and other research to coincide with periodic natural phenomena that may only be visible at certain times of the day or year. When not conducting field research, astronomers typically work in offices or laboratories where they evaluate data and create models of various phenomena. There are many observation locations located in the United States, but many research astronomers also travel abroad to take advantage of astronomical equipment located in other countries or to collaborate with researchers working on complimentary projects. Many astronomical research programs involve collaborations between scientists working in different countries or regions and astronomers frequently have the opportunity to travel abroad for work, whether for short-term research projects or to live and work overseas for extended periods.

Profile

Interests: Data
Working Conditions: Work Inside
Physical Strength: Light Work
Education Needs: Bachelor's Degree, Master's Degree, Doctoral Degree
Licensure/Certification: Usually Not Requiredd
Physical Abilities Not Require: Not Climb, Not Kneel, Not Hear and/or Talk
Opportunities For Experience: Military Service, Volunteer Work, Part Time Work
Holland Interest Score*: IRE

* See Appendix A

Occupation Interest

Individuals interested in pursuing astronomy should have a strong interest in the physical and natural sciences and should be able to demonstrate exceptional skill in mathematics and physics. Astronomers are often drawn to their field because of a strong curiosity about the natural world and astronomical phenomena and should enjoy attempting to investigate unexplained phenomena. Astronomers typically have advanced degrees beyond the undergraduate level, including both postgraduate and doctoral degrees, and prospective astronomers should therefore have strong interest in conducting research and academic study. In addition, astronomy, like most sciences, is a collaborative field in which researchers succeed by working together and building on research conducted by past and contemporary professionals, both locally and around the world.

A Day in the Life–Duties and Responsibilities

Much of the typical work day for an astronomer is spent in the laboratory conducting research and studying data. Astronomers may conduct experiments using a variety of equipment including particle accelerators, lasers, and radio systems and astronomers often use data to create models and formulate theories about space phenomena. Using mathematics and physics, astronomers will attempt to discover new objects, study cosmic forces, and chart the observable universe. In addition to laboratory work, astronomers may also spend weeks or longer working outdoors or in remote locations, operating equipment such as large optical and radio telescopes to collect data to support their research.

Drawing on data from experiments and other researchers, astronomers may then spend time formulating hypotheses and writing and publishing scholarly papers on their research. Astronomers may also be asked to give reports to government agencies (such as NASA), and other scientific bodies or organizations. Astronomers must often present their findings and theories to their peers—and, to an extent, the general public—an activity that often occurs at universities, astronomy-oriented conferences, or within the organization at which the astronomer is employed. In light of this responsibility, astronomers benefit from strong communication and presentation skills and the ability to explain complex data to inexperienced audiences.

Along with their research pursuits, many astronomers have more managerial and technical responsibilities. Some astronomers, for example, work in planetariums, where they are responsible for providing non-technical presentations on space to students and other visitors. Other astronomers must maintain research equipment, a responsibility which includes cleaning optical telescope lenses, calibrating radio dishes, and coordinating satellite-based technologies. In some cases, professional astronomers also act as managers, overseeing students, assistants, and research technicians who assist in conducting research.

Duties and Responsibilities

- Developing theories, projects and ways to test them
- Testing theories through observation and analysis of results
- Developing conclusions based on test results
- Teaching classes in astronomy and/or physics
- Developing mathematical tables and charts for navigational and other purposes
- Designing new optical instruments for observation

WORK ENVIRONMENT

Immediate Physical Environment

Most astronomical work is performed indoors, in temperature controlled laboratories and observatories. In both of these settings, the environment must be clean and well-organized in order to prevent corruption of data and/or equipment malfunctions and facility accidents. Astronomers may also spend time traveling to various observatories and other facilities around the country or internationally to conduct their research and may spend extended periods at remote locations while conducting observational research.

Transferable Skills and Abilities

Communication Skills
- Speaking effectively
- Writing concisely

Interpersonal/Social Skills
- Being able to work independently

Organization & Management Skills
- Making decisions
- Paying attention to and handling details

Research & Planning Skills
- Creating ideas

Technical Skills
- Performing scientific, mathematical and technical work
- Working with data or numbers

Plant Environment

Astronomers work in small, medium, and large laboratories, observatories, and similar facilities. These research facilities may be based in academia, such as at a research university or college, where astronomers are also responsible for writing grants to fund research and for teaching and supervising students. Alternatively, astronomers may work at government-funded labs and national observatories, such as those managed by NASA or other governmental astronomical organizations. Astronomers can also work in planetariums and museums that make scientific discoveries and information accessible to the public and to students of various ages.

Human Environment

Astronomers must work with a number of other team members, collaborating on research and operating equipment. Astronomers will work with fellow astronomers, engineers, physicists, and mathematicians. They will also work with other non-scientific personnel, such as facilities managers and directors. Furthermore, professional astronomers may be joined by interns, university students, and computer scientists. Astronomers employed as professors at research universities or teaching colleges must interact with the students they are teaching and advising.

Technological Environment

Astronomers use a wide range of technological equipment both in observational research and when conducting experiments and analyzing data in a laboratory or office. Astronomers typically learn how to operate optical and radio telescopes, lasers, particle accelerators, and other large-scale equipment typically used to collect physical or astronomical data. Astronomers also need a strong familiarity with computer science as complex computer systems and software are common tools used to manage, manipulate, and evaluate data. In addition, astronomers need a general knowledge of office tools and technology, including word processing, presentation, and spreadsheet software, and must be proficient in the use of digital communication and networking tools.

EDUCATION, TRAINING, AND ADVANCEMENT

High School/Secondary

High school students who wish to become astronomers can best prepare by studying mathematics through pre-calculus levels in order to develop a strong groundwork for complex mathematics courses as the postsecondary and graduate levels. Additionally, secondary students should take courses in chemistry and physics and other physical and natural sciences. Many students take physics and mathematics at the advanced placement (AP) level, although such training is not required. To further their early understanding of astronomy, students should also consider joining science-related groups at their school, participating in a state-sponsored junior academy of science, or simply participating in activities through an amateur astronomy club or organization. Lastly, many professional astronomers begin their careers as amateur astronomers, using telescopes and other tools to begin learning the process of observing and studying natural astronomical objects and phenomena.

Suggested High School Subjects
- Algebra
- Applied Math
- Applied Physics
- Calculus
- Chemistry

- Algebra
- Applied Math
- Applied Physics
- Calculus
- Chemistry
- Earth Science
- English
- Mathematics
- Physical Science
- Physics
- Science
- Trigonometry

Related Career Pathways/Majors

Science, Technology, Engineering & Mathematics Cluster

- Science & Mathematics Pathway

Postsecondary

Because astronomy is often considered a subfield of physics, students at the collegiate and postgraduate levels will study other subsets or branches within this field, including magnetism, atomic and nuclear physics, thermodynamics, statistical mechanics, and quantum physics and theory. College students should also continue to build on their mathematical skills, including courses in advanced algebra, calculus, and trigonometry. Additionally, the fact that twenty-first-century astronomy relies on computers for data collection and model building means that undergraduate college students must study computer science to help them explore new concepts in this field. Some colleges and universities might offer undergraduate degrees in astronomy, while other institutions might only offer related physics degrees, which can also be used to apply for post-graduate training programs.

After the undergraduate level, students hoping to become professional astronomers will need to obtain at least a master's degree, while most professional researchers obtain a doctorate degree in astronomy or a specific subfield. In addition to the continuation of core courses in physics, astronomy, and astrophysics, much of the work at this level is research-oriented, and students must design and pursue their own individual projects under the supervision of senior researchers.

Related College Majors
- Astronomy
- Astrophysics
- Chemistry, General
- Earth & Planetary Sciences
- Physics, General

Adult Job Seekers

People become astronomers after many years of educational training and many astronomers find employment by networking through educational or professional organizations. Professional associations such as the American Astronomical Society (AAS) and similar regional organizations often provide networking opportunities and resources for professionals seeking employment.

Professional Certification and Licensure

In the United States, there are no specific licenses or certification requirements for professional astronomers, however, in order to operate and maintain some astronomical equipment, such as radio telescopes, some facilities require professionals to participate in a training program that grants a certification of expertise. Requirements for astronomers working abroad vary according to national and regional laws and astronomers hoping to conduct research or work in foreign nations must research the specific national laws and guidelines for scientific research and foreign employment.

Additional Requirements

Astronomers pursue knowledge about the fundamental nature, history, and future of the universe and successful astronomers need to be intellectually curious, and dedicated enough to invest significant time attempting to find difficult and elusive information, and should be open minded and willing to learn about new and emerging theories. In addition to this exploratory mindset, astronomers must be patient as astronomical research and discovery can move at a very gradual pace. Astronomers may spend long periods working in remote observatories and may spend years trying to validate or disprove a single hypothesis, some of which may have been created before most contemporary astronomers were born.

EARNINGS AND ADVANCEMENT

According to the Bureau of Labor Statistics (BLS), astronomers working in the United States earned a median annual wage of $104,740 in 2016, though salaries in the field are highly dependent on the specifics of an astronomer's employment and their relative level of seniority, and salaries in the field can range from less than $50,000 to over $180,000. Astronomers typically work for institutions or organizations that provide paid vacations, holidays, and sick days; life and health insurance; and retirement benefits. In many cases, researchers are paid a standard salary and can receive additional funds by winning grants from organizations and institutions that support scientific research. Astronomers who are skilled in grant writing can therefore earn far higher salaries in a given year and will be able to fund and support more extensive research projects and studies.

EMPLOYMENT AND OUTLOOK

According to the BLS, employment of astronomers and physicists is expected to grow by 7 percent between 2014 and 2024, which is average growth compared to the 6-7 percent predicted for all US occupations during this same period. Increases or decreases in federal funding for scientific research can have a significant effect on the astronomical research industry. Political and cultural developments that inspire higher levels of interest in space exploration and/or research therefore lead to more opportunities for professionals in the field. Due to average growth, compared to levels of interest at the student level, competition for permanent research postings can be significant and researchers with prestigious educational backgrounds or who have accrued more work experience might therefore have an advantage in the field. Given strong competition in the United States, an increasing number of US trained researchers might consider applying for positions with foreign universities or scientific institutions.

Related Occupations
- College Faculty Member
- Meteorologist
- Physicist

MORE INFORMATION

American Association of Amateur Astronomers
P.O. Box 7981
Dallas, TX 75209-0981
www.astromax.com

American Astronomical Society
2000 Florida Avenue, NW, Suite 400
Washington, DC 20009-1231
202.328.2010
www.aas.org

National Aeronautics and Space Administration
NASA Headquarters, Suite 5K39
Washington, DC 20546-0001
202.358.0001
www.nasa.gov

Sky and Telescope **Magazine**
Sky Publishing
90 Sherman Street
Cambridge, MA 02140
617.864.7360
www.skyandtelescope.com

Michael Auerbach/Editor,
updated by Micah Issitt

Botanist

Snapshot

Career Cluster(s): Agriculture, Food & Natural Resources, Science, Technology, Engineering & Mathematics

Interests: Plant life, plant biology, environmental studies, nature, working outdoors

Earnings (Yearly Average): $60,520

Employment & Outlook: Slower Than Average Growth Expected

OVERVIEW

Sphere of Work

Botanists are scientists who study plants and plant characteristics as well as the environments in which plants grow, studying how chemical and biological factors within ecosystems affect plant growth and development. Some botanists specialize in the study of plant life processes or cultivate useful plants for food, while others focus on the structure of plants, species hierarchy, or how different plants react to adverse environmental

conditions. Botanists are employed by universities, government agencies, and private organizations where they conduct research and prepare professional publications. Some botanists help to bring botanical knowledge to the public by working for botanical gardens and other educational botanical programs.

Work Environment

Depending on a botanist's specialization and employer, he or she may conduct much of their work in office or laboratory environments or may spend most of their time working outdoors, in the field, studying plants and the environments in which they grow. To locate species for research, botanists may travel and spend time in remote locations and many research and field botanists travel internationally and spend much of their time in the field hiking or otherwise traveling to interesting botanical areas. Back in the office or laboratory, botanists spend time examining plants and conducting experiments on various botanical behaviors and characteristics. Some botanists working in academic environments might also spend time teaching students at the undergraduate and postgraduate levels. Zoos, museums, arboretums, and botanical gardens hire botanists to conduct research, to create interesting botanical communities, and to participate in educational programs.

Profile

Interests: Data, Things
Working Conditions: Work Outside, Work Inside and Outside
Physical Strength: Light Work
Education Needs: Bachelor's Degree, Master's Degree
Licensure/Certification: Usually Not Requiredd
Physical Abilities Not Require: Not Climb, Not Hear and/or Talk
Opportunities For Experience: Internship
Holland Interest Score*: IRS

* See Appendix A

Occupation Interest

Botanists, like most biologists, are usually drawn to their careers through a personal, profound interest in environmentalism and natural history. Plants of various types are the basis of all life on earth, forming the basis of food chains that fuel the emergence and diversification of animal species and ultimately provide the material basis for human life and culture. While some botanists study plants because of a relatively pure interest in plant life, others take a different approach, utilizing their knowledge of plant biology to improve agriculture or to fuel plant-based economic industries and botanists may therefore approach their careers from a variety of basic perspectives and levels of interest. Though some botanists work primarily in laboratories or offices, most botanists spend much of their time in the field, studying plants as they occur in nature, and successful botanists therefore tend to have a profound and enduring love of nature and outdoor activities in addition to strong intellectual curiosity and an appreciation for the scientific process.

A Day in the Life—Duties and Responsibilities

Botanists conduct basic or applied research on trees, mosses, flowering plants, fungi, algae, and other types of plants. In basic research, inquiry is driven by curiosity; in applied research, study is geared towards testing a specific theory or advancing the development of a product and therefore has a specific purpose in society.

In order to conduct their research, whether it is basic or applied, many botanists spend considerable time in remote locations. Many botanists specialize in certain plant groups or families and may therefore travel domestically or internationally to research different species within a family. For instance, a specialist in the plant family Cactaceae, which contains many species of cactus and succulents, might conduct research in many locations around the United States, but might also travel to South America, Africa, or many other international locations where unique species of cactus occur in nature. When conducting research, botanists collect samples, observe and document growth and distribution patterns, and take measurements of environmental variables, such as level of light, soil quality, and the availability of water.

Returning to the laboratory, the type of research conducted by a botanist can vary widely. Taxonomic botanists preserve and study plant samples in an effort to organize various species into different taxonomic groups, like genera or species, while plant physiologists conduct experiments on living plants or tissues, studying how plants metabolize, grow, and behave within their environments. Many botanists work for non-profit institutions such as universities and scientific foundations and, in these environments, botanists typically need to contribute to funding their own research projects by applying for grants and/or research fellowships. Research botanists may therefore spend considerable time researching and applying for various types of funds to support their studies.

Many botanists are also employed by government agencies, such as the US Department of Agriculture and the US Department of the Interior and these botanists help the government gain a better understanding of current trends in environmental degradation, the impact of droughts and crop disease outbreaks, and other environmental incidents and trends. The US Department of Agriculture is also active in many international locations, helping to organize and evaluate agricultural programs and working on research to preserve natural resources.

A large number of botanists work in museums, botanical gardens, and zoological institutions. These botanists present scientific information about plant life to daily visitors, helping the general public to better understand the natural world. Botanists who are members of university faculties present this type of information to undergraduate and graduate students, conduct classes and seminars, and perform independent research.

Duties and Responsibilities

- Conducting research in laboratories, greenhouses, agricultural areas and forest
- Analyzing plant specimens

OCCUPATION SPECIALTIES

Plant Pathologists

Plant Pathologists conduct research in nature, case and control of plant diseases and decay of plant products.

Cytologists

Cytologists study structure, function, and life history of plant and animal cells.

Paleobotanists

Paleobotanists study fossilized remains of plants and animals found in geological formations to trace evolution and development of past life.

Mycologists

Mycologists study all types of fungi to discover those that are useful to medicine, agriculture and industry.

WORK ENVIRONMENT

Immediate Physical Environment

Botanists conduct frequent research, examining species in forests, in farm country, and a variety of other locations. A great deal of time is also spent in the laboratory, studying samples and analyzing data. Additionally, botanists often work in classroom settings, museums, botanical gardens, and similar venues, where they present information to students and the general public.

Transferable Skills and Abilities

Communication Skills
- Speaking effectively
- Writing concisely

Interpersonal/Social Skills
- Being able to work independently
- Working as a member of a team

Organization & Management Skills
- Organizing information or materials
- Paying attention to and handling details

Technical Skills
- Working with machines, tools or other objects
- Working with your hands

Work Environment Skills
- Working outdoors

Human Environment

In the field, botanists work in teams with other scientists, assistants, and students. In the laboratory, botanists interact with equipment technicians and other scientists as well as administrators and laboratory managers. In some cases, botanists provide information to government representatives, legislators, farmers, and foresters, and botanists are sometimes asked to deliver presentations at official functions, scientific meetings, or to panels of legislators.

Technological Environment

Botanists use a variety of manual and computerized tools to gather and analyze data, including microscopes, spectrometers, photometers, cameras, and preservation materials. Computers and research-related software, such as word processing, spreadsheet, and presentation programs, are typically used to share research results and theories with other scientists. In addition, there are many software programs that can be used to compile or manipulate data on genetics, ecological distribution, and climate modeling. The type of equipment used by a botanist may depend on his or her specialization and specific areas of interest.

EDUCATION, TRAINING, AND ADVANCEMENT

High School/Secondary

High school students interested in careers in botany should take classes in biology, chemistry, mathematics, physics, and geography and should, in general, prepare to pursue postsecondary education after graduation. Basic writing classes help future scientists learn how to write research papers, a skill they will need throughout their careers, and an introduction to computer science is increasingly important in preparing for scientific careers. Because botanists often travel internationally and to remote locations, a grounded understanding of foreign languages and culture can be helpful as well. Secondary students might also consider participating in local forestry, botanical, or biological clubs and societies in their area and many professional biologists begin learning to locate and collect data on animals and plants as amateur enthusiasts before becoming educated professionals.

Suggested High School Subjects

- Algebra
- Biology
- Calculus
- Chemistry
- Earth Science
- English
- Geometry
- Physics
- Science
- Social Studies
- Trigonometry

Related Career Pathways/Majors

Agriculture, Food & Natural Resources Cluster
- Plant Systems Pathway

Science, Technology, Engineering & Mathematics Cluster
• Science & Mathematics Pathway

Postsecondary

Botanists need to obtain a bachelor's degree in botany, biology, or a related natural science. Some individuals supplement their scientific coursework with studies in other disciplines, such as engineering, environmental studies, and agriculture. Most research botanists obtain a doctorate in botany, receiving training in plant taxonomy and physiology, as well as other specific sub-fields. Doctoral work is usually followed by independent research (a post-doctoral position at a college or university).

Related College Majors
• Biology, General
• Botany
• Forestry, General
• Wildlife & Wildlands Management
• Zoology, General

Adult Job Seekers

No matter the phase of life an individual decides to pursue a career in botany, all botanists must follow the same academic path. Those with the appropriate academic credentials may apply directly to universities with open faculty positions. Those trained in another biological science who wish to transition to studying botany may return to their education, taking classes in plant studies to supplement their biological knowledge. Furthermore, botanists may join professional botany organizations, such as the Botanical Society of America, where they network with peers and other scientific professionals and can often find opportunities for employment.

Professional Certification and Licensure

Botanists seeking positions with government agencies may be required to obtain professional licenses and certification, such as a professional engineer's license or a certificate to operate specific research equipment. Consult credible professional associations within the field, and follow professional debate as to the relevancy and value of any certification program. Botanists living and working abroad may also be required to adhere to specific national guidelines for foreign workers or for conducting scientific research and prospective international workers must therefore take time to research relevant requirements and procedures.

Additional Requirements

Botanists should be excellent critical thinkers, with an ability to analyze complex concepts and a strong interest in understanding the natural world. Botanists should also have an understanding of the government regulatory environment, as well as an appreciation of the industries affected by their work (such as agriculture and forestry). Botany is a collaborative field and so botanists need to be comfortable working with others and presenting complex information to specialists and non-specialists alike. Because botanists conduct frequent field research, they should endeavor to remain reasonably physically fit, as they may need to hike great distances in challenging weather and terrain to conduct certain types of research.

Fun Fact

It takes 70 percent less energy to produce a ton of paper from recycled paper than from trees.

Source: hightechscience.org

EARNINGS AND ADVANCEMENT

According to the Bureau of Labor Statistics (BLS), botanists in the United States earned median salaries of approximately $60,520 per year, with a range of less than $39,000 to over $98,000. The highest paid positions for botanists in the United States are typically found in governmental agencies and corporations, where botanists typically conduct applied botanical research or development. Academic and local government positions are less lucrative but may enable a botanist to focus on pure botanical research rather than designing research programs according to economic or developmental interests. In many situations, botanists may receive paid vacations, holidays, and sick days; life and health insurance; and retirement benefits supplemented by their employer. Pay for botanists varies widely in countries around the world and botanists living and working abroad may earn higher, lower, or similar salaries to those in the United States, depending on their specific field and specialization.

EMPLOYMENT AND OUTLOOK

The BLS estimates that employment of biological and wildlife researchers will grow by 4 percent between 2014 and 2024, which is slower than the 6-7 percent average for all US occupations during this same period. As more and more nations around the world adopt stronger environmental protection policies as a result of research indicating that human activity is leading to climate change and vast environmental degradation, there may be increased demand for botanists and other researchers with knowledge of climate and biosphere interactions. In addition, the expansion of the human population has created a growing demand for agricultural innovation and reform and botanists may play a key role in the future as climate change furthers food and water shortages around the world and necessitates changes in global agricultural policies and processes. Due to slower than average growth, biologists may face increasingly difficult competition when searching for employment and those with specialist expertise, higher degrees, and higher levels of experience will therefore have an advantage when seeking employment.

Related Occupations
- Agricultural Engineer
- Agricultural Scientist
- Biological Scientist
- Forester & Conservation Scientist
- Marine Biologist
- Microbiologist
- Oceanographer
- Range Manager
- Soil Scientist
- Wildlife Biologist

MORE INFORMATION

**American Bryological and
Lichenological Society**
P.O. Box 7065
Lawrence, KS 66044-8897
785.843.1234
www.abls.org

**American Phytopathological
Society**
3340 Pilot Knob Road
St. Paul, MN 55121-2097
651.454.7250
aps@scisoc.org
www.apsnet.org

**American Society of Plant
Biologists**
15501 Monona Drive
Rockville, MD 20855-2768
301.251.0560
info@aspb.org
www.aspb.org

**American Society of Plant
Taxonomists**
University of Wyoming
Department of Botany
1000 E. University Avenue
Laramie, WY 82071
307.766.2556
aspt@uwyo.edu
www.sysbot.org

Botanical Society of America
P.O. Box 299
St. Louis, MO 63166-0299
314.577.9566
bsa-manager@botany.org
www.botany.org

Ecological Society of America
1990 M Street, NW, Suite 700
Washington, DC 20006-3915
202.833.8773
esahq@esa.org
www.esa.org

**National Biological Information
Infrastructure**
USGS Biological Informatics Office
302 National Center
Reston, VA 20192
703.648.4216
www.nbii.gov

Torrey Botanical Society
P.O. Box 7065
Lawrence, KS 66044-8897
800.627.0326
www.torreybotanical.org

U.S. Botanic Garden
245 First Street SW
Washington, DC 20024
202.225.8333
www.usbg.gov

U.S. Department of Agriculture
1400 Independence Avenue SW
Washington, DC 20250
202.720.2791
www.usda.gov

Michael Auerbach/Editor,
updated by Micah Issitt

Microbiologist

Snapshot

Career Cluster(s): Agriculture, Food & Natural Resources, Health Science, Science, Technology, Engineering & Mathematics
Interests: Science, research and analysis, observation, microbiology, microorganisms, biotechnology
Earnings (Yearly Average): $66,850
Employment & Outlook: Slower than average growth expected

OVERVIEW

Sphere of Work

Microbiologists study organisms such as bacteria, fungi, algae, protozoa, and viruses, which are only visible with the aid of microscopes. They research and analyze the structure, development, reproduction, and other characteristics of microorganisms and observe and record the ways in which microorganisms influence the lives of plants and animals and affect the physical environment of the planet. While some

microbiologists study the way that microorganisms exist in nature and interact with their environments, others focus on applied research, studying microbiology in an effort to improve human culture or out of an interest in the industrial use of microscopic life. A microbiologist's specific focus and area of expertise will determine the type of research and the type of research environments that a microbiologist utilizes in his or her work.

Work Environment

Microbiologists spend the majority of their time in the laboratory, conducting research using a wide array of microscopes and other analytical equipment. Laboratory environments are typically temperature controlled, well lit, safe and sterile. Some microbiologists also spend time working outdoors collecting samples and conducting field experiments on microorganisms that occur in nature. Fieldwork may require travel to remote locations, hiking over rugged terrain, or working in difficult weather conditions, and many microbiologists travel internationally to conduct field research on various microorganisms. Microbiologists who hold positions at universities and colleges split their time between the classroom, the laboratory, and the office and may spend considerable time teaching and mentoring students at the undergraduate or graduate levels in addition to conducting their own research. Microbiologists usually work a regular forty-hour week, with extra hours typically required only when deadlines approach or an emergency occurs.

Profile

Interests: Data, Things
Working Conditions: Work Inside
Physical Strength: Light Work
Education Needs: Doctoral Degree
Licensure/Certification: Usually Not Requiredd
Physical Abilities Not Require: Not Climb, Not Kneel
Opportunities For Experience: Internship
Holland Interest Score*: IRS

* See Appendix A

Occupation Interest

Microbiologists study the smallest organisms, an area of science that is currently evolving at a fast pace. New and exciting discoveries in the areas of clinical microbiology and biotechnology are common. Microbiologists sometimes advise government agencies or private companies and organizations about issues involving microorganisms, including environmental protection, remediation, and the spread of germs and disease. Because there are a variety of pure and applied research topics within microbiological research, professionals in the field may approach their careers from different background and areas of interest.

A Day in the Life—Duties and Responsibilities

Microbiologists work primarily in laboratories, using many different types of research and analytical tools to study microorganisms and formulate hypotheses about various facets of microbiological form, function, and ecological interactions. Data collected from observations and experiments is typically compiled and stored in specialized biological databases and may be used to create theoretical or ecological models of microbial interactions and development. Senior microbiologists working in laboratories may supervise the activities of lab technicians, assistants, and junior level scientists.

Microbiologists often write technical reports, academic papers, and books based on their findings and accumulated data. Some of these reports are submitted to government agencies to help formulate appropriate public policies and regulations or to assist medical researchers and doctors in isolating and delivering effective treatments for certain diseases. Research results and writings may be published in technical journals or simply shared with other biologists, ecologists, and microbial specialists to further future research programs.

When they are not in the laboratory, many microbiologists teach at colleges and universities. They provide classroom instruction to undergraduates and graduate students, conduct lectures, host lab sessions, and advise students on independent projects. Many microbiologists also present papers and theories at academic conferences and departmental meetings.

Duties and Responsibilities

- Growing organisms in liquid or solid media
- Injecting cultures or infected body fluids in lab animals
- Observing effects of new drugs or known disease-causing microorganisms
- Cultivating microorganisms that produce products such as alcohol or industrial solvents

WORK ENVIRONMENT

Immediate Physical Environment

Microbiologists work primarily in laboratories operated by the governmental organizations, public and private universities, and private scientific or industrial organizations. They may also conduct field research, which may involve traveling to remote locations or spending long periods traveling or exploring various environments to search for and study microbial colonies.

Because a clean, sterile environment is necessary to ensure the validity of research results, laboratories have strict rules governing personal hygiene, surface cleanliness, clothing, and air quality. Despite these protocols, some microbiologists may experience a slight risk of exposure to dangerous chemicals or germs when conducting their research. Microbiologists working in the field might also be subject to environmental hazards, inclement weather, and potential exposure to microbial pathogens.

Human Environment

Depending on their areas of expertise, microbiologists interact and collaborate with a wide range of individuals, including laboratory technicians, assistants and interns, environmental scientists, medical doctors and researchers, government officials, and university students and professors.

Transferable Skills and Abilities

Communication Skills
- Writing concisely

Interpersonal/Social Skills
- Being able to work independently
- Being patient
- Working as a member of a team

Organization & Management Skills
- Paying attention to and handling details

Research & Planning Skills
- Analyzing information

Technical Skills
- Performing scientific, mathematical and technical work

Technological Environment

Microbiologists use a wide range of tools and technology to complete their work, including a variety of microscopes and visualization tools, sampling tools and equipment, centrifuges, infrared spectrometers, heating blocks, incubators, slides and test tubes, and sterilization equipment. Additionally, they must use medical database systems, analytical software, and general office software (including word proessing, spreadsheet, and presentation programs).

EDUCATION, TRAINING, AND ADVANCEMENT

High School/Secondary

High school students who wish to become microbiologists should take as many classes as possible in biology, chemistry, physics, physiology, and other natural sciences. Computer science training is also helpful, as are mathematics courses like algebra, calculus, and statistics. English and other classes that teach presentation and communication skills are highly useful and those planning on working or studying abroad might consider taking foreign language and culture courses to supplement their basic education and preparation for higher education.

Suggested High School Subjects

- Biology
- Chemistry
- English
- Physical Science
- Physiology
- Science

Related Career Pathways/Majors

Agriculture, Food & Natural Resources Cluster
- Environmental Service Systems Pathway
- Food Products & Processing Systems Pathway

Agriculture, Food & Natural Resources Cluster
- Plant Systems Pathway

Health Science Cluster
- Biotechnology Research & Development Pathway

Science, Technology, Engineering & Mathematics Cluster
- Science & Mathematics Pathway

Postsecondary

Some entry-level positions in applied research and product development only require a bachelor's degree, but in general, microbiologists should obtain at least a master's degree and preferably a doctorate degree in their field. Microbiologists who have obtained doctoral degrees are typically qualified to teach in academic environments as well as to conduct research. Such educational training includes work in the classroom, the field, and the laboratory. Those who choose to pursue a subfield of microbiology may need additional or specialized training, typically available only at the postgraduate level. For instance, microbiologists interested in pathogens and clinical microbiology, the study of how microbes affect human health and wellness, may study both microbiology and medicine through MD/PhD programs offered by many medical education institutions around the world.

Related College Majors

- Biochemistry
- Cell Biology
- Epidemiology

- Medical Microbiology
- Microbiology/Bacteriology
- Virology
- Wildlife & Wildlands Management

Adult Job Seekers

Qualified microbiologists may apply directly to universities and colleges with openings and may also attempt to find employment through university placement offices. Microbiologists who desire employment with state or federal government agencies may respond to postings on agency websites. Joining and networking through professional microbiology associations, such as the American Society for Microbiology, can be a useful job search strategy.

Professional Certification and Licensure

Some states in the United States require microbiologists and other laboratory workers handling potentially dangerous materials to obtain state-sponsored certification. Interested individuals should consult the department of health in the state where they seek employment. Legal and licensing requirements for microbiologists living and working overseas vary according to national and regional laws and prospective professionals should research any relevant requirements when searching for employment with international companies or research programs.

Additional Requirements

Microbiologists should demonstrate exceptional research and analytical skills and the ability to formulate theories and hypotheses based on their own and previously obtained data. Strong knowledge of medical science is also useful, especially for microbiologists who work in virology, immunology, and similar subfields. Microbiologists must possess strong interpersonal and public speaking skills in order to collaborate on research and present research results to colleagues. They should be innately curious and find satisfaction in investigating microscopic life and broadening general understanding of it.

EARNINGS AND ADVANCEMENT

According to the Bureau of Labor Statistics (BLS), microbiologists working in the United States earned annual median salaries of $66,850 in 2016. Salaries range widely depending on a professional's particular field, specialization, level of experience, seniority, and ability to obtain funding for research through grants and scientific organizations. Those at the lower end of the income spectrum earned less than $39,000, while the highest paid microbiologists, typically those working in senior federal government or in applied research or commercial positions, might earn over $120,000 annually. Microbiologists advance by gaining seniority within their field, which may involve publishing or completing important research, leading academic departments or programs, or taking on management roles in laboratories or commercial microbial divisions.

EMPLOYMENT AND OUTLOOK

The BLS estimates that employment of microbiologists will grow by 4 percent between 2014 and 2024, which is slower than the 6-7 percent predicted for all US occupations during the same period. Medical research and the pressing need to combat diseases and pathogens drives demand for microbiologists, but slow growth in the field limits opportunities and results in strong competition for available positions. Those specializing in clinical microbiology, pathology, immunology, and applied research will have more opportunities for employment than microbiologists studying the ecological factors of microbial life. Though some positions require only a bachelor's degree for entry-level positions, high competition means that those with higher level degrees will have an advantage when seeking acceptance to various professional positions.

Related Occupations
- Biological Scientist
- Botanist
- Medical Scientist
- Oceanographer
- Soil Scientist
- Veterinarian
- Wildlife Biologist
- Zoologist

Conversation With . . .
ROBERT F. GARRY, PHD

Professor of Microbiology and Immunology
Tulane School of Medicine
New Orleans, Louisianna
Research scientist, 40 years

1. What was your individual career path in terms of education/training, entry-level job, or other significant opportunity?

I majored in biology at Indiana State University and had a great experience in a great research lab studying virology. I was encouraged by a graduate student and a postdoctoral researcher who must have seen some potential and took me under their wings. I got fascinated by the field of virology and how you can discover things and make a difference. The possibilities are endless. I enjoyed the camaraderie in the lab. I wouldn't want to be doing anything else.

I received my PhD in microbiology with a focus on virology at the University of Texas in Austin. I remained for my postdoctoral research and worked in an area that was off the beaten track at the time, on a retrovirus, reticuloendotheliosis virus (REV), that can cause immunosuppression in chickens. It turned out to be a fortunate choice because about the time I was finishing my postdoc, a new disease called AIDS appeared. All of a sudden, my work on this obscure avian retrovirus became very relevant because what we were studying—immune suppression—was exactly what we were seeing in AIDS patients.

I received a National Institutes of Health (NIH) grant to study in humans what I had worked on in birds. There just weren't that many people who knew about this. I went on to join an NIH study section, reviewing and funding grants. It's really what happens to move the field forward, and I learned the process of doing science.

I also moved to New Orleans and became an assistant professor, associate professor, and, later, professor at Tulane University.

I worked on AIDS up until 10 or 15 years ago when work on HIV shifted mostly to vaccine discovery, which really isn't my field. This was coincident with 9-11, and concerns about anthrax. Funding shifted as did concern that something like Ebola was a potential bioweapon of mass destruction.

I had worked on tests to determine if people had HIV and learned a lot about the diagnostic industry. NIH was basically looking to fund grants relating to diagnostics, vaccinations, and therapeutics for these viruses of new concern. So I moved into research on the Lassa virus, a hemorrhagic fever similar to Ebola. Unlike Ebola, which occurs in outbreaks that burn themselves out, Lassa is endemic in West Africa. That means you can study it.

I am principal investigator of the Viral Hemorrhagic Fever Consortium, and set up a lab at Kenema Government Hospital (KGH) in eastern Sierra Leone in 2005. I go four to six times a year for two to three weeks at a time with a team and work with clinicians. In the U.S., we'd be working in a biosafety four-level lab—the high-level labs where you wear a space suit—but there are no rubber suits in Africa. The doctors don't have the opportunity to put on that kind of protection so you have to be pretty brave, as well as the mindset you're going to use as many proper precautions as you can.

In March 2014, the World Health Organization announced the Ebola outbreak in Guinea and Liberia, a three- or four-hour drive from KGH. Lassa and Ebola have similar symptoms, and on May 25, our hospital received its first sample that was positive for Ebola. West Africa is different from the interior of Africa because it is more populated and mining companies – such as those that mine diamonds—have built good roads. People can travel around Sierra Leone, as opposed to a village you could ring off from the spread of disease.

I was at KGH by May 27 with diagnostics and personal protective equipment. The cases kept coming. We were overwhelmed. Kenema had several thousand patients.

Over the past couple of years, we've been able to get back to our Lassa program. But we lost team members to Ebola, including the only virologist in Sierra Leone and the hospital's head nurse. That certainly motivates me to put these diseases behind us.

In addition to my work with the consortium, I am Assistant Dean for Graduate Studies in Biomedical Sciences at Tulane.

2. What are the most important skills and/or qualities for someone in your profession, particularly someone who decides to work overseas?

Persistence: not being discouraged if an experiment doesn't work the first time, a grant doesn't get funded, or a paper is not accepted.

3. What do you wish you had known before deciding to work abroad?

I wish I had known about the opportunities for work overseas earlier in my career. Until we got involved in Sierra Leone, my work was laboratory-based. When you see what's happening on the ground, you see what the stakes are.

4. **Are there many job opportunities overseas in your profession? In what specific geographic? areas?**

    Yes, in all developing low- and middle-income countries (LMICs).

5. **Will the willingness of professionals in your career to travel and live overseas change in the next five years?**

    Yes, I think it will increase. We are seeing more awareness of the need for enhancing basic healthcare infrastructure and for epidemic preparedness.

6. **What role will technology play in those changes, and what skills will be required?**

    Researchers have to be computer literate, but basic lab skills are a must. So is maturity.

7. **What do you enjoy most about your job? What do you enjoy least about your job?**

    I most enjoy the eureka moments. I least enjoy paperwork and budgeting.

8. **Can you suggest a valuable "try this" for students considering a career overseas in your profession?**

    Do work-study or volunteer in a lab. Do a study-abroad program or join the Peace Corps. A research university is probably the most likely place to start if you're interested in going overseas. Public health schools are doing a lot of work in developing countries.

MORE INFORMATION

American Society for Biochemistry and Molecular Biology
11200 Rockville Pike, Suite 302
Bethesda, MD 20852-3110
240.283.6600
www.asbmb.org

American Society for Microbiology
1752 N Street, NW
Washington, DC 20036-2904
202.737.3600
www.asm.org

Biotechnology Industry Organization
1201 Maryland Avenue, SW
Suite 900
Washington, DC 20024
202.962.9200
info@bio.org
www.bio.org

Northeast Association for Clinical Microbiology and Infectious Disease
19 Sylvester Avenue
Chelsea, ME 04330
www.nacmid.unh.edu

Society for Industrial Microbiology
3929 Old Lee Highway, Suite 92A
Fairfax, VA 22030-2421
703.691.3357
www.simhq.org

Michael Auerbach/Editor, updated by Micah Issitt

Zoologist

Snapshot

Career Cluster(s): Agriculture, Food & Natural Resources, Science, Technology, Engineering & Mathematics
Interests: Zoology, Biology, Animal Behavior, Research (field and laboratory), Environmental Studies
Earnings (Yearly Average): $60,520
Employment & Outlook: Slower than average growth expected

OVERVIEW

Sphere of Work

Zoologists are biologists who focus on the study of animal life, conducting experiments in animal behavior, physiology, ecological distribution, and other subjects. In addition to studying animal anatomy and physiology, zoologists monitor and inventory animal populations, study the impact of industrial development on natural habitats and wild animal populations, and analyze the relationship between animal

species and their immediate environments. Zoologists are usually classified by the animal groups they specialize in studying, such as mammals (mammalogy), birds (ornithology), fish (ichthyology), reptiles (herpetology), or the study of certain aspects of animal life, such as the development of animals from fertilized cell to birth or hatching (embryology). Zoologists frequently conduct field research, which may involve traveling to and working in remote locations and many travel internationally to conduct research. Many zoologists are also college or university professors and so spend time teaching and mentoring students and obtaining funding to support academic departments and specific research programs/projects.

Work Environment

Zoologists work in offices, laboratories, academic buildings, government agencies, private companies, natural animal habitats, and zoological parks. Although they spend time in laboratories, offices, and classrooms, they must also spend a great deal of time outdoors conducting research, hiking rough terrain, and working in different weather conditions in order to study animals in their natural habitats.

Profile

Interests: Data, Things
Working Conditions: Work Outside, Work Both Inside and Outside
Physical Strength: Light Work
Education Needs: Doctoral Degree
Licensure/Certification: Usually Not Requiredd
Physical Abilities Not Require: N/Al
Opportunities For Experience: Internship, Volunteer Work
Holland Interest Score*: IRE

* See Appendix A

Occupation Interest

Zoologists are scientists, and so should have strong intellectual curiosity and an appreciation for the scientific process. Unlike many scientific fields, however, zoologists and wildlife biologists spend much of their time in nature studying wild populations and so many are drawn to the field through a profound love of nature, environmentalism, and animals. Some zoologists are professors, teaching others while conducting their own research, and those working in academia should have an interest in spreading knowledge and sharing their interests with others. Others work in zoos and animal sanctuaries, where they may help to share their knowledge and love of animals with the general public and also engage in conservation and population management. Still others contribute to efforts to protect the environment, working for not-for-profit or government agencies and providing input on policies that safeguard threatened species and their habitats.

A Day in the Life—Duties and Responsibilities

A considerable portion of the work performed by zoologists is research or laboratory work. In the field, zoologists set up observation camps from which to study animals in their natural habitats, taking photos, taking samples, and keeping daily records of animals' interrelationships, development, and health. In the laboratory, they dissect animals, prepare tissue slides, study samples, and classify species. They also write reports and articles for their employers and for publication in scholarly journals. As biological scientists, zoologists may be invited to present their findings at academic and environmental conferences.

When they are not in the field or laboratory, most zoologists are university or college professors, committed to both research and teaching responsibilities. Some zoologists work in zoos, animal sanctuaries, and nature preserves. Others are hired by government agencies to study how animals and their habitats are affected by pollution and industrial development, as well as make recommendations as to how better protect these species. Pharmaceutical and biological supply companies employ some zoologists to conduct applied research.

Duties and Responsibilities

- Studying animals
- Performing research on animal behaviors, such as mating and eating habits
- Teaching courses at the secondary and college level

WORK ENVIRONMENT

Immediate Physical Environment

When conducting research in the field, zoologists often travel to remote locations in all types of terrain and weather conditions, sometimes to areas where their research puts them in close proximity to dangerous environmental conditions. Zoologists also work in academic offices and laboratories while conducting research and analyzing data from field or laboratory studies. A zoologist's specific specialty will determine the amount of time that he or she spends in various environments, such as the classroom, laboratory, and field.

Transferable Skills and Abilities

Research & Planning Skills
- Analyzing information
- Gathering information

Technical Skills
- Performing scientific, mathematical and technical work

Work Environment Skills
- Working with plants or animals

Human Environment

Depending on their job specialization, zoologists interact with many different people. When traveling to animal habitats to do research in the field, they may work with guides and local residents; in the laboratory, they work with lab technicians, graduate students, and interns. At zoos, they work with zookeepers, veterinarians, and the general public. In government agencies, zoologists interact with elected as well as appointed officials, public administrators, and fellow scientists. In private organizations, they work with executives, other scientists, and administrators.

Technological Environment

In the field, zoologists use traps, nets, and other devices to capture live specimens. They also use special containers and other sampling equipment. In the laboratory, zoologists use microscopes, reactive chemicals, and other test equipment and substances. In addition, zoologists should be competent with modeling, map-generating, and database computer software. Zoologists also need to be able to use a variety of basic office and management software, including word processing, presentation, and spread sheet software programs.

EDUCATION, TRAINING, AND ADVANCEMENT

High School/Secondary

High school students interested in pursuing a career in zoology attempt to gain a strong foundational education in the biological and physical sciences and in scientific theory and practice. This should include any available classes in biology and/or ecology, as well as classes in physics, chemistry, mathematics, environmental science, sociology, anthropology, archaeology, and geology. Computer science skills are critical to the recording and sharing of scientific data and training in foreign languages and culture will be helpful for zoologists who travel to conduct research or who interact with other scientists and specialists from different cultures.

Suggested High School Subjects
- Biology
- Chemistry
- Computer Science
- English
- Geography
- Mathematics
- Physical Science
- Physics
- Physiology
- Science

Related Career Pathways/Majors
Agriculture, Food & Natural Resources Cluster
- Animal Systems Pathway

Science, Technology, Engineering & Mathematics Cluster
- Science & Mathematics Pathway

Postsecondary

A doctoral degree is required for most positions in zoology, so it is critical to earn a bachelor's degree in a biological science and plan for continued study in master's and doctoral programs within the natural sciences. There are many different subspecialties within zoology, and students at the graduate level will generally focus on a specific subfield or area of interest. Zoologists may choose a subfield based on a specific type of animal or animal group, such as ornithology, primatology, mammology, or marine biology, or may focus on environmental subfields, such as ecology, behavior, or population dynamics.

Related College Majors
- Biology, General
- Human & Animal Physiology
- Zoology, General

Adult Job Seekers

Qualified individuals seeking zoologist positions should apply directly to universities, zoos, and other organizations with posted openings. The US Department of the Interior, for example, posts open positions through the department's website. Joining professional or scientific organizations can be a helpful way to network and to learn about job opportunities.

Professional Certification and Licensure

While there are no specific licenses or certifications required for zoologists in the United States, some fields utilize specific equipment that may require specialized training or certification. For instance, a marine biologist may need to study and receive certification in scuba diving or in operating boats, submersibles, and other marine vehicles and equipment. Legal and professional requirements for zoologists conducting research or living and working in foreign countries will depend on specific national laws regarding foreign workers or scientific research and professionals should research relevant laws and regulations before applying for positions that involve foreign travel or working abroad.

Additional Requirements

Zoologists should demonstrate natural curiosity, a strong ability to analyze complex issues and problems, and strong written, research, and verbal skills. When and if necessary in the course of their work, they should be physically fit and prepared to conduct physically demanding work, sometimes in the face of environmental dangers.

Fun Fact

Ebola was discovered in 1976 in the Democratic Republic of the Congo, near the Ebola River. It is transmitted to people from wild animals, then spreads from human to human.

Source: globalhealth.musc.edu

EARNINGS AND ADVANCEMENT

According to the Bureau of Labor Statistics (BLS), zoologists in the United States earned a median annual salary of $60,520 in 2016, with a range of less than $39,000 to over $98,000 possible in the field. Higher paid positions can be found in the federal government and in research and development organizations, while state government, education, and private research institutions provide lower pay, but may supplement with opportunities for different types of research. Zoologists may receive paid vacations, holidays, and sick days; life and health insurance; and retirement benefits, supported by their employer. In many cases, zoologists conducting research contribute to their own earnings by writing grant proposals and applying for funding through various scientific and research funding organizations. Researchers who are successful in obtaining grants will receive a bonus in pay as well as being able to fund more expensive or complex research programs that may involve hiring technicians, assistants, and students.

EMPLOYMENT AND OUTLOOK

The BLS estimates that employment of zoologists and other types of wildlife and field biologists will grow by approximately 4 percent between 2014 and 2024, which is slower than the average of 6-7 percent growth expected for all occupations in the United States during the same period. In the United States, scientific organizations limit funding for pure research on animal behavior and physiology, and concentrate funding on projects that can demonstrate human interest, including applied research and animal research that has industrial or commercial applications. Other nations place increased emphasis on pure ecological and wildlife research and professionals interested in this aspect of zoology might therefore apply for research positions or grants from foreign governments or scientific organizations. As growth in the industry is slow, there is expected to be significant competition for jobs in the United States and those with advanced degrees and experience will therefore have a distinct advantage when seeking employment.

Related Occupations
- Biological Scientist
- Microbiologist
- Wildlife Biologist

MORE INFORMATION

American Physiological Society
Education Office
9650 Rockville Pike
Bethesda, MD 20814-3991
301.634.7164
webmaster@the-aps.org
www.the-aps.org

American Society for Microbiology
1752 N Street, NW
Washington, DC 20036-2904
202.737.3600
www.asm.org

American Zoo and Aquarium Association
8403 Colesville Road, Suite 710
Silver Spring, MD 20910-3314
301.562.0777
generalinquiry@aza.org
www.aza.org

Biotechnology Industry Organization
1201 Maryland Avenue, SW
Suite 900
Washington, DC 20024
202.962.9200
info@bio.org
www.bio.org

Botanical Society of America
P.O. Box 299
St. Louis, MO 63166-0299
314.577.9566
bsa-manager@botany.org
www.botany.org

Society for Integrative and Comparative Biology
1313 Dolley Madison Boulevard
Suite 402
McLean, VA 22101
800.955.1236
SICB@Burklnc.com
www.sicb.org

The Wildlife Society
5410 Grosvenor Lane, Suite 200
Bethesda, MD 20814-2144
301.897.9770
tws@wildlife.org
www.wildlife.org

Wildlife Conservation Society
2300 Southern Boulevard
Bronx, NY 10460
718.720.5100
www.wcs.org

Zoological Association of America
P.O. Box 511275
Punta Gorda, FL 33951-1275
941.621.2021
www.zaoa.org

Michael Auerbach/Editor, updated by Micah Issitt

TRAVEL, TOURISM, AND HOSPITALITY

The International Travel and Tourism Industry

The international travel, tourism, and hospitality industries account for hundreds of separate occupations. In the United States, the travel, tourism, and hospitality industries support more than 7.6 million jobs, with more than $1.6 trillion in revenue in 2015. The industry is so large, in fact, that one out of every 18 Americans is employed in one of the nation's travel and tourism-related businesses. Travel agents, tour guides, pilots, flight attendants, chefs, hotel managers, and many other careers are included in the broader hospitality industry, which, collectively supports and facilitates millions of tourists traveling abroad each year for work, entertainment, and exploration.

Travel and Tourism

The international air travel industry began to develop before commercial airliners were in general use. The first vessel to ferry tourists across the Atlantic Ocean was the Graf Zeppelin, which flew from Germany to the United States between October 11 and October 15th of 1928. The birth of this new industry, international air travel, created new careers as well, including the pilots who operated the airships, and later airplanes, as well as the cabin crew, called variously stewardesses, stewards, cabin attendants, or flight attendants. The world's first cabin attendant was Heinrich Kubis, who tended to passengers aboard zeppelins operated by DELAG Airlines beginning in 1912. United Airlines hired the first female flight attendant, nurse Ellen Church, in 1930.

Pioneers like Kubus and Church paved the way for the more than 113,000 professional flight attendants working in the U.S. side of the industry in 2016, on both domestic and international flights. Flight attendants and the pilots carrying passengers internationally do not typically live overseas, but their work carries them to many international locations where they may spend hours or days before returning to their native nations. There are no special qualifications, typically, for cabin crew or pilots who operate international flights, and the airline companies typically provide assistance in obtaining any needed permits or licenses needed by the crew to travel back and forth between nations. However, those interested in careers in international who have experience with foreign languages or international travel may have an advantage when seeking employment.

There are also opportunities for U.S. airline professionals to work overseas by working for foreign airlines or travel companies. Though the airline industry in the United States has experienced diminishing growth, many nations have a shortage of trained pilots in comparison to the growth of their airline industries. This has created a significant international demand for pilots willing to work overseas. In some cases, foreign companies offer higher-than-average salaries and bonuses in an effort to attract pilots from other nations. For instance, in 2016, China was experiencing a severe shortage in qualified pilots, needing between 4,000 to 5,000 new pilots each year to accommodate the nation's rapidly growing airline industry. That year, the Chinese travel company Chengdu Airlines advertised positions for trained pilots offering to pay $25,000 per month, with a $36,000 signing bonus for completing a three-year contract for the company. By contrast, domestic pilots in some U.S. regions might earn less than $25,000 per year for a similar level or even higher level of flight time. While international companies have far less need for cabin crew, there are a variety of foreign airlines and travel companies that do occasionally hire U.S. professionals for other crew positions.

International Tourist Services

There are other careers in tourism in which professionals may live and work overseas for extended periods. For instance, in nations that see high levels of tourism from the United States, there are typically hotels, resorts, and other tourism services and facilities that cater to U.S. natives and offer English-language assistance and help with the logistics of traveling abroad. Similarly, many U.S. based companies operate abroad, providing tour guides, translators, drivers/transportation experts, and other services for foreign visitors.

Many U.S.-based hotel and resort chains also have international locations and offices and these businesses often hire U.S. workers for certain positions. There are also professional companies that specialize in placing U.S. based professionals in international hospitality positions and typically such companies will help prospective hospitality workers to obtain visas and other work permits. Some companies staffing overseas locations also offer student and intern positions, training programs, and other services to help U.S. residents find work in overseas hospitality. Specifically, many U.S.-based hotel chains operating in foreign nations hire U.S.-natives for executive and management positions in their international locations. Hotels may also hire U.S.-natives to serve as concierges, guides, translators, or for security positions.

The culinary industry is another field that may offer opportunities for overseas work, especially for U.S.-trained chefs and restaurant managers. U.S. hotels operating overseas, for instance, regularly hire U.S.-native chefs to work in their restaurants. Some international chalets and resorts also advertise positions for other food service specialists, such as kitchen managers/porters, bartenders, servers, and food industry managers. While some companies hiring international professionals for culinary jobs offer job training and guidance, many positions require significant prior experience and training. Those looking to work abroad as chefs, for instance, might consider attending a culinary education program through a U.S. based institution. Culinary schools often offer students opportunities for internships and summer programs overseas, which can be a good way to explore working overseas without committing to full employment in another nation.

Growing Opportunities Abroad

International hospitality is a rapidly growing field, fueled in part by the increasing number of other businesses operating internationally. The increasing number of business travelers from the United States traveling overseas for work, or living overseas for extended periods, creates a higher demand for hospitality specialists as well. The growth of international economies has therefore also fueled growth in international travel and tourism and it is therefore likely that opportunities for overseas work in travel and tourism will increase in the future. Students interested in a career in international hospitality and travel have numerous options, but might begin by seeking out summer internship or other hospitality-based temporary work programs overseas. In terms of education, international hospitality specialists may or may not need to meet specific requirements, but training on foreign languages and a familiarity with international culture and customs is an advantage to those seeking work overseas in hospitality, travel, or any other field.

Works Used

Grossman, Dan. "The World's First Flight Attendant." *Airships*. DanGrossman. Jul 9 2010. Web. 1 Aug 2017.

Mullen, Jethro. "Want to earn $300,000 tax free? Try flying a plane in China." *CNN Money*. Nov 15 2016. Web. 1 Aug 2017.

"Travel, Tourism & Hospitality Spotlight." *SelectUSA*. International Trade Administration. 2016. Web. 1 Aug 2017.

Cook/Chef

Snapshot

Career Cluster(s): Hospitality & Tourism

Interests: Culinary arts, food, being independent, being creative

Earnings (Yearly Average): $43,180

Employment & Outlook: Faster than average growth expected

OVERVIEW

Sphere of Work

Cooks and chefs prepare culinary dishes for restaurant clientele, private parties, and other customers and oversee kitchen activities and operation. Chefs and cooks design menus and dishes, order supplies and grocery items, prepare food, organize ingredients, set staff schedules, and direct other chefs and kitchen personnel. Chefs and cooks also ensure that kitchens are efficient, safe, and abide by health department standards. Cook

and chef job descriptions vary based on their experience, the place of employment, and the staff size.

Work Environment

The kitchen is the primary work environment for chefs and cooks. They work in restaurants, banquet halls, hospitals, school dining halls and cafeterias, and similar venues. The kitchen environment may be stressful, as chefs and cooks are required to prepare many dishes simultaneously while coordinating with other kitchen and restaurant staff. Kitchens may be hot, uncomfortable, and dangerous at times and chefs and cooks must learn how to safely and securely work in the kitchen environment. In some cases, hours may be long—chefs and cooks must arrive early to sign for orders and prepare foods, and they must stay late after hours to clean up and take inventory. Though most chefs live and work in their native nations, there are many opportunities for chefs to travel, live, and work abroad. Cruise ships and international hotels are the most common venues for international food service employment and each of these venues features a unique environment with its own benefits and challenges. In addition, chefs and cooks in training, especially those training in certain types of global cuisine, often seek out opportunities to train abroad with native chefs in other nations.

Profile

Interests: Data, People, Things
Working Conditions: Work Inside
Physical Strength: Medium Work
Education Needs: On-The-Job Training, High School Diploma or G.E.D., High School Diploma with Technical Education, Apprenticeship
Licensure/Certification: Usually Not Required
Physical Abilities Not Require: Not Climb, Not Kneel, Not Hear and/or Talk
Opportunities For Experience: Apprenticeship, Military Service, Volunteer Work, Part Time Work
Holland Interest Score*: ESR, RES, RSE

* See Appendix A

Occupation Interest

The best chefs and cooks are culinary artists. There are a wide range of venues in which chefs and cooks can express this artistry and love of food, including upscale and chain restaurants, cruise ships, hotels, local bistros, and corner delis. Although the work is very challenging, chefs and cooks take ownership of the dishes they prepare, which can be very empowering. Generally, individuals who become chefs and cooks simply love food and food preparation.

A Day in the Life—Duties and Responsibilities

The work of chefs and cooks varies based on the size of the kitchen staff as well as the professional level at which they work. Chefs meet with food suppliers to determine the quality and price of their food supplies, prepare vendor orders, and meet deliveries (inspecting them for quality). In the early morning, chefs organize food ingredients so that they are easily located during peak business hours and prepare certain food items (such as marinating meats, chopping vegetables, and preparing sauces). Chefs and cooks also design menu items, food displays, and individual plates, directing garnishment and food arrangement. Chefs and cooks are also accountable for managing food costs, balancing supply costs with labor costs and menu prices.

During meal times, cooks and chefs work at the stoves and ovens, cooking ingredients to order, arranging plates, and placing them where servers can easily find them. Additionally, head chefs direct the activities of other chefs and cooks at the facility, ensuring that all orders are being prepared quickly and properly. Between meal rushes, chefs and cooks work on daily accounting, staff schedules, new menus, and dish recipes. They also inspect equipment to ensure that it is working and has been cleaned properly.

Duties and Responsibilities

- Planning menus
- Selecting and developing recipes
- Preparing raw food for cooking
- Weighing, measuring and mixing ingredients
- Seasoning foods
- Observing and testing food being cooked
- Baking
- Carving and serving portions of foods

OCCUPATION SPECIALTIES

Chefs de Froid

Chefs de Froid design and prepare decorated foods and artistic food arrangements for buffets in formal restaurants.

Bakers

Bakers prepare bread, rolls, muffins and biscuits and supervise other bakers in various institutions.

Short Order Cooks

Short Order Cooks prepare and cook to order foods requiring short preparation time.

Specialty Fast Food Cooks

Specialty Fast Food Cooks prepare such foods as fish and chips, tacos and pastries for window or counter service.

Pie Makers

Pie Makers prepare and bake pies, tarts and cobblers.

Institutional Cooks

Institutional Cooks prepare soups, meats, vegetables, salads, dressings and desserts in large quantities for schools, cafeterias, hospitals and other institutions.

WORK ENVIRONMENT

Immediate Physical Environment

Chefs primarily work in the kitchens, but there are many different types of venues with different kitchen designs and amenities. Depending on their specific job, chefs may work in restaurants, banquet halls, cafeterias, cruise ships, hotels, or in any of a variety of other venues. Some chefs and cooks, such as personal chefs, work in private homes or may travel between homes owned by a number of clients. Kitchens can be busy, loud, and potentially dangerous environments and all kitchen staff need to be trained in safety procedures and practices.

Transferable Skills and Abilities

Interpersonal/Social Skills
- Cooperating with others
- Working as a member of a team

Organization & Management Skills
- Managing time
- Meeting goals and deadlines
- Organizing information or materials
- Paying attention to and handling details

Technical Skills
- Working with machines, tools or other objects
- Working with your hands

Unclassified Skills
- Performing work that produces tangible results
- Preparing food

Human Environment

Chefs and cooks work with many other people, depending on the size and nature of the venue at which they work. Among those on the kitchen staff with whom chefs and cooks may interact are sous chefs, line and prep cooks, stewards, servers, bartenders and sommeliers, restaurant managers or owners, and dishwashers. In addition, chefs and cooks work with deliverymen, vendors, suppliers, and the public. Chefs working overseas may additionally need to contend with linguistic barriers that might make it more difficult to communicate with clients or other members of a kitchen staff.

Technological Environment

Chefs and cooks should be able to use stoves, fryers, ovens, grills, mixers, and other kitchen tools and appliances. Their knowledge of these kitchen tools should extend to legal rules on operation, cleaning, and maintenance, so that the facility complies with local health and safety regulations. Increasingly, chefs need to know how to use digital tools and computers, including software programs designed to aid kitchen workers in handling various facets of the job, such as inventory and staff management.

EDUCATION, TRAINING, AND ADVANCEMENT

High School/Secondary

Interested high school students are encouraged to take food preparation and cooking courses. They may also benefit from health and nutrition classes. Higher-level cooks, such as head chefs and sous chefs, oversee the management of the kitchen – high school students seeking to reach such professional levels should take business courses as well. Most important, though, is on-the-job training. High school students interested in a culinary degree should find a job in food service to understand the atmosphere, the pace, and dynamics of a working kitchen. Those interested in international opportunities might also take language courses as well as classes in international business.

Suggested High School Subjects
- Business
- Business Math
- International business
- English
- Family & Consumer Sciences
- First Aid Training
- Food Service & Management
- Foods & Nutrition

- Health Science Technology
- Foreign Languages

Related Career Pathways/Majors
- Hospitality & Tourism Cluster
- Restaurants & Food/Beverage Services Pathway

Postsecondary

Most cooks and chefs begin working in a kitchen right after high school, although many high-level chefs and cooks pursue a postsecondary degree. Many of these degrees can be earned at vocational schools, where students can receive culinary training. Two- and four-year colleges offer more extensive training for individuals seeking positions in fine-dining and upscale restaurants. For those seeking international experience, training in languages and international culture might lead to better employment opportunities.

Related College Majors
- Culinary Arts/Chef Training

Adult Job Seekers

The most important qualification an aspiring chef or cook can have is experience. Adults seeking to become senior-level chefs and cooks must begin by pursuing jobs at lower levels, such as line or prep cook, which give them the experience and professional guidance they need to advance. Qualified chefs and cooks also find opportunities by networking through culinary and restaurant trade organizations, such as the National Restaurant Association and local affiliates of the American Culinary Federation. Those interested in overseas opportunities might concentrate their job search on companies or organizations that operate abroad or that have connections to international restaurants.

Professional Certification and Licensure

While most countries do not require chefs and cooks to be licensed, many nations require that chefs receive training and certification in food safety and regulatory compliance. This certification process addresses such subjects as food storage, preparation, and service.

Interested individuals should research food safety and other certification requirements specific to their target region or nation. Some cooks and chefs receive optional certification in specialized cooking skills, such as professional pastry-makers, personal chefs, and teachers of culinary arts. Such certification may enhance a job candidate's credentials.

Additional Requirements

Chefs and cooks are food lovers, knowledgeable about a wide range of different food styles and origins. They should know and have an appreciation for flavors, textures, techniques, and styles. Successful cooks often have a creative and artistic attitude, which helps in meal presentation. Cooks and chefs must have a tolerance for a busy and often chaotic atmosphere. Many chefs are enterprising, seeking to own and operate their own business or create their own unique style of dining experience. For those who seek this path, an understanding of business and management is essential, as many restaurants fail within the first three years of opening.

EARNINGS AND ADVANCEMENT

Earnings depend on the type, size, and geographic location of the employer, and the employee's experience and skill. Wages generally are highest in elegant restaurants and hotels, where many executive chefs are employed, and in major metropolitan areas. In the United States, annual earnings of fast food, restaurant and short order cooks were $43,180 in 2016. For those working internationally, salaries may vary widely depending on the venue and economic environment of the chef or cook's host nation. In some cases, international chefs may be able to earn higher salaries than possible in the United States, while, in other cases, those working in international positions may need to accept lower pay for the opportunity to live and work abroad.

Cooks and chefs may receive paid vacations, holidays, and sick days; life and health insurance; and retirement benefits. These are usually paid by the employer. Cooks may also receive free meals and uniforms and laundry service.

EMPLOYMENT AND OUTLOOK

In the United States, the food service industry was expected to grow by more than 9 percent between 2014 and 2024, marking higher than average growth in comparison to the 6-7 percent for all occupations. While the number of overseas chef and cook positions is unknown, web recruitment has increased opportunities for chefs and cooks looking to work abroad and there are many growing tourist centers around the world that may accept international applications. Opportunities for overseas employment are more common in nations with thriving hospitality industries, such as in Europe and Asia. US-based food and hospitality organizations can be helpful in assisting cooks or chefs in locating opportunities for working abroad.

Related Occupations
- Dietitian & Nutritionist
- Food & Beverage Service Worker
- Food Service Manager

Related Military Occupations
- Food Service Specialist

Conversation With . . .
PETER LAUFER

Executive Chef
27 years in the industry

1. What was your individual career path in terms of education/training, entry-level job, or other significant opportunity?

I started my career back in Germany with a three-year apprentice program working in a small hotel, working through all areas of the kitchen, while at the same time going to school at the Hotel Restaurant Bauer, where I graduated in 1986. Then my journey began. My goal was to get as much training as possible with the goal of moving up in position and title–*commis de cuisine, chef de partie*, sous chef, executive sous chef until, finally, executive chef.

It was important to me to not to stay at the same place too long until I established myself. My first job, in Munich, was preparing cold appetizers and platters, with beautiful presentation using decorative pieces like mirrors, for a famous wine restaurant in Munich. I stayed there one year, and for each of the next seven years, I stayed just one year at each job: junior chef, first cook, *chef entremetier*, first assistant to the chef. I worked in Germany and Switzerland and for Norwegian Cruise Line out of Miami. I worked on cruise ships from 1993 to 2001. At 25 years old, I was one of the youngest executive chefs in the cruise industry. I worked on ships serving up to 2,400 guests and 1,000 crew members. I then worked at Sandals Resort in Montego Bay, followed by two years at a hotel in Miami. In 2012, I joined the Royal Sonesta in Houston.

2. What are the most important skills and/or qualities for someone in your profession?

Creativity, an eye for color, and attention to the details are all important for a chef. You must be able to work long hours and be capable of handing stress. An executive chef will be responsible for menus, training and leading staff, purchasing, and more.

If you enjoy cooking at home and for friends, you may be a candidate. If you love to be around food and like to spend time at a farmers market, butcher shop or produce row, you may be a candidate. If you like working with your hands and have an artistic drive, you may be a candidate. If you don't mind working long hours and like to be surrounded by an intense environment, you may be a candidate. If you would like to see the world and work in different places, you may be a candidate.

3. What do you wish you had known going into this profession?

This profession changes your personal life. It influences your circle of friends, as you work late nights, weekends and holidays.

4. Are there many job opportunities in your profession? In what specific areas?

The nice thing about this job is that you can work anywhere in the world. Working for a large company gives you the chance to branch out in different parts of the world. Restaurants, hotels and the cruise industry are always looking for talented chefs.

5. How do you see your profession changing in the next five years? What role will technology play in those changes, and what skills will be required?

Food trends are changing every year, with new things cropping up all the time: Peruvian Asian fusion, or farm-to-table, and tail-to-nose cooking (that is, eating the entire animal). A good chef needs to keep up with the trends and follow the patterns of his local customers.

With the implementation of low temperature cooking, re-thermo banquet cooking, and high tech smoking, a lot more skills are required in order to get the feeling for cooking with these techniques.

Also, the demand for nutritional value is getting more important, so some of the training needs to be geared to the whole healthy living aspect of food.

6. What do you enjoy most about your job? What do you enjoy least?

No day is the same. During my time working on cruise ships, I enjoyed being able to see the world and working with different cultures. What I enjoy least about this job is dealing with paperwork.

7. Can you suggest a valuable "try this" for students considering a career in your profession?

Ask your favorite restaurant, bakery or hotel if you can stay in the kitchen for a couple of days and see what it's like to work as a chef.

Try to copy a dish from a fine dining restaurant that you frequent and serve it to your friends.

Take a whole fish or chicken and try to de-bone it.

Attend a local American Culinary Federation (ACF) Chefs chapter meeting and get information about pros and cons in the industry.

MORE INFORMATION

American Culinary Federation
180 Center Place Way
St. Augustine, FL 32095
800.624.9458
acf@acfchefs.net
www.acfchefs.org

Asian Chef Association
3145 Geary Boulevard, #112
San Francisco, CA 94118
408.634.9462
www.acasf.com

**International Association of
Culinary Professionals**
1100 Johnson Ferry Road, Suite 300
Atlanta, GA 30342
404.252.3663
info@iacp.com
www.iacp.com

James Beard Foundation
167 West 12th Street
New York, NY 10011
212.675.4984
www.jamesbeard.org

JBF Awards:
www.jamesbeard.org/index.php?q=awards

JBF Scholarships:
www.jamesbeard.org/index.
php?q=james_beard_scholarships

**National Restaurant Association
Educational Foundation**
175 West Jackson Boulevard
Suite 1500
Chicago, IL 60604-2814
800.765.2122
info@foodtrain.org
www.nraef.org

UNITE HERE! Headquarters
275 7th Avenue
New York, NY 10001-6709
212.265.7000
www.unitehere.org

**United States Personal Chef
Association**
5728 Major Boulevard, Suite 750
Orlando, FL 32819
800.995.2138
www.uspca.com

Michael Auerbach/Editor,
updated by Micah Issitt

Flight Attendant

Snapshot

Career Cluster(s): Transportation, Distribution & Logistics
Interests: Aviation, travel, communicating with others, handling emergency situations
Earnings (Yearly Average): $48,500
Employment & Outlook: Slower Than Average Growth Expected

OVERVIEW

Sphere of Work

A flight attendant is an airline professional that ensures the overall security and safety of the airplane cabin, as well as the safety and comfort of its passengers. They will also attend to passenger's needs, and are responsible for serving food and beverages to the passengers and crew. A flight attendant guarantees successful compliance with standard aviation safety regulations and protocols, and must thoroughly understand the ways in which airplanes operate. Flight attendants report to a

flight supervisor and also to the captain of the aircraft on which he or she is working.

Work Environment

Flight attendants spend most of their time aboard an aircraft, and are assigned a home base location from which they generally operate. Generally, they are away from their home base location for at least one third of their working time, per month. Most flight attendants are expected to work nights, holidays, and weekends, in addition to regular hours during the week. They usually spend sixty-five to eighty-five hours per month in flight (with shifts lasting up to fourteen hours), with the ability to request additional hours, and another fifty hours per month on the ground performing tasks such as flight and report preparation.

Profile

Interests: People, Things
Working Conditions: Work Inside, Work Both Inside and Outside
Physical Strength: Light Work
Education Needs: High School Diploma or G.E.D., Junior/Technical/Community Colleg
Licensure/Certification: Required
Physical Abilities Not Require: Not Kneel
Opportunities For Experience: Military Service, Part Time Work
Holland Interest Score*: ESA

* See Appendix A

Occupation Interest

Potential flight attendants need to possess outstanding communication skills as communicating with crew and passengers is central to the occupation. Flight attendants must interact with diverse and, at times, difficult passengers, and must project a pleasant and personable attitude, regardless of the circumstances. In an emergency, flight attendants must be able to remain calm and collected in order to ensure the safety of their passengers. Those working on international flights may encounter a variety of different passengers from different environments and should be comfortable communicating across various cultural barriers. While flight attendants may spend most of their time aboard an airplane or in an airport, the job offers opportunities to spend time in many different locations and, in some cases, flight attendants can arrange to spend extended periods in various regions or nations. Prospective flight attendants should therefore have a strong interest in exploration and travel.

A Day in the Life—Duties and Responsibilities

When a flight attendant reports for duty, he or she will typically meet with the captain and other crew members one hour before take-off to discuss evacuation procedures, airline crew coordination, flight duration, relevant passenger information (such as health or mobility issues), and anticipated weather conditions. Before passengers board the airplane, flight attendants take inventory of and prepare food and beverages and check first aid kits and emergency equipment. Once passengers begin boarding, flight attendants are responsible for greeting them, helping them find their seats, and assisting with the storage of carry-on luggage. Before take-off, flight attendants check the aircraft for any dangerous materials and note any passengers exhibiting odd or potentially threatening behavior. They welcome passengers aboard the flight, and provide information regarding safety procedures and emergency escape routes.

A flight attendant ensures the safety and security of the passengers and attends to their comfort and satisfaction from the time they board the aircraft until they depart. This includes assisting sick or injured passengers, providing food and beverages, answering any questions passengers might have, and preparing the passengers and plane for a safe landing. To further ensure passenger satisfaction, a flight attendant might also calm the nerves of anxious passengers and supervise small children. Prior to departure, flight attendants also collect audio headsets and trash, as well as take inventory. Once the plane is on the ground, flight attendants assist passengers exiting the aircraft and report the condition of cabin equipment. The lead flight attendant supervises crewmembers aboard the airplane in addition to performing his or her own regular duties.

Duties and Responsibilities

- Attending a briefing session with crew members on weather conditions, number of passengers and route
- Checking the cabin for supplies, emergency equipment and food and beverages
- Greeting passengers and assisting them with coats and small baggage
- Verifying passengers' tickets
- Recording destinations
- Issuing a general welcome and explaining and demonstrating the use of emergency equipment
- Providing passengers with newspapers, magazines, pillows and blankets
- Heating and serving cooked meals, sandwiches or other light refreshments and beverages

WORK ENVIRONMENT

Immediate Physical Environment

The majority of a flight attendant's work takes place inside the cabin of an airplane. He or she is required to wear a uniform representing the airline for which he or she works, and must stand for long periods of time. A flight attendant also spends time in or around airline terminals. Constant exposure to re-circulated air, repetitive lifting and pushing motions, and the lack of safety restraints as the airplane encounters turbulence all contribute to a higher than average rate of job-related illness and injury.

Transferable Skills and Abilities

Communication Skills
- Speaking effectively
- Writing concisely

Interpersonal/Social Skills
- Cooperating with others
- Working as a member of a team

Organization & Management Skills
- Demonstrating leadership

Managing time
- Meeting goals and deadlines
- Performing duties which change frequently
- Performing routine work

Unclassified Skills
- Keeping a neat appearance

Work Environment Skills
- Traveling

Human Environment

Flight attendants work and deal with large groups of passengers, as well as other crewmembers. They report to flight supervisors and captains. Because they interact with so many people on a daily basis, flight attendants are exposed to a variety of pathogens that may cause illness. In spite of work-related stressors, flight attendants must remain visibly positive, friendly, and accessible, and must address passenger requests in a cordial yet authoritative manner.

Technological Environment

In addition to learning and understanding the basic functions of an airplane, flight attendants must learn how to use a variety of industry-related equipment such as intercoms, compact food and beverage carts, movie and music systems, first aid kits, and other emergency safety equipment such as breathing masks and flotation devices. Flight attendants must also know how to use computers and digital tools, which are increasingly used for business communication, scheduling, and other logistics.

EDUCATION, TRAINING, AND ADVANCEMENT

High School/Secondary

High school students who wish to become flight attendants can prepare by studying foreign languages, foods and nutrition, psychology, and public speaking. They should also take a basic first aid training and certification course. An understanding of the fundamentals of aviation, emergency procedures, and airplane operation and maintenance is useful. As flight attendants work with the public, participation in any activities that involve communicating with groups and customer service will be helpful for those seeking employment as members of a cabin crew.

Suggested High School Subjects

- English
- First Aid Training
- Food Service & Management
- Foreign Languages
- Mathematics
- Psychology
- Speech
- Public Speaking

Related Career Pathways/Majors

Transportation, Distribution & Logistics Cluster
- Transportation Operations Pathway

Postsecondary

In the United States, flight attendants are required to have earned a high school diploma or its equivalent. Certain schools and colleges also offer flight attendant training, but a postsecondary degree is generally not required; however, increasingly often, some airlines give preference to those candidates with a college degree or who have already completed some kind of related training. Flight attendants may find it helpful to study postsecondary subjects related to the hospitality industry, such as communications and travel and tourism. Flight attendants who wish to work for an international airline are usually proficient in at least one foreign language and may also benefit from courses in foreign culture and history.

Related College Majors
- Flight Attendant Training

Adult Job Seekers

Potential flight attendants should have extensive experience working with the public and should demonstrate the ability to think on their feet and remain calm during a dispute or crisis. Most airlines require that flight attendants be at least eighteen to twenty-one years of age, undergo thorough background checks, and pass stringent medical evaluations. Those seeking employment through an international airline must research the specific laws, educational, and licensing requirements of their potential host nation before applying for advertised positions.

Professional Certification and Licensure

In the United States, flight attendants must complete a training program through the Federal Aviation Administration (FAA), providing flight attendant certification. Successful certification depends on a flight attendant's ability to fulfill specific training requirements, set forth by the FAA and the Transportation Security Administration, including safety procedures, evacuations, and medical emergencies. Each nation has its own licensing and certification requirements for airline personnel and, in most cases, international companies advertising for foreign flight attendants will provide information on specific national requirements and may assist international applicants in completing the necessary applications and/or certification procedures.

Additional Requirements

Some flight attendants are constantly traveling to and from exotic destinations, while others may be just making a run between regional airports. Due to their schedule, flight attendants and other members of the aircrew are often away from home for long periods of time and potential flight attendants should consider that they may never experience a "normal" schedule, and will have to leave family members and loved ones for extended periods.

Successful flight attendants possess an interest in working with people and a willingness to learn about other cultures. Though air travel is not usually dangerous, some flights may be unpleasant because of turbulence, mechanical failure, or other mishaps. Because of this, flight attendants must handle themselves with poise and confidence under severe pressure or duress. Most airlines require that applicants be physically fit in proportion to their height, and stay within a certain weight range throughout their years of service. In the United States, most flight attendants pay union dues and belong to the Association of Flight Attendants, the Transport Workers Union of America, or the International Brotherhood of Teamsters. Other nations also have unions and associations for flight personnel and these organizations can help working professionals to find job opportunities and to address any employment-related problems that arise.

Fun Fact

Back in the 1980s, a cost-cutting move by American Airlines saved $40,000 a year ... the removal of a single olive from each in-flight salad.
Source: huffingtonpost.com

EARNINGS AND ADVANCEMENT

According to the Bureau of Labor Statistics, flight attendants working in the United States earn an annual median wage of $48,500, with a range less than $26,000 to over $78,000. Higher pay is typically associated with boutique and specialty airline service. While the US airline industry has been growing at a slower rate than many other industries in the nation, thus placing limits on potential pay and job opportunities, there may be more lucrative opportunities for those willing to work overseas.

Depending on their employer, flight attendants may receive paid vacations, holidays, and sick days; life and health insurance; and retirement benefits. In many cases, airlines provide flight attendants with free or reduced air fares for themselves and their families. Flight attendants are required to purchase uniforms and wear them while on duty. The airlines usually pay for uniform replacement items and may provide a small allowance to cover cleaning and upkeep of the uniforms.

EMPLOYMENT AND OUTLOOK

As of 2017, the US flight attendant and cabin crew industries were expected to grow by 2 percent between 2014 and 2024, which is far slower than the average of 6-7 percent predicted for all U.S. industries. Population growth and an improving economy are expected to increase the number of airline passengers. As airlines enlarge their capacity to meet rising demand by increasing the number and size of planes in operation, more flight attendants will be needed. However, this growth will be tempered by higher fuel prices. Competition for jobs as flight attendants is expected to remain very strong because the number of applicants is expected to greatly exceed the number of job openings. While international airlines regularly advertise positions for foreign workers trained as pilots or aviation specialists, opportunities for cabin crew positions with foreign companies are relatively rare.

Related Occupations
- Food & Beverage Service Worker
- Waiter/Waitress

Related Military Occupations
- Transportation Specialist

MORE INFORMATION

Air Transport Association of America
Office of Communications
1301 Pennsylvania Avenue, NW
Suite 1100
Washington, DC 20004-1707
202.626.4000
ata@airlines.org
www.air-transport.org

Association of Flight Attendants
501 3rd Street, NW
Washington, DC 20001
202.434.1300
info@afacwa.org
www.afanet.org

Transport Workers Union of America
501 3rd Street, NW, 9th Floor
Washington, DC 20001
202.719.3900
www.twu.org

U.S. Department of Transportation
Federal Aviation Administration
800 Independence Avenue SW
Washington, DC 20591
866.835.5322
www.faa.gov

Briana Nadeau/Editor,
updated by Micah Issitt

Pilot

Snapshot

Career Cluster(s): Transportation, Distribution & Logistics
Interests: Aviation, navigation, geography, engineering technology, physics, math and geometry
Earnings (Yearly Average): $105,720
Employment & Outlook: Average Growth Expected

OVERVIEW

Sphere of Work

Pilots are vehicular experts trained to operate airplanes and other flying vehicles. While airline pilots typically transport passengers between airports, pilots may also operate air vehicles for a variety of other reasons, such as assisting with rescue operations, conducting aerial photography or research operations, or assisting in disaster response. The main vehicles used by pilots are large commercial airplanes, smaller fixed-wing aircraft, jets, military aircraft, and helicopters. Each type of

vehicle requires specific training and experience and pilots may spend years in training before qualifying to fly certain aircraft or to participate in certain types of aerial activities.

Work Environment

Pilots work in a variety of environments. Most pilots work in the airline industry, flying regional, national, and international routes for major commercial airlines. Many pilots are in the military, using their aircraft for attacks and rescues, as well as surveillance and mapping purposes. Commercial pilots operate aircraft for commercial purposes and most commercial pilots transport cargo between destinations though other commercial pilots may work in agriculture or forestry, using aircraft to spray pesticides or drop seeds. Other professional pilots work in the media industry, flying over traffic and incident scenes or working with photographers to film or photograph scenes from an aerial perspective. Because pilots may fly internationally or between a variety of local environments, pilots may work in a variety of different environments and may cope with a wide range of environmental conditions.

Profile

Interests: Data, People, Things
Working Conditions: Work Inside
Physical Strength: Light Work
Education Needs: Junior/
  Technical/Community College,
  Bachelor's Degree
Licensure/Certification: Required
Physical Abilities Not Require: Not
  Climb, Not Kneel
Opportunities For Experience:
  Military Service
Holland Interest Score*: IRE

* See Appendix A

Occupation Interest

Piloting aircraft is a complex and potentially dangerous activity and work in the field can be personally demanding, requiring that pilots spend long periods away from their homes and families. However, flying aircraft can also be exhilarating and enjoyable and many professional pilots first take up flying as a personal interest. As a rule, the pilot in command (PIC)—of any aircraft, small or large—has a legal obligation for and the final authority of that aircraft under national and/or regional regulations. This means that the PIC is responsible for the safety of the aircraft, ultimately determines the aircraft's route, commands the flight crew, and holds the responsibility for the safe passage of any passengers. In the case of an emergency, the pilot is in command and has the authority to deviate from standard practice or make a decision that differs from the direction given by the control tower.

A Day in the Life—Duties and Responsibilities

The specific responsibilities of a pilot vary a great deal based on the industry in which he or she works. Overall, however, a pilot's primary responsibilities are to ensure the safety of the plane and its passengers and satisfy the requirements of his or her employers. To this end, pilots will conduct thorough safety and systems checks on a plane before departing, a process known as a "pre-flight," or pre-flight inspection. During such reviews, the pilot will use a checklist to make sure all safety equipment, navigation technology, and other systems are operating normally. The pilot will check the plane's logs to review any issues the plane may have had in its previous flights and review weather reports and flight plans. A pilot oversees the plane's "pushback" and taxi from a gate or terminal before takeoff. During flight, the pilot will communicate with passengers, the flight crew, and air traffic control with any updates. When it is time to land, a pilot runs another series of checks, communicating with the tower of the receiving airport and re-checking landing gear and systems.

In addition to sharing many of the responsibilities described above, pilots who do not work for airlines have a number of other tasks. Helicopter pilots, for example, often photograph accident sites and conduct tours while flying their vehicles. Crop dusters and seeders must often load their payloads in addition to operating their airplanes. Many pilots who do not work for a major airline must also perform their own administrative tasks and business development activities in addition to flying.

Duties and Responsibilities

- Reviewing and examining papers to determine necessary flight data
- Performing pre-flight inspection of the aircraft and its cargo
- Contacting control tower by radio to receive instructions
- Controlling the airplane in flight
- Logging flight information

OCCUPATION SPECIALTIES

Navigators

Navigators establish the position of the plane and direct the course of airplanes on flights, using navigational instruments, atmospheric observations or basic reasoning.

Agricultural Aircraft Pilots

Agricultural Aircraft Pilots fly airplanes or helicopters, at low altitudes, over agricultural fields in order to dust or spray them with seeds, fertilizers or pesticides.

Commercial Airplane Pilots

Commercial Airplane Pilots fly passenger, mail or freight planes.

Airplane-Patrol Pilots

Airplane-Patrol Pilots fly airplanes over pipelines, tracks and communications systems to detect and radio the location and nature of the damage they are investigating.

Test Pilots

Test Pilots fly new or modified aircraft to evaluate the plane's airworthiness, performance, systems operation and design.

Executive Pilots

Executive Pilots fly company-owned aircraft to transport company officials or customers. They file a flight plan with airport officials and obtain and interpret weather data based upon the flight plan.

Helicopter Pilots

Helicopter Pilots fly helicopters for purposes such as transporting passengers and cargo, search and rescue operations, fighting fires and reporting on traffic and weather conditions.

WORK ENVIRONMENT

Immediate Physical Environment

Airline pilots primarily work in airports or other aviation centers. Military pilots may also be found on aircraft carriers and other naval ships or may work at an airbase. Each of these environments tend to be complex and busy, with many different professionals performing tasks around the clock. Pilots for commercial airlines will often have layovers where they may spend hours or days waiting for their next flight and this creates opportunities for a pilot to explore a variety of environments in the course of his or her job.

Transferable Skills and Abilities

Communication Skills
- Speaking effectively
- Writing concisely

Organization & Management Skills
- Making decisions
- Meeting goals and deadlines
- Performing duties which change frequently

Research & Planning Skills
- Using logical reasoning

Technical Skills
- Performing scientific, mathematical and technical work
- Working with machines, tools or other objects

Human Environment

Pilots must work with a wide range of people on the ground and on board their planes, including maintenance crews, security personnel, flight attendants, air traffic controllers, luggage handlers, and passengers. Pilots spend much of their time communicating with other members of a cabin or ground crew and, in some cases, also work directly with passengers. In general, pilots are expected to have excellent communication skills and to be able to work as part of a team, though pilots are also managers who are ultimately responsible for ensuring that their aircraft and flight crew functions efficiently and effectively in both normal and emergency flight conditions.

Technological Environment

Aircraft are complex machines that contain many specialized controls and pieces of equipment that pilots must both understand and know how to operate. Increasingly, digital computing technology is an important part of aircraft maintenance and operation and pilots must receive specialized training to learn to use various types of digital and traditional controls. As part of the pre-flight check, they must carefully examine each of these systems to ensure that they are running properly. During flight, they must be skilled with automatic pilot systems, weather gauges, communications equipment, and safety measures. Specialized pilots, such as those in the military, or working in aerial firefighting or agricultural work, are also expected to operate industry-specific systems, such as weapons systems, payload devices, and aerial photographic equipment.

EDUCATION, TRAINING, AND ADVANCEMENT

High School/Secondary

High school students interested in becoming pilots are encouraged to physics, math, geometry, and geography. Additionally, because communication with passengers, ground personnel, and passengers is critical to many pilots, aspiring pilots are encouraged to take courses that build verbal skills, such as English. Those interested in operating international flights, or in working as pilots in foreign nations, might also benefit from classes in foreign language or culture.

Suggested High School Subjects
- Algebra
- Applied Math
- Applied Physics
- College Preparatory
- English
- Geography

- Geometry
- Physics
- Trigonometry
- Foreign Languages
- Public Speaking

Related Career Pathways/Majors
Transportation, Distribution & Logistics Cluster
- Transportation Operations Pathway

Postsecondary

Many pilots receive postsecondary certification, such as an associate's degree, from a junior and/or community college. However, as the field of aviation is extremely competitive, prospective pilots are encouraged to obtain at least a bachelor's degree in a related field and/or to obtain direct pilot training through the military or civilian flight schools. In the past, many commercial pilots were ex-military. While no longer the trend, the military is a viable option for those seeking pilot training. For those seeking to pilot international airlines, training in foreign language and culture is essential and will enhance opportunities for employment.

Related College Majors
- Aircraft Piloting & Navigation (Professional)

Adult Job Seekers

Professional pilot positions are difficult to obtain in the United States due to high competition and slow domestic growth. It is essential for pilots, particularly those aspiring to gain employment with a major airline, to log the most flight hours possible in order to have a chance at obtaining a better job. Many pilots begin their careers at small, regional carriers or train through the military before seeking employment through a commercial flight company or airline. There are some regions and nations in which the airline flight industry is growing at a faster average pace than in the United States and this creates opportunities for U.S. trained pilots willing to work and/or live abroad. The Chinese airline industry, for instance, advertises much higher than average wages for U.S.-trained commercial airline pilots, due to a shortage of native pilots and fast national growth in tourism and commercial air travel.

Professional Certification and Licensure

In the United States, the central authority regulating pilots in the civilian arena is the Federal Aviation Administration (FAA). U.S.-based pilots must receive their licenses from the FAA by completing a series of tests (including a written exam as well as a physical examination) and by logging a certain number of hours of active flight time both in simulators and in aircraft accompanied by FAA officials. During the course of their careers, pilots can also receive certification in specialized flight techniques, such as navigating only using instruments, and may also gain certification in different classes of airlines. Airline pilots must also log 1,500 hours of FAA-approved flight time and certification in instrument and night flying. Physical exams and additional training are required on a yearly basis. Requirements for professional licensing and certification vary by country and each nation may have different physical and professional guidelines for professional pilots. Companies hiring foreign-born or trained pilots will typically assist prospective employees in completing the requirements needed for professional certification.

Additional Requirements

Pilots should demonstrate a strong attention to detail and be able to work long hours in stressful situations. In many nations, pilots must demonstrate a certain minimum level of hearing and eyesight before obtaining their license. Because professional pilots need to meet certain physical and mental benchmarks to maintain professional certification, pilots may retire earlier, on average, than employees in many other fields. Pilots working in international travel must be comfortable navigating in foreign cultures and communicating across linguistic and cultural lines. Knowledge of foreign languages is a helpful tool for those seeking overseas employment or working with a domestic airline specializing in international travel.

EARNINGS AND ADVANCEMENT

Salaries for pilots vary widely depending on the type of position and/or company, with U.S. pilots earning an average annual salary of around $105,720, with a range of between $65,000 and over $200,000. Private and specialty pilots typically earn higher wages than commercial or airline pilots. Because of high international demand, pilots willing to work for foreign aviation organizations or corporations have the potential to earn much higher salaries than are typically available in the United States, though pilots applying for international positions may need to commit to a minimum contract of one to several years.

Pilots often receive paid vacations, holidays, and sick days; life and health insurance; and retirement benefits, though the benefits vary according to employer, or may receive no benefits if operating independently. Commercial airline companies typically provide pilots and other crew members with accommodations while traveling for work and many receive an expense account for situations in which the pilot must spend an extended period in another area or country. Pilots employed by airlines may also receive free or reduced fare flights for themselves and family members.

EMPLOYMENT AND OUTLOOK

According to the Bureau of Labor Statistics (BLS), the U.S. airline pilot industry is expected to grow by 5 percent between 2014 and 2024, which constitutes average of slightly slower than average growth in comparison to the 6-7 percent estimated for all U.S. occupations during the same period. In an effort to remain competitive, U.S. airlines have reduced the number of routes and flights offered, which limits employment growth and opportunities for prospective professionals. By contrast, opportunities for commercial pilots have expanded in the 2010s, with 10 percent growth expected between 2014 and 2024.

Pilots attempting to get jobs at the major airlines will face strong competition, as those firms tend to attract many more applicants than they have jobs. Pilots who have logged the greatest number of flying hours in the more sophisticated equipment typically have the best prospects. For this reason, military pilots often have an advantage over other applicants. The international market for U.S. trained pilots is growing faster than the domestic market, which has created a variety of opportunities for airline, commercial, and specialty pilots in certain parts of the world. Trained pilots unable to find work in the United States, or who are interested in experimenting with international living, can therefore also seek employment by looking for job opportunities with foreign companies.

Related Military Occupations
- Air Crew Member
- Airplane Navigator
- Airplane Pilot
- Helicopter Pilot
- Radar & Sonar Operator
- Space Operations Officer
- Special Operations Officer

MORE INFORMATION

Aircraft Owners and Pilots Association
421 Aviation Way
Frederick, MD 21701
301.695.2000
www.aopa.org

Air Line Pilots Association, International
1625 Massachusetts Avenue, NW
Washington, DC 20036
703.689.2270
www.alpa.org

Federal Aviation Administration
800 Independence Avenue, SW
Washington, DC 20591
866.835.5322
www.faa.gov

International Society of Women Airline Pilots
723 S. Casino Center Boulevard
2nd Floor
Las Vegas, NV 89101-6716
www.iswap.org

Michael Auerbach/Editor,
updated by Micah Issitt

Travel Agent

Snapshot

Career Cluster(s): Hospitality & Tourism, Transportation, Distribution & Logistics

Interests: Travel, Event Planning, Tourism

Earnings (Yearly Average): $36,460

Employment & Outlook: Decline Expected

OVERVIEW

Sphere of Work

Travel agents are customer service experts who specialize in travel and vacation planning and scheduling and offer their services to prospective travelers, helping them with the logistics of vacation or business trips, whether domestic or international. While many different types of travelers once utilized the services of travel agents to organize their trips, web-based tools and direct airline-to-customer tools have reduced the need for professional travel agents,

though travel agent expertise is still utilized for certain types of travel. Travel agents help to book airfare or other forms of travel, organize lodging, help travelers obtain certificates needed to travel to certain destinations, and work with customers to organize travel plans that meet certain budgetary needs. Some travel agents form partnerships with certain resorts or hospitality companies, receiving payment for leading customers towards services offered by certain companies.

Work Environment

Travel agents typically work in clean, comfortable, and well-lit offices. Self-employed travel agents often work out of home offices. Most work alone or among a small staff of administrative personnel and/or other travel agents. It is customary for travel agents to work at least forty hours per week; however, many work overtime, especially during peak travel seasons. Travel agents may spend most of a typical day behind a desk, coordinating and negotiating with airlines, cruise lines, hotels, and tourism companies via phone and Internet. Being a travel agent is also highly interactive and travel agents spend much of their time working directly with their clients to schedule trips or to handle logistical issues that arise during a scheduled travel package.

Profile

Interests: Data, People
Working Conditions: Work Inside
Physical Strength: Light Work
Education Needs: Junior/
  Technical/Community College
Licensure/Certification: Required
Physical Abilities Not Require: Not
  Climb, Not Kneel
Opportunities For Experience:
  Military Service, Part Time Work
Holland Interest Score*: ECS

* See Appendix A

Occupation Interest

The travel industry is often demanding and challenging. Successful transactions frequently rely on speed, effective communication, and in-depth knowledge of national and international destinations. Prospective travel agents should enjoy working with people, even when this becomes a challenge, and should be comfortable working with and communicating with people from a variety of backgrounds and cultures. Since people tend to hold idealized views of vacation trips, customer expectations are often difficult to fulfill. When unforeseen events occur, travel agents are sometimes blamed for a customer's poor travel experiences and a travel agent must therefore be able to calmly and diplomatically address complains and issues that arise. Travel agents are typically expected to have detailed knowledge about a variety of national and international travel locations, recommending lodging, food, and tourist destinations to their customers as well as providing cultural information that might affect travelers.

A Day in the Life—Duties and Responsibilities

Travel agents spend most of the workday at a desk, on the phone, and on the computer and often function as liaisons between travelers and travel or hospitality companies. Travel agents may also spend part of a typically day consulting with travelers about desired destinations, availability, budget restrictions, and any special travel requirements they might have in addition to conducting introductory meetings with customers considering utilizing a travel agency for an upcoming trip. Travel agents also provide customers with information regarding national and international regulations, including travel advisories, money exchange rates, and required documentation like passports and visas. For long-term or high-profile clients, some travel agents make themselves available on an "on-call" basis to deal with any travel-related issues that arise during a client's trip.

In some cases, travel agents may travel to specific destinations to research the quality of a travel experience themselves, which further bolsters their credibility with clients. Many travel agents specialize in a specific geographic area or region, demographic group, or cultural preference and specialization has become more common and increasingly advantageous due competition for travel agent positions and clients. Travel agents specializing in arranging international travel will benefit from specific linguistic and cultural knowledge about their specialty area. For instance, travel agents who specialize in booking travel in Latin America will benefit from a knowledge of Spanish and from specific experience with the resorts, tourist destination, and other specifics of travel within that region.

Duties and Responsibilities

- Collecting payment for tickets and tour packages
- Promoting, advertising and selling travel services
- Advising on travel sites and weather conditions
- Arranging hotel reservations, car rentals, tours and recreation
- Informing clients on customs, regulations, passports, medical certificates and currency exchange rates
- Using computers for fares and schedules
- Visiting hotels and travel attractions for evaluations

OCCUPATION SPECIALTIES

Government Travel Clerks

Government Travel Clerks plan itineraries and schedule travel accommodations for government personnel and relatives.

Automotive Club Travel Counselors

Automotive Club Travel Counselors plan trips for members, providing maps and brochures.

Reservation Clerks

Reservation Clerks make travel and hotel accommodations for guests and employees of businesses.

Hotel Travel Clerks

Hotel Travel Clerks provide travel information and arrange accommodations for tourists.

WORK ENVIRONMENT

Transferable Skills and Abilities

Communication Skills
- Persuading others
- Speaking effectively
- Writing concisely

Interpersonal/Social Skills
- Being able to work independently
- Cooperating with others
- Working as a member of a team

Organization & Management Skills
- Paying attention to and handling details
- Selling ideas or products

Technical Skills
- Using technology to process information
- Working with data or numbers
- Working with machines, tools or other objects

Work Environment Skills
- Traveling

Immediate Physical Environment

Most travel agents work in an office or out of their own homes and may conduct much of their work via telephone or email. In many cases, a travel agent may want to have access to a location where potential customers can meet in person to discuss a travel itinerary.

Human Environment

Travel agents constantly communicate with clients and customer service personnel over the phone, in person, and through e-mail. In some cases, travel agents may need to cope with difficult individuals and interactions and must be able to maintain an outwardly pleasant attitude and an accommodating demeanor at all times. In larger offices, travel agents interact with other office personnel, administrators, and other travel agents.

Technological Environment

Travel agents use basic office equipment to help them complete their daily tasks. They routinely use phones, fax machines, calculators, and digital communication tools. In addition, travel agents should be proficient with scheduling and spreadsheet software and must learn to use a variety of web-based software systems used to book various types of accommodation, hospitality, and travel. Travel agents should also be highly proficient at reading and understanding maps as they often help customers navigate in unfamiliar areas and should know how to use web and software based map programs.

EDUCATION, TRAINING, AND ADVANCEMENT

High School/Secondary

High school students who wish to become travel agents should enroll in academic courses that emphasize business, communications, geography, foreign languages, world history, and social studies. Students should also participate in extracurricular clubs and student groups that focus on travel and tourism or that sharpen skills with customer service and/or social interaction. It is also helpful for students to travel as much as possible, even to local or regional attractions, in order to develop a sense of how to evaluate and critique locations and exhibitions. Students can gain valuable research experience by investigating online travel sources, deals, itineraries, and popular tourist attractions across the globe.

Suggested High School Subjects

- Applied Communication
- Bookkeeping
- Business & Computer Technology
- Business Math
- College Preparatory
- Computer Science
- English
- Foreign Languages
- Geography
- History
- Mathematics
- Science
- Social Studies
- Speech

Related Career Pathways/Majors

Hospitality & Tourism Cluster

* Travel & Tourism Pathway

Transportation, Distribution & Logistics Cluster

* Sales & Service Pathway

Postsecondary

After graduating from high school, most prospective travel agents find it helpful to enroll in full- or part-time travel agent programs offered through vocational schools, public adult education programs, local community colleges, and distance learning programs. Travel agent programs provide students with a solid understanding of sales and marketing, ticketing and reservations, tour planning and development, and world geography, as well as introducing helpful software typically used in the industry. A small number of colleges and universities offer bachelor's and master's degrees travel and tourism and individuals looking for an employment advantage should consider enrolling in a higher degree program.

Related College Majors

* Tourism & Travel Services Marketing Operations
* Travel-Tourism Management

Adult Job Seekers

Though a postsecondary degree is not considered a requirement for prospective travel agents, many employers give hiring preference to those jobseekers with demonstrated experience in the field of travel and tourism. In addition, those who have personal travel experience and proven knowledge of a specific geographic region or foreign country are likely to have an easier time finding employment. Prospective travel agents can participate in mentorships with local travel agencies and some travel agents begin their careers as reservation clerks or agent assistants with local travel agencies.

Professional Certification and Licensure

Experienced travel agents who have worked in larger offices and wish to start their own businesses might need professional accreditation through a known travel organization, like the Airlines Reporting Corporation and the International Airlines Travel Agency Network.

Various cruise lines, and railways might also accredit certain travel agents or agencies. In order to receive approval, a travel agent's business must be financially viable and must employ at least one experienced manager or travel agent. Accreditation is meant to ensure quality in the industry and thus assure customers that the agent working with them is a professional in his or her field.

Additional Requirements

As more and more travel information becomes available via online sources, agents must continually add to their existing knowledge of cultures, destinations, lodging, procedures, government regulations, and attractions. They must possess impeccable research and computer skills, and they must also be able to effectively relay updated and new information to clients as it becomes available. As travelers more regularly arrange their own trips, travel agents must adapt to fill specific niches within the broader tourism and hospitality industry. To accomplish this, some travel agents specialize in organizing large group or business travel packages while others attempt to attract clients by offering specialize knowledge of a certain region, nation, or type of travel.

Fun Fact

The travel industry is one of the world's largest, contributing $7.6 trillion to the global economy in 2016. Worldwide, 1.24 billion international tourists were estimated to have arrived at their destinations that year.

Source: statista.com

EARNINGS AND ADVANCEMENT

In the United States, travel agents earn an average annual salary of $36,460, with a range of between $20,000 and 60,000. Higher wages can be found in prestigious travel agencies or by working directly with businesses to help organize conferences and business travel packages.

Travel agents usually receive paid vacations, holidays, and sick days; life and health insurance; and retirement benefits. These are usually paid by the employer. Self-employed agents must provide these benefits for themselves. In some companies, travel agents may also benefit from reduced cost for travel and lodging.

EMPLOYMENT AND OUTLOOK

According to the Bureau of Labor Statistics (BLS), the travel agent industry is expected to decline by approximately 12 percent between 2014 and 2024. A combination of factors, most notably the ease of booking travel and other activities through online travel companies, has contributed to the decline of the industry. Due to the overall decline in the industry, competition is expected to be significant for remaining positions. As web-booking services have emergent, the travel agent industry has begun to evolve with agencies and independent agents increasingly specializing in certain types of travel or in helping customers with complex travel arrangement that may involve multiple locations and layovers, various types of lodging and transportation, or specialized needs.

Related Occupations
- Reservation and Ticket Agent

Related Military Occupations
- Transportation Specialist

Conversation With . . .
KATE HOWE

Ski Instructor / Trainer / Examiner
Owner, katehowe.com
Aspen-based, teaches around the globe
11 years in profession

1. What was your individual career path in terms of education/training, entry-level job, or other significant opportunity ?

I was an athlete as a kid, a figure skater who learned to earn time with coaches by proving I was worth it. I developed an understanding of skill acquisition and the psychology of performing under pressure.

I went on to college at the Art Center College of Design in Pasadena, CA, but left to open a rock climbing gym with my husband. We ran that for five years, then moved to Montana.

I became a ski instructor almost by accident, when I took my 5-year-old son to a local ski area for a lesson. The supervisor offered me a job working with kids. I had told him I was a figure skating coach—and lousy skier—and he said, "We need people who can teach; we will teach you to ski."

That was 11 years ago. I started as an entry level instructor, making $7.25 an hour at Bridger Bowl Ski Area. I admired instructors who could take private guests to the top of Bridger Ridge (double black difficulty)—they earned more and had fun skiing difficult terrain.

I decided that if I wanted to get good quickly, I should train as if I were trying out for the Professional Ski Instructors of America (PSIA) National Alpine Team. I took advantage of my employer's in-house training with a talented instructor, an alumnus of the national team. I also read every book and watched every video I could about technique, and attended the PSIA National Academy to be trained by current team members.

In two years, I passed all three levels of certification by the PSIA and was recruited to teach on Aspen Mountain in Colorado. I am now an Examiner for PSIA. This means I give certification exams to ski instructors. I'm also a trainer at Aspen Snowmass.

I have a full calendar of private clients who ski with me for three to 25 days. My company, KH Global Ski Adventures, takes clients adventure/back country skiing all over the globe, from Japan to British Columbia to Switzerland … wherever they want to go.

I made my own career path and sought out the coaching and opportunities I needed. Starting a new, expensive career with two kids under 5 was scary.

2. What are the most important skills and/or qualities for someone in your profession, particularly if working overseas?

You need to manage guest relations and to always improve so you can better serve your guests. As a teacher, everything you do must be in service to your students' improvement and ability. Guest-centered teaching creates trust, and your guests will return.

You have to have the ability to be coached. You must be able to be critiqued and criticized without taking it personally. You can practice this skill in high school. It's about getting as good as you can at everything they put in front of you. Always move your goal ahead so that when you cross one line, you're already training for the next goal.

When working overseas, make friends with everyone. Overcome your fear of the unknown by saying yes as often as you can. Help others out. When I'm at an unfamiliar ski area, if someone has fallen or has trouble with their skis, I offer help. Be humble and grateful and cultivate friendships and doors will open for you. Because of this philosophy, I was the first woman and the seventh person to go heli skiing on the island of Hokkaido, Japan, invited by a tour operator I had made friends with by helping clear breakfast dishes.

3. What do you wish you had known before deciding to work abroad?

Plan for visas, which can be difficult. Always hire a local guide. You don't have to know the language to succeed. Google Maps can get you around a new country without a hitch. Figure out a way to fly business class so that you are rested and ready to work.

4. Are there many job opportunities overseas in your profession? In what specific geographic areas?

There's as much work as you want. To access it, put yourself in a position where people want to hire you. Skiing in China is booming right now.

5. Will the willingness of professionals to travel and live overseas need to change in the next five years? What role will technology play, and what skills will be required?

All instructors dream of traveling overseas with a private client for heli skiing, the pinnacle of our profession. I don't see that changing, but I do see the snow changing. Climate change is a real threat. There is less powder. Seasons are shorter. To stay relevant in the travel ski industry, you must seek the snow, and find clients who are willing to travel to find it.

6. What do you enjoy most about your job? What do you enjoy least about your job?

Skiing deep powder out of a helicopter off the top of an un-skied peak is the most incredible sensation I have ever experienced, topped only by watching a guest I have trained do the same. The next best piece is traveling, making friends, experiencing new things and embracing the scary, stressful chaos of being somewhere you don't understand.

The worst is being cold and getting frostbitten feet. And being exhausted from giving my all 24/7 from the moment I leave my house until the day I return. I usually sleep for two or three days when I get back from a trip.

7. Can you suggest a valuable "try this" for students considering a career overseas in your profession?

Go to Rookie Academy in New Zealand to get certified as a Level 2 instructor. Practice being coachable, ego-less, humble, and hard working. Apply to ski schools in Japan and China, where a lot of ski schools are just opening. They hire lower level instructors.

MORE INFORMATION

Airlines Reporting Corporation
3000 Wilson Boulevard, Suite 300
Arlington, VA 22201-3862
703.816.8000
www.arccorp.com

American Society of Travel Agents
1101 King Street, Suite 200
Alexandria, VA 22314
703.739.2782
askasta@astahq.com
www.asta.org

International Airlines Travel Agency Network
703 Waterford Way, Suite 600
Miami, FL 33126
877.734.2826
www.iatan.org

National Association of Career Travel Agents
1101 King Street, Suite 200
Alexandria, VA 22314
877.226.2282
www.nacta.com

Specialty Travel Agents Association
12381 Fenton Road
Fenton, MI 48430
810.629.2386
www.specialtytravelagents.com

The Travel Institute
148 Linden Street, Suite 305
Wellesley, MA 02482
800.542.4282
tech@thetravelinstitute.com
www.thetravelinstitute.com

Briana Nadeau/Editor

What Are Your Career Interests?

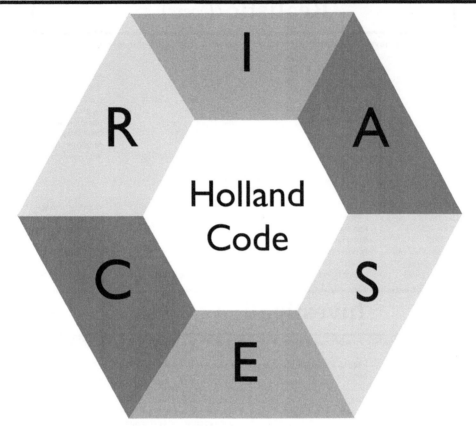

This is based on Dr. John Holland's theory that people and work environments can be loosely classified into six different groups. Each of the letters above corresponds to one of the six groups described in the following pages.

Different people's personalities may find different environments more to their liking. While you may have some interests in and similarities to several of the six groups, you may be attracted primarily to two or three of the areas. These two or three letters are your "Holland Code." For example, with a code of "RES" you would most resemble the Realistic type, somewhat less resemble the Enterprising type, and resemble the Social type even less. The types that are not in your code are the types

you resemble least of all.

Most people, and most jobs, are best represented by some combination of two or three of the Holland interest areas. In addition, most people are most satisfied if there is some degree of fit between their personality and their work environment.

The rest of the pages in this booklet further explain each type and provide some examples of career possibilities, areas of study at MU, and co-curricular activities for each code. To take a more in-depth look at your Holland Code, take a self-assessment such as the SDS, Discover, or a card sort at the MU Career Center with a Career Specialist.

Realistic *(Doers)*

People who have athletic ability, prefer to work with objects, machines, tools, plants or animals, or to be outdoors.

Are you?	independent	**Can you?**	**Like to?**
practical	ambitious	fix electrical things	tinker with machines/vehicles
straightforward/frank	systematic	solve electrical problems	work outdoors
mechanically inclined		pitch a tent	be physically active
stable		play a sport	use your hands
concrete		read a blueprint	build things
reserved		plant a garden	tend/train animals
self-controlled		operate tools and machine	work on electronic equipment

Career Possibilities
(Holland Code):

Air Traffic Controller (SER)	Dental Technician (REI)	Laboratory Technician (RIE)	Property Manager (ESR)
Archaeologist (IRE)	Farm Manager (ESR)	Landscape Architect (AIR)	Recreation Manager (SER)
Athletic Trainer (SRE)	Fish and Game Warden (RES)	Mechanical Engineer (RIS)	Service Manager (ERS)
Cartographer (IRE)	Floral Designer (RAE)	Optician (REI)	Software Technician (RCI)
Commercial Airline Pilot (RIE)	Forester (RIS)	Petroleum Geologist (RIE)	Ultrasound Technologist (RSI)
Commercial Drafter (IRE)	Geodetic Surveyor (IRE)	Police Officer (SER)	Vocational Rehabilitation
Corrections Officer (SER)	Industrial Arts Teacher (IER)	Practical Nurse (SER)	Consultant (ESR)

Investigative *(Thinkers)*

People who like to observe, learn, investigate, analyze, evaluate, or solve problems.

Are you?	intellectually self-confident	**Can you?**	Like to?
inquisitive	Independent	think abstractly	explore a variety of ideas
analytical	logical	solve math problems	work independently
scientific	complex	understand scientific theories	perform lab experiments
observant/precise	Curious	do complex calculations	deal with abstractions
scholarly		use a microscope or computer	do research
cautious		interpret formulas	be challenged

Career Possibilities
(Holland Code):

Actuary (ISE)	Chemical Engineer (IRE)	Geologist (IRE)	Physician, General Practice (ISE)
Agronomist (IRS)	Chemist (IRE)	Horticulturist (IRS)	Psychologist (IES)
Anesthesiologist (IRS)	Computer Systems Analyst (IER)	Mathematician (IER)	Research Analyst (IRC)
Anthropologist (IRE)	Dentist (ISR)	Medical Technologist (ISA)	Statistician (IRE)
Archaeologist (IRE)	Ecologist (IRE)	Meteorologist (IRS)	Surgeon (IRA)
Biochemist (IRS)	Economist (IAS)	Nurse Practitioner (ISA)	Technical Writer (IRS)
Biologist (ISR)	Electrical Engineer (IRE)	Pharmacist (IES)	Veterinarian (IRS)

Artistic *(Creators)*

People who have artistic, innovating, or intuitional abilities and like to work in unstructured situations using their imagination and creativity.

Are you?
creative
imaginative
innovative
unconventional
emotional
independent
Expressive

original
introspective
impulsive
sensitive
courageous
complicated
idealistic
nonconforming

Can you?
sketch, draw, paint
play a musical instrument
write stories, poetry, music
sing, act, dance
design fashions or interiors

Like to?
attend concerts, theatre, art exhibits
read fiction, plays, and poetry
work on crafts
take photography
express yourself creatively
deal with ambiguous ideas

**Career Possibilities
(Holland Code):**

Actor (AES)
Advertising Art Director (AES)
Advertising Manager (ASE)
Architect (AIR)
Art Teacher (ASE)
Artist (ASI)

Copy Writer (ASI)
Dance Instructor (AER)
Drama Coach (ASE)
English Teacher (ASE)
Entertainer/Performer (AES)
Fashion Illustrator (ASR)

Interior Designer (AES)
Intelligence Research Specialist (AEI)
Journalist/Reporter (ASE)
Landscape Architect (AIR)
Librarian (SAI)

Medical Illustrator (AIE)
Museum Curator (AES)
Music Teacher (ASI)
Photographer (AES)
Writer (ASI)
Graphic Designer (AES)

Social *(Helpers)*

People who like to work with people to enlighten, inform, help, train, or cure them, or are skilled with words.

Are you?
friendly
helpful
idealistic
insightful
outgoing
understanding

cooperative
generous
responsible
forgiving
patient
kind

Can you?
teach/train others
express yourself clearly
lead a group discussion
mediate disputes
plan and supervise an activity
cooperate well with others

Like to?
work in groups
help people with problems
do volunteer work
work with young people
serve others

**Career Possibilities
(Holland Code):**

City Manager (SEC)
Clinical Dietitian (SIE)
College/University Faculty (SEI)
Community Org. Director (SEA)
Consumer Affairs Director (SER)Counselor/Therapist (SAE)

Historian (SEI)
Hospital Administrator (SER)
Psychologist (SEI)
Insurance Claims Examiner (SIE)
Librarian (SAI)
Medical Assistant (SCR)
Minister/Priest/Rabbi (SAI)
Paralegal (SCE)

Park Naturalist (SEI)
Physical Therapist (SIE)
Police Officer (SER)
Probation and Parole Officer (SEC)
Real Estate Appraiser (SCE)
Recreation Director (SER)
Registered Nurse (SIA)

Teacher (SAE)
Social Worker (SEA)
Speech Pathologist (SAI)
Vocational-Rehab. Counselor (SEC)
Volunteer Services Director (SEC)

E̲nterprising *(Persuaders)*

People who like to work with people, influencing, persuading, leading or managing for organizational goals or economic gain.

Are you?	ambitious	**Can you?**	**Like to?**
self-confident	agreeable	initiate projects	make decisions
assertive	talkative	convince people to do things	be elected to office
persuasive	extroverted	your way	start your own business
energetic	spontaneous	sell things	campaign politically
adventurous	optimistic	give talks or speeches	meet important people
popular		organize activities	have power or status
		lead a group	
		persuade others	

**Career Possibilities
(Holland Code):**

Advertising Executive (ESA)
Advertising Sales Rep (ESR)
Banker/Financial Planner (ESR)
Branch Manager (ESA)
Business Manager (ESC)
Buyer (ESA)
Chamber of Commerce Exec (ESA)

Credit Analyst (EAS)
Customer Service Manager (ESA)
Education & Training Manager (EIS)
Emergency Medical Technician (ESI)
Entrepreneur (ESA)

Foreign Service Officer (ESA)
Funeral Director (ESR)
Insurance Manager (ESC)
Interpreter (ESA)
Lawyer/Attorney (ESA)
Lobbyist (ESA)
Office Manager (ESR)
Personnel Recruiter (ESR)

Politician (ESA)
Public Relations Rep (EAS)
Retail Store Manager (ESR)
Sales Manager (ESA)
Sales Representative (ERS)
Social Service Director (ESA)
Stockbroker (ESI)
Tax Accountant (ECS)

C̲onventional *(Organizers)*

People who like to work with data, have clerical or numerical ability, carry out tasks in detail, or follow through on others' instructions.

Are you?	practical	**Can you?**	**Like to?**
well-organized	thrifty	work well within a system	follow clearly defined
accurate	systematic	do a lot of paper work in a short	procedures
numerically inclined	structured	time	use data processing equipment
methodical	polite	keep accurate records	work with numbers
conscientious	ambitious	use a computer terminal	type or take shorthand
efficient	obedient	write effective business letters	be responsible for details
conforming	persistent		collect or organize things

**Career Possibilities
(Holland Code):**

Abstractor (CSI)
Accountant (CSE)
Administrative Assistant (ESC)
Budget Analyst (CER)
Business Manager (ESC)
Business Programmer (CRI)
Business Teacher (CSE)
Catalog Librarian (CSE)

Claims Adjuster (SEC)
Computer Operator (CSR)
Congressional-District Aide (CES)
Cost Accountant (CES)
Court Reporter (CSE)
Credit Manager (ESC)
Customs Inspector (CEI)
Editorial Assistant (CSI)

Elementary School Teacher (SEC)
Financial Analyst (CSI)
Insurance Manager (ESC)
Insurance Underwriter (CSE)
Internal Auditor (ICR)
Kindergarten Teacher (ESC)

Medical Records Technician (CSE)
Museum Registrar (CSE)
Paralegal (SCE)
Safety Inspector (RCS)
Tax Accountant (ECS)
Tax Consultant (CES)
Travel Agent (ECS)

BIBLIOGRAPHY

Arts, Media, and Entertainment

Boslaugh, Sarah. *Careers and Occupations*. Gale Cengage, 2015. Print.

Burdick, Jan E. *Creative Careers in Museums*. New York: Constable & Robinson, 2012. Internet resource.

Careers in Focus. New York: Ferguson's, 2012. Print.

Careers in Popular Music: Perfomers, Recording Artists, Writers. Chicago: Institute for Career Research, 2006. Internet resource.

Careers in Writing. Paw Prints, 2010. Print.

Congdon, Lisa, Meg M. Ilasco, and Jonathan Fields. *Art, Inc: The Essential Guide for Building Your Career As an Artist*. San Francisco: Chronicle Books, 2014. Print.

Fine Art As a Career: Painter, Sculptor, Printmaker : Portrait of the Artist As an Intriguing Individual. Chicago, Ill: Institute for Career Research, 2005. Internet resource.

Inkson, Kerr, Nicky Dries, and John Arnold. *Understanding Careers*. Los Angeles: Sage, 2015. Print.

Mathieu, Chris. *Careers in Creative Industries*. New York: Routledge, 2015. Print.

Melber, Leah M., ed. *Teaching the Museum: Careers in Museum Education*. New York: Routledge, 2009.

Schlatter, N. Elizabeth. *Museum Careers: A Practical Guide for Students and Novices*. Washington, DC: American Alliance of Museums, 2014. Print.

Education

Anonymous. *The Secret Lives of Teachers*. Chicago: University of Chicago Press, 2015.

Armstrong, Thomas. *The Power of the Adolescent Brain: Strategies for Teaching Middle and High School Students*. Alexandria, VA: ASCD, 2016.

Bain, Ben. *What the Best College Teachers Do*. Cambridge, MA: Harvard University Press, 2004.

Baker, Nicholson. *Substitute: Going to School with a Thousand Kids*. New York: Blue Rider Press, 2016.

Brinkley, Alan, et al. *The Chicago Handbook for Teachers: A Practical Guide to the College Classroom*, 2nd ed. Chicago: University of Chicago Press, 2011.

Brown, Dave F. and Trudy Knowles. *What Every Middle School Teacher Should Know*, 3rd ed. Portsmouth, NH: Heinemann, 2014.

Fourie, Dennis and Nancy E. Loe. *Libraries in the Information Age: An Introduction and Career Exploration*. Santa Barbara, CA: Libraries Unlimited, 2016.

Goldstein, Dana. *The Teacher Wars: A History of America's Most Embattled Profession*. New York: Anchor Books, 2014.

Gordon, Howard R.D. *The History and Growth of Career and Technical Education in America*, 4th ed. Long Grove, IL: Waveland Press, 2014.

Green, Tena. *How to Be Successful in Your First Year of Teaching Elementary School.* Ocala, FL: Atlantic Publishing, 2010.

Gutkind, Lee, ed. *What I Didn't Know: True Stories of Becoming a Teacher.* Pittsburgh: In Fact Books, 2016.

Kellough, Richard D. and Noreen G. Kellough. *Secondary School Teaching: A Guide to Methods and Resources,* 4th ed. Upper Saddle River, NJ: Pearson, 2010.

Littrell, John M. and Jean Sunde Peterson. *Portrait and Model of a School Counselor.* New York: Routledge, 2004.

Lortie, Dan C. *Schoolteacher: A Sociological Study.* Chicago: University of Chicago Press, 2002.

Melber, Leah M., ed. *Teaching the Museum: Careers in Museum Education.* Washington, DC: American Alliance of Museums, 2014.

Mondale, Sarah, ed. *School: The Story of American Public Education.* Boston: Beacon Press, 2002.

Morrison, George S. *Early Childhood Education Today,* 13th ed. Upper Saddle River, NJ: Pearson Higher Education, 2014.

Parkay, Forrest W. *Becoming a Teacher,* 10th ed. Boston: Pearson, 2015.

Ravitch, Diane. *The Death and Life of the Great American School System,* 3rd ed. New York: Basic Books, 2016.

Schlatter, N. Elizabeth. *Museum Careers: A Practical Guide for Students and Novices.* New York: Routledge, 2009.

Smith, Deborah Deutsch and Naomi Chowdhuri Tyler. *Introduction to Special Education: Making a Difference,* 9th ed. Upper Saddle River, NJ: Pearson Higher Education, 2009.

Toor, Ruth and Hilda K. Weisberg. *Being Indispensable: A School Librarian's Guide to Becoming an Invaluable Leader.* Chicago: American Library Association, 2011.

Underwood, Joseph W., ed. *Today I Made a Difference: A Collection of Inspiring Stories from America's Top Educators.* Avon, MA: Adams Media, 2009.

Medicine

American Medical Association, Health Care Careers Directory. Chicago: American Medical Association, 2013.

Agabegi, Steven S., and Elizabeth D. Agabegi. *Step-Up to Medicine,* 3rd ed. Philadelphia: Lippincott Williams & Wilkins, 2012.

Association of American Medical Colleges, *Medical School Admission Requirements (MSAR): Getting Started.* Washington, D.C.: Association of American Medical Colleges, 2013.

DeLaet, Roxann, *Introduction to Health Care & Careers.* Philadelphia: Lippincott, Williams & Wilkins, 2011.

Gawande, Atul, *Complications: A Surgeon's Notes on an Imperfect Science.* London: Picador, 2003.

Gerdin, Judith, *Health Careers Today, 5th ed.* Maryland Heights, MO: Mosby, 2011.

Groopman, Jerome, *How Doctors Think.* Boston: Mariner, 2008.

Jauhar, Sandeep, *Intern: A Doctor's Initiation.* New York: Farrar, Strauss & Giroux, 2009.

Laine, Christine, and Michael A. LaCombe, eds., *On Being a Doctor 3: Voices of Physicians and Patients.* Philadelphia: American College of Physicians, 2007.

Makely, Sherry, Shirley Badasch, and Doreen S. Chesebro, *Becoming a Health Care Professional*. Upper Saddle River, NJ: Prentice Hall, 2013.

Miller, Robert H., and Daniel M. Bissell, *Med School Confidential: A Complete Guide to the Medical School Experience: By Students, for Students*. New York: St. Martin's/Griffin, 2006.

Smart, John, Stephen Nelson, and Julie Doherty, *Planning a Life in Medicine: Discover If a Medical Career is Right for You and Learn How to Make It Happen*. Framingham, MA: Princeton Review, 2011.

Sweet, Victoria, *God's Hotel: A Doctor, a Hospital, and a Pilgrimage to the Heart of Medicine*. New York: Riverhead Books, 2013.

Transue, Emily R., *On Call: A Doctor's Days and Nights in Residency*. New York: St. Martin's Press, 2005.

Nursing & Nursing Assistants

Carter, Pamela J., *Lippincott's Essentials for Nursing Assistants: A Humanistic Approach to Caregiving*, 3d ed. Philadelphia: Lippincott Williams & Wilkins, 2012.

Chenevert, Melodie, *Mosby's Tour Guide to Nursing School*, 6th ed. Maryland Heights, MO: Mosby, 2010.

Fitzpatrick, Joyce, and Emerson E. Ea, 201 *Careers in Nursing*. New York: Springer, 2011.

Gutkind, Lee, ed., *I Wasn't Strong Like This When I Started Out: True Stories of Becoming a Nurse*. Pittsburgh: In Fact Books, 2013.

Katz, Janet R., *A Career in Nursing: Is It Right for Me?* Maryland Heights, MO: Mosby, 2007.

Peterson's, *Nursing Programs 2014*. Lawrenceville, NJ: Peterson's, 2013.

Shalof, Tilda, *A Nurse's Story: Life, Death, and In-Between in an Intensive Care Unit*. Toronto: Emblem Editions, 2005.

Sports and Athletics

Acsm's Resources for the Personal Trainer. [Place of Publication Not Identified]: Lww, 2010. Print.

Armour, Kathleen M., and Robyn L. Jones. "Physical Education Teachers' Lives and Careers : PE, Sport, and Educational Status." *Physical Education Teachers' Lives and Careers : PE, Sport, and Educational Status*. N.p., n.d. Web.

Cook, Colleen Ryckert. "Dream Jobs in Coaching." *Dream Jobs in Coaching*. N.p., n.d. Web.

Do You Want to Work in Baseball? Advice to Acquire Employment in Mlb and Mentorship in Scouting and Player Development. N.p.: Bookbaby, 2017. Print.

Edelman, Marc, Geoffrey Christopher, Rapp, and American Bar Association. Forum on the Entertainment and Sports Industries,. *Careers in Sports Law*. N.p.: n.p., 2014. Print.

Ferguson Publishing. *Careers in Focus. Coaches and Fitness Professinals*. New York: Ferguson, 2008. Print.

Goodman, Jonathan. *Ignite the Fire : The Secrets to Building a Successful Personal Training Career (Revised, Updated, and Expanded)*. N.p.: Createspace, 2015. Print.

Institute for Career Research. *Careers in Nutrition : Dietitian, Nutritionist.* Chicago: Institute for Career Research, 2011. Print.

La, Bella Laura. "Dream Jobs in Sports Fitness and Medicine." *Dream Jobs in Sports Fitness and Medicine.* N.p., n.d. Web.

Shadix, Kyle W ,, Milton Stokes, Catherine Cioffi, Kyle W. Shadix, and Academy of Nutrition and Dietetics,. *Launching Your Career in Nutrition and Dietetics : How to Thrive in the Classroom, the Internship, and Your First Job.* N.p.: n.p., 2016. Print.

Wong, Glenn M. *The Comprehensive Guide to Careers in Sports.* Burlington, MA: Jones & Bartlett Learning, 2013. Print.

INDEX